Teacher's Book

Contents

Introduction	p. 2
Overview of the components	p. 4
GoGetter for your classroom	p. 6
Extra Online Practice and how to use it	p. 7
Assessment for Learning	p. 8
GoGetter videos	p. 10
A unit of the Students' Book	p. 11
Workbook overview	p. 18
Students' Book contents	p. 20
Starter Unit	p. 22
Unit 1	p. 28
Get Culture! English around the world	p. 38
Unit 2	p. 40
Skills Revision 1&2	p. 50
Unit 3	p. 52
Get Culture! Houses in the UK	p. 62
Unit 4	p. 64
Skills Revision 3&4	p. 74
Unit 5	p. 76
Get Culture! Kid's London	p. 86
Unit 6	p. 86
Skills Revision 5&6	p. 98
Unit 7	p. 100
Get Culture! Pets in the UK	p. 110
Unit 8	p. 102
Skills Revision 7&8	p. 122
Extra reference: Answers, Student A activities	p. 124
Extra reference: Songs and raps	p. 125
Extra reference: Pairwork activities, Student B activities	p. 126
Get more on Geometry!	p. 127
Get more on Science!	p. 128
Get more on Music!	p. 129
Get more on Sports!	p. 130
Students' Book Word list	p. 131
Audio and video scripts	p. 135
Workbook answer key	p. 141
Photocopiable resources – teaching notes	p. 145
Photocopiable resources – Vocabulary	p. 148
Photocopiable resources – Grammar	p. 152
Photocopiable resources – Communication	p. 168
Play – *Where's the chocolate?*	p. 176
Project worksheets	p. 179
Grammar video roleplays	p. 181

Introduction

GoGetter for students

GoGetter is a new four-level English course for upper primary and lower secondary children, taking them from an A1 to B1 level of English. Students in this age range are in a transitional period between childhood and their teens and are still developing intellectually and emotionally. They live in a fast moving, very dynamic world governed by new technologies. Each level of the *GoGetter* series has been carefully tailored to the modern student's cognitive needs and has been designed to create an enjoyable and engaging environment for effective learning. Multimedia teaching and learning tools offer teachers and students a wide range of options for the classroom and home. They include videos, animations and exciting digital content on MyEnglishLab, Extra Online Practice and ActiveTeach activities.

GoGetter for teachers

GoGetter has been created on the basis of tried and tested methodology for effective teaching. It builds on existing EFL methods adapted to the reality of today. A variety of language presentation context and very rich multimedia content will help keep students engaged and motivated. Seamlessly integrated exam preparation, an online gradebook in MyEnglishLab and a unique assessment package will help your students get great results and prepare for future exams.

GoGetter has also been created with busy teachers in mind. Teaching with *GoGetter* will require minimal preparation time due to the open-and-teach formula in the Students' Book and at-a-glance organisation of materials within the Teacher's Book.

Features of the course

Grammar

Grammar is clearly presented in a scaffolded, step-by-step approach with two contextualised grammar presentations per unit: a photo story with teenage characters, which is also available as a video, in Lesson 2, and a cartoon in Lesson 3. Grammar boxes contain clear, student-friendly examples of the target structures and provide a reference point for students as they learn and practise. *Get Grammar!* animations support every grammar lesson. The likeable, captivating characters make learning grammar fun! Further consolidation practice is available in the Workbook.

Vocabulary

Each unit starts with and eye-catching visual presentation of vocabulary, which gets students' attention right from the start. It is followed by step-by-step engaging practice. As well as appealing to students, vocabulary sets reflect typical exam topic areas. The *I know that!* feature at the start of the unit allows for quick revision of lexical items students are very likely to know from previous school years, which is a great confidence-booster. *I remember that!* activities engage students, as they are personalised and effectively help students remember new words. Each Students' Book page has a corresponding Workbook page allowing for lots of additional practice. Finally, there is a *Word blog* in the Workbook at the end of every unit that consolidates the vocabulary of the unit.

Skills

There are separate skills lessons that also take step-by-step approach:

Communication lessons: using videos or audio material, dialogues are modelled and brought to life, which encourages students to use natural English in their own dialogues.

Reading lessons: engaging and age-appropriate texts in different genres motivate and inspire students.

Listening and Writing lessons: students need to use their critical thinking skills in order to complete the listening comprehension activities. *GoGetter* provides clear writing models to help students write their own text on the same topic.

A lot of support, such as prompts, dialogue frames to fill in etc., is provided in free speaking and writing tasks.

There are also four *Skills Revision* sections in each level that consolidate skills work from each two units.

Motivating content

GoGetter offers a great variety of context and teaching modes. Language is presented through real life dialogues, videos, cartoons, animations and exciting reading texts and audio material. The topics are all up-to-date and were carefully chosen to appeal to the age-groups concerned.

Each level of *GoGetter* contains four fascinating *Get Culture!* lessons with authentic BBC video content that takes students on an world wide journey, opening their eyes to different parts of the English-speaking world and motivating them to find out more.

Multimedia content

GoGetter is a fully blended course with exciting digital and video content that will engage your students. They will really look forward to their lessons! Every student who uses the print Workbook has access to additional language practice through Extra Online Practice (for more information, see page 7). If you do not have easy access to a classroom computer or a projector, you can still run successful lessons as the material has been designed in such a way that you can use print and audio material only.

Content and Language Integrated Learning (CLIL)

There are four CLIL sections in *GoGetter* 1. They are titled: *Get more on Science!*, *Get more on Music!*, *Get more on Sports!* and *Get more on Geometry!* These lessons are included in the Workbook and ActiveTeach and they are designed be used in class or can be assigned for homework. They teach students practical language connected to a wide range of subjects that they will be learning about in their native language at the same time. There are four CLIL sections per level.

Support for mixed ability classes

GoGetter supports teachers who work with mixed-ability classes in a number of ways. The Teacher's Book includes teaching tips for mixed ability classes, as well as extra worksheets for grammar, vocabulary and communication lessons. In the Workbook challenging activities are labelled with an asterisk, which makes it easier for the teacher to assign homework to students at different language level.

The Global Scale of English in *GoGetter*

The Global Scale of English (GSE) is a standardised, granular scale which measures English language proficiency. Unlike some other frameworks which describe attainment in broad bands, the Global Scale of English identifies what a learner can do at each point on the scale across speaking, listening, reading and writing skills.

The scale is designed to motivate learners by giving a more granular insight into the learning progress. Teachers can use the Global Scale of English to match a student to the right course materials for their exact level and learning goals.

The badging on the back of your coursebook shows the range of objectives that are covered within the content. Knowing this range helps you select course materials with the right level of support and challenge for your students to help them progress. It does not mean that students need to have mastered all the objectives below the range before starting the course, or that they will all be 'at' the top of the range by the end.

For more information about how using the GSE can support your planning and teaching, your assessment of your learners, and in selecting or creating additional materials to supplement your core programme, please go to www.english.com/gse.

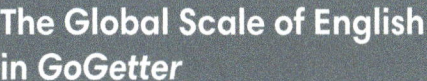

Exam preparation

The table below shows the correlation between the language level of each part of *GoGetter* series and the requirements for Pearson Test of English and Cambridge exams.

Course level	CEFR	GSE	PTE	CAMBRIDGE
GoGetter 1	<A1/A1	17–29	YL Springboard	YLE Starters
GoGetter 2	A1/A2	27–36	YL Quickmarch	YLE Movers
GoGetter 3	A2/A2+	33–41	YL Breakthrough	YLE Flyers
GoGetter 4	A2+/B1	38–46	General Level 1	Key for Schools

The *GoGetter* course provides a lot of opportunities for students to get acquainted with the formats of the Pearson Test of English for Young Learners and Cambridge English: Young Learners tests. In every unit of the Students' Book there are exercises flagged *Exam Spot* which help students to prepare for the exams. *Skills Revision* sections in the Students' Book and Workbook enable students to regularly check their progress through exam-style exercises. Additionally, the *Skills Revision* section in the Students' Book includes an *Exam Language Bank*, collating key language from the unit. There is an *Exam Practice* section in the Workbook, which provides additional exam practice. The assessment package includes two exam-style tests for those students who are preparing for PTEYL or CYLET.

21st century skills

Today's learners require materials that will help them develop skills they need to survive and succeed in the rapidly changing world. They need to be challenged and inspired by their learning. They also need to learn how to work with peers, using modern technologies they are familiar with and enjoy. *GoGetter* helps develop not just English language skills, grammar and vocabulary, but also all those skills modern learners need to build to become fully rounded citizens of the global community.

The key skills focused on in *GoGetter* are: *Communication, Collaboration, Creativity, Cultural Awareness, Critical Thinking, Digital Literacy, Assessment for Learning* and *Autonomy*.

Communication, Collaboration and Creativity: There are a lot of pairwork and groupwork activities integrated in the core lessons in each unit. Project work at the end of *Get Culture!* lessons involves team work so students can learn how to collaborate with peers in order to successfully complete a task.

Cultural Awareness: In an increasingly globalised world, it is important that students gain an understanding of different cultures through the medium of English. *Get Culture!* lessons and exciting videos provide students with a wider perspective of cultural aspects. They also provide an opportunity to compare a foreign culture to their own.

Critical Thinking: Problem solving and reasoning skills are developed throughout the course, especially via the reading and listening activities. These activities are flagged in the teaching notes in every lesson. Interactive cliff-hanger endings in the video story create a great opportunity to analyse and predict.

Autonomy and Personal Initiative: *Get Culture!* sections end with project work which requires some simple data collating or research in order to complete the task. Students are also encouraged to present their own view on the topic from the lesson.

Students are prompted to reflect on and take responsibility for their own progress through the regular Self-assessment sections in the Students' Book and Workbook.

Assessment for Learning: see page 8 for more information.

Digital Literacy: In *Get Culture!* lessons students are encouraged to create their own projects such as presentations, photo albums, leaflets or even mini videos. Photocopiable project worksheets (in the Teacher's Book) provide step-by-step guidelines on how to complete the tasks.

Extra Online Practice or the online Workbook on MyEnglishLab enable students to practise what they have learnt in a digital environment.

Overview of the components

Students' Book

- Nine units with 70–120 hours of teaching material, including a *Get Started!* unit
- Clear lesson objectives ('*I can …*')
- Thorough vocabulary learning programme with motivating presentations and helpful wordlists
- Videos with every unit providing meaningful context in grammar and communication lessons
- Four *Get Culture!* lessons with BBC culture videos and projects
- Exam spot tasks preparing for *Pearson Test of English for Young Learners* (PTEYL) and *Cambridge English: Young Learners of English Tests* (CYLET) throughout the book
- *Language Revision* after every unit and *Skills Revision* with exam-style tasks after every two units
- Songs and chants
- Students' Book is also available with access code to MyEnglishLab and Extra Online Practice. For details on MyEnglishLab and Extra Online Practice, see relevant sections further down and on the next page.

Class Audio CDs

- Students' Book audio material for use in class

Students' eBook

- The full Students' Book in digital format
- All audio tracks and videos embedded into the exercises
- Students' eBook is also available with access code to MyEnglishLab and Extra Online Practice. For details on MyEnglishLab and Extra Online Practice, see relevant sections down below and on the next page.

Workbook

- Additional grammar, vocabulary and skills practice to reinforce the material in the Students' Book
- Practice activities for all Students' Book sections
- *Check yourself!* in each unit to help students prepare for Language Tests
- Four *Skills Revisions* and two *Exam Practice* sections to enable students to check their progress with PTEYL and CYLET exam-style tasks
- *Word blogs* with games and fun activities to consolidate the vocabulary from each unit
- Four *Get more on …!* lessons which cover CLIL topics
- Each print Workbook provides access to Extra Online Practice powered by MyEnglishLab. For details on Extra Online Practice see the relevant section on the next page.

MyEnglishLab

Student's area

- Interactive online Workbook with instant feedback and audio tracks embedded in the listening exercises
- Remediation activities and tips for grammar exercises
- Extra Online Practice activities
- All Students' Book videos
- Downloadable Workbook audio material

Teacher's area

- Access to Assignments module, from which the teacher can assign Workbook activities to students
- Access to the Gradebook, which gives the teacher possibility to monitor students' work
- Access to the complete Students' eBook
- Teachers resources: all photocopiable activities from the Teacher's Book, as well as all Tests in PDF and Word format
- Test audio material
- Skills Test, Mid- and End-of-Year Tests in a digital format

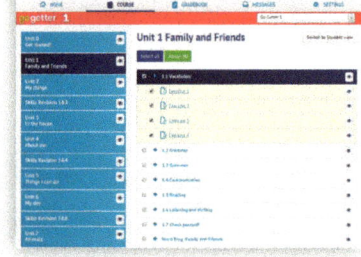

Extra Online Practice (powered by MyEnglishLab)

- Extra activities, based on Students' Book Grammar and Communication lessons videos, with embedded videos, as well as additional revision activities helping students to prepare for Language Tests
- All Students' Book videos
- Downloadable Workbook audio material
- Students access the activities through a code printed on the inside front cover of the Workbook. Please see section Extra Online Practice on page 7 for more details.

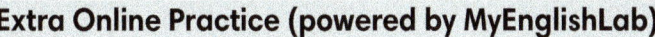

Teacher's Book with DVD-ROM

Teacher's Book

- Embedded Students' Book pages with overwritten answers
- Unit-by-unit teaching notes with extra activities and tasks for fast finishers for all Students' Book lessons and *Get more on …!* (CLIL) lessons in the Workbook
- Practical tips on how to implement Assessment for Learning in the classroom
- Students' Book and Workbook audio and video scripts
- Workbook answer key
- Photocopiable resources with teaching notes and answer key including: grammar, vocabulary, communication and project worksheets, a play and grammar video roleplays
- Teacher's Book provides access code to MyEnglishLab and Extra Online Practice.

Teacher's DVD-ROM

- Students' Book videos with video scripts
- Class and Workbook audio material in MP3 format with audio scripts
- All photocopiable resources from the Teacher's Book, including teaching notes and answer key
- Flashcards

ActiveTeach

- Students' Book pages with embedded audio material and videos and 'Show Answers' functionality
- Workbook pages with embedded audio tracks and 'Show Answers' functionality
- Class and Workbook audio material with audio scripts and time coding (audioscript section is highlighted while played)
- All Students' Book videos, with subtitles which can be switched on and off
- Additional interactive exercises for every unit
- Vocabulary games
- Teacher's tool box for creating personalised vocabulary games, notes and adding internet links
- Teacher's Resources: phonetic chart, photocopiable activities, flashcards, score board and stop watch
- Interactive Whiteboard toolbar including a virtual keyboard, a felt pen and highlighter, a curtain and a spotlight

Tests

- Types of tests included in a printed booklet: Placement Test, eight Vocabulary and Grammar Checks, nine Language Tests, four Skills Tests, Mid-Year and End-of-Year Tests, two Exam Tests, four sets of Speaking Tasks and eight Writing Tasks
- All tests in PDF and editable formats, as well as tests audio material available at www.MyEnglishLab.com
- There are A and B versions available for most of the tests.

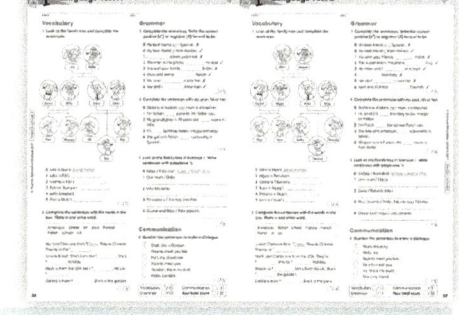

Website

- Additional information and support available at http://pearsonELT.com/gogetter

GoGetter for your classroom

There are many different ways to teach English. Your choice will be influenced by your specific teaching context and preferred teaching style; the number of students in your class; their level and background (the school or Ministry requirements) and access to broadband internet in class, amongst other reasons. *GoGetter* content was designed so you can easily adapt it to your own unique situation. Here are a few possible ways to access the comprehensive set of *GoGetter* materials:

CLASSIC

The classic option is recommended for teachers who prefer to use the printed version of the Students' Book in class and would like their students to do their Workbook homework on paper in the Workbook itself. If students have access to the internet at home or on their own mobile devices, they can access Extra Online Practice (powered by MyEnglishLab) and do additional language exercises in digital format. To access the Extra Online Practice activities, they will need to use the code printed on the inside cover of their Workbook.

If teachers have access to a computer with a projector or an interactive white board in the classroom, they can also use ActiveTeach for front of class presentation of the Students' Book and Workbook materials. They will also find all the coursebook audio material and videos on ActiveTeach. For classrooms with DVD and CD players, teachers can use the Teacher's DVD ROM and Class Audio CDs.

BLENDED

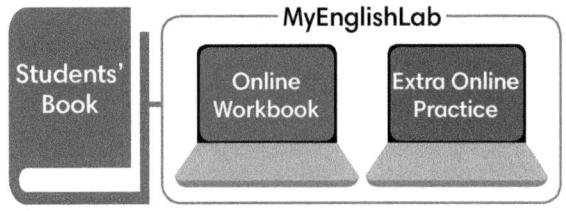

This solution is recommended for teachers who would prefer their students to do their Workbook homework in the online digital Workbook accessed from MyEnglishLab. Their work will be automatically corrected and reported to the teacher. Additional content and the complete coursebook video material can be accessed in Extra Online Practice. In this option the teacher can assign the class all the content available online from their account on MyEnglishLab. Teachers can also use the ActiveTeach either with an interactive whiteboard or from their laptop with a projector. For classrooms with DVD and CD players, teachers can use the Teacher's DVD ROM and Class Audio CDs.

DIGITAL

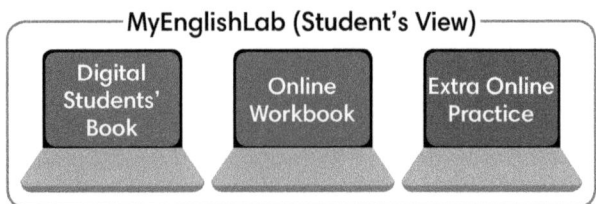

In fully digital classrooms, where students have their own tablets or computers, *GoGetter* can be used in a fully digital configuration. Students can use the digital Students' Book in the classroom and do all their homework online on MyEnglishLab, where they will find all the Workbook activities and also Extra Online Practice. Workbook and Extra Online Practice content can be assigned by the teacher from their account on MyEnglishLab.

Teachers can use the ActiveTeach either with an interactive whiteboard or from their laptop with a projector. There they will find all the Students' Book and Workbook pages with interactive exercises, as well as all the course audio material and videos.

Extra Online Practice and how to use it

What is Extra Online Practice?

Extra Online Practice is a collection of carefully structured digital activities that give students further practice of the core content in the Students' Book and the Workbook. These motivating interactive activities encourage students to make the most of *GoGetter's* multimedia resources by watching the course videos on their own.

Extra Online Practice includes:

- Video-based interactive activities related to the Grammar and Communication videos in the Students' Book.

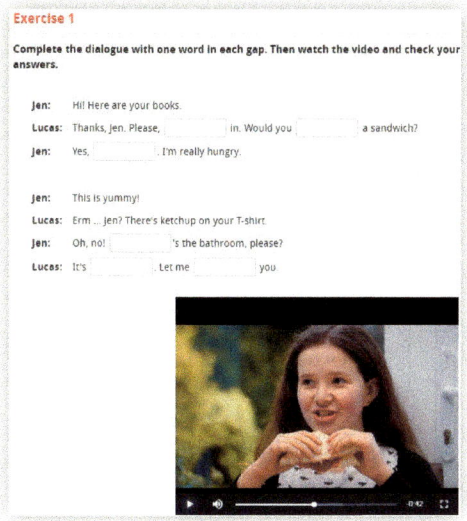

- A collection of revision activities for each unit, which provide further practice of the target language.
- All videos in *GoGetter* 1: Grammar and Communication videos, *Get Grammar!* animations and *Get Culture!* BBC videos.
- The downloadable Workbook audio materials.
- Students can find reference to Extra Online Practice in selected lessons of the Workbook.

Unit 1.2 Video and Grammar	2 exercises
Unit 1.4 Video and Communication	2 exercises
Unit 1 Language Revision	3 exercises
Unit 2.2 Video and Grammar	2 exercises
Unit 2.4 Video and Communication	2 exercises
Unit 2 Language Revision	3 exercises
Unit 3.2 Video and Grammar	2 exercises
Unit 3.4 Video and Communication	2 exercises
Unit 3 Language Revision	3 exercises
Unit 4.2 Video and Grammar	2 exercises
Unit 4.4 Video and Communication	2 exercises
Unti 4 Language Revision	3 exercises
Unit 5.2 Video and Grammar	2 exercises
Unit 5.4 Video and Communication	2 exercises
Unit 5 Language Revision	3 exercises
Unit 6.2 Video and Grammar	2 exercises
Unit 6.4 Video and Communication	2 exercises
Unit 6 Language Revision	3 exercises
Unit 7.2 Video and Grammar	2 exercises
Unit 7.4 Video and Communication	2 exercises
Unit 7 Language Revision	3 exercises
Unit 8.2 Video and Grammar	2 exercises
Unit 8.4 Video and Communication	2 exercises
Unit 8 Language Revision	3 exercises
TOTAL	**56 exercises**

How to access Extra Online Practice

Extra Online Practice can be accessed through the MyEnglishLab platform by both the student and the teacher. The access codes are provided in the course materials. The table below shows where to find relevant codes and what content they activate.

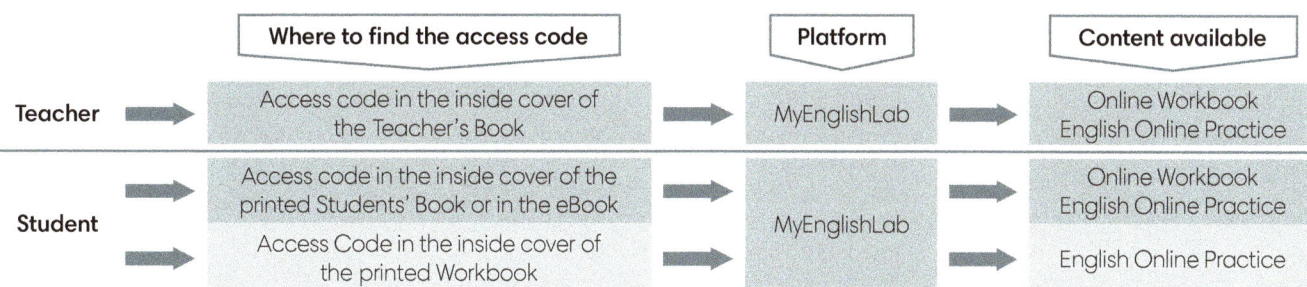

How to work with Extra Online Practice in different classroom settings

- If your students are using online Workbooks with Extra Online Practice (both powered by MyEnglishLab), you will be able to assign all the online activities and monitor the performance of your students in an online gradebook.
- If your students are using printed Workbooks and therefore only have access to Extra Online Practice on MyEnglishLab, you will have to tell them which exercises from Extra Online Practice you want them to do. You cannot monitor students' performance in an online gradebook in this configuration.

How to register your Extra Online Practice access code

To register go to www.myenglishlab.com and click *Register*. Follow the instructions on the screen.

Assessment for Learning (AFL)

Traditionally, assessment aims to find out what students already know in order to diagnose what their linguistic proficiency is. Thanks to assessment procedures, teachers can monitor the progress students make and prepare them for tests which in many countries await students at the end of their respective educational stage. What is more, the results of assessment procedures provide information for students and their parents about their progress in learning; information to teachers about the effectiveness of their teaching and school management about the efficacy of their teachers. There are two main types of assessment: formative and summative.

Formative assessment refers to the strategies and procedures used by teachers during the students' learning process in order to provide the teachers with feedback. Teachers can use this information to modify teaching and learning activities where necessary, keeping up student motivation levels and maximising attainment. Summative assessment, on the other hand, is usually administered at the end of a teaching period to find out whether the progress students made is very good, good, satisfactory or unsatisfactory. Formative assessment is often described as Assessment for Learning rather than assessment of learning. The lists below present the main differences between formative and summative assessment.

Assessment for Learning (formative)
- while teaching
- continuous
- aim: to observe student's progress and his/her strengths and weaknesses, to provide constructive feedback
- students' intrinsic motivation: to achieve success/self-fulfilment
- feedback: information about how to improve performance (usually expressed in a descriptive way, orally or in writing)

Assessment of learning (summative)
- after teaching (usually in the form of tests)
- periodical
- aim: to evaluate student's progress, to give grades
- students' instrumental motivation: to be rewarded or to avoid being punished
- feedback: information about student's results (usually expressed in grades)

Main strategies of formative assessment

The main strategies of formative assessment enable students to focus better and make it easier for them to understand what learning is about. Each student is more involved in the process of learning and invited to answer three questions which are important for their education:
1 *Where am I going?*, i.e. *What am I going to learn?*
2 *Where am I now?*, i.e. *Can I do what is expected of me? Am I on the right track?*
3 *How can I get better?*

The strategies of formative assessment refer to all three stages listed above. The table below presents the most useful techniques that teachers might consider using during English lessons.

Strategies of formative assessment	Recommended techniques used for formative assessment
SETTING AIMS and CRITERIA FOR SUCCESS At the beginning of each lesson, students are informed about the learning objectives. The teacher tells them what they are going to learn, why they are going to learn it, and then makes it clear what the required standards of good work are.	• **Key question:** an intriguing/interesting problem posed to get students involved in the lesson, inspire them and make the lesson memorable, e.g. *Why is English an international language?*, *Why are there so many English words in our native language?* • **Lesson objectives presentation:** The teacher explains lesson aims in a way appropriate to students' linguistic and cognitive development. Brief lesson objectives are written on board. • **'What Am I Looking For?' (WILF):** The teacher draws students' attention to the most important elements in the lesson and provides examples of model work.
MONITORING STUDENTS' LEARNING The teacher observes how students participate in classes during pairwork or groupwork, assesses their written work, evaluates project work or oral tasks. The data, which is collected regularly, enables the teacher to give feedback to each student. **GIVING CONSTRUCTIVE FEEDBACK** is a kind of a dialogue between the student and the teacher which aims at helping the student to find his/her best way of learning. The teacher first accentuates the positive aspects of a student's work and then tells him/her what he/she should improve on and eventually what he/she should focus on in order to get better.	As students are discouraged to volunteer, in order to encourage them all to answer the teacher's questions, there are the following techniques that can be used instead: • **Lollipop stick technique:** students write their names on lollipop sticks and put them in a cup. Teacher asks one student to pick a stick and a student whose name is on the stick responds to a question. • **ABC, True/False, Yes/No, Stop/Go, ☺/☺/☹** response cards to monitor whether all students can understand the different exercises and questions and keep up with the lesson. Each student has his/her own set of cards to choose from. • **Traffic Lights Cards:** students show 'Green' if they know how to do an exercise or understand the topic, 'Yellow' when they need some help, and 'Red' when they need re-teaching the language point. • **Thumbs up/down technique:** teacher asks students to make a thumbs up/down gesture to get feedback on what's correct/true/false etc. • **Basketball technique:** a student gives the answer, then throws a ball to another student to give his/her answer and so on. The teacher only gives feedback after all the students involved have spoken. • **Observation form:** teacher collects data about students' work by filling observation forms or reading written assignments to adjust teaching procedures where necessary. • **Stand up and change places:** students stand up and change places if they agree with the statement teacher reads out about the lesson. Students can explain why they agree or disagree.

PEER LEARNING Working together in pairs or groups, completing cooperative teaching-learning tasks and peer assessment gives students opportunity to share knowledge and learn how to be more attentive and objective.	• **Think-pair-share:** students first individually think of the answer to a question, then discuss their ideas in pairs and eventually pairs present their ideas to a group or a class. Students can express their ideas and consider those of others. • **Pairwork/Groupwork:** students 'study' each other's work and do tasks specified by the teacher. • **Two stars and a wish:** students identify two positive aspects of the work of a peer and express a wish about what the peer might do next time to improve their work. • **Expert Envoy:** individual students are 'experts' who share their knowledge and understanding with pairs or groups. Choose strong students to help others.	
INDEPENDENT LEARNING This strategy is based on a number of reflective questions which promote autonomous, more independent learning. Students need to be aware of their aims and be convinced that they truly have an influence on what and how they learn. They need to know that the teacher appreciates their involvement and efforts. Gradually, students take more responsibility for the progress they make and for the pace of their learning.	• **Summative questions:** at the end of a unit, module or lesson students are encouraged to think about the lesson, revise what was being taught and reflect on their successes and difficulties. They can be given a number of sentences to finish, e.g. *Today I have learned …, I can …, I am good at …, I haven't managed …, I don't understand …, I have difficulty in …* • **Thought-provoking questions:** students gradually develop autonomy in learning by answering such questions as *How successful is my learning? How am I learning it? How can I improve? What are we going to do next? What would I like to learn next?* • **Three facts and a fib:** students write three facts and one fib about the topic of the lesson and share them in pairs, groups or with the class. Then they try to indentify the 'fib'. • **Learning diary:** the teacher can ask students to write down their questions and make notes about their learning in special notebooks. • **Portfolio:** a collection of student work and related material which presents a student's activities, achievements, self-evaluation and reflection.	

Assessment for Learning in *GoGetter*

Assessment for Learning techniques are clearly presented in all components of *GoGetter*. The table below shows how each component of the course helps to put these strategies into practice.

	Setting aims/criteria for success	Monitoring/Giving feedback	Peer learning	Independent learning
Students' Book	• **Unit and lesson objectives** are specified in a simple and straightforward way. • **Model texts, plans, prompts and examples** show students what they are expected to produce in each exercise.	• **Variety of contexts and exercises** (e.g. videos, animations, games, role-plays etc.) gives teacher opportunity to monitor students' progress in a lot of different ways.	• **Communicative games** at the end of the lessons encourage peer feedback and correction. • **Projects** are a great way to introduce peer assessment.	• *I know that!* and *I remember that!* exercises help students check what they know and what they are expected to learn. • **Projects** give students opportunity to take responsibility for their work. • *Exam Language Banks* show students the most important language required at tests. • *Check yourself!* boxes encourage students to reflect on their learning.
Workbook with Extra Online Practice	• **Examples, grammar tables and model answers** provide useful information on what students should produce in each exercise.			• *Check yourself!*, *Skills Revision* and *Exam Practice* sections give students opportunity to check their progress and assess themselves regularly. • **Extra Online Practice** allows students to check their progress after every unit.
MyEnglishLab		• The teacher can **monitor students' progress** and find out if certain language points need re-teaching or more practice.		• **Instant feedback** and possibility for students to monitor their own progress develop students independence and responsibility for their work. • **Remediation activities** help students improve when they have problems with grammar.
Active Teach	• It is a great tool to **get students' focus** at the start of the lesson to set aims and inform about the expected outcomes.	• Possibility to **display the answers, audio and video scripts** opens more ways for teacher to provide feedback.	• Displaying the answers on IWB makes **peer correction easier**.	
Teacher's Book with DVD-ROM	• **Introduction** to AFL presents strategies and techniques with practical ideas about how they can be used in class. • **Teaching notes** for every lesson provide plenty of quick and easy-to-use AFL tips for various lesson stages (flagged with symbols:). • **AFL-specific flashcards** (available on DVD-ROM and ActiveTeach) help with feedback.			

GoGetter videos

There are three types of videos in *GoGetter*. All of the videos are available on the DVD-Rom attached to the Teacher's Book, on ActiveTeach and MyEnglishLab. There are 45 videos per level!

Grammar and Communication videos

A specially shot, entertaining soap-opera-type drama about a group of pre-teens, their families and friends. The video presents the key language of the lesson for one of the Grammar lessons in each unit and each Communication lesson. Real-life dialogues provide natural and memorable language models.

The purpose of this video is to present the target language of the lesson that is truly engaging and meaningful. When new language is backed-up by visual clues and context (the location, the action, the body language and facial expression), it transforms the learning experience so that language is 'acquired' (in the long-term memory) rather than merely 'learnt' (in the short-term memory). This will improve students' receptive accuracy. Interactive cliff-hanger endings in the grammar videos engage students in prediction activities and encourage critical thinking.

All the video episodes are also available in audio-only format on the Class Audio CDs for those classrooms where video is not readily available. Students can access the videos on Extra Online Practice where they can also do extra comprehension and practice exercises.

Get Grammar! animations

These are funny animated clips about the adventures of Hammy, a cute hamster, and his friends Max and Anna. The video presents the key grammar structures taught in each Grammar lesson. It is divided into two parts – a short scene from Hammy's life and a *Look and Learn!* section presenting the key grammar structures.

The animations provide a great opportunity for the teacher to explain new grammar structures in an entertaining and meaningful way that will motivate students and get their attention for longer. The videos can be used multiple times both as an effective presentation tool and a quick revision of grammar structures.

Get Culture! BBC videos

A series of inspiring culture videos which recycle the topics and language of the preceding units. These videos appear in *Get Culture!* lessons following Units 1, 3, 5 and 7. Extracts of high-quality BBC footage are introduced by the popular British presenter Maddie Moate at an appropriate level for the learner.

The purpose of these motivating authentic videos is to present the diversity of the English-speaking world, sparking students' imaginations and curiosity. This will encourage them to continue learning English independently.

A unit of the Students' Book

- A clear summary of content and video material is available for the unit.
- Clear lesson objectives are included at the beginning of each lesson.
- *I know that!* revision activities boost motivation.
- Vocabulary sets are placed in clearly organised boxes. All lexical items are recorded for students to listen and repeat.

- Varied practice activities, including listening exercises, help students remember new vocabulary.
- *Look!* boxes draw students' attention to important language points.
- Vocabulary consolidation at the end of the lesson are based on personalised memorisation activities.

A unit of the Students' Book

Grammar is presented through video. Real-life dialogues provide a natural context and help students memorise the language. The lesson can also be run using the audio track of the presentation dialogue only.

Grammar tables highlight target structures.

***Look!* boxes provide useful language tips.**

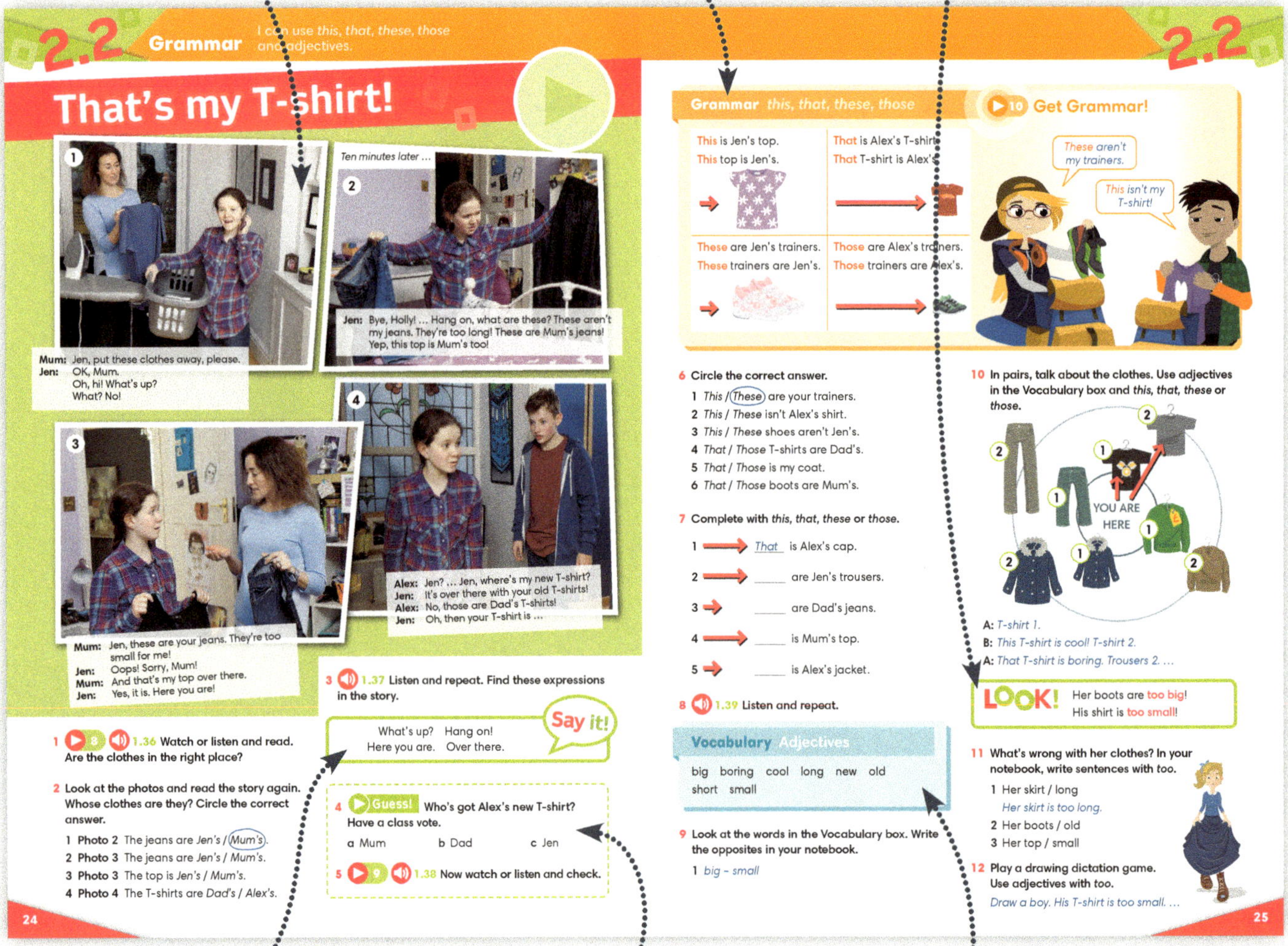

Everyday phrases and expressions from the video presentation are included in *Say it!* boxes.

***Guess!* activities based on the cliff-hanger endings in the video story encourage curiosity and stimulate critical thinking.**

Key lexis is placed in vocabulary boxes for easy reference and to help memorisation. All items are recorded for students to listen and repeat.

Grammar is presented through an exciting comic strip with amusing characters.

Humorous grammar animations motivate students to focus on new structures and give them real enthusiasm for learning!

2.3 Grammar I can ask and answer questions with the verb *to be*.

The Terrific Two — Dug's new suit

Girl: Are they OK?
Superdug: Yes, they are.
Girl: Thank you!
Boy: Is he a superhero?
Kit: Yes, he is. He's Superdug!

Kit: Dug! Your suit is too small!

Dug: This suit is cool! Size M? No. Size XL!
Kit: Are you sure, Dug?
Dug: Yes, I am.
Kit: XL is too big for you.
Dug: No, I'm a superhero! I'm big!

Two days later …

Kit: Thank you.
Dug: Is this box for me?
Kit: Yes, it is. What is it?
Dug: It's my new suit!

Dug: Ready! Am I cool in this suit?
Kit: No, you aren't. The suit is too big! Hm … Hang on!

Dug: Fantastic. You're a clever cat, Kit!

1 Look at the cartoon. Where does Dug buy his superhero suits from?

2 🔊 1.40 Listen and read. What size is Dug's new suit?

3 Read the sentences. Circle T (true) or F (false).
1 The dogs are OK. **T** / F
2 The girl is a superhero. T / F
3 Dug's new suit is in the box. T / F
4 Dug is cool in his new suit. T / F

2.3

Grammar *to be* questions and short answers ▶ 11 Get Grammar!

?	Short answers
Am I OK?	Yes, I **am**. / No, I**'m not**.
Are you OK?	Yes, you **are**. / No, you **aren't**.
Is he/she/it OK?	Yes, he/she/it **is**. / No, he/she/it **isn't**.
Are we OK?	Yes, you **are**. / No, you **aren't**.
Are you OK?	Yes, we **are**. / No, we **aren't**.
Are they OK?	Yes, they **are**. / No, they **aren't**.

What **is** it?   It**'s** my new suit.

Is this shirt OK?
No, it isn't.

4 Write questions. Who's asking the question? Write *boy, girl, Dug* or *Kit*.
1 they OK Are ?   *Are they OK?*   *girl*
2 he a superhero Is ?   _____   ____
3 you Are sure ?   _____   ____
4 for me is this box ?   _____   ____
5 it What is ?   _____   ____
6 cool I Am ?   _____   ____

5 Look at the cartoon. Answer the questions in Exercise 4.
1 *Superdug: Yes, they are.*

6 Complete the questions and the short answers.
1 **Boy:** ___*Are*___ you a superhero?
   Kit: No, I **'m not**.
2 **Kit:** _____ we best friends?
   Dug: Yes, we _____ .
3 **Dug:** _____ my new suit cool?
   Kit: No, it _____ .
4 **Kit:** _____ I clever?
   Dug: Yes, you _____ .
5 **Girl:** _____ Superdug your brother?
   Kit: No, he _____ .
6 **Kit:** _____ they your dogs?
   Girl: Yes, they _____ .

7 🔊 1.41 Listen to the questions and circle the correct answer.
1 (Yes, it is.) / No, they aren't.
2 Yes, you are. / No, they aren't.
3 Yes, I am. / No, you aren't.
4 Yes, they are. / No, he isn't.
5 Yes, they are. / No, you aren't.
6 Yes, we are. / No, they aren't.

8 Write questions in your notebook. Then ask the questions and give true answers in pairs.
1 you / ten years old?   *Are you ten years old?*
2 you / happy?
3 we / friends?
4 Superdug and Kit / cool?
5 you / clever?
6 I / a superhero?

A: *Are you ten years old?*
B: *Yes, I am. / No, I'm not.*

9 🔊 1.42 🔊 1.43 Go to page 107. Listen and chant Kit's Rap.

Step-by-step practice and a variety of exercises improve accuracy.

Regular *Fun Spot* activities provide an engaging context for consolidation of the new language.

A unit of the Students' Book

Functional dialogues are presented through video. Real-life dialogues provide natural and memorable language models. The lesson can also be run by just using the audio track of the presentation dialogue.

Key vocabulary from the reading text is collected in boxes for easy reference. All lexical items are recorded in audio format for students to listen and repeat.

Practice tasks in exam-like format help students prepare for exams.

2.4 Communication — I can ask for and give personal information.

What's your name?

Mr Wood: What's your name?
Lucas: Lucas Ortiz. That's O-R-T-I-Z.
Mr Wood: Good. And how old are you, Lucas?
Lucas: I'm eleven years old.
Mr Wood: Welcome to the school band.

Lian: Where are you from, Lucas?
Lucas: I'm from Madrid, Spain.
Lian: What's your favourite music?
Lucas: Good question. Rock, I think.
Lian: Who's your favourite singer?
Lucas: Erm ... Ed Sheeran.
Lian: High five! He's my favourite too!

1 ▶ 1.44 Watch or listen and read. Where is Lucas from?

2 🔊 1.45 Listen and repeat.

Communication
Asking for personal information
What's your name?
How old are you?
Where are you from?
What's your favourite music/sport/film?
Who's your favourite actor/singer/sports person?

3 🔊 1.46 Listen to the dialogues. Circle the correct answer.
1 Star Wars. / (Superman.)
2 Nick Carr. That's C-A-double R. / Carl Neal. That's N-E-A-L.
3 Warsaw, Poland. / Paris, France.
4 I'm twelve. / I'm thirteen.
5 Alicia Keys. / Taylor Swift.

4 **Exam Spot** Complete the dialogues with questions in the Communication box.
1 A: _What's your favourite music?_
  B: Pop, I think.
2 A: _____?
  B: I'm twelve years old.
3 A: _____?
  B: My name's Fred Allen. That's A- double L-E-N.
4 A: _____?
  B: Football.
5 A: _____?
  B: I'm from Glasgow, Scotland.

5 In pairs, ask and answer questions in the Communication box. Give crazy answers!
A: What's your name?
B: My name's Queen Coco!
A: Where are you from?
B: I'm from Chocolateland!

2.5 Reading — I can understand a text about a super backpack.

1 🔊 1.47 Listen and repeat. Then label pictures 1–6 with the words in the Vocabulary box.

Vocabulary My things
backpack   games console   laptop computer
mobile phone   mountain bike   skateboard

1 _games console_   2 _____   3 _____

4 _____   5 _____   6 _____

2 🔊 1.48 Read and listen to the article. Why is the backpack a super backpack?

3 Read the sentences. Circle T (true) or F (false).
1 Jamie is from London in the UK.   T /(F)
2 Super backpack is a jumper too.   T / F
3 Super backpack is too small for a laptop computer.   T / F
4 Fiona is Jamie's pet.   T / F

4 **Exam Spot** Look at the picture in the text and answer the questions.
1 What colour is the super backpack?   _It's red._
2 What colour is the mountain bike?   _____
3 Is the jacket red or blue?   _____
4 Is the cat in the pocket big or small?   _____

5 Work in groups. Invent a supergadget! Draw it and present it to the class.
It's a school bag. It's a skateboard too.

Jamie Cooper's 13.
He's from Liverpool in the UK.
Jamie's super backpack is our gadget of the week. Why? Read on.
CONGRATULATIONS, JAMIE!

Super backpack!

What's in the picture? Yes, that's right. It's a red backpack. It's a super backpack! It's very very cool.

Look again. This super backpack is also a mountain bike. It's small but it isn't too small. It's fantastic! And that's not all. Think about it. You're in the park with your friends. You're cold and your jumper is at home. No problem. This super backpack is a big jacket too.

What about your other things? Don't worry! Super backpack is just the right size for your laptop computer, your mobile phone, your new games and other favourites. There's even a pocket for a small pet like my cat Fiona. How cool is that?

Key functional language from the presentation are included in boxes which are easy to find on the page.

Practice tasks in exam-like format help students prepare for exams.

Manageable texts on up-to-date, engaging topics relevant to students' age motivate students to read.

Practice tasks in exam-like format help students prepare for exams.

Example texts provide a model for students to follow in the free writing task at the end of the lesson.

Language Revision at the end of each unit provides effective and engaging revision of the grammar, vocabulary and communication language from the unit.

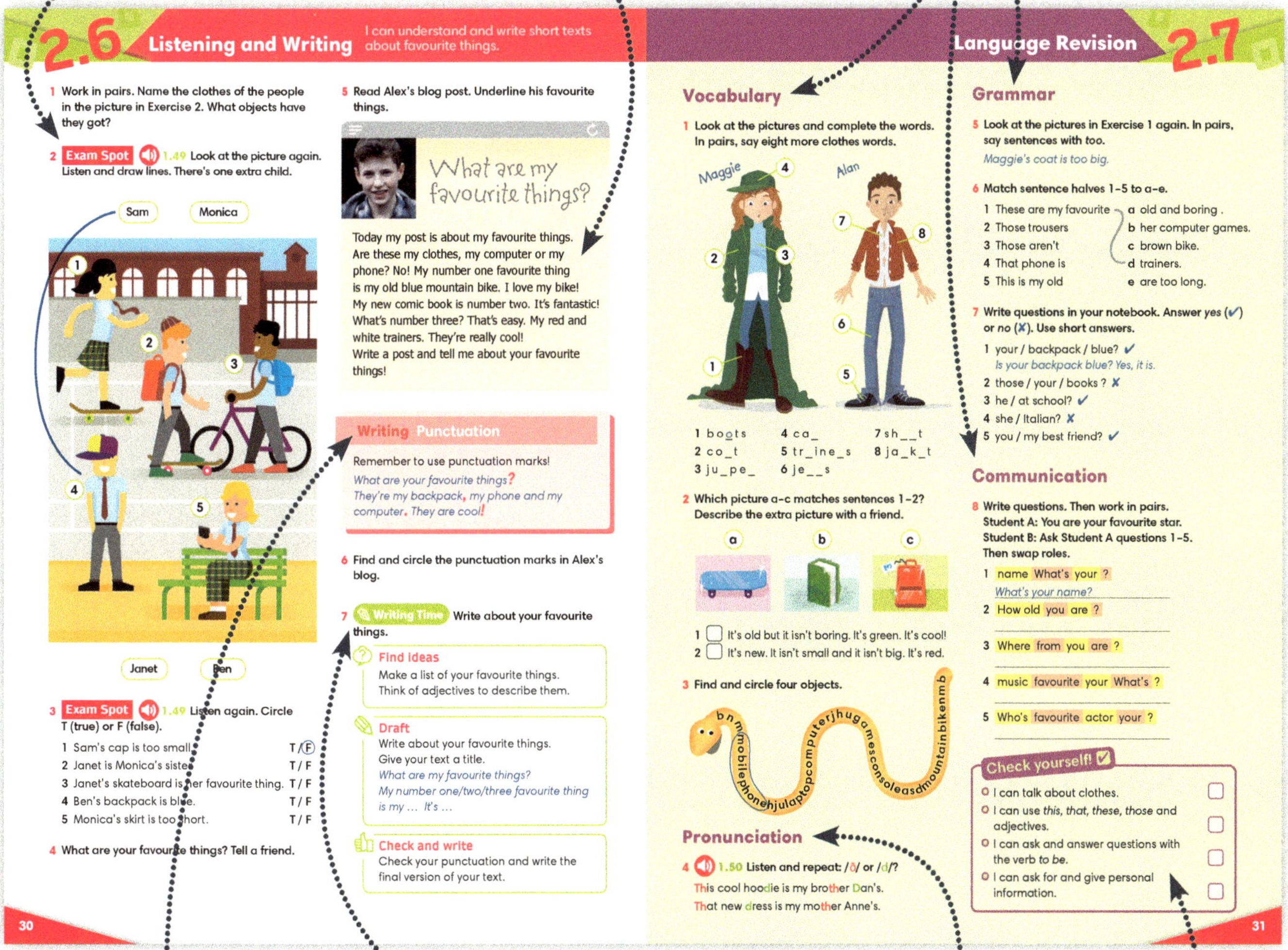

2.6 Listening and Writing
I can understand and write short texts about favourite things.

1 Work in pairs. Name the clothes of the people in the picture in Exercise 2. What objects have they got?

2 **Exam Spot** 1.49 Look at the picture again. Listen and draw lines. There's one extra child.

Sam   Monica

Janet   Ben

3 **Exam Spot** 1.49 Listen again. Circle T (true) or F (false).
1 Sam's cap is too small. T / F
2 Janet is Monica's sister. T / F
3 Janet's skateboard is her favourite thing. T / F
4 Ben's backpack is blue. T / F
5 Monica's skirt is too short. T / F

4 What are your favourite things? Tell a friend.

5 Read Alex's blog post. Underline his favourite things.

What are my favourite things?

Today my post is about my favourite things. Are these my clothes, my computer or my phone? No! My number one favourite thing is my old blue mountain bike. I love my bike! My new comic book is number two. It's fantastic! What's number three? That's easy. My red and white trainers. They're really cool!
Write a post and tell me about your favourite things!

Writing Punctuation
Remember to use punctuation marks!
What are your favourite things?
They're my backpack, my phone and my computer. They are cool!

6 Find and circle the punctuation marks in Alex's blog.

7 **Writing Time** Write about your favourite things.

🔍 **Find Ideas**
Make a list of your favourite things. Think of adjectives to describe them.

✏️ **Draft**
Write about your favourite things. Give your text a title.
What are my favourite things?
My number one/two/three favourite thing is my ... It's ...

👍 **Check and write**
Check your punctuation and write the final version of your text.

2.7 Language Revision

Vocabulary
1 Look at the pictures and complete the words. In pairs, say eight more clothes words.

Maggie   Alan

1 b o o ts   4 ca_   7 sh__t
2 co_t   5 tr_ine_s   8 ja_k_t
3 ju_pe_   6 je__s

2 Which picture a–c matches sentences 1–2? Describe the extra picture with a friend.

a   b   c

1 ☐ It's old but it isn't boring. It's green. It's cool!
2 ☐ It's new. It isn't small and it isn't big. It's red.

3 Find and circle four objects.

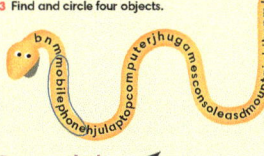

b n m o b i l e p h o n e h j u l a p t o p c o m p u t e r j h u g o m e s c o n s o l e a s d m o u n t a i n b i k e n m b

Pronunciation
4 🔊 1.50 Listen and repeat: /ð/ or /d/?
This cool hoodie is my brother **D**an's.
That new **d**ress is my mother Anne's.

Grammar
5 Look at the pictures in Exercise 1 again. In pairs, say sentences with *too*.
Maggie's coat is too big.

6 Match sentence halves 1–5 to a–e.
1 These are my favourite   a old and boring.
2 Those trousers   b her computer games.
3 Those aren't   c brown bike.
4 That phone is   d trainers.
5 This is my old   e are too long.

7 Write questions in your notebook. Answer *yes* (✔) or *no* (✘). Use short answers.
1 your / backpack / blue? ✔
  Is your backpack blue? Yes, it is.
2 those / your / books ? ✘
3 he / at school? ✔
4 she / Italian? ✘
5 you / my best friend? ✔

Communication
8 Write questions. Then work in pairs.
Student A: You are your favourite star.
Student B: Ask Student A questions 1–5.
Then swap roles.
1 name What's your ?
  What's your name?
2 How old you are ?
3 Where from you are ?
4 music favourite your What's ?
5 Who's favourite actor your ?

Check yourself! ✅
○ I can talk about clothes. ☐
○ I can use *this, that, these, those* and adjectives. ☐
○ I can ask and answer questions with the verb *to be*. ☐
○ I can ask for and give personal information. ☐

Comprehensive writing tips with examples help students develop writing skills.

Writing Time activities with prompts and examples provide step-by-step guidelines to help students write their own texts.

Fun pronunciation activities focus on different sounds and help students improve their pronunciation.

The *Check yourself!* section allows for quick and effective self-assessment.

Get Culture!

In the Students' Book, there are four *Get Culture!* lessons. They appear after Unit 1, 3, 5 and 7 and they include fascinating material which will help your students broaden their knowledge of the English-speaking countries.

Inspiring BBC culture videos with authentic footage and BBC presenters encourage curiosity in the English-speaking world.

Reading texts include a lot of fascinating information about English-speaking countries.

In every *Get Culture!* lesson students listen to peers living in English-speaking countries.

Culture projects teach students about different aspects of British culture. They also develop students' creativity, artistic and ICT skills and give them the opportunity to practise planning and working in a team.

Skills Revision

Skills Revision activities after every second unit consolidate skills taught in the preceding two units.

Clear prompts and examples enable students of all abilities to write their own texts.

A list of key vocabulary and expressions taught in the two preceding units helps students organize their learning and prepare for tests.

1&2 Skills Revision

Reading and Writing

Cheryl is my new school friend. She's twelve. Her favourite colour is pink. Cheryl's pink mobile phone is her favourite thing. A lot of her clothes are pink too. Her pet dog, Rafs, isn't pink! He's grey and black.

Cheryl's family is very big. Sarah and Daniela are her sisters. Her brothers are Rob and Mick. Her dad is a guitarist in a band. Sometimes he's on TV shows! Her mum's a singer. She's very cool. Her granny and grandad are from Spain. They aren't boring. They are actors. They are in films! Are they all happy? Yes, they are!

1 Work in pairs. Say what you can see in the photo.

2 Exam Spot Read the text. Circle the correct title.
   a Cheryl's new dog.   b My new school friend.

3 Read the sentences. Answer the questions.
   1 How old is Cheryl?   *Cheryl is twelve.*
   2 What's her favourite thing?
   3 Is Cheryl's family small?
   4 Who are Rob and Mick?
   5 Is Cheryl's mum boring?
   6 Where is her grandmother from?

4 Exam Spot Look and read. Tick (✓) for *yes* or put a cross (✗) for *no*.

1 ✓ This is a dog. 2 ☐ This is a skirt.

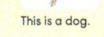 
3 ☐ These are shoes. 4 ☐ These are skateboards.

5 ☐ This is a party. 6 ☐ These are jeans.

5 Exam Spot Write 40–50 words about your friend. Use these questions to help you.
   1 What's his/her name?
   2 How old is he/she?
   3 What's his/her favourite colour?
   4 What are his/her favourite things?
   5 Where is his/her family from?

My good friend is … He/She is … years old.
His/Her favourite colour is … His/Her favourite things are … His/Her family is from …

Listening

6 Exam Spot 🔊 1.51 Read the questions. Listen and write a name or a number.

1 What's the man's surname?   *Smith*
2 What's the boy's name?
3 Who is the boy's best friend?
4 How old is the boy?
5 What's the number of the boy's house?

Communication

7 Exam Spot Look at the pictures. Match a–h to 1–6. There are two extra sentences.

1 e   2

3   4

5   6

a Nice to meet you.
b Who's your favourite actor?
c This is my mum.
d Caz, this is Jack.
e Hello Caz!
f He's my neighbour.
g What's your favourite music?
h Nice to meet you too, Mrs Smith.

8 Exam Spot Work in pairs. Ask and answer the questions.
1 What are your favourite weekend clothes?
2 What colour is your T-shirt/top today?
3 What's in your schoolbag today? (Don't look!)
4 What is your favourite place?

Exam Language Bank

Family	Places
mother	at home
mum	at school
father	at a party
dad	in the garden
parents	in the park
grandfather	on holiday
grandad	
grandmother	**Clothes**
granny	boots — shirt
son	cap — shoes
daughter	coat — skirt
brother	dress — T-shirt
sister	hoodie — top
aunt	jacket — tracksuit
uncle	jeans — trainers
cousin	jumper — trousers

Countries and nationalities	Adjectives
the UK / British	big — new
Spain / Spanish	boring — old
Poland / Polish	cool — short
the USA / American	long — small
Italy / Italian	**My things**
France / French	backpack
China / Chinese	games console
	laptop computer
	mobile phone
	mountain bike
	skateboard

Introductions
Mum, this is *Lucas*.
He's my *friend/classmate*.
Lucas, this is *my mum*.
Nice to meet you.
Nice to meet you too.

Asking questions
What's your name?
How old are you?
Where are you from?
What's your favourite *music/sport/film*?
Who's your favourite *actor/singer/sportsperson*?

Practice tasks in exam-style format help students prepare for exams.

Personalised questions motivate students to talk.

Workbook overview

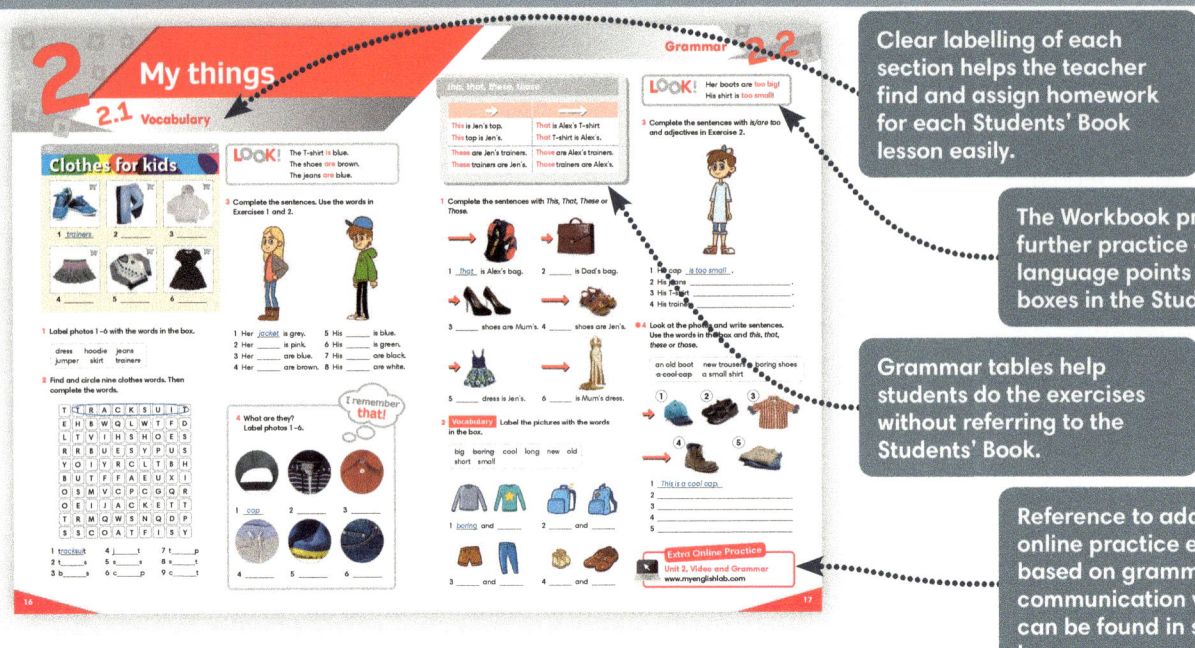

Clear labelling of each section helps the teacher find and assign homework for each Students' Book lesson easily.

The Workbook provides further practice of the language points from *Look!* boxes in the Students' Book.

Grammar tables help students do the exercises without referring to the Students' Book.

Reference to additional online practice exercises based on grammar and communication videos can be found in selected lessons.

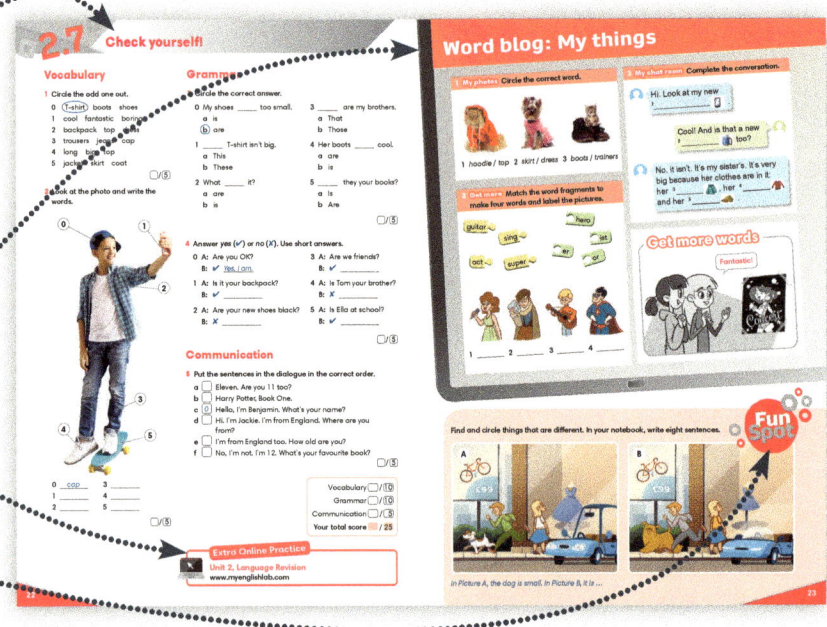

Check yourself! provides further practice on grammar, vocabulary and functional language from the unit.

Word blogs with games and fun activities consolidate and extend the vocabulary from the unit.

Additional revision exercises for each *Check yourself!* lesson help students get ready for the Language Test.

Fun Spot activities provide engaging context for revision activities.

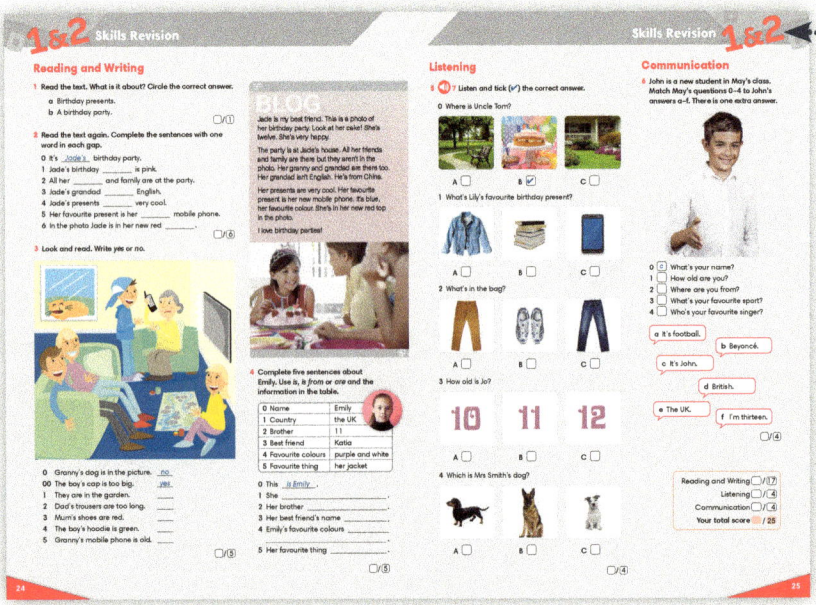

Four *Skills Revision* sections provide further practice of the skills material from two preceding units and help students prepare for *Skills Tests*.

Students can check answers to the *Check yourself!* and *Skills Revision* lessons.

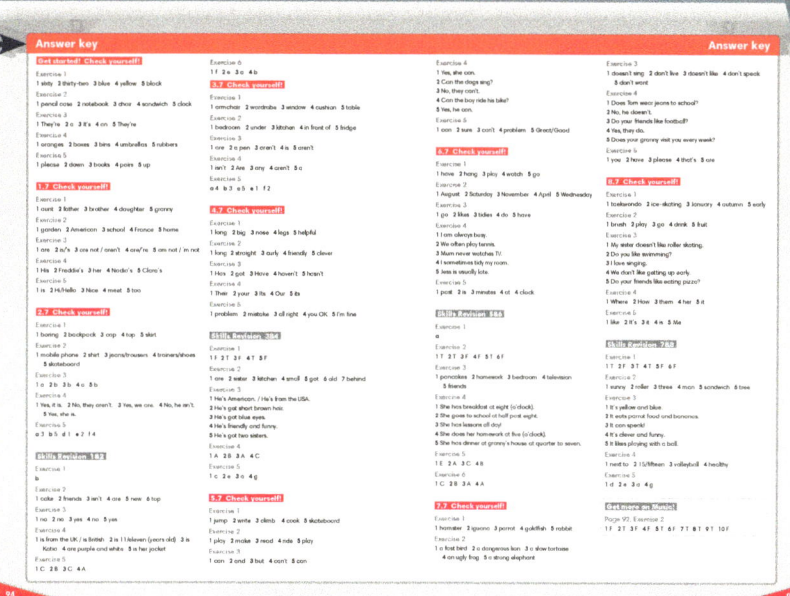

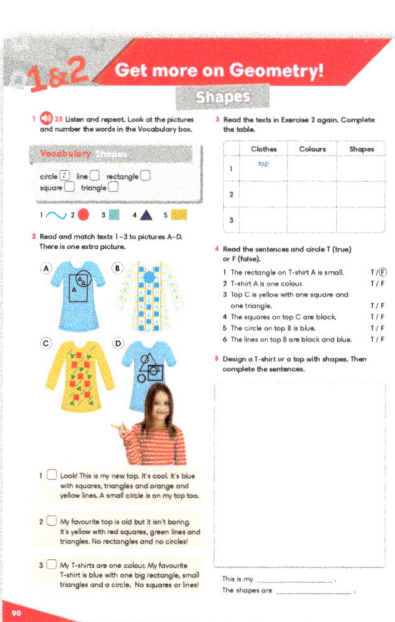

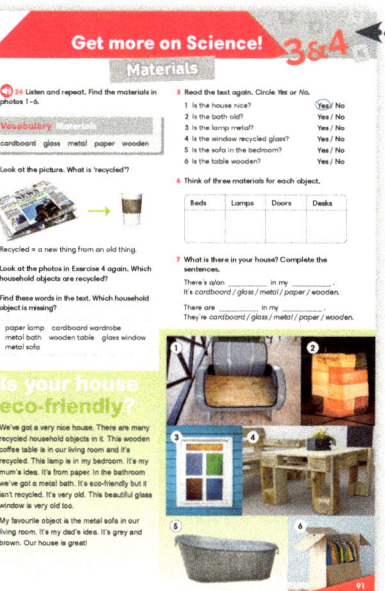

Four *Get more on ...!* lessons are tailored to the Students' Book material for Content and Language Integrated Learning (CLIL). They are also available on ActiveTeach to be used in class.

Two *Exam Practice* sections provide additional revision material in exam-style format.

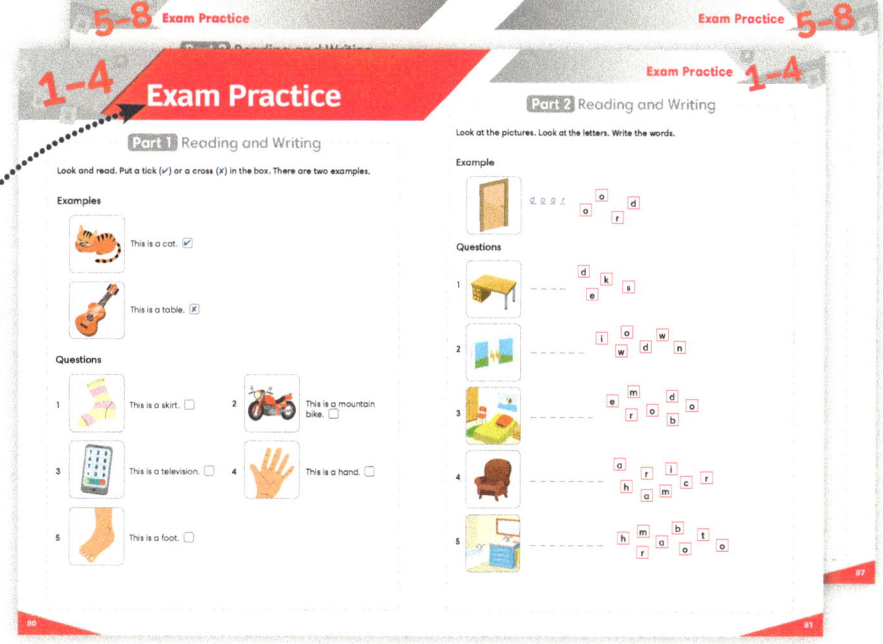

19

Contents

▶ Grammar/Communication video ▶ Grammar animation ▶ Culture video

Unit	Vocabulary	Grammar	Skills	Revision
0 Get Started! p. 4	• The alphabet • Numbers • Colours • In my bag • Classroom objects	• *a/an* • Plural nouns • *My/your*	• Classroom language • Spelling words/names • Simple introductions (*I'm … / My name is … ; This is …*)	
1 Family and friends p. 10	• Family • Countries and nationalities • Places	• Possessive *'s* • *to be* affirmative ▶▶ • Possessive adjectives *my, your, his, her* • *to be* negative ▶	**Communication:** Introductions [Exam] ▶ **Reading:** My family album [Exam] **Listening:** Best friends [Exam] **Writing:** Me and my best friend; Capital letters	Language Revision Pronunciation: /v/ and /b/
p. 20	**BBC Get Culture!**		English around the world ▶ This is the UK Project: English around the world (presentation)	
2 My things p. 22	• Clothes • Adjectives • My things	• *this/that/these/those* ▶▶ • *too big/small* • *to be* questions and short answers ▶	**Communication:** Asking for personal information [Exam] ▶ **Reading:** Super backpack! [Exam] **Listening:** Favourite things [Exam] **Writing:** My favourite things; Punctuation	Language Revision Pronunciation: /ð/ and /d/
p. 32	Skills Revision 1&2 [Exam]			
3 In the house p. 34	• In the house • Prepositions of place • Household objects	• *there is / there are* affirmative ▶▶ • *there is / there are* negative and questions • *a/an, any* ▶	**Communication:** Having a guest [Exam] ▶ **Reading:** A skateboarder's dream [Exam] **Listening:** My bedroom [Exam] **Writing:** My bedroom; Apostrophes	Language Revision Pronunciation: /ɪ/ and /iː/
p. 44	**BBC Get Culture!**		Houses in the UK ▶ Hampton Court Palace Project: Houses in my area (presentation)	
4 About me p. 46	• Face and hair • Parts of the body • Personality adjectives	• *have got* affirmative and negative [Exam] ▶▶ • Regular and irregular plural • *have got* questions and short answers ▶ • Possessive adjectives *its, our, your, their*	**Communication:** Apologising [Exam] ▶ **Reading:** Personality quiz **Listening:** Cartoon characters **Writing:** My favourite character; Paragraphs	Language Revision Pronunciation: /h/
p. 56	Skills Revision 3&4 [Exam]			

Contents

Unit	Vocabulary	Grammar	Skills	Revision
5 **Things I can do** p. 58	• Action verbs **Exam** • Collocations with *make, play* and *ride*	• *can* affirmative and negative • *can* questions and short answers	**Communication:** Suggestions **Exam** **Reading:** Sign language **Listening:** After-school clubs **Exam** **Writing:** After-school club ad; *and, but*	Language Revision Pronunciation: /aː/ and /æ/
p. 68	**BBC Get Culture!** Kids' London ▶ Free time activities Project: Fun things to do in your town (leaflet)			
6 **My day** p. 70	• Daily activities • Days of the week • Months	• Present Simple affirmative • Adverbs of frequency	**Communication:** Telling the time **Reading:** A day with … *Dreamtime Traveler!* **Listening:** My typical weekend **Exam** **Writing:** My typical weekend; *before, after*	Language Revision Pronunciation: /s/, /z/ and /ɪz/
p. 80	Skills Revision 5&6 **Exam**			
7 **Animals** p. 82	• Wild animals • Pets • Money • Adjectives	• Present Simple negative • Present Simple questions and short answers	**Communication:** Buying a ticket **Reading:** Amazing animals! **Exam** **Listening:** Pets **Exam** **Writing:** An email to a friend; Starting and ending an email	Language Revision Pronunciation: /s/
p. 92	**BBC Get Culture!** Pets in the UK ▶ The London Zoo Project: Our pets (digital photo album)			
8 **I like that!** p. 94	• Sports **Exam** • Seasons and weather • Healthy lifestyle	• *love/like/don't like/hate + -ing* • object pronouns • Question words **Exam**	**Communication:** Talking about the weather **Exam** **Reading:** Teen health **Exam** **Listening:** My healthy lifestyle **Exam** **Writing:** My lifestyle; Checking for grammar mistakes	Language Revision Pronunciation: /r/
p. 104	Skills Revision 7&8 **Exam**			
p. 106	Extra reference: Answers, Student A activities			
p. 107	Extra reference: Songs and raps			
p. 108	Extra reference: Pairwork activities, Student B activities			
p. 109	Wordlist			

0.1

In this lesson

Lesson aims:
- Vocabulary: the alphabet
- Communication: saying and spelling first name and surname

Homework:
- Workbook Unit 0, p. 4

Assessment for Learning in this lesson
- Setting aims and criteria for success: Warm-up
- Giving feedback: Exercise 2 and 10
- Peer learning: Exercise 5
- Independent learning: Finishing the lesson

Warm-up
- (*Books closed*) Introduce yourself to different Ss. Say *Hello! I'm …* and *Hi! My name's …* Encourage Ss to use the same expressions to reply.
- Write *Hello!* on the board. (L1/L2) Explain this is the title of the first lesson. Ask the class *What is in this lesson?* Then say the following sentences one by one: *My name is … I like animals. I'm ten years old. My mum is a teacher. My hobby is dancing.* Ask Ss to give thumbs up/down signals to show you which of these sentences they think fit in with the title of the lesson. (*Books open*) Ss read the lesson objectives, look at pages 4–5 and check their predictions.
- (L1/L2) Explain the lesson objectives.

Lead-in
- (*Books open*) Use the photos to find out what your Ss know. E.g. pointing to the photo of Jen, say *Look. This is a … (girl).* Point at her hair and say *What colour is this? (Brown.)* Encourage Ss who seem confident to say colours and to name as many objects/clothes as they can.
- Use the photos to check *computer*, *cupcakes* and *skateboard*.

Get started!

How do you spell that? I can say and spell my name and surname.

In this unit
- I'm … / My name is …
- This is …
- My/your
- The alphabet
- Spelling words/names
- Numbers
- Colours
- In my bag
- Classroom objects
- Classroom language

1 ▶1 🔊 **1.2** Watch or listen and read. Who is not from the UK?
Lucas.

2 Look at the photos and read. Complete the children's hobbies.
1 Jen <u>making cupcakes</u>
2 Alex computers and <u>computer</u> games
3 Lian all <u>sports</u>
4 Lucas <u>music</u> and Maths

- Check Ss understand *the UK*. Point to the photo of Lian, shake your head and say *She isn't in* (your city/town). *I think she's in London. It's in … (the UK)*.

Exercise 1   1.2
- Play the video. If you don't have access to a computer and projector, play the recording.
- Ask a student to justify the answer by referring to the text.

Answer → student page

Exercise 2
- Ask pairs to complete what they can. Then play the video/recording again for Ss to check. 💬 Use the Lollipop Stick technique to choose different Ss to write the answers on the board.

Answers → student page

- 💬 Get to know your class as soon as you can. You could now use the Traffic Lights technique to find out how easy/difficult they found the first two exercises.

3 **Game!** Stand in a line. Ask and answer.
 A: *Hi, I'm Mario. What's your name?*
 B: *I'm Isabella. Hi, I'm Isabella. What's your name?*
 C: *My name's David. …*

4 🔊 1.3 🔊 1.4 Listen and do the Alphabet Rap.

, , , D,

E, F, G,

 Say the alphabet, say it with me!

H, I, J, K, L, M, N, O, P,

 is funny as you can see.

R, S, T, U and V

four more letters and we're free.

W, X, Y and – Shh …

is sleepy, so are we!

5 Complete the words with the letters in the box. Say the letters.

| t h g x l s |

1 <u>g</u>irl   2 bo<u>x</u>   3 <u>s</u>andwich

4 <u>t</u>able   5 <u>l</u>ion   6 fis<u>h</u>

6 🔊 1.5 Listen and tick (✔) the letters you hear.

1 A ✔   E ✔   I ☐
2 G ✔   J ☐   C ✔
3 W ✔   U ✔   Y ☐
4 B ✔   D ☐   P ✔
5 M ✔   N ✔   F ☐
6 I ✔   J ☐   Y ✔

7 Work in pairs. Say the alphabet. Stop when the teacher tells you. Your partner says what comes next.

 A, B, C, D, …   *Stop!*   *E!*

LOOK! LL = double L

8 🔊 1.6 Listen to the surnames. Complete the missing letters. Check with your partner.
 1 N <u>E</u> W M <u>A</u> N
 2 O R <u>T</u> I Z
 3 C A <u>V</u> E N D I S H
 4 H I G <u>G</u> I N S

9 Work in pairs. Ask for your partner's surname. Write it down.
 A: *What's your surname?*
 B: *Brown.*
 A: *How do you spell that?*
 B: *B-R-O-W-N.*

10 Have a class spelling competition.

Apple. A-double P-L-E. Apple.

5

Exercise 7
- One student in each pair listens and the other says the alphabet. Say *Stop*. Ss change roles after the listener says the next letter of the alphabet.
- Alternatively, you could ask Ss to work in groups of three. Student A is 'teacher'. He/She says *Go!* Student B says the alphabet. Student A says *Stop!* and Student C says the next letter. Ss continue, changing roles each time.

Look!
- Explain we say *double* before two of any letter.

Exercise 8 🔊 1.6
- After, ask Ss to spell the surnames to each other.

Answers → student page

Exercise 9
- Ask Ss to repeat the two questions in chorus after you before they start.

Exercise 10
- Divide the class into four teams. Say a word Ss know. One student from each team writes it on the board and then spells it. 💬 Use the Thumbs up/down technique to check which are correct with the class. Continue with different words/Ss.

Finishing the lesson
- Pairs discuss which predictions they made in the Warm-up were correct. Ask *Can you say and spell your name and surname?* Students show self-assessment response cards (☺, 😐, ☹).
- Ss copy the objectives into their notebooks and draw the emoticons that reflect their progress.

⏳ Fast finishers
- (*Books closed*) Ss label all the objects they know in the photos on page 4.

Exercise 3
- Ask the class to repeat *What's your name?* and *I'm … / My name's …* after you in chorus before they start. Draw Ss attention to the contractions by using your fingers. E.g. say *I* (hold up one finger) *am* (hold up a second finger). Then say *I'm* (bring your fingers together).
- Alternatively, Ss ask and answer in rows / on their tables.

Exercise 4 🔊 1.3 🔊 1.4
- Encourage Ss to clap/beat the rhythm as they listen and/or teach them some gestures, e.g. laugh for *funny*, yawn for *sleepy*.
- When Ss are familiar with the rap, play the karaoke version. Ss make the gestures as they rap.

Exercise 5
- 💬 Pairs help each other complete. Then they listen to each other say the words.

Answers → student page

Exercise 6 🔊 1.5
- Play the recording two or three times if your class seems weak.

Answers → student page

Extra activity
- Ss write down six-eight letters of the alphabet at random. They say them to a partner who writes them down. Tell Ss they can't repeat the letters! They check, swap roles and continue.

23

0.2

In this lesson

Lesson aims:
- Vocabulary: numbers 1–100, colours

Homework:
- Workbook Unit 0, p. 5

Assessment for Learning in this lesson
- Setting aims and criteria for success: Warm-up
- Giving feedback: Exercise 3 and 11
- Peer learning: Exercise 4 and 9
- Independent learning: Finishing the lesson

Warm-up

- (*Books closed*) Write English surnames on slips of paper and give one slip/surname to each student. Ss stand up and mingle. They ask each other *What's your surname?* and *How do you spell that?* Alternatively, do this activity in groups of four. Possible surnames: Smith, Jones, Williams, Taylor, Davies, Evans, Wilson, Thomas, Johnson, Roberts, Robinson, Thompson, Wright, Hughes, Walker, White, Edwards, Green, Hall, Lewis, Harris, Clarke, Patel, Jackson, Wood, Turner. You could give Ss English first names too!
- (*Books open*) Pairs look at pages 6–7 and discuss what they will do in this lesson. (*L1/L2*) Explain the lesson objectives.

Lead-in

- (*Books open*) Ask the class to look at the picture and to name any objects they can. Ask different Ss to spell them! Use the picture to check Ss understand *dog* and *cat* too.

Exercise 1 1.7
- Before you play the recording, ask the class to predict the answer.
- After, ask a student to justify the answer by pointing to the picture / referring to the text.

Answer → student page

0.2 **Numbers and colours** — I can say numbers 0–100 and name basic colours.

Meet Dug and Kit

This is Dug. Dug is also Superdug. Superdug is a superhero.

This is Kit. Kit is very clever. She is Dug's best friend.

1 🔊 1.7 Listen and read. Look at the picture. Then circle the correct answer.

(Dug) / Kit is a superhero.

2 🔊 1.8 Listen and repeat.

Vocabulary Numbers 1–20

1 one		11 eleven	
2 two		12 twelve	
3 three		13 thirteen	
4 four		14 fourteen	
5 five		15 fifteen	
6 six		16 sixteen	
7 seven		17 seventeen	
8 eight		18 eighteen	
9 nine		19 nineteen	
10 ten		20 twenty	

3 Complete the numbers.

1 o n e   7 s e v e n
2 t w o   8 e i g h t
3 t h r e e   9 n i n e
4 f o u r   10 t e n
5 f i v e   11 e l e v e n
6 s i x   12 t w e l v e

4 Write the answers in words.

1 six + six = twelve
2 eighteen − three = fifteen
3 two + eleven = thirteen
4 twenty − nine = eleven
5 seventeen − three = fourteen
6 two + seven = nine
7 five + two = seven
8 sixteen − twelve = four

Exercise 2 1.8
- Find out if your class knows some numbers first. You could count the Ss in the class aloud. Either encourage all Ss to say the numbers with you or ask different Ss to say each number with the class'/your help if necessary.
- Give Ss time to look at the Vocabulary box before you play the recording.

Exercise 3
- Tell Ss to check the spelling by referring to the Vocabulary box and not to guess / use their memories. Then use the Lollipop Stick technique to choose different Ss to say and spell each word.

Answers → student page

Exercise 4
- Pairs help each other work out and write the answers. Then ask pairs to stand up and to check their answers with two other pairs.

Answers → student page

- (*Books closed*) Challenge a strong class. Teach Ss how to say '+' (*plus/and*) and '−' (*minus*). Ask different Ss the sums in Exercise 4. E.g. *What's eighteen minus three?* (Fifteen.)

Exercise 5 1.9
- You could challenge pairs in a strong class to cover the words first and to help each other say the numbers.

5 🔊 **1.9** Listen and repeat.

Vocabulary Numbers 10–100

10 ten	60 sixty
20 twenty	70 seventy
30 thirty	80 eighty
40 forty	90 ninety
50 fifty	100 a hundred

6 Circle the correct number.
1 forty   14 /⑭
2 fifteen   ⑮/ 50
3 thirteen ⑬/ 30
4 eighty   18 /⑱
5 twenty   12 /⑳
6 sixteen   ⑯/ 60

7 🔊 **1.10** Listen and write the number you hear.
a _20_   d _40_   g _8_
b _7_   e _12_   h _19_
c _13_   f _50_

8 🔊 **1.11** Listen and repeat.

Vocabulary Colours

black blue brown green grey
orange pink purple red
white yellow

9 Look at Exercise 3. Write numbers which are this colour. There are two numbers for one of the colours.

red	_9_	green	_5_	pink	_1, 11_
grey	_6_	white	_12_	black	_10_
blue	_4_	purple	_8_	brown	_2_
orange	_7_	yellow	_3_		

10 Game! Student A: Listen to Student B and guess! Then swap roles.

A: *What's your favourite colour?*
B: *Not pink, not brown, not white, not yellow, not green, not red, not blue, not grey, not black, not orange.*
A: *It's purple!*

11 Look at the picture below. Match 1–8 to a–h.
1 The elephants are —— a blue.
2 The flowers are —— b black and white.
3 The zebras are —— c red.
4 The sky is —— d grey.
5 The oranges are —— e green.
6 The lemons are —— f pink.
7 The trees are —— g orange.
8 The flamingoes are —— h yellow.

12 Game! Finish the sentences.
A: *The elephants are …*
B: *… green.*
C: *No! They're grey. The flowers are …*
D: *Red!*
E: *Yes! The zebras are …*

Exercise 10
- Tell the class Student A should let Student B say at least eight–nine colours before he/she guesses.

Exercise 11
- First, make sure Ss know the names of the objects and animals in points 1–8. Say each object/animal in turn and get a different student to hold up his/her book and point.
- 💬 Ss do the exercise individually. Use the Traffic Lights technique to monitor.

Answers → student page

Exercise 12
- Make sure Ss understand that the student who completes a sentence can say a colour that's either correct or wrong.
- Alternatively, ask Ss to work in groups of three.

Finishing the lesson
- Ask the class *Can you say numbers 1–100? Can you name basic colours?* Students show self-assessment response cards after each question (☺, 😐, ☹).
- Ss copy the objectives into their notebooks and draw the emoticons that reflect their progress.

⏳ **Fast finishers**
- Ss label the colours in the cartoon.
- Ss label the objects and animals in the picture on page 7.

Exercise 6
- Ss read and circle individually.
- When checking answers, help Ss with pronunciation. Write *forty/fourteen* on the board to show them where the stress is. If your class is strong, you could ask Ss to practise saying each pair of words to a partner.

Answers → student page

Exercise 7 🔊 1.10
- After Ss listen, ask them to compare their answers with a partner. Then play the recording again. Pause after each number and ask different Ss to write them on the board.

Answers → student page

Extra activity
- Make a 'ball' from a piece of waste paper. Say *One!* Throw it at random to a student and encourage him/her to say *Two!* He/She then throws it at random to another student who says *Three!* and so on. Challenge Ss by asking them to say odd/even numbers or multiples of five, etc.

Exercise 8 🔊 1.11
- Before you play the recording, point to different objects in the classroom and elicit any colours Ss know.

Exercise 9
- Use the example to make sure Ss understand they should first find the colour.
- 👥 Pairs help each other do the exercise.

Answers → student page

0.3

In this lesson

Lesson aims:
- Vocabulary: objects in a schoolbag, classroom objects
- Communication: classroom language

Resources:
- Tests: Get Started! Language Test

Homework:
- Workbook Unit 0, pp. 6–7

Assessment for Learning in this lesson
- 🎯 Setting aims and criteria for success: Warm-up
- 💬 Giving feedback: Exercise 1, 5 and 9
- 👥 Peer learning: Exercise 6 and 10
- 🎓 Independent learning: Finishing the lesson

Warm-up
- (*Books closed*) Divide the class into two teams. Write an easy sum on the board, e.g. 50 − 5 = … (45). A student from one team writes, then says and spells the answer to win a point. Ask different Ss from each team in turn to work out different sums.
- 🎯 (*Books open*) Give pairs time to look at pages 8–9. (*L1/L2*) Explain the lesson objectives.

Lead-in
- (*Books open*) Point to the different objects in the picture above Exercise 1. Ask different Ss to say the colours.
- The class names any objects they can.

Exercise 1 🔊 1.12
- As Ss repeat, ask *What's the number?* or say it yourself and ask Ss to point.

Answers → student page

- 💬 (*Books closed*) After Ss label the pictures, say the numbers at random and use the Lollipop Stick technique to choose Ss who give the names of the objects.

0.3 In the classroom

I can talk about classroom objects and understand classroom instructions.

Extra activity
- Play *I Spy* with the class. Secretly choose an object in the classroom. Say *I spy with my little eye something beginning with …* (say the first letter of the object). Different Ss guess the object. The student who guesses first, goes next.

Look!
- (*L1/L2*) Explain we use *an* before nouns beginning with *a, e, i, o, u*.

Exercise 2
- Ask the class to underline the words beginning with a vowel first.
- Ask pairs to compare answers.

Answers → student page

Look!
- Tell Ss we add *-s* to most nouns to form the plural, including nouns ending in *e*. We need to add *-es* to some nouns, e.g. those ending in *x* and *ch*.

Exercise 3
- Pairs race to answer! Then ask different Ss to write the answers on the board.

Answers → student page

Exercise 4 🔊 1.13
- As Ss repeat, ask them to point at the objects in the classroom or do it yourself.

26

6 Work in pairs. Guess what these objects are. Then go to page 106 and check.

1 It's a <u>pencil case.</u>

2 They're <u>scissors.</u>

3 <u>It's a bin.</u>

4 <u>It's a desk.</u>

5 <u>They're chairs.</u>

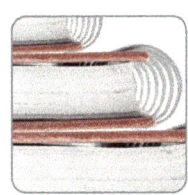
6 <u>They're notebooks</u>.

9 🔊 1.15 Match 1–5 to a–e. Listen and check. Act out the dialogues in pairs.

1 [e] Can you repeat that, please?
2 [d] Can you help me, Miss?
3 [a] How do we say *elefante* in English?
4 [b] I'm ready!
5 [c] What does *amazing* mean?

a We say *elephant*.
b Good. Class, are you ready too?
c It means *really good*.
d Yes, Maria. How can I help you?
e Yes, Tomas. Giraffe. Giraffe. OK?

7 🔊 1.14 Listen and repeat.

Communication Classroom language

Close your books.
Listen (*to the story*).
Look (*at the photo*).
Open your books.
Read (*the text*).
Sit down.
Stand up.

Work in pairs.
Write (*your name*).

Can you help me?
Can you repeat (that)?
I'm ready.
What's *kredka* in English?

8 Read the expressions in the Communication box again. Who usually says them: Teacher or Student?

LOOK! Can you help me, please?
Stand up, please!

Fun Spot

10 Game! Be a teacher. Tell other students what to do. Use the expressions in the Communication box.

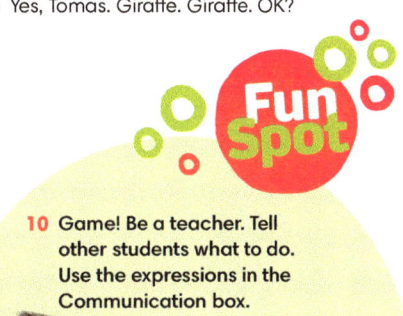

Write your name, please.

Exercise 8
- Ask Ss to write *T* (*Teacher*) or *S* (*Student*) next to each expression. Then ask them to compare their answers with a partner.

Answers
The first nine expressions in the Communication box are what a teacher might say. The last four are for Ss.

Look!
- Remind Ss it's polite to say *please* in English.

Exercise 9 🔊 1.15
- After Ss do the exercise individually, they compare answers with a partner.
- 💬 Use the Traffic Lights technique to find out how easy/difficult Ss found the exercise. Explain the expressions again if necessary.

Answers → student page

Exercise 10
- Ss work in groups of four and take turns to be the teacher. Remind Ss to use appropriate intonation. Challenge strong Ss to close their books.
- 🐫 Each group votes for the best teacher. One student reports and explains his/her group's decision to the class.

Finishing the lesson
- 📖 Read the lesson objectives. Ss show self-assessment response cards (😊, 😐, ☹).
- 📖 Ss copy the objectives into their notebooks and draw the emoticons that reflect their progress.

⏳ Fast finishers
- Ss write what objects they've got in their schoolbags and say how many. E.g. *Three books.*

Exercise 5
- Pairs point at the objects, say a number and the corresponding word in the Vocabulary box. E.g. *Twenty-five chairs!*
- 💬 Alternatively, use the Lollipop Stick technique to choose different Ss to do it.

Look!
- After Ss read the information, use your fingers to show the contraction *it's* = *it is* and *they're* = *they are*.
- **Critical thinking** Say *It's! Singular or plural?* You could hold up one pen to explain *singular*, and two or more pens to explain *plural*. Repeat.

Exercise 6
- 🌐 Pairs discuss each answer before they write. Before they check, you could write down Ss' ideas on the board for each question and vote!

Answers → student page

Exercise 7 🔊 1.14
- As Ss listen to each expression, make an appropriate gesture. E.g. mime opening/closing a book with your hands for *books open/closed*. You may need to explain the last four expressions in L1.
- (*L1/L2*) Draw Ss' attention to intonation. Tell them appropriate intonation is very important or they might seem rude.

1.1

In this lesson

Lesson aims:
- Vocabulary: family members

Resources:
- Vocabulary worksheet 1.1, p. 148
- Tests: Vocabulary Check 1.1

Homework:
- Workbook Unit 1, p. 8

Assessment for Learning in this lesson
- Setting aims and criteria for success: Warm-up
- Giving feedback: Exercise 3 and 8
- Peer learning: Exercise 6
- Independent learning: Finishing the lesson

Warm-up
- (*Books closed*) Play *Snowman* with words from Unit 0. On the board, write a dash for each letter of a word. Ss work in two teams and take turns to guess the letters of the word. Draw a part of the snowman for each wrong guess (snowballs, sticks for arms, a hat, eyes, a nose, a mouth, buttons). The team who guesses the word before the snowman is complete wins a point. If a team makes a wrong guess and you draw the last part of a snowman, it loses a point.
- Write *Family and friends* on the board. Volunteers predict what they will learn.
- (L1/L2) Explain the lesson objective. Ss predict what they will be able to say in English at the end of the lesson.

Lead-in
- (*Books closed*) Brainstorm family words with the class.

Exercise 1
- Choose one word from the box, translate it and say *I know that!* with a thumbs up gesture. Volunteers continue.

Exercise 2 🔊 1.16
- Ss look at page 10. Say *This is Mark. This is Mark's family.*
- (L1/L2) Pairs use the colours of each character's clothes to work out who they are.

Answers → student page

1 Family and friends

Vocabulary I can talk about people in a family.

In this unit

Vocabulary
- Family
- Countries and nationalities
- Places

Grammar
- possessive *'s*
- *to be* affirmative
- possessive adjectives
- *to be* negative

1.2 Grammar video

1.2 Grammar animation

1.3 Grammar animation

1.4 Communication video

BBC Culture video

1 Read these words. What do they mean?

brother   dad   grandad   granny   mum   sister

I know that!

- Play the recording. Pause for Ss to repeat each word and to point to the corresponding person. Alternatively, with a weak class get different volunteers to hold up their books and point. Explain where necessary.

Exercise 3
- Make sure Ss understand that the words on the left are masculine and those on the right feminine.
- Pairs complete.
- Use the Lollipop Stick technique to pick individuals who write the answers on the board.

Answers → student page

Exercise 4
- Ss do the matching exercise individually.
- Pairs compare answers.

Answers → student page

- (L1/L2) Ask *Are words 1–4 formal or informal?* (Formal.) *Are words a–d formal or informal?* (Informal.)
- **Critical thinking** (L1/L2) Class discussion. Compare the words with formal and informal family words in your language.

Look!
Using the picture on page 10, point at Mark and then at his dad. Say *Mark. Dad. Mark's dad.* Explain that in this example *'s* is not a short form of *to be*. It is used to express relationship between people.

28

2 🔊 **1.16** Listen and repeat. Find the people in Mark's family pyramid on page 10. Use the colours to help you.

Vocabulary Family

mother mum father dad parents
grandfather grandad grandmother granny
son daughter brother sister
aunt uncle cousin

3 Complete the family words. Use the Vocabulary box to help you.

He	She
father	mother
grandfather	grandmother
son	daughter
brother	sister
uncle	aunt
cousin	cousin

4 Match 1–4 to a–d.
1 father — a grandad
2 grandmother — b dad
3 mother — c granny
4 grandfather — d mum

LOOK! Paul = Mark's father
Lucy = Rose's daughter

5 Look at the family pyramid on page 10 and write the names.

1 Mark's grandfather — John
2 Mark's sister — Lucy
3 Mark's aunt — Julia
4 Mark's brother — David
5 Mark's cousins — Tom, Anna
6 Mark's grandmother — Agatha
7 Mark's uncle — Peter
8 Mark's parents — Rose, Paul

6 Look at the family pyramid again. Complete the sentences. Use the names in the box.

Mark's Julia's Rose's Tom's Paul's Peter's

1 Peter is _Mark's_ uncle.
2 Julia is _Paul's_ sister.
3 David is _____ son. Rose's / Paul's
4 Anna is _____ daughter. Peter's / Julia's
5 John and Agatha are _____ parents. Julia's / Paul's
6 Lucy is _____ cousin. Tom's / Anna's

7 🔊 **1.17** Listen and circle T (true) or F (false). Then listen again and check your answers.

1 John — T / **F**
2 Anna — **T** / F
3 Julia — T / **F**
4 Agatha — T / **F**
5 Paul — **T** / F
6 Mark — **T** / F

8 Draw your family pyramid. Write the names of the people from your family.

I remember that!

Exercise 5
- Ss complete in pairs. Then divide the class into two groups. Ask one student from each group to come up. Raise the book and say *Mark's (uncle)*. The student who first points at the right person in the picture wins a point for his/her group. Continue with other pairs.

Answers → student page

Exercise 6
- Help weak Ss by pairing them with strong ones.
- 🌐 Ss complete individually. Then they check each other's answers and give feedback.

Answers → student page

Extra activity
- (*Books open*) The class look at Mark's family pyramid for one minute.
- (*Books closed*) Divide the class into two teams, A and B. Invite one student from each team to the front. Secretly show Student A the pyramid. He/She imitates one of the character's posture and/or facial expression. Student B guesses who it is. E.g. *Mark's uncle* (one point) or *Mark's uncle, Peter* (two points). Continue with different Ss/roles!

Exercise 7 🔊 1.17
- Pause after the example to make sure Ss understand the exercise.
- Ss work individually. (Pause after each question to help a weak class.) Then they compare their answers in pairs.
- Get a strong class to correct the false answers.

Answers → student page

Exercise 8
- Ss do the activity in their notebooks. Alternatively, if you have class time, Ss could make a poster.
- 💬 Pairs or small groups point and tell each other about their family. As you monitor, try to give positive feedback and challenge strong Ss to use complete sentences. E.g. *My dad is Marek. My sisters are …*

Finishing the lesson
- 📕 Ss circle the new words in the Vocabulary box they have learnt. Remember to praise and encourage. (*L1*) Tell weak Ss they will be able to practise the words again in the other units and activities.
- 📕 Ask *Can you talk about people in a family?* Students show self-assessment response cards (☺, 😐, ☹). Then they copy the objective into their notebooks and draw the emoticon that reflects their progress.

⏳ Fast finishers
- Pairwork. (*Book open*) Student A names someone in Mark's family. (*Book closed*) Student B says his/her relationship to Mark, e.g. *Mark's uncle*. They swap roles and continue.
- Ss close their books and write all the family words they can remember in their notebook. They open their books and check.
- Ss write sentences about a friend's family, e.g. *Martin is Anna's brother* or *Martin – Anna's brother*.

1.2

In this lesson

Lesson aims:
- Grammar: *to be* affirmative; *my, your, his, her*

Resources:
- Grammar worksheet 1.2, p. 152
- Tests: Grammar Check 1.2

Homework:
- Workbook Unit 1, p. 9
- Extra Online Practice Unit 1

Assessment for Learning in this lesson
- Setting aims and criteria for success: Warm-up
- Giving feedback: Exercise 2, 11 and 12
- Peer learning: Exercise 6 and 9
- Independent learning: Finishing the lesson

Warm-up
- (*Books closed*) Pointing to your lips, say *Look!* Mouth a family word but don't say it aloud. The class guesses the word by reading your lips. Pairs continue.
- Write a few sentences with *to be* on the board. E.g. *I am your teacher. You are students.* Ask *What's the verb?* (L1/L2) Explain the lesson objectives.

Lead-in
- (*Books open*) Pointing to the photos on page 12, ask *Who is he/she?* (*Alex./Jen.*) Ss guess who the new characters are.
- Use the photos to pre-teach *cake, present* and *card*. A strong student translates *Spain*.

Exercise 1 ▶2 🔊 1.18
- Read the questions. The class predicts the answers.
- Play the video. If you don't have access to a computer and projector, play the recording.
- Check answers by writing on the board: *1 seven, seventy, seventeen; 2 Granny's son, Alex's cousin, Alex's brother.* Ss queue in front of the correct answers.

Answers → student page

1.2 Grammar

I can use the affirmative form of the verb *to be* and *my, your, his, her*.

It's Granny's birthday!

Today is Sophie's birthday. She is seventy years old. Sophie is Jen and Alex's grandmother. They are at her house.

Sophie: I'm so happy you're here.

Alex: It's aunt Megan!
Megan: Hello, Alex! Hold this, please! Be careful! It's Granny's birthday cake.
Alex: It's OK. I've got it!

Megan: Happy birthday, Mum! Here's your present.
Sophie: Thank you, my darling. Where's your son?
Megan: Jason is in Spain with his class. They're on a school trip. Here's a card from him.
Sophie: Oh, it's a lovely card!
Dad: Hello, sister!

Dad: We're ready for the cake!
Mum: Oh, no!

1 ▶2 🔊 **1.18** Watch or listen and read. Answer the questions.
1. How old is Jen and Alex's granny today? *70.*
2. Who is Jason? *Megan's son. / Jen and Alex's cousin.*

2 Read the sentences. Circle T (true) or F (false). Correct the false sentences.
1. Granny's name is Sophie. (T)/ F
2. They are at Jen and Alex's house. T /(F)
3. There's a present for Granny in the box. T /(F)
4. Jason is at home. T /(F)
5. Dad is Aunt Megan's brother. (T)/ F

3 🔊 **1.19** Listen and repeat. Find these expressions in the story.

> Hold this, please! Be careful!
> I've got it!

Say it!

4 ▶ **Guess!** Jen and Alex's mum says 'Oh, no!' Why? Have a class vote. Choose a, b or c.
a The cake is a mess. (b) It's not Granny's cake.
c There's a mouse in the box.

5 ▶3 🔊 **1.20** Now watch or listen and check.

12

Exercise 2
- Check answers using T/F response cards.

Answers → student page

Correct sentences:
2 They are at Sophie's/Granny's house. 3 There's a birthday cake in the box. 4 He's in Spain.

Exercise 3 🔊1.19 ▶2
- Play the recording, pausing for Ss to repeat each expression.
- Play the video again. Ss shout *STOP!* when they hear each expression. Alternatively, Ss underline the expressions in the dialogue.

Exercise 4
- Pre-teach *mess* (show) and *mouse* (draw).
- **Critical thinking** Say *Hands up for a/b/c!* (L1/L2) Individuals explain their choice. Don't confirm yet!

Answer → student page

Exercise 5 ▶3 🔊 1.20
- Play the video or recording to check.

Video/Audio script
Dad: What?
Mum: Look at the cake.
Megan: Oh, no! It's the wrong cake.
Jen: It's a baby's cake! Look!
Sophie: 'Happy birthday baby Luke!'
Alex: Luke is one today!
Dad: And the cake is yummy!
Jen and Alex: Dad!

1.2

Grammar *to be affirmative*

Long form	Short form
I **am** ten.	**I'm** ten.
You **are** ten.	**You're** ten.
He/She/It **is** ten.	**He/She/It's** ten.
We **are** ten.	**We're** ten.
You **are** ten.	**You're** ten.
They **are** ten.	**They're** ten.

▶ 4 **Get Grammar!**

We're friends!
Hammy is my pet hamster.

6 Find the sentences in the story. Write the missing word.
1 They _are_ at her house.
2 'I _'m_ so happy!'
3 'You _'re_ here!'
4 'It _'s_ Granny's birthday cake.'
5 'Jason _is_ in Spain.'
6 'We _'re_ ready for the cake!'

7 Circle the correct answer.
1 You (are)/ is ready.   4 Jason (is)/ am Jen's cousin.
2 I is /(am)here.   5 It are /(is) a present for you.
3 We am /(are)happy!   6 Jen and Alex is /(are) at their Granny's house.

8 Rewrite sentences 1, 2, 3 and 5 in Exercise 7 using short forms of the verb *to be*.
1 *You're ready.*

LOOK!
I → my	It's **my** birthday. **I'm** ten!
you → your	It's **your** birthday. **You're** eleven!
he → his	It's **his** birthday. **He's** twelve.
she → her	It's **her** birthday. **She's** nine.

9 Complete with *my, your, his* or *her*.
1 Alex: 'Granny, here's _your_ birthday card!'
2 Dad: 'It's my mother's birthday. We are at _her_ house.'
3 Sophie: 'I'm very happy! _My_ family is here!'
4 Megan: 'Jason is in Spain with _his_ class.'
5 Alex: '_Your_ birthday cake is in this box, Granny.'

10 🔊 1.21 How old are they? Follow the lines and complete the sentences. Then listen and check.
1 Lucas: 'I _'m_ _eleven_.'   10
2 Lian: 'Alex and I _are_ _twelve_.'   16
3 Lucas: 'My brother _is_ _sixteen_.'   11
4 Lian to Jen: 'You _are_ _ten_, right?'   12

11 Read and complete with *am, are* or *is*.

My name ¹ _is_ Lian and I ² _'m/am_ twelve years old. Alex and I ³ _are_ best friends and classmates. His sister, Jen, ⁴ _is_ ten years old. We ⁵ _'re/are_ friends too.

12 Look at Exercise 11. Write about you and your friends.
My name's … and I …

13 Read the poem. Make changes to talk about a friend or a classmate.

I'm ten today.
Hip, hip, hooray!
Let's have a break.
And eat my cake!

Ola's eleven today. …

Extra video activity ▶ 2
- (Books closed) Play a short scene, e.g. 2, with no sound. Pause after each character speaks. Elicit what they say, using gesture. Pairs/groups act it out. Weak Ss read the lines in their books.

Get Grammar! ▶ 4
- Introduce Hammy and the characters.
- Play the Get Grammar! video. If you don't have access to a computer and projector, continue.
- The class repeats the examples after you in chorus.
- Explain contractions. E.g. say *I am ten.* Hold up one finger on each hand. Then say *I'm ten.* Bring both fingers together.

Exercise 6
- 💬 Ss work individually and then compare their answers in pairs.

Answers → student page

Exercise 7
- Pairs in a weak class underline the subject of each sentence first.

Answers → student page

Exercise 8
- Ss write in their notebooks.
- Choose Ss to read their answers.

Answers
2 I'm here. 3 We're happy.
5 It's a present for you.

Look!
Ask Ss if they know the difference between, e.g. *your* and *you're*. Make sure Ss understand which are the possessive forms.

Exercise 9
- 💬 Ss complete and then work in pairs. They look at each other's answers, discuss and decide what's wrong and why.

Answers → student page

Exercise 10 🔊 1.21
- Pairs do the exercise.
- Play the recording. Ss check.

Answers → student page

Exercise 11
- Pre-teach/elicit *classmates* by pointing to different pairs.
- 💬 Use the Traffic Lights technique to check who needs more support.

Answers → student page

Exercise 12
- Ss write in their notebooks.
- 💬 When monitoring, explain why work is good or needs improvement.

Extra activity
- Pairs write three sentences about a classmate similar to those in Exercise 12. They read the sentences to another pair/the class but they don't say the classmate's name. Ss guess who it is.

Exercise 13
- Read the poem aloud with Ss, clapping a rhythm as you read. Pairs continue, changing the words in red.

Finishing the lesson
- 💬 Ask individuals to say sentences with *to be*. Then ask the class *Can you use the verb 'to be'?* Students show self-assessment response cards (☺, 😐, ☹).
- 💬 Ss copy the objectives into their notebooks and draw the emoticons that reflect their progress.

⌛ **Fast finishers**
- Ss write more T/F sentences about the photo story. They ask the class at the end of the activity/lesson.
- Ss look at the pictures in the photo story and write down the words they know.

1.3

In this lesson

Lesson aims:
- Grammar: *to be* negative
- Vocabulary: countries and nationalities

Resources:
- Grammar worksheet 1.3, p. 153
- Tests: Grammar Check 1.3, Vocabulary Check 1.3

Homework:
- Workbook Unit 1, p. 10

Assessment for Learning in this lesson
- Setting aims and criteria for success: Warm-up
- Giving feedback: Exercise 3, 4 and 5
- Peer learning: Exercise 7
- Independent learning: Finishing the lesson

Warm-up

- (*Books closed*) Write on the board: *1 The bag __ blue. 2 Alex __ twelve. 3 I __ in my classroom. 4 You __ the teacher. 5 We __ cool. 6 Dug and Kit __ best friends.* Different Ss come to the board and complete the sentences with *am/are/is*. Ask Ss to reflect on how much they remember from Lesson 1.2.
- (*Books open*) Pairs look at pages 14–15. (L1) Ask *What will you learn in this lesson?* Volunteers give their ideas. Explain the lesson objectives. Then Ss look at the board again. Ask who can make the sentences negative.

Lead-in

- (*Books open*) Pointing to Picture 1 in the cartoon, ask *Who's he? (Superdug.) Who's she? (Kit.)* Ss tell you what they know about them. (*Superdug is a superhero. Kit is his best friend.*)
- Ss tell you what they can see in the other pictures. Use Picture 1 to pre-teach *family album*. Pre-teach/Elicit *happy*. Point to Picture 3, shake your head and say *Dug isn't … (happy)!* Pre-teach *hungry*. Rubbing your stomach, say *I'm … (hungry)!*

1 Look at the cartoon. How many types of dogs can you see?

2 🔊 1.22 Listen and read. What nationality is Uncle Roberto? *Spanish.*

3 Read the sentences. Circle T (true) or F (false).
1 Uncle Roberto is a superhero. **T** / F
2 Aunt Gigi is French. **T** / F
3 Dug's parents are superheroes. T / **F**
4 Dug is happy in the photo. T / **F**
5 Dug's mum is British. T / **F**

Exercise 1
- **Critical thinking** Tell pairs to look at each picture carefully. Make this a race!

Answer
There are eight types of dogs.

Exercise 2 🔊 1.22
- Write on the board *British, French, Polish* and *Spanish* for a weak class and elicit the meaning.
- Play the recording. Ss listen and read.
- Have a class discussion and ask Ss to justify their answers.

Answer → student page

Exercise 3
- Pairs do the exercise.
- Check answers using the Basketball technique.

Answers → student page

Get Grammar!
- Play the Get Grammar! video. If you don't have access to a computer and projector, continue.
- The class repeats the examples after you in chorus.
- Use your fingers to draw Ss' attention to the contractions. (See Lesson 1.2, Get Grammar! notes.)
- It's advisable not to teach the alternative negative forms *you're not, he's not*, etc. This could be confusing.

Grammar *to be* negative

Long form	Short form
I **am not** Spanish.	I'**m not** Spanish.
You **are not** Spanish.	You **aren't** Spanish.
He/She/It **is not** Spanish.	He/She/It **isn't** Spanish.
We **are not** Spanish.	We **aren't** Spanish.
You **are not** Spanish.	You **aren't** Spanish.
They **are not** Spanish.	They **aren't** Spanish.

▶ 5 **Get Grammar!**

Hammy isn't orange.

No, I'm not orange and I'm not fat.

4 In your notebook, write negative sentences. Use the long form of the verb *to be*.
1 Dug is French. *Dug is not French.*
2 Kit is a dog. *Kit is not a dog.*
3 Dug's parents are superheroes. *Dug's parents are not superheroes.*
4 Dug: 'I am happy.' *Dug: 'I am not happy.'*
5 Kit: 'You are in the photo, Dug'. *Kit: 'You are not in the photo, Dug.'*
6 Dug is hungry. *Dug is not hungry.*

5 Rewrite the sentences in Exercise 4 in your notebook. Use the short form of the verb *to be*.
1 *Dug isn't French.*

6 🔊 1.23 Look, listen and repeat.

Vocabulary
Countries and nationalities

🇬🇧 the UK / British   🇮🇹 Italy / Italian
🇪🇸 Spain / Spanish   🇫🇷 France / French
🇵🇱 Poland / Polish   🇨🇳 China / Chinese
🇺🇸 the USA / American

7 Look at the flags. Complete the sentences about Dug's family with *is* or *isn't*. Correct the false sentences.
1 🇪🇸 Aunt Teresa *isn't* Spanish. *She is Polish.*
2 🇮🇹 Grandad Umberto *isn't* Chinese. *He is Italian.*
3 🇫🇷 Cousin Lulu *is* French.
4 🇨🇳 Cousin Chen *isn't* British. *She is Chinese.*
5 🇺🇸 Granny Flossie *is* American.

8 In your notebook, write sentences about Kit's friends and family.

I'm not from Italy. I'm from the UK.

1 Italy ✗   the UK ✔

We …

2 Spain ✗   the UK ✔

Granny Susie …

3 France ✗   the UK ✔

My cousins …

4 the USA ✗   China ✔

9 Choose your nationality and play Three Guesses game.
A: *You're Spanish!*
B: *No, I'm not Spanish.*
A: *You're British!*
B: *No, I'm not British.*
A: *You're Italian!*
B: *Yes, I'm Italian.*

Fun Spot

15

Exercise 4
• Pairs write.
• 💬 Choose Ss to write the answers on the board. Involve the class. Ask *Is this correct?* The class helps if necessary.

Answers → student page

Exercise 5
• Ss write in their notebooks.
• 💬 When monitoring, remember to praise as well as correct. Explain why Ss' work is good or needs improvement. Make positive comments first.

Answers
2 Kit isn't a dog. 3 Dug's parents aren't superheroes. 4 Dug: 'I'm not happy.' 5 Kit: 'You aren't in the photo, Dug.' 6 Dug isn't hungry.

Exercise 6 🔊 1.23
• Pre-tech the words if necessary.
• Play the recording, pausing for Ss to repeat each word in chorus.

Exercise 7
• Make sure Ss understand the flags show the characters' nationalities.
• 🌐 Divide Ss into groups of five, making sure that one person in each group is strong / 'an expert'. Ss complete and 'the expert' assists them if necessary.

Answers → student page

Exercise 8
• Pairs write in their notebooks.
• Invite different pairs to write the answers on the board.

Answers
2 We aren't from Spain. We're from the UK. 3 Granny Susie isn't from France. She's from the UK. 4 My cousins aren't from the USA. They're from China.

Extra activity
• Ss write negative and affirmative sentences about their friends and family similar to those in Exercise 8.
• Strong students could write about world celebrities instead. They find words they don't know in a dictionary.

Exercise 9
• Choose a confident pair to demonstrate the activity.
• Pairs continue, taking turns to guess.

Finishing the lesson
• Say affirmative sentences about this lesson that are false. Individuals correct you. E.g. *Dug's mum is British.* (No, she isn't. She's Polish.) *Cousin Chen is French.* (No, he isn't. He's Chinese.) *Granny Flossie is Spanish.* (No, she isn't. She's American.)
• 📧 Read the lesson objectives. Ss show self-assessment response cards (☺, 😐, ☹). Then Ss copy the objectives into their notebooks and draw the emoticons that reflect their progress.

⏳ **Fast finishers**
• Ss look at the pictures in the cartoon and write down the names of the things they know.
• Ss find the English names of three more countries/nationalities in a dictionary.

33

1.4

In this lesson

Lesson aims:
- Communication: making introductions

Resources:
- Communication worksheet 1.4, p. 168

Homework:
- Workbook Unit 1, p. 11
- Extra Online Practice Unit 1

Assessment for Learning in this lesson
- Setting aims and criteria for success: Warm-up
- Giving feedback: Exercise 3 and 4
- Independent learning: Finishing the lesson

Culture notes
Pre-teens in the UK may call a married woman they don't know well or a teacher *Mrs* + surname, e.g. *Mrs Hall*.

Warm-up
- (*Books closed*) Pairs write three negative sentences about a character from the book. One is false. They read the sentences to another pair who say *True* or *False*.
- Speak to two Ss. Say: *X, this is Y. He's/She's my student. Y, this is X. He's/She's my friend.* Then ask the class to guess what they will learn and explain the lesson objective.

Lead-in
- (*Books open*) Pointing to the photo, ask *Who's she?* (Jen.) *Where are they?* (At home.) Pre-teach/Elicit *neighbour*. Draw two houses with two people by each. Say *They are … (neighbours).*

Exercise 1 1.24
- Play the video. Students watch. If you don't have access to a computer and projector, play the recording.

Answer → student page

Exercise 2 1.25
- Make sure Ss understand all the phrases in the box first.

1.4 Communication — I can make introductions.

Nice to meet you!

Jen: Hi, Mum!
Mum: Hi, kids!
Jen: Mum, this is Lucas. He's our new neighbour. Lucas, this is my mum.
Mum: Hello, Lucas. Nice to meet you.
Lucas: Nice to meet you too, Mrs Newman.
Mum: Jen, your bag!
Jen: Sorry, Mum. Let's go, Lucas.

1 ▶ 6 🔊 1.24 Watch or listen and read. What's Jen's family name? *Newman.*

2 🔊 1.25 Listen and repeat.

Communication — Introductions

A: *Mum*, this is *Lucas*.
   He is *my friend/classmate*.
   Lucas, this is *my mum*.
B: Hello, *Lucas*. Nice to meet you.
C: Nice to meet you too.

3 🔊 1.26 Put the dialogue in the correct order. Then listen and check.
1 [b] 2 [d] 3 [c] 4 [a]

a Desi: Nice to meet you too, Lisa.
b Adam: Lisa, this is Desi. He's my best friend.
c Lisa: Hello, Desi. Nice to meet you.
d Adam: Desi, this is my cousin, Lisa.

4 In groups of three, act out the dialogue in Exercise 3.

5 Exam Spot Circle the best answer.
1 A: Hello, I'm George.
   B: a Very well, thanks. b I've got it.
   (c) Nice to meet you, George.
2 A: Mum, this is Sam.
   B: a He's my classmate. (b) Hello, Sam.
   c Hold this, please.
3 A: Kate, this is my sister, Lisa.
   B: a Be careful! (b) Hi, Lisa. Nice to meet you.
   c She's my friend.

6 Write the names of three famous people. Then introduce them to your friends!

Famous pop star _____
Famous film star _____
Famous sports person _____

Fun Spot

Tom, this is my friend, Zac Efron. He's a famous film star!

16

Extra activity
- Ss invent new names and work in two independent groups. Each student says hello to the student on his/her left, then introduces himself/herself and all the Ss that have spoken so far. E.g. S1: *Hello. I'm X.* S2: *Hello. I'm Y. This is X.* S3: *Hello. I'm Z. This is X and this is Y.* The first group to make a mistake loses.

Exercise 3 1.26
- Pairs write their answers on response cards. Appoint Ss to justify their answers.

Answers → student page

Exercise 4
- Monitor. Don't correct immediately. Try to give positive feedback first.

Exercise 5
- This is preparation for CYLET Movers, Reading and Writing Part 2.

Answers → student page

Exercise 6
- SS work in groups of four. The celebrity should speak, too.

Finishing the lesson
- Ss copy the lesson objective into their notebooks and draw the emoticon that reflects their progress (☺, 😐, ☹).

Fast finishers
- Ss write a dialogue. They introduce two friends to each other.

Reading 1.5

I can understand a text about family photos.

My family album

I'm Alice! I'm twelve.
I'm from London in the UK.
This is my family album.

A

This is my favourite photo.
I'm four and my sister, Isabel, is six! We aren't at home in this photo. We're at my granny's house in London. Granny is Dad's mum. She's fun!

B

My cousin Tommy, Isabel and I are in this photo.
We're in the park near my house. I'm nine, Tommy's ten and Isabel's eleven.

C

And this is my family: Mum, Dad, Isabel and I.
I'm eleven and Isabel's thirteen. We're on holiday in France. My mum and my Aunt Jackie (Mum's sister) are French. Vincent's in the photo too. He's Aunt Jackie's dog. He's great.

---

1 🔊 **1.27** Read and listen to Alice's blog. Find Alice in photos A, B and C.

2 Complete the sentences about the text with one word.
1. Isabel is Alice's _sister_.
2. Alice's mum and aunt are _French_.
3. Vincent is _Aunt_ Jackie's dog.
4. Tommy is Isabel's _cousin_.
5. Granny is _Dad_'s mum.

3 🟥 **Exam Spot** Read the sentences. Circle T (true) or F (false).
1. Alice is eleven in Photo C. (T)/ F
2. They're on holiday in France in Photo A. T /(F)
3. They are in the park in Photo B. (T)/ F
4. Tommy is eleven in Photo B. T /(F)
5. Photo A is Alice's favourite. (T)/ F

4 🔊 **1.28** Listen and repeat.

Vocabulary Places
at home   at school   at a party
in the garden   in the park   on holiday

5 Look at the pictures and write the places.

a  b
in the park   _at school_

c  d
on holiday   _at a party_

e  f
at home   _in the garden_

6 🔊 **1.29** Listen and match conversations 1–4 to places a–f in Exercise 5. There are two extra places.
1 _d_   2 _f_   3 _b_   4 _e_

7 Work in pairs. Student A: Go to page 106. Student B: Go to page 108.

1.5

In this lesson

Lesson aims:
- Reading: understanding a text about family photos
- Vocabulary: places

Resources:
- Tests: Vocabulary Check 1.5

Homework:
- Workbook Unit 1, p. 12

Assessment for Learning in this lesson
- 🎯 Setting aims and criteria for success: Warm-up
- 💬 Giving feedback: Exercise 2, Finishing the lesson
- 🔄 Peer learning: Exercise 3 and 7
- 📖 Independent learning: Finishing the lesson

Warm-up
- (*Books closed*) Different groups of four act out introducing a celebrity for the class (See Lesson 1.4, Exercise 6).
- (*L1/L2*) Ask *Do you read blogs? What about?* Have a class discussion.
- 🎯 (*Books open*) Ss look at page 17. Ask what they expect to learn in this lesson. Explain the lesson objectives.

Lead-in
- (*Books open*) Pairs look at each photo and say the words they know.
- Ss predict how old the people in each photo are.

Exercise 1 🔊 1.27
- Pairs find Alice in the photos.
- Ss underline Alice's age in each paragraph. (*Four, nine, eleven.*)
- Write *fun, near* and *great* on the board. Ss find the words in the text. Pairs use the context to guess the meaning. Ss tell you their ideas.

Answers → student page

Exercise 2
- Pairs complete.
- 💬 Use the Lollipop Stick technique to check answers. Ask *Are you sure?* and challenge students to justify their answers.

Answers → student page

Exercise 3
- This is preparation for CYLET Starters, Reading and Writing Part 2.
- 🔄 Ss work individually. Then they compare each answer with a different student.

Answers → student page

Exercise 4 🔊 1.28
- Ss read the words before listening. Challenge strong Ss to translate words they know.

Exercise 5
- In a weak class, ask different students for the answers first.

Answers → student page

Exercise 6 🔊 1.29
- Play the recording twice, stopping if necessary.

Answers → student page

Exercise 7
- 🔄 Pairs describe their photos to each other. Encourage Ss to help each other.

Finishing the lesson
- 💬 (*L1/L2*) Use the Traffic Lights technique to find out how difficult Ss found the text.
- 📖 Read the lesson objective. Ss show self-assessment response cards (☺, 😐, ☹).
- 📖 Ss copy the objective into their notebooks and draw the emoticon that reflects their progress.

⏳ **Fast finishers**
Ss write sentences about the pictures in Alice's blog.

1.6

In this lesson

Lesson aims:
- Listening: understanding a radio show about friends
- Writing: a text about a best friend; capital letters

Resources:
- Tests: Writing Task Unit 1

Homework:
- Workbook Unit 1, p. 13

Assessment for Learning in this lesson
- Setting aims and criteria for success: Warm-up
- Giving feedback: Exercise 4
- Peer learning: Lead-in, Exercise 5 and 6
- Independent learning: Finishing the lesson

Culture notes
International Friendship Day is celebrated on different dates around the world.

Warm-up
- (*Books closed*) Play *Chinese Whispers* with the new words in Lesson 1.5. Ss form two lines. Whisper a word to the last student in each line. Each student whispers it to the person directly in front of him/her once. The students at the front say the word aloud!
- (*Books open*) (*L1/L2*) Explain the lesson objectives.

Lead-in
- (*Books closed*) (*L1/L2*) Write on the board *Why are friends important?* Pairs discuss. Then groups of four compile a list. Have a class discussion.

Exercise 1
- Pairs look and decide.
- Appoint a student to explain International Friendship Day.

Answer → student page

Exercise 2 1.30
- Play the recording twice if necessary. Ss write down key words.

Answers → student page

1.6 Listening and Writing
I can understand and write short texts about best friends.

1 Look at the website. What is the radio show about? *It's about friends / best friends.*

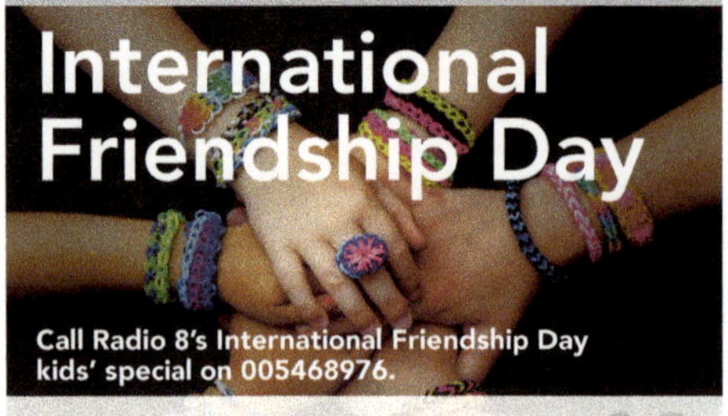

International Friendship Day
Call Radio 8's International Friendship Day kids' special on 005468976.
Tell us about your best friends!

2 1.30 Listen to the radio show. Match callers 1–3 to photos of their best friends A–C.

1 Tom *C*   2 Maria *B*   3 Juan *A*

3 Exam Spot 1.30 Read the questions. Listen again. Write a number or a country.
1 How old is Monica? *11*
2 Where is Monica now? *(in) the UK*
3 How old is Jack? *two*
4 Where are Giorgia and Toni from? *Italy*

4 Who's your best friend? Tell the class.

18

---

5 Read Jen's blog and complete the table.

Me and my best friend

(M)y name's (J)en. (I)'m ten and (I)'m from the (U)K. (I)'m (B)ritish. (M)y best friend is my neighbour, (L)ucas. (H)e's eleven. (L)ucas and his family are from (S)pain. (T)hey're (S)panish.

	Name	Age	Nationality	Country
Me	*Jen*	*10*	*British*	*the UK*
My best friend	*Lucas*	*11*	*Spanish*	*Spain*

Writing Capital letters
Use a capital letter for names of people, countries and nationalities.
Use a capital letter for the pronoun *I* and at the beginning of every sentence too.

(M)y best friend is (J)ack.   (I)'m from (F)rance.
(G)iorgia and (T)oni are (I)talian.

6 Find and circle capital letters in Jen's blog in Exercise 5.

7 Writing Time Write about you and your best friend.

? Find ideas
Find a photo of you and your best friend. Make notes.

✎ Draft
Write about your name, age, country and nationality.
My name's …   I'm (ten/eleven/twelve …)
I'm from …
Write the same about your best friend.

✓ Check and write
Check all the capital letters and write the final version of your text.

Exercise 3 1.30
- This is preparation for CYLET Starters, Listening Part 2.
- First, pairs think if they know any answers.

Answers → student page

Exercise 4
- Write these prompts on the board: *1 Name 2 Age 3 Classmate/Neighbour/Family?*
- Ask Ss to use these prompts to tell the class about their best friend. Appoint a student to take notes on the board.

Exercise 5
- Ss read and complete individually. Then pairs compare answers.

Answers → student page

Writing
- Pre-teach/check *capital letter*.

Exercise 6
- Challenge pairs to compare the rules from the Writing box with the rules in L1.

Answers → student page

Exercise 7
- Try to indicate the good aspects of Ss' work and list things to improve.

Finishing the lesson
- Read the lesson objectives. Ss show self-assessment response cards (☺, 😐, ☹).

Fast finishers
- Ss find capital letters in the text on page 17.

Language Revision 1.7

Vocabulary

1 Complete the family words. What seven other family words do you know?

1 g r a n d **a** d
2 g r a n **n** y
3 u n c **l** e
4 a **u** n t
5 m **u** m
6 d **a** d
7 c o **u** s i n
8 s **i** s t e r
9 b r **o** t h e r

2 Circle the odd one out.

1 a (Chinese)   b Spain   c the UK
2 a the USA   (b) Italian   c the UK
3 a France   b Poland   (c) American
4 a Spanish   b British   (c) China
5 a French   (b) the USA   c Polish

3 Look at the pictures. Circle a, b or c.

1.   a in the park   (b) at school   c in the garden
2.   a at home   b on holiday   (c) at a party
3.   (a) on holiday   b at home   c in the garden

Pronunciation

4 🔊 1.31 Listen and repeat: /v/ or /b/?

Viv's **b**est friends, **V**incent and **B**rad, are a **b**ad **b**rown dog and a **v**ery **b**ig cat!

Grammar

5 Write sentences with possessive 's.

1 Luke / cake   It's _Luke's cake_ .
2 Granny / birthday   It's _Granny's birthday_
3 Megan / son   Jason is _Megan's son_ .
4 Dad / sister   Megan is _Dad's sister_ .

---

6 Read and complete Maria's profile with *am*, *are* or *is*.

My name's Maria.

I ¹_am_ thirteen. I ²_am_ from the USA. My best friend ³_is_ Isabel. Her family ⁴_is_ English. We ⁵_are_ classmates. Her two brothers ⁶_are_ my friends too.

7 Match 1–5 to a–e.

1 [c] Jane's best   a your schoolbag.
2 [d] Your brother is   b George is eleven.
3 [e] It's my   c friend is her neighbour.
4 [a] That isn't   d in my class.
5 [b] His cousin   e birthday today!

8 Write negative sentences. Which sentences are true for you? Tell your partner.

1 I'm fifteen. / _I'm not fifteen_ .
2 My best friend is my cat. / _My best friend isn't my cat._
3 My brother's name is Ben. / _My brother's name isn't Ben._
4 We're at home. / _We aren't at home._
5 It's my birthday. / _It isn't my birthday._
6 My neighbours are my classmates. / _My neighbours aren't my classmates._

Communication

9 Complete the dialogue with the words in the box. Then act out the dialogue in groups of three.

Nice   ~~this~~   meet   this

Jamie: Mum, ¹_this_ is my friend, David. David, ²_this_ is my mum.
David: Hello, Mrs Smith. ³_Nice_ to meet you.
Mum: Nice to ⁴_meet_ you too, David.

Check yourself! ✅

- I can talk about people in a family.
- I can talk about countries and nationalities.
- I can use possessive 's.
- I can use the affirmative and negative forms of the verb *to be*.
- I can use possessive adjectives *my*, *your*, *his*, *her*.
- I can make introductions.

19

1.7

In this lesson

Lesson aims:
- Revising Vocabulary, Grammar and Communication from Unit 1.
- Pronunciation: /v/ and /b/

Resources:
- Tests: Language Test Unit 1

Homework:
- Workbook Unit 1, pp. 14–15
- Extra Online Practice Unit 1

Assessment for Learning in this lesson
- 🎯 Setting aims and criteria for success: Warm-up
- 💬 Giving feedback: Exercise 9
- 👥 Peer learning: Exercise 6 and 8
- 📖 Independent learning: Finishing the lesson

Warm-up

- (*Books closed*) Divide the class into two teams. Ask each team in turn these questions: *1 My mum's sister is my …* (Aunt.) *2 Who is Sophie?* (Alex and Jen's granny.) *3 How old is Sophie?* (70.) *4 What nationality is Uncle Roberto?* (Spanish.) *5 Who is Kit?* (She's Dug's best friend.)
- 🎯 Explain the objective is to remember language from Unit 1.

Lead-in

- (*Books open*) (*L1/L2*) Ask *What are your favourite lessons in this unit? Why?* Encourage Ss to explain.

Exercise 1
- Groups race to do this activity.

Answers → student page

Other family words:
grandfather, grandmother, mother, father, parents, son, daughter

Exercise 2
- Explain the example first. (A – nationality; b, c – countries.)

Answers → student page

Extra activity
- Pairs make up two more 'odd one out' questions.

Exercise 3
- Strong Ss tell you what's in the pictures first.

Answers → student page

Exercise 4 🔊 1.31
- (L1) Tell Ss when we say /v/, our top teeth touch our bottom lip. When we say /b/ our teeth don't touch our lips.

Exercise 5
- Individuals do the exercise.

Answers → student page

Extra activity
- Pairs use Lesson 1.3 to say possessive sentences about Dug and Kit.

Exercise 6
- 👥 Pairs help each other complete. They look at Lesson 1.2 and 1.3 to help.

Answers → student page

Exercise 7
- Pairs compare answers.

Answers → student page

Exercise 8
- 👥 Ask Ss to swap partners twice.

Answers → student page

Exercise 9
- 💬 Monitor pairs as they speak. Give positive feedback.

Answers → student page

Finishing the lesson
- 📖 Read Check yourself! statements. Ss show their response cards (☺, 😐, ☹). Then Ss tick the statements.

⏳ **Fast finishers**
- Ss do one of the extra activities suggested.

37

Get Culture

In this lesson

Lesson aims:
- Culture focus: *English around the world*
- BBC video: *This is the UK* (optional)
- Project: presenting an English-speaking country

Resources:
- Project worksheet p. 179

Assessment for Learning in this lesson
- Setting aims and criteria for success: Warm-up
- Giving feedback: Lead-in, Exercise B and C.
- Peer learning: Exercise 3 and the Project
- Independent learning: Finishing the lesson

Culture notes
The photos above Exercise 1 are of (from left to right): the Statue of Liberty, New York, the USA; Big Ben, London, the UK; the Sydney Opera House, Australia.
The buses in the BBC video photo are London's famous double-decker buses.

Warm-up
- (*Books closed*) Play *Snowman* with the names of countries on page 15. On the board, write a dash for each letter of a word. Ss work in two teams and take turns to guess the letters of the word. Draw a part of the snowman for each wrong guess. (See Lesson 1.1, Warm-up.)
- Then find out what other countries Ss know.
- (*Books open*) Get Ss to look at pages 20–21 and discuss with the class what they will do in this lesson.

Lead-in
- (*Books open*) Use the photo above Exercise 1 to teach *map* and to check *flag*. Use the Thumbs up/down technique to find out which flags Ss recognise.

Get Culture!
English around the world

1 Look at the map. Label countries 1–3 with the words in the box.

the UK   the USA   Australia

2 🔊 1.32 People in the UK, the USA and Australia speak the same language. What language is it? Read, listen and check.   *English.*

Who speaks English?

The UK   The capital city of the United Kingdom, or UK, is London. The UK is four different countries: England, Wales, Scotland and Northern Ireland. There are about 65 million people in the UK and English is the official language.

The USA   The USA is short for the United States of America. The capital of the USA is Washington. There are 324 million people in the USA. They speak English but about 37 million people speak Spanish too.

Australia   24 million people live in Australia. Its capital city is Canberra and Sydney is its biggest city. Most people speak English in Australia. Here's an interesting fact: when it's winter in the UK and the USA, it is summer in Australia.

3 Look at the map and read the text again. Read tasks 1–6 and follow the instructions.
1 Circle the Australian flag.
   a 🇬🇧   b 🇺🇸   **c** 🇦🇺
2 Complete the sentence.
   Scotland is in *the UK*.
3 Number the countries from 1 to 3 (very big, big, small number of people).
   [2] The UK   [1] The USA   [3] Australia
4 Write T (true) or F (false).
   Christmas is in the summer in Australia. *T*
5 Circle the correct answer.
   Sydney is in (*Australia*) / the USA.
6 Complete the sentence.
   Many people speak Spanish in *the USA*.

4 🔊 1.33 Listen and match 1–4 to a–d.
1 [c] Erin   a is from the USA.
2 [a] Peter   b is from Australia.
3 [b] Ollie   c is from the UK.
4 [d] Mary   d is from London, UK.

5 Game! Say three facts about the UK, the USA or Australia for your partner to guess the country.
A: *The capital city is Canberra.*
B: *It's Australia!*

20

Exercise 1
- Pairs help each other label.
- Ask different Ss to say each answer. Then challenge the class to name the icons in the photos next to each gap. (See Culture notes.)

Answers → student page

Exercise 2 🔊 1.32
- Teach *speak* before Ss do the exercise. E.g. say *In (Poland) we speak (Polish)*.

Answer → student page

Extra activity
- Write these words on the board: *capital city, live, most people, the biggest, different, winter, summer*. Ask Ss to find and underline them in the text. Then pairs discuss what they mean and make their own sentences with these words.

Exercise 3
- Pairs discuss and write their answers.
- Then pairs swap notebooks and review each other's answers.

Answers → student page

Exercise 4 🔊 1.33
- Before you play the recording, ask the class to predict the answers.

Answers → student page

This is the UK

A ▶ 7 Watch the video and answer the presenter's questions. Who is Harry?
Prince William's brother. / Prince Charles' son. / Queen Elisabeth's grandson.

B ▶ 7 Watch the video again. Circle the correct answer a, b or c.
1 The UK is: The United Kingdom of Great Britain and …
   a Scotland.   b Wales.   **(c)** Northern Ireland.
2 People from the UK are …
   (a) British.   b English.   c American.
3 There are … million people in London.
   a 4   **(b)** 9   c 64
4 Queen Elizabeth is Prince William's
   a grandson.   **(b)** grandmother.   c aunt.

C Discuss in class. What new things did you learn from the video? Would you like to visit the UK? Why/Why not?

PROJECT

- Work in four groups. Prepare a digital presentation about one of these countries.

  The Republic of Ireland   New Zealand
  The Republic of South Africa   Canada

- Write information about the country. Use these questions to help you.

  How many people live in this country?
  What is the capital city? What are other big cities?
  What language(s) do people speak there?

- Add a map of the country, its flag and photos of important and/or interesting places.
- Share your presentation with the class.

English around the world
- The capital of *Canada* is …
- Its biggest city is / cities are …
- … million people live in …
- People speak …

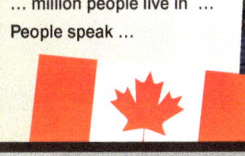

Exercise 5
- Alternatively, pairs choose 3 facts for another pair to guess.

BBC video

Video script → see Teacher's Book p. 138
Presenter's questions
1 (01:23) Wow! 64 million! That's a lot of people. What about your country?
2 (01:45) What's the name of the capital of your country?
3 (02:19) What is the name of the UK flag? Is it a) The Union John or b) The Union Jack?

Note: if you can't show the video, spend more class time on preparing the Project.

Exercise A ▶ 7
- Brainstorm what Ss know about the UK.
- Ss read the question. Then play the video.
- First, pause after each of the presenter's questions and ask the class for their ideas.

Answers
Question 3: b

- Then check the answer to Exercise A.

Answer → student page

Exercise B ▶ 7
- First, Ss answer any questions they can.
- 💬 After Ss watch, use the Stand up and Change Places technique to check answers.

Answers → student page

Exercise C
- 💬 After pairs discuss the questions, use the Lollipop Stick technique to choose Ss to explain their answers and have a class discussion.

🌐 Project

Setting the project up
- Allocate at least 10 minutes for setting up the project.
- Choose groups of three/four and ask them to read the instructions.
- Allocate one country per group, or write them on separate slips of paper and give one at random to each group.
- Ask groups to decide what each student is going to be responsible for (map, flag, photos, text, design, research about interesting places).
- Give Ss the Project worksheets to help them prepare.
- Choose how the presentation will be shared: via the class projector, a file sharing service, email or on the school website.
- If your class can't make digital presentations, ask Ss to prepare posters. Follow the same steps for setting up the project, but ask Ss to draw their map, flag and pictures or print some photos and write by hand.
- Set a date for giving presentations.

Sharing the project
- Before Ss give their presentations, let them practise for a while. Make sure everybody is involved. Take notes. You could comment on: design, interest, accuracy, pronunciation. Remember to praise first.
- Have a class vote for the most popular country!

Finishing the lesson
- The class tells you what they enjoyed most and why.
- 💾 Check what Ss have learnt in this lesson using Three Facts and a Fib technique.

⏳ Fast finishers
- Ss use a dictionary and label the pictures in the text in Exercise 2. *(A cup of tea, a (cowboy) hat, a kangaroo.)* Then they choose an object to represent their country.

2.1

In this lesson

Lesson aims:
- Vocabulary: clothes

Resources:
- Vocabulary worksheet 2.1, p. 148
- Tests: Vocabulary Check 2.1

Homework:
- Workbook Unit 2, p. 16

Assessment for Learning in this lesson
- Setting aims and criteria for success: Warm-up
- Giving feedback: Exercise 4, 5 and 10
- Peer learning: Exercise 6
- Independent learning: Look!, Finishing the lesson

Warm-up

- (*Books closed*) Play *Touch and Guess* with the class to revise vocabulary. Put six–eight objects in a bag (include one or two objects to introduce the unit topic), e.g.: a book, a pencil case, an apple, a small umbrella, a phone, a T-shirt. Blindfold a student and give him/her an object from the bag to feel. He/She guesses what it is, e.g. *Is it a phone?* Continue with different objects and Ss.
- Point to your objects and say *These are my things.* Then write *My things* on the board. Ss predict what they will learn.
- (L1/L2) Explain the lesson objective. Ask *Why do you need to learn clothes words in English?* (*To go shopping in a foreign country / to talk to foreign friends.*)

Lead-in

- (*Books closed*) Brainstorm clothes words with the class. Challenge Ss who know more words to translate for weak Ss.

Exercise 1

- Pairs help each other find the clothes.
- Say the clothes and ask Ss who are wearing them to stand up.

Answers → student page

---

2 My things

Vocabulary I can talk about clothes.

In this unit

Vocabulary
- Clothes
- Adjectives
- My things

Grammar
- *this, that, these, those*
- *too big/small*
- *to be* questions and short answers

▶ 8–9 2.2 Grammar video
▶ 10 2.2 Grammar animation
▶ 11 2.3 Grammar animation
▶ 12 2.4 Communication video

1 Find these clothes in the picture. Which are you wearing today?

I know that!

coat	jeans	shoes	skirt	T-shirt	trousers
4	5	15	11	1	10

22

Exercise 2 🔊 1.34

- Play the recording, pausing for Ss to repeat each word and find it in the picture.

Answers → student page

- Say the colour each item is in the picture and use gestures for Ss to guess the word. T: *Green!* (Point to your head.) Ss: *Cap!*

Exercise 3 🔊 1.35

- Ss read the words before they listen.
- Pause to ask individuals for the answers.
- Play pairs of words that Ss find difficult again.

Answers → student page

Look!

- Read the examples. After each, ask the class *Why 'is/are'?* and elicit the answer. Encourage learner autonomy by referring weak Ss to the Grammar box in Lesson 1.2.

Exercise 4

- Ask pairs to complete the table.
- Draw the table on the board. Use the Lollipop Stick technique and select individuals to write the words. Tell them the order isn't important. The class says if each word is correct. If it isn't, choose a student to explain why.

Answers → student page

2 🔊 **1.34** Listen and repeat. Find the clothes in the picture on page 22.

Vocabulary Clothes

boots	cap	coat	dress	hoodie	jacket
jeans	jumper	shirt	shoes	skirt	T-shirt
top	tracksuit	trainers	trousers		

(numbered: 7 boots, 3 cap, 4 coat, 2 dress, 6 hoodie, 12 jacket, 11 jeans, 5 jumper, 15 shirt, 8 shoes, 16 skirt, 1 T-shirt, 14 top, 13 tracksuit, 9 trainers, 10 trousers)

3 🔊 **1.35** Listen and circle the word you hear.

1 (T-shirt) / shirt   4 shoes / (skirt)
2 jacket / (jumper)   5 cap / (coat)
3 (trainers) / trousers   6 (boots) / hoodie

LOOK!
The T-shirt **is** blue.
The shoes **are** brown.
The jeans **are** blue.

4 Complete the table with the words in the Vocabulary box.

is	are
T-shirt, *cap*, *coat*, *dress*, *hoodie*, *jacket*, *jumper*, *shirt*, *skirt*, *top*, *tracksuit*	shoes, *boots*, *trainers*, jeans, *trousers*

5 Complete the sentences with *is* or *are*. Then look at the picture on page 22. Tick (✔) for *yes* or put a cross (✘) for *no*.

1 ✘ The tracksuit *is*   black.
2 ✔ The dress *is*   yellow.
3 ✘ The trainers *are*   red.
4 ✘ The hoodie *is*   grey.
5 ✔ The boots *are*   brown.
6 ✘ The trousers *are*   green.

6 Look at your clothes and tell a partner.
My jeans are blue, my T-shirt is green and white and my trainers are red.

7 Choose a student from your class and name his or her clothes. Ask your partner to guess.
A: *White T-shirt, blue skirt.*
B: *It's Natasha!*

8 Adam and Adele are in the sports centre. Are their clothes OK? Complete the list. Tick (✔) for *yes* or put a cross (✘) for *no*.

Adam: 1 *T-shirt* ✔   2 *jacket* ✘
      3 *trousers* ✘   4 *trainers* ✔
Adele: 5 *cap* ✔   6 *hoodie* ✔
      7 *skirt* ✘   8 *boots* ✘

9 Dress Adam and Adele for a party. Write two lists of clothes. Then compare in pairs.
Adam: *white T-shirt, …*
Adele: *pink dress, …*

10 Make lists of clothes you wear at school and at the weekend.

I remember that!

at school	at the weekend

23

Exercise 9
- Alternatively, Ss work in groups of four and race to do the exercise. Brainstorm lists to the board. A change of focus like this can help you manage a restless class.

Extra activity
- ⟦Critical thinking⟧ Class discussion. Ask *Is it OK to wear jeans and trainers at a party?* (L1/L2) Ss name different clothes for different types of parties.

Exercise 10
- Pre-teach *school uniform* if your school has one. Check *weekend*. Say *Saturday and Sunday is the … (weekend)*.
- 💬 Ss write. Monitor. Correct spelling. Praise neat, tidy work as well as good spelling. This could help boost weak Ss' confidence.

Extra activity
- Ss draw themselves wearing their favourite clothes. They label the picture. You could make a class poster.

Finishing the lesson
- 🎓 Ss circle the new words in the Vocabulary box they have learnt. Remember to praise and encourage.
- 🎓 Ask *Can you talk about clothes?* Students show self-assessment response cards (☺, 😐, ☹).
- 🎓 Ss copy the objective into their notebooks and draw the emoticon that reflects their progress.

⏳ **Fast finishers**
- (*Books closed*) Ss write all the clothes words they know.
- Ss list what they are wearing. Strong Ss write sentences following the example: *My hoodie is red. My jeans are …*

Exercise 5
- Ss do the exercise in pairs.
- 💬 Ask individuals to read the sentences. After each sentence use the ✔/✘ response cards to check answers. Ask Ss to correct the wrong sentences. You could make more T/F sentences about the picture and continue the activity. E.g. *The coat is blue.* (✔) *The jumper is white.* (✘) *The skirt is orange.* (✘)

Answers → student page

Exercise 6
- 🙋 A confident student demonstrates the exercise. Pairs continue. Encourage them to correct each other if necessary.

Exercise 7
- Alternatively, divide the class into two teams. A student from one team names a classmate's clothes. A student from the other team guesses who he/she is.

Exercise 8
- Ss in a weak class name the clothes first.
- Pairs do the exercise.
- Encourage Ss to say complete sentences. E.g. *Adam's T'shirt is OK.*

Answers → student page

41

2.2 In this lesson

Lesson aims:
- Grammar: *this, that, these, those*
- Vocabulary: adjectives

Resources:
- Grammar worksheet 2.2, p. 154
- Tests: Grammar Check 2.2, Vocabulary Check 2.2

Homework:
- Workbook Unit 2, p. 17
- Extra Online Practice Unit 2

Assessment for Learning in this lesson
- Setting aims and criteria for success: Warm-up
- Giving feedback: Exercise 1, 7 and 12
- Peer learning: Exercise 11
- Independent learning: Finishing the lesson

Warm-up
- (*Books closed*) Divide the class into two teams. A student from team A stands facing the board. A student from team B names the clothes a classmate is wearing, e.g. *A black hoodie*. Student A guesses who it is. Continue with different pairs.
- (*Books open*) Pairs look at pages 24–25. They discuss what they think they will learn. Brainstorm ideas from the class. (*L1/L2*) Explain the lesson objectives.

Lead-in
- (*Books open*) Pointing to the photos, ask *Where is Jen?* (*At home.*) *Who's the woman?* (*Alex and Jen's mum.*) *Is she happy?* (*No!*)
- Use the photos to pre-teach *long*, *old* and *new*.

Exercise 1 1.36
- Read the question. Ss look at the pictures and guess the answer.
- Play the video. If you don't have access to a computer and projector, play the recording.

2.2 Grammar — I can use *this*, *that*, *these*, *those* and adjectives.

That's my T-shirt!

1
Mum: Jen, put these clothes away, please.
Jen: OK, Mum.
Oh, hi! What's up?
What? No!

2 *Ten minutes later …*
Jen: Bye, Holly! … Hang on, what are these? These aren't my jeans. They're too long! These are Mum's jeans! Yep, this top is Mum's too!

3
Mum: Jen, these are your jeans. They're too small for me!
Jen: Oops! Sorry, Mum!
Mum: And that's my top over there.
Jen: Yes, it is. Here you are!

4
Alex: Jen? … Jen, where's my new T-shirt?
Jen: It's over there with your old T-shirts!
Alex: No, those are Dad's T-shirts!
Jen: Oh, then your T-shirt is …

1 🎬 8 🔊 1.36 Watch or listen and read. Are the clothes in the right place?
No, they aren't.

2 Look at the photos and read the story again. Whose clothes are they? Circle the correct answer.
1 Photo 2 The jeans are Jen's / **Mum's**.
2 Photo 3 The jeans are **Jen's** / Mum's.
3 Photo 3 The top is Jen's / **Mum's**.
4 Photo 4 The T-shirts are **Dad's** / Alex's.

3 🔊 1.37 Listen and repeat. Find these expressions in the story.

What's up?   Hang on!
Here you are.   Over there.

Say it!

4 ▶ **Guess!** Who's got Alex's new T-shirt? Have a class vote.
a Mum   **b** Dad   c Jen

5 🎬 9 🔊 1.38 Now watch or listen and check.

24

- Use the Lollipop Stick technique to choose Ss to give the answer and justify it.

Answer → student page

Exercise 2
- Ask pairs to look, agree and circle.

Answers → student page

Exercise 3 1.37
- Play the recording, pausing for Ss to repeat each expression.
- Play the video again. Ss shout *STOP!* when they hear each expression. Alternatively, Ss find and underline the expressions in the dialogue.

Exercise 4
- **Critical thinking** T: *Hands up for a/b/c!* (*L1/L2*) Individuals explain their choice. Don't confirm yet!

Answer → student page

Exercise 5 1.38
- Play the video or recording to check.

Video/Audio script
Alex: Dad! That's my T-shirt!
Dad: Yes, it's cool, isn't it? My T-shirts are boring!
Alex: But dad …
Dad: Bye now!
Jen: … it's too small for you …

2.2

Grammar *this, that, these, those* ▶ 10 **Get Grammar!**

| **This** is Jen's top. | **That** is Alex's T-shirt. |
| **This** top is Jen's. | **That** T-shirt is Alex's. |

| **These** are Jen's trainers. | **Those** are Alex's trainers. |
| **These** trainers are Jen's. | **Those** trainers are Alex's. |

These aren't my trainers.
This isn't my T-shirt!

6 Circle the correct answer.
1 This /(These) are your trainers.
2 (This)/ These isn't Alex's shirt.
3 This /(These) shoes aren't Jen's.
4 That /(Those) T-shirts are Dad's.
5 (That)/ Those is my coat.
6 That /(Those) boots are Mum's.

7 Complete with *this, that, these* or *those*.
1 ➡ _That_ is Alex's cap.
2 ➡ _Those_ are Jen's trousers.
3 ➡ _These_ are Dad's jeans.
4 ➡ _That_ is Mum's top.
5 ➡ _This_ is Alex's jacket.

8 🔊 1.39 Listen and repeat.

Vocabulary Adjectives

big boring cool long new old
short small

9 Look at the words in the Vocabulary box. Write the opposites in your notebook.
1 big – small
boring – cool, long – short, new – old

10 In pairs, talk about the clothes. Use adjectives in the Vocabulary box and *this, that, these* or *those*.

YOU ARE HERE

A: *T-shirt 1.*
B: *This T-shirt is cool! T-shirt 2.*
A: *That T-shirt is boring. Trousers 2. …*

LOOK! Her boots are *too big*!
His shirt is *too small*!

11 What's wrong with her clothes? In your notebook, write sentences with *too*.
1 Her skirt / long
   Her skirt is too long.
2 Her boots / old *Her boots are too old.*
3 Her top / small *Her top is too small.*

12 Play a drawing dictation game. Use adjectives with *too*.
Draw a boy. His T-shirt is too small. …

25

Extra activity
• (*Books open*) Groups act out one or two scenes from the photo story.

Get Grammar! ▶10
• Play the Get Grammar! video. If you don't have access to a computer and projector, continue.
• Ss repeat the examples after you in chorus.
• Use gesture to reinforce meaning, e.g. point to the other end of the room and say *Those (books)*. Draw Ss' attention to the pronunciation of *this* /ɪ/ and *these* /iː/.

Exercise 6
• Ss circle. Pairs compare answers.

Answers → student page

Exercise 7
• 💬 Pairs complete, Use the Traffic Lights technique to monitor the exercise.

Answers → student page

• Ask pairs to write three sentences about the objects in the classroom, e.g. *This is my pen. Those are (Mark's) books.*

Exercise 8 🔊 1.39
• Play the recording, pausing for Ss to repeat each word in chorus.
• Ask individuals to use these words in sentences about the objects in the classroom, e.g. *My bag is new.*

Exercise 9
• Pairs help each other.

Answers → student page

Exercise 10
• Ss use the Grammar box for help.

Answers
(*Jumper 1*) This jumper is new.
(*Jumper 2*) That jumper is old.
(*Coat 1*) This coat is small.
(*Coat 2*) That coat is big.
(*Trousers 1*) These trousers are short. (*Trousers 2*) Those trousers are long.

Look!
• Use your clothes, e.g. a coat, to demonstrate the meaning of *too big*. Ss repeat the examples after you in chorus.

Exercise 11
• Individuals write.
• Ask pairs to swap notebooks.
• 🌐 Write the answers on the board. Ss correct each other's sentences.

Answers → student page

Exercise 12
• Describe a person and the clothes he/she is wearing for Ss to draw. E.g. *Draw a boy. His jeans are too short. They're black. His red T-shirt is cool.*
• 💬 Ss raise their drawings. Pick one and ask another student to describe it. Repeat with other descriptions.

Finishing the lesson
• 🎓 Ask individuals for examples of sentences with demonstrative pronouns. Ask *Can you use this/that/these/those?* Students show self-assessment response cards (☺, 😐, ☹).
• 🎓 Individuals say sentences with *too* + adjective to describe clothes in the photo story.
• 🎓 Ss copy the objectives into their notebooks and draw the emoticons that reflect their progress.

⏳ Fast finishers
• Ss look at the pictures in the photo story and write down the words they know.
• Ss underline the new adjectives in the photo story.

43

2.3

In this lesson

Lesson aims:
- Grammar: *to be* questions and short answers

Resources:
- Grammar worksheet 2.3, p. 155
- Tests: Grammar Check 2.3

Homework:
- Workbook Unit 2, p. 18

Assessment for Learning in this lesson
- Setting aims and criteria for success: Warm-up
- Giving feedback: Exercise 2, 3 and 8
- Peer learning: Exercise 4
- Independent learning: Finishing the lesson

Warm-up

- (*Books closed*) Divide Ss into three teams of six–eight. Give each team a set of adjectives from Lesson 2.2 on separate cards so that each student has one or two cards. When you say a sentence with *this/these*, e.g. *This (shirt) is small*, Ss with *small* run to you. When you say a sentence with *that/those*, e.g. *Those (shoes) are big*, Ss with *big* run to the back of the room. Ss who go to the right place win a point.
- (*Books open*) Pairs look at pages 26–27. (*L1/L2*) Ask *What will you learn in this lesson?* Volunteers give their ideas. Ask a student *Are you OK?* When he/she answers (probably using only *Yes* or *No*), ask the class if the answer is correct. Then explain the lesson objectives.

2.3 Grammar — I can ask and answer questions with the verb *to be*.

The Terrific Two — Dug's new suit

1 Look at the cartoon. Where does Dug buy his superhero suits from? *From www.supersuits.get.*

2 🔊 1.40 Listen and read. What size is Dug's new suit? *XL.*

3 Read the sentences. Circle T (true) or F (false).
1 The dogs are OK. (T)/ F
2 The girl is a superhero. T /(F)
3 Dug's new suit is in the box. (T)/ F
4 Dug is cool in his new suit. T /(F)

Lead-in

- (*Books closed*) Write *Dug's new suit* on the board. (*L1*) Ss guess what *suit* means.
- (*Books open*) Ss look at the pictures and check/work out the meaning. Translate if necessary.
- Then Ss tell you what they can see in the pictures.
- Pre-teach *box* (Picture 4). Point to Dug's suit in Picture 5 and ask *What size is it? M, L or XL?* Ss guess. Elicit/Translate *clever*. Point to Kit in Picture 6. Nod, make the thumbs up sign and say *Kit is … (clever)*.

Exercise 1

- Critical thinking Individual Ss race to write the answer on a piece of paper and to raise it.

Answer → student page

Exercise 2 🔊 1.40

- Ask *What size is Dug's new suit?* Don't confirm Ss' answers yet.
- After Ss do the exercise, ask an individual to point to the text and justify the answer.

Answer → student page

Exercise 3

- Individuals do the exercise.
- To check answers, read the sentences. Ss stand up for *T* and sit down for *F*.
- Ss refer to the text and justify the answers.

Answers → student page

Extra activity

- Groups of four act out the cartoon.

2.3

Grammar to be questions and short answers ▶11 **Get Grammar!**

?	Short answers
Am I OK?	Yes, I **am**. / No, I**'m not**.
Are you OK?	Yes, you **are**. / No, you **aren't**.
Is he/she/it OK?	Yes, he/she/it **is**. / No, he/she/it **isn't**.
Are we OK?	Yes, you **are**. / No, you **aren't**.
Are you OK?	Yes, we **are**. / No, we **aren't**.
Are they OK?	Yes, they **are**. / No, they **aren't**.
What **is** it? It**'s** my new suit.	

Is this shirt OK?

No, it isn't.

4 Write questions. Who's asking the question? Write boy, girl, Dug or Kit.
1 they OK Are ? — Are they OK?   girl
2 he a superhero Is ? — Is he a superhero?   boy
3 you Are sure ? — Are you sure?   Kit
4 for me Is this box ? — Is this box for me?   Dug
5 it What is ? — What is it?   Kit
6 cool I Am ? — Am I cool?   Dug

5 Look at the cartoon. Answer the questions in Exercise 4.
1 Superdug: Yes, they are.

6 Complete the questions and the short answers.
1 Boy: _Are_ you a superhero?
  Kit: No, I _'m not_ .
2 Kit: _Are_ we best friends?
  Dug: Yes, we _are_ .
3 Dug: _Is_ my new suit cool?
  Kit: No, it _isn't_ .
4 Kit: _Am_ I clever?
  Dug: Yes, you _are_ .
5 Girl: _Is_ Superdug your brother?
  Kit: No, he _isn't_ .
6 Kit: _Are_ they your dogs?
  Girl: Yes, they _are_ .

7 🔊 1.41 Listen to the questions and circle the correct answer.
1 (Yes, it is.) / No, they aren't.
2 Yes, you are. / (No, they aren't.)
3 (Yes, I am.) / No, you aren't.
4 Yes, they are. / (No, he isn't.)
5 (Yes, they are.) / No, you aren't.
6 (Yes, we are.) / No, they aren't.

8 Write questions in your notebook. Then ask the questions and give true answers in pairs.
1 you / ten years old? Are you ten years old?
2 you / happy? Are you happy?
3 we / friends? Are we friends?
4 Superdug and Kit / cool? Are Superdug and Kit cool?
5 you / clever? Are you clever?
6 I / a superhero? Am I a superhero?

A: Are you ten years old?
B: Yes, I am. / No, I'm not.

Fun Spot

9 🔊 1.42 🔊 1.43 Go to page 107. Listen and chant Kit's Rap.

27

Exercise 6
- Pair weak and strong Ss.
- Different pairs read the dialogues to the class.

Answers → student page

Exercise 7 🔊 1.41
- Get Ss to underline the pronouns in the answers.
- When you check the answers, play the recording again. Pause after each question and get Ss to tell you what the pronouns they underlined refer to.

Answers → student page

Exercise 8
- 💬 Ss work individually. Use the Traffic Lights technique to check when Ss need help. Try to give positive feedback. Check answers before Ss ask and answer so Ss are practising correct language.

Answers → student page

Exercise 9 🔊 1.42 🔊 1.43
- Play Kit's rap. Ss clap the beat and chant!
- When Ss are familiar with the rap, play the karaoke version and ask them to chant.

Finishing the lesson
- 📖 Ask Ss to think and write one sentence summing up what they have learnt (L1). Then read the lesson objectives. Ss show self-assessment response cards (☺, 😐, ☹).
- 📖 Ss copy the objectives into their notebooks and draw the emoticons that reflect their progress.

⏳ Fast finishers
- Ss look at the pictures in the cartoon and write down the words they know.
- Ss use these prompts to write questions for Dug with to be: *1 You/famous? 2 Your suit/new? 3 Your friends/superheroes? 4 Kit/short?* Ss ask the class at the end of the lesson.

Get Grammar! ▶11
- Play the Get Grammar! video. If you don't have access to a computer and projector, continue.
- Ss repeat the examples after you in chorus.
- Point out we invert the subject and verb to form a question.
- Tell Ss people use short answers in everyday English, not just Yes/No which can be rude.
- Tell Ss we don't use contractions for affirmative short answers. Write on the board *Yes, we're.* (✘) *Yes, we are.* (✓)

Exercise 4
- Pair weak and strong Ss. They write, find, underline the questions in the dialogue and decide who asks them.
- 👥 Different individuals write the answers on the board. Involve the class. Ask *Is it correct?* (*Yes, it is. / No, it isn't.*) *Are you sure?* (*Yes, I am. / No, I'm not.*)

Answers → student page

Exercise 5
- Ss write individually. They check by finding and underlining the answers in the text.

Answers
2 Kit: Yes, he is. 3 Dug: Yes, I am. 4 Kit: Yes, it is.
5 Dug: It's my new suit. 6 Kit: No, you aren't.

2.4

In this lesson

Lesson aims:
- Communication: asking for and giving personal information

Resources:
- Communication worksheet 2.4, p. 169

Homework:
- Workbook Unit 2, p. 19
- Extra Online Practice Unit 2

Assessment for Learning in this lesson
- Setting aims and criteria for success: Warm-up
- Giving feedback: Exercise 3
- Peer learning: Exercise 5
- Independent learning: Exercise 4, Finishing the lesson

Culture notes
Pre-teens in the UK may call an adult man they don't know well / a teacher *Mr* + surname, e.g. *Mr Wood*.

Warm-up

- (*Books closed*) Ss work in pairs. Student A chooses an object / item of clothing in the room. Student B: *Is it big/blue/ Maria's …?* Student A: *Yes, it is. / No, it isn't*.
- Write *What's your name?* on the board. Elicit more personal information questions. Then Ss predict what the lesson is about. (*Books open*) Ss look at page 28 to check. (*L1/L2*) Explain the lesson objectives.

Lead-in

- (*Books open*) Ask the class questions about the photos. E.g. *Where are they?* (Ss guess.) *Who's he/she?* (*Lucas./Lian.*)

Exercise 1 ▶12 🔊 1.44
- Have a class vote!
- Play the video. If you don't have access to a computer and projector, play the recording.

Answer → student page

Exercise 2 🔊 1.45
- Make sure Ss understand all the phrases before you play the recording.

Extra activity
- Groups of three practise the dialogue in Exercise 1.

Exercise 3 🔊 1.46
- Before Ss listen, elicit the questions they think will be asked in the recording.
- (*L1/L2*) Use the Traffic Lights technique to check how difficult Ss found the exercise.

Answers → student page

Exercise 4
- This is preparation for PTEYL Springboard, Task Three Reading and Writing.

- When monitoring, give Ss an opportunity to self-correct. T: *Is this right?*

Answers → student page

Exercise 5
- Ss note two things they liked and one thing they didn't like about their partner's answers. Then they discuss.

Finishing the lesson
- Ss copy the lesson objectives into their notebooks and draw the emoticons that reflect their progress (☺, 😐, ☹).

Fast finishers
- Ss write a dialogue with an imaginary new classmate.

2.4 Communication

I can ask for and give personal information.

What's your name?

1
Mr Wood: What's your name?
Lucas: Lucas Ortiz. That's O-R-T-I-Z.
Mr Wood: Good. And how old are you, Lucas?
Lucas: I'm eleven years old.
Mr Wood: Welcome to the school band.

2
Lian: Where are you from, Lucas?
Lucas: I'm from Madrid, Spain.
Lian: What's your favourite music?
Lucas: Good question. Rock, I think.
Lian: Who's your favourite singer?
Lucas: Erm … Ed Sheeran.
Lian: High five! He's my favourite too!

1 ▶12 🔊 1.44 Watch or listen and read. Where is Lucas from? *Madrid, Spain.*

2 🔊 1.45 Listen and repeat.

Communication
Asking for personal information

What's your name?
How old are you?
Where are you from?
What's your favourite *music/sport/film*?
Who's your favourite *actor/singer/sports person*?

3 🔊 1.46 Listen to the dialogues. Circle the correct answer.
1 Star Wars. / (Superman.)
2 Nick Carr. That's C-A-double R. / (Carl Neal. That's N-E-A-L.)
3 Warsaw, Poland. / (Paris, France.)
4 (I'm twelve.) / I'm thirteen.
5 Alicia Keys. / (Taylor Swift.)

4 **Exam Spot** Complete the dialogues with questions in the Communication box.
1 A: *What's your favourite music?*
  B: Pop, I think.
2 A: *How old are you* ?
  B: I'm twelve years old.
3 A: *What's your name* ?
  B: My name's Fred Allen. That's A- double L-E-N.
4 A: *What's your favourite sport* ?
  B: Football.
5 A: *Where are you from* ?
  B: I'm from Glasgow, Scotland.

Fun Spot

5 In pairs, ask and answer questions in the Communication box. Give crazy answers!
A: *What's your name?*
B: *My name's Queen Coco!*
A: *Where are you from?*
B: *I'm from Chocolateland!*

I can understand a text about a super backpack. **Reading** 2.5

1 🔊 **1.47** Listen and repeat. Then label pictures 1–6 with the words in the Vocabulary box.

Vocabulary My things

backpack   games console   laptop computer
mobile phone   mountain bike   skateboard

1 _games console_   2 _backpack_   3 _skateboard_
4 _mobile phone_   5 _laptop computer_   6 _mountain bike_

2 🔊 **1.48** Read and listen to the article. Why is the backpack a super backpack?

3 Read the sentences. Circle T (true) or F (false).
1 Jamie is from London in the UK.   T / **F**
2 Super backpack is a jumper too.   T / **F**
3 Super backpack is too small for a laptop computer.   T / **F**
4 Fiona is Jamie's pet.   **T** / F

4 **Exam Spot** Look at the picture in the text and answer the questions.
1 What colour is the super backpack?   _It's red._
2 What colour is the mountain bike?   _It's grey._
3 Is the jacket red or blue?   _It's blue._
4 Is the cat in the pocket big or small?   _It's small._

5 Work in groups. Invent a supergadget! Draw it and present it to the class.

It's a school bag. It's a skateboard too.

Jamie Cooper's 13.
He's from Liverpool in the UK.
Jamie's super backpack is our gadget of the week. Why? Read on.
CONGRATULATIONS, JAMIE!

Super backpack!

What's in the picture? Yes, that's right. It's a red backpack. It's a super backpack! It's very very cool.

Look again. This super backpack is also a mountain bike. It's small but it isn't too small. It's fantastic! And that's not all. Think about it. You're in the park with your friends. You're cold and your jumper is at home. No problem. This super backpack is a big jacket too.

What about your other things? Don't worry! Super backpack is just the right size for your laptop computer, your mobile phone, your new games and other favourites. There's even a pocket for a small pet like my cat Fiona. How cool is that?

29

2.5

In this lesson

Lesson aims:
- Reading: understanding a text about a super backpack
- Vocabulary: personal/ favourite objects

Resources:
- Tests: Vocabulary Check 2.5

Homework:
- Workbook Unit 2, p. 20

Assessment for Learning in this lesson
- Setting aims and criteria for success: Warm-up
- Giving feedback: Exercise 1 and 3
- Peer learning: Exercise 2 and 5
- Independent learning: Finishing the lesson

Warm-up
- (*Books closed*) Brainstorm personal information questions with the class. Write prompts on the board, e.g. *Name?/ Age?/Where from?* Pairs interview each other.
- (*Books open*) Pairs look at page 29, discuss what they will do/learn and note their ideas. Don't explain the objectives! Review Ss' predictions at the end of the class.

Lead-in
- (*Books closed*) Write *My things* on the board. Brainstorm any words Ss know.

Exercise 1 🔊 **1.47**
- Pairs do the labelling exercise.
- Use the Lollipop Stick technique to check answers.

Answers → student page

Extra activity
- One student mimes using a thing from the Vocabulary box for his/her partner to guess what it is.

Exercise 2 🔊 **1.48**
- Use the picture to pre-teach *pocket*.
- Before Ss listen/read, they work individually and guess two reasons the backpack is 'super'. Then they snowball their ideas in pairs and think of four. Finally, two pairs join up and think of eight ideas.

Answer
The backpack is a mountain bike, a jumper and a jacket. There's a pocket for a pet and space for your things.

Exercise 3
- Check answers using T/F response cards. Different individuals justify each answer.

Answers → student page

Exercise 4
- This is preparation for CYLET Starters, Reading and Writing Part 5.

Answers → student page

Exercise 5
- Bring enough sheets of A3 or A4 for groups of four.
- Ss brainstorm ideas.
- One student draws. The others plan what they will say.
- Ss give their comments on their friends' posters after they present them. Ask them to use the Two Stars and a Wish technique.

Finishing the lesson
- Pairs refer to the lesson objectives they predicted in the Warm-up. Were they correct?
- Ss copy the objective into their notebooks and draw the emoticon that reflects their progress (☺, 😐, ☹).

⏳ Fast finishers
- Ss write a list in their notebooks: 'My things'.

47

2.6 In this lesson

Lesson aims:
- Listening: understanding a conversation about classmates
- Writing: a text about favourite things; punctuation

Resources:
- Tests: Writing Task Unit 2

Homework:
- Workbook Unit 2, p. 21

Assessment for Learning in this lesson
- Setting aims and criteria for success: Warm-up
- Giving feedback: Exercise 3 and 6
- Peer learning: Exercise 1 and 7
- Independent learning: Finishing the lesson

Warm-up
- (*Books closed*) Review Lesson 2.5. Ask: *What is the gadget of the week?* (*A super backpack.*) *Why is it super?* (See Lesson 2.5, Exercise 2.) *Who's Fiona?* (*Jamie's pet cat.*)
- (*Books open*) Pairs look at page 30 and discuss what they will learn. (*L1/L2*) Explain the lesson objectives.

Lead-in
- (*Books closed*) Write P _ A _ _ _ O _ _ D on the board. Ss suggest letters to complete the word. (*Playground.*) Explain.

Exercise 1
- Pairs help each other name the objects and clothes. Then they compare answers with another pair. Finally, collect Ss' answers on the board.

Answers → student page

Exercise 2 🔊 1.49
- This is preparation for CYLET Starters/Movers, Listening Part 1.

Answers → student page

Exercise 3 🔊 1.49
- This is preparation for CYLET Starters, Reading and Writing Part 2.

2.6 Listening and Writing
I can understand and write short texts about favourite things.

1 Work in pairs. Name the clothes of the people in the picture in Exercise 2. What objects have they got? *Shirt, cap, trousers, skirt, shoes. Backpack, bike, mobile phone, skateboard.*

2 **Exam Spot** 🔊 1.49 Look at the picture again. Listen and draw lines. There's one extra child.

(Sam — Monica — Janet — Ben)

3 **Exam Spot** 🔊 1.49 Listen again. Circle T (true) or F (false).
1 Sam's cap is too small. — T / **F**
2 Janet is Monica's sister. — T / **F**
3 Janet's skateboard is her favourite thing. — **T** / F
4 Ben's backpack is blue. — **T** / F
5 Monica's skirt is too short. — T / **F**

4 What are your favourite things? Tell a friend.

- Use Ss' T/F response cards to check answers.

Answers → student page

Exercise 4
- Pairs tell each other. Then ask Ss to stand up and talk to three other Ss.

Exercise 5
- Ss predict Alex's favourite things first.

Answers → student page

Writing
- Ss read. Elicit the rules. Then ask the class (*L1/L2*) *Why is punctuation important?* (*It helps us understand a text.*)

---

5 Read Alex's blog post. Underline his favourite things.

What are my favourite things?

Today my post is about my favourite things. Are these my clothes, my computer or my phone? No! My number one favourite thing is my <u>old blue mountain bike</u>. I love my bike! My <u>new comic book</u> is number two. It's fantastic! What's number three? That's easy. My <u>red and white trainers</u>. They're really cool! Write a post and tell me about your favourite things!

Writing — Punctuation
Remember to use punctuation marks!
*What are your favourite things ?
They're my backpack , my phone and my computer . They are cool !*

6 Find and circle the punctuation marks in Alex's blog.

7 **Writing Time** Write about your favourite things.

Find ideas
Make a list of your favourite things. Think of adjectives to describe them.

Draft
Write about your favourite things. Give your text a title.
*What are my favourite things?
My number one/two/three favourite thing is my … It's …*

Check and write
Check your punctuation and write the final version of your text.

Exercise 6
- Ask Ss how difficult they found the exercise.

Answers → student page

Extra activity
- Ss draw and label two favourite things.

Exercise 7
- Pairs review each other's work and check punctuation marks.

Finishing the lesson
- Ss read the lesson objectives and show self-assessment response cards (☺, 😐, ☹).

Fast finishers
- Ss write sentences about the picture in Exercise 2.

Language Revision 2.7

Vocabulary

1 Look at the pictures and complete the words. In pairs, say eight more clothes words.

Maggie Alan

1 b**oo**ts   4 ca**p**   7 sh**irt**
2 co**at**   5 tr**ainers**   8 ja**ck**et
3 j**u**mpe**r**   6 je**a**n**s**

2 Which picture a–c matches sentences 1–2? Describe the extra picture with a friend.

a   b   c

1 [b] It's old but it isn't boring. It's green. It's cool!
2 [c] It's new. It isn't small and it isn't big. It's red.

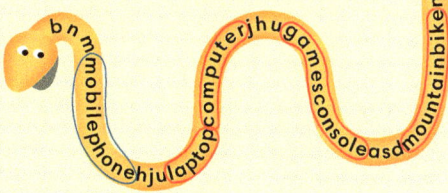

3 Find and circle four objects.

(word snake: mobilephone, laptop, computer, games console, mountain bike)

Pronunciation

4 🔊 1.50 Listen and repeat: /ð/ or /d/?

This cool hoo**d**ie is my bro**th**er **D**an's.
That new **d**ress is my mo**th**er Anne's.

Grammar

5 Look at the pictures in Exercise 1 again. In pairs, say sentences with *too*.
Maggie's coat is too big.

6 Match sentence halves 1–5 to a–e.
1 These are my favourite — a old and boring.
2 Those trousers — b her computer games.
3 Those aren't — c brown bike.
4 That phone is — d trainers.
5 This is my old — e are too long.

7 Write questions in your notebook. Answer *yes* (✔) or *no* (✘). Use short answers.
1 your / backpack / blue? ✔
  Is your backpack blue? Yes, it is.
2 those / your / books? ✘
3 he / at school? ✔
4 she / Italian? ✘
5 you / my best friend? ✔

Communication

8 Write questions. Then work in pairs.
Student A: You are your favourite star.
Student B: Ask Student A questions 1–5.
Then swap roles.
1 name What's your ?
  What's your name?
2 How old you are ?
  How old are you?
3 Where from you are ?
  Where are you from?
4 music favourite your What's ?
  What's your favourite music?
5 Who's favourite actor your ?
  Who's your favourite actor?

Check yourself! ✓
○ I can talk about clothes. ☐
○ I can use *this, that, these, those* and adjectives. ☐
○ I can ask and answer questions with the verb *to be*. ☐
○ I can ask for and give personal information. ☐

31

Exercise 1
• Refer Ss to page 23 for help.

Answers → student page

Exercise 2
• 💬 Use the Lollipop Stick technique and choose a student to describe the extra picture.

Answers → student page
Suggested description:
It's new and it's very cool. It's blue.

Extra activity
• Pairs write a riddle about a favourite thing.

Exercise 3
• Pairs race to find the words.

Answers → student page

Exercise 4 🔊 1.50
• Say /ð/ and show that your tongue touches your top teeth.

Exercise 5
• 💬 When Ss speak, monitor and give positive feedback.

Answers
Maggie's boots are too big. Maggie's coat/cap is too big. Maggie's jumper's too small. Alan's trainers are too big. Alan's jeans are too long. Alan's shirt/jacket is too small.

Exercise 6
• Ss work individually.

Answers → student page

Exercise 7
• 🔄 Ss review each other's work.

Answers
2 Are those your books? No, they aren't. **3** Is he at school? Yes, he is. **4** Is she Italian? No, she isn't. **5** Are you my best friend? Yes, I am.

Exercise 8
• Check answers before Ss speak.

Answers → student page

Finishing the lesson
• 📖 Read Check yourself! statements. Ss show their response cards (☺, 😐, ☹). Then Ss tick the statements.

⏱ **Fast finishers**
• Ss do the Extra activity individually.

2.7
In this lesson

Lesson aims:
○ Revising Vocabulary, Grammar and Communication from Unit 2
○ Pronunciation: /ð/ and /d/

Resources:
○ Tests: Language Test Unit 2

Homework:
○ Workbook Unit 2, pp. 22–23
○ Extra Online Practice Unit 2

Assessment for Learning in this lesson
◎ Setting aims and criteria for success: Warm-up
💬 Giving feedback: Exercise 2 and 5
🔄 Peer learning: Exercise 7
📖 Independent learning: Finishing the lesson

Warm-up
• (*Books closed*) Ss write their names and favourite things on slips of paper. They give them to you. Read the favourite things out but don't say whose they are. The class guesses.
• ◎ Ask Ss to work in groups and write down what they have learnt in this unit. (L1/L2) Explain the lesson objectives.

Lead-in
• (*Books open*) (L1/L2) Ask *What are your favourite lessons in this unit? Why?* Encourage Ss to explain.

1 & 2 In this lesson

Lesson aims:
- Skills practice: Reading, Writing, Listening and Communication
- Exam practice: CYLET and PTEYL

Resources:
- Tests: Skills Test Units 1&2, Speaking Tasks Units 1&2

Homework:
- Workbook Skills Revision 1&2, pp. 24–25

Assessment for Learning in this lesson
- Setting aims and criteria for success: Warm-up
- Giving feedback: Exercise 3 and 7
- Peer learning: Exercise 5
- Independent learning: Finishing the lesson

Exam Language Bank
This lists the key language from Units 1–2. Here are some ideas to help you make the most of it.
- Encourage Ss to be independent learners. They tick the words they know and check the meaning of the words they can't remember in a dictionary.
- Ss try to memorize a section, close the book and write down all the words they can remember.
- Make a quick two-minute test. (*Books closed*) Say different words/expressions in English from one section. Ss write or say sentences with them.
- Fast finishers test each other.
  Student A: *What's 'uncle' in (Polish)?*
  Student B: …
  Student B: *How do you spell 'Chinese'?*
  Student A: *C-H-I-N-E-S-E.*

Warm-up
- (*Books closed*) Name one of your favourite things and one 'false' one. Ss guess which is false. Choose different Ss to do the same. Help with vocabulary as necessary.

1 & 2 Skills Revision

Reading and Writing

Cheryl is my new school friend. She's twelve. Her favourite colour is pink. Cheryl's pink mobile phone is her favourite thing. A lot of her clothes are pink too. Her pet dog, Rafs, isn't pink! He's grey and black.

Cheryl's family is very big. Sarah and Daniela are her sisters. Her brothers are Rob and Mick. Her dad is a guitarist in a band. Sometimes he's on TV shows! Her mum's a singer. She's very cool. Her granny and grandad are from Spain. They aren't boring. They are actors. They are in films! Are they all happy? Yes, they are!

1 Work in pairs. Say what you can see in the photo.
There is a girl with a dog.

2 **Exam Spot** Read the text. Circle the correct title.
a Cheryl's new dog.   **b** My new school friend.

3 Read the sentences. Answer the questions.
1 How old is Cheryl? *Cheryl is twelve.*
2 What's her favourite thing? *A mobile phone.*
3 Is Cheryl's family small? *It's big.*
4 Who are Rob and Mick? *Cheryl's brothers.*
5 Is Cheryl's mum boring? *She's very cool.*
6 Where is her grandmother from? *Spain.*

4 **Exam Spot** Look and read. Tick (✔) for *yes* or put a cross (✘) for *no*.

1 ✔ This is a dog.
2 ✘ This is a skirt.
3 ✔ These are shoes.
4 ✘ These are skateboards.
5 ✔ This is a party.
6 ✘ These are jeans.

5 **Exam Spot** Write 40–50 words about your friend. Use these questions to help you.
1 What's his/her name?
2 How old is he/she?
3 What's his/her favourite colour?
4 What are his/her favourite things?
5 Where is his/her family from?

My good friend is … He/She is … years old. His/Her favourite colour is … His/Her favourite things are … His/Her family is from …

Listening

6 **Exam Spot** 🔊 1.51 Read the questions. Listen and write a name or a number.

1 What's the man's surname?   *Smith*
2 What's the boy's name?   *Shaun*
3 Who is the boy's best friend?   *David*
4 How old is the boy?   *12*
5 What's the number of the boy's house?   *13*

32

- Write *Skills Revision* on the board. Ask what it means. (*Books open*) Pairs look and check. Tell Ss this lesson will help prepare them for CYLET and/or PTEYL too. (See the Introduction.)

Exercise 1
- Pointing to the picture, ask *What's this?* Elicit *dog, girl, pink T-shirt.* Say *This is Cheryl.*

Answer → student page

Exercise 2
- This is preparation for CYLET Movers, Reading and Writing Part 3.
- Remind Ss they don't need to understand details yet, just the key ideas.

Answer → student page

Exercise 3
- Use the Traffic Lights technique to monitor.

Answers → student page

Extra activity
- (*Books closed*) Divide Ss into two teams. Ask each team in turn true/false questions about the text in Exercise 1. E.g. *Rafs is Cheryl's brother.* (F – her dog.) *Cheryl's favourite colour is pink.* (T) *Sarah and Daniela are her cousins.* (F – sisters.) *Her mum is a guitarist.* (F – her dad.)

Skills Revision 1 & 2

Communication

7 Exam Spot Look at the pictures. Match a–h to 1–6. There are two extra sentences.

1. e
2. d
3. f
4. a
5. g
6. b

a Nice to meet you.
b Who's your favourite actor?
c This is my mum.
d Caz, this is Jack.
e Hello Caz!
f He's my neighbour.
g What's your favourite music?
h Nice to meet you too, Mrs Smith.

8 Exam Spot Work in pairs. Ask and answer the questions.

1 What are your favourite weekend clothes?
2 What colour is your T-shirt/top today?
3 What's in your schoolbag today? (Don't look!)
4 What is your favourite place?

Exam Language Bank

Family
mother
mum
father
dad
parents
grandfather
grandad
grandmother
granny
son
daughter
brother
sister
aunt
uncle
cousin

Countries and nationalities
the UK / British
Spain / Spanish
Poland / Polish
the USA / American
Italy / Italian
France / French
China / Chinese

Places
at home
at school
at a party
in the garden
in the park
on holiday

Clothes
boots   shirt
cap   shoes
coat   skirt
dress   T-shirt
hoodie   top
jacket   tracksuit
jeans   trainers
jumper   trousers

Adjectives
big   new
boring   old
cool   short
long   small

My things
backpack
games console
laptop computer
mobile phone
mountain bike
skateboard

Introductions
Mum, this is *Lucas.*
He's my *friend/classmate.*
Lucas, this is *my mum.*
Nice to meet you.
Nice to meet you too.

Asking questions
What's your name?
How old are you?
Where are you from?
What's your favourite *music/sport/film*?
Who's your favourite *actor/singer/sportsperson*?

33

Exercise 4

- This is preparation for CYLET Starters, Reading and Writing Part 1.
- Ss do the exercise individually.
- Ss say the answers. Ask them to say a negative sentence if the answer is '✘' and to name the object.

Answers → student page

Extra activity
- Play *I Spy* with objects in your classroom. (See Lesson 0.3, Extra activity.)

Exercise 5

- This is preparation for PTEYL Springboard, Task 6 Writing.
- (*Books closed*) Pairs tell each other what they can remember about using capital letters and punctuation. Then they look at pages 18 and 30 to check.
- Then Ss write individually. They exchange notebooks and review each other's work using the Two Stars and a Wish technique.

Extra activity
- Ss read their texts to the class now or at the end of the lesson. If the friend is in the class, the student doesn't say his/her name. The class guesses.

Exercise 6 🔊 1.51

- This is preparation for CYLET Starters, Listening Part 2.
- Ss guess where the man and boy in the picture are.
- Ss read the questions. Tell them to only write one name or number.
- Play the recording. Ss listen and write. With a weak class, pause for pairs to discuss and write the answers.
- Play the recording again for Ss to check. (Ss hear it twice in the exam.)

Answers → student page

Exercise 7

- This is preparation for PTEYL Firstwords/Springboard, Task Four Reading.
- Ss in a weak class tell you what they can see in the pictures before they match.
- Remind Ss there are two extra sentences.
- Use the Lollipop Stick technique to check answers.

Answers → student page

Exercise 8

- This is preparation for CYLET/PTEYL Speaking.
- Ask Ss to take notes.

Extra activity
- Divide Ss into two groups. Ss use their notes and take turns to say T/F sentences about their partners for the other group to guess.

Finishing the lesson

- Write the headings *Reading and Writing, Listening, Communication* on the board. Read each out. Ss show self-assessment response cards (☺, 😐, ☹). Then they write one sentence about what they did well in each section and one about what they could improve.

Fast finishers
- Ss write sentences like those in Exercise 5 about a different friend.
- Ss study the Exam Language Bank.

3.1

In this lesson

Lesson aims:
- Vocabulary: furniture and parts of the house

Resources:
- Vocabulary worksheet 3.1, p. 149
- Tests: Vocabulary Check 3.1

Homework:
- Workbook Unit 3, p. 26

Assessment for Learning in this lesson
- Setting aims and criteria for success: Warm-up
- Giving feedback: Exercise 2 and 3
- Peer learning: Exercise 4 and 5
- Independent learning: Exercise 7 and Finishing the lesson

Culture notes
A lot of people live in houses in the UK. They often have a garden.

Warm-up

- (*Books closed*) Spelling game! Divide the class into three or four teams. Say a new word from Unit 2. One student from each team writes it on the board. Check spelling. Each correctly spelt word wins a point. Continue with a different word and different Ss from each team.
- (*L1/L2*) Say Unit 3 is 'In the house'. Ask different Ss to predict what they will learn. List predictions on the board.
- Explain the lesson objective. Then ask Ss to predict what they will be able to say in English at the end of the lesson.

Lead-in

- **Critical thinking** (*Books closed*) Ask *What house words do you know?* Different Ss say a word and write it on the board with the class'/your help. Translate if the class is weak.

In this unit

Vocabulary
- In the house
- Prepositions of place
- Household objects

Grammar
- there is / there are affirmative, negative and questions
- a/an, any

3 In the house

Vocabulary I can talk about my house.

1 How many of these objects can you find in the photos?

1	4	1	3	1	2	12
bed	chair	desk	door	sofa	table	window

I know that!

Exercise 1
- Choose one word from the box, translate it and say *I know that!* with a thumbs up gesture. Encourage Ss to continue.
- Pairs count and note the number of objects by the corresponding words.
- (*L1/L2*) Check answers by asking different pairs.

Answers → student page

Exercise 2 2.1
- Give Ss time to read the words.
- Play the recording. Pause after each word. Ss repeat it and find the item in the photos. Ask different Ss in a weak class to hold up their books and point at the objects.

Exercise 3
- Ss do the exercise individually. Then pairs compare answers.
- Ask different Ss for the answers. They justify their answers by holding up their book, pointing and naming objects.

Answers → student page

Exercise 4 2.2
- Play the recording. Pause after number 1. One student reads the example aloud.
- Play until the end, pausing for pairs to discuss and note their answers.
- Alternatively, do this as a whole class activity. Ss tell you their ideas. Vote and check!

Answers → student page

2 🔊 **2.1** Listen and repeat. Find the items in the Vocabulary box in the photos on page 34.

> **Vocabulary** In the house
>
> **Parts of the house**
> bathroom   bedroom   door   floor   garage
> garden   kitchen   living room   wall   window
>
> **Inside the house**
> armchair   bath   bed   chair   desk   fridge
> sofa   table   wardrobe

3 Which part of the house are the photos from? Circle the correct answer.

1 living room / (bedroom)    2 (bathroom) / kitchen

3 (garage) / garden    4 bedroom / (living room)

5 living room / (garden)    6 floor / (wall)

4 🔊 **2.2** Listen to the sounds. Where are you? Write in your notebook.

1 *In the living room.*
2 *In the kitchen.*   5 *In the garden.*
3 *In the garage.*   6 *In the bathroom.*
4 *In the bedroom.*

5 Complete the word. Read the sentence, look at the photos on page 34 and circle T (true) or F (false).

1 b <u>e</u> d
   It's in the bathroom.   T / (F)
2 f <u>r</u> i <u>d</u> g e
   It's in the kitchen.   (T) / F
3 a <u>r</u> m <u>c</u> h <u>a</u> i <u>r</u>
   It's in the kitchen.   T / (F)
4 w <u>a</u> r <u>d</u> r <u>o</u> b e
   It's in the bedroom.   (T) / F
5 t <u>a</u> b <u>l</u> e
   It's in the garden.   T / (F)
6 b <u>a</u> t <u>h</u>
   It's in the bathroom.   (T) / F
7 c <u>h</u> a <u>i</u> r
   It's in the kitchen   (T) / F

6 In your notebook, correct the false sentences in Exercise 5.

1 *The bed is in the bedroom.*

7 Look at the photos on page 34.
Student A: Say a sentence about an object inside the house.
Student B: Find the object in the photos. Is Student A's sentence true? Correct the false sentences.
Then swap roles.

A: *An armchair is in the bathroom.*
B: *No, it isn't. It's the living room!*

8 Draw where things are in your Crazy House. Then make lists and compare in pairs.

The kitchen: a sofa, …

I remember that!

3.1

Exercise 8
- Ask *What's in your crazy house?* Volunteers give you two or three examples.
- Ss imagine, draw and write lists. They compare in pairs. You could ask them to tell the class. Have a class vote: *Whose house is the craziest?*

Finishing the lesson
- 💬 Ss circle the new words in the Vocabulary box they have learnt. Remember to praise and encourage. (*L1*) Tell weak Ss they will be able to practise the words again in the other units and activities.
- 💬 Ask *Can you talk about your house?* Ss show self-assessment response cards (☺, 😐, ☹). Then they copy the objective into their notebooks and draw the emoticon that reflects their progress.

⏳ **Fast finishers**
- Ss choose a photo on page 34. They write all the words they know. They look up words they don't know in a dictionary.
- Ss write how many objects from the Vocabulary box on page 35 are in their house. E.g. *Twelve chairs,* …

Exercise 5
- Do the example with the class, then Ss do the exercise individually. Point out the words they need are in the Vocabulary box.
- 👥 Ss then stand up and compare each answer with a different student, discussing and correcting each other's answers.

> Answers → student page

Exercise 6
- Ask a weak class where the items are in the photos first. Ss write individually and pairs compare answers.
- Ask different Ss to write the answers on the board.

> **Answers**
> 3 *It's in the living room.* 5 *It's in the kitchen.*

Exercise 7
- Ss find the armchair in the photos.
- A confident pair reads the example.
- Pairs decide who is A and B and continue, changing roles.
- 💬 Challenge strong Ss to do the activity without referring to the example.

Extra activity
- Game! Write an object on the board, e.g. *chair*. Pairs have thirty seconds to write where we usually find chairs. Check. The pair with the most places wins. Continue.

3.2

In this lesson

Lesson aims:
- Grammar: *there is / there are* affirmative
- Vocabulary: prepositions of place

Resources:
- Grammar worksheet 3.2, p. 156
- Tests: Grammar Check 3.2, Vocabulary Check 3.2

Homework:
- Workbook Unit 3, p. 27
- Extra Online Practice Unit 3

Assessment for Learning in this lesson
- Setting aims and criteria for success: Warm-up
- Giving feedback: Exercise 2
- Peer learning: Exercise 6 and 11
- Independent learning: Finishing the lesson

Warm-up
- (*Books closed*) Game! Divide the class into groups of four. Give Ss two minutes to list house words from Lesson 3.1. The team with the longest (correct) list wins.
- Say a true sentence about your classroom with *there is/are*, e.g. *There's a desk next to the door.* Explain the lesson objectives.

Lead-in
- (*Books open*) Ask the class questions about the photo story, e.g. *Who is he?* (Alex.) *Is Jen Lian's sister?* (No, she isn't!) *Are they at Alex and Jen's house?* (Yes, they are.)
- Use the photos to pre-teach any vocabulary you think Ss will find difficult, e.g.: *milk, carton, orange juice, sweets.*

3.2 Grammar
I can use there is / there are *and prepositions of place.*

There's a phone on the sofa!

1
Alex: Jen, where's the orange juice?
Jen: It's in the fridge.
Alex: Where?
Jen: It's in front of you.
Alex: No, it isn't.
Jen: Right there! There's a carton next to the milk.
Alex: Oh, there it is!

2
Alex: Where's my phone?
Lian: There's a phone on the sofa.
Jen: No, that's my phone.
Lian: Maybe it's under the table.
Jen: No, it isn't.

3
Lian: Is it behind the sofa?
Alex: No, it isn't but there are two DVDs.
Jen: Hey! Those are my DVDs!

4
Alex: Wait! There are some sweets under the sofa.
Jen: Yuck! They're old!
Alex: But where's my phone?
Lian: Hang on!

1 ▶13 🔊 2.3 Watch or listen and read. What is Alex looking for? Circle the correct answer.
a a book (**b**) his phone c a DVD

2 Answer the questions.
1 Photo 1 Where are the three friends? *They're in the kitchen.*
2 Photo 2 Where are they now? *In the living room.*
3 Photo 2 Is it Jen's phone? *Yes, it is.*
4 Photo 3 Are they Alex's DVDs? *No, they aren't.*
5 Photo 4 What's wrong with the sweets? *They're old.*

3 🔊 2.4 Listen and repeat. Find these expressions in the story.

> Right there! There it is!
> Wait! Yuk!

Say it!

4 ▶ Guess! Where is Alex's phone? Make a guess. Use *in*, *on* or *under*. *It is in the fridge.*

5 ▶14 🔊 2.5 Now watch or listen and check.

36

Exercise 1 ▶13 🔊 2.3
- Read the question. Ss predict the answer. Have a class vote!
- Play the video. If you don't have access to a computer and projector, play the recording. Ss check their predictions.

Answer → student page

Exercise 2
- Pairs write the answers they know.
- Play the video again (stopping it in appropriate places) or refer Ss to the photo story to confirm the answers.
- Check answers using the Basketball technique.

Answers → student page

Exercise 3 🔊 2.4 ▶13
- Play the recording, pausing for Ss to repeat.
- Play the video again. Ss shout *STOP!* when they hear each expression. Alternatively, Ss find and underline the expressions in the dialogue.

Exercise 4
- Write *in*, *on* and *under* on the board. Point to objects in the photos that exemplify each and elicit/give examples. E.g. *The orange juice is in the fridge.*
- **Critical thinking** The class guesses where Alex's phone is. Don't confirm yet!

Answer → student page

54

3.2

Grammar
there is / there are affirmative

▶ 15 **Get Grammar!**

➕ There's (There is) a phone on the sofa.
There are two DVDs behind the sofa.
There are some sweets under the sofa.

There are two rats under the table.
There's a rat under the sofa.

6 Complete with *There is* or *There are*. Then look at the photos on page 36 and tick (✔) the true sentences.

1 ✔ *There is* a fridge.
2 ✔ *There is* one chair.
3 ✘ *There is* a bed.
4 ✘ *There are* four phones.
5 ✘ *There are* two windows.
6 ✔ *There is* a sofa.

7 Look around. Say how many of them there are in your classroom.

| door | window | board | desk |
| boys and girls | teacher | wall | |

There's one door. There are two windows.

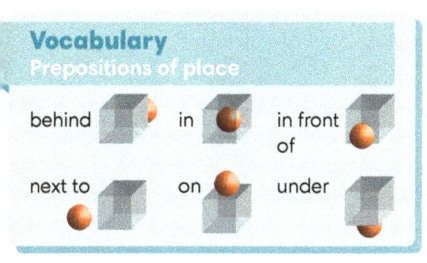

8 🔊 2.6 Look, listen and repeat.

Vocabulary
Prepositions of place

behind | in | in front of
next to | on | under

9 Look at the photos on page 36. Circle the correct preposition.

1 Photo 1 There are two phones *under* / **on** the kitchen table.
2 Photo 1 Alex is *behind* / **in front of** the fridge.
3 Photo 1 There is a carton of juice **in** / *next to* the fridge.
4 Photo 1 Jen is *behind* / **next to** Alex.
5 Photo 2 There are some books **under** / *on* the small table.

10 Look at pictures A and B. Complete the sentences.

1 *There's* a chair …
A *in front of* the desk. B *on* the bed.
2 *There's* a box …
A *behind* the desk. B *in front of / next to* the door.
3 *There's* a bag …
A *next to* the door. B *in* the box.
4 *There are* some books …
A *in* the bag. B *under* the desk.
5 *There are* some T-shirts …
A *on* the bed. B *under* the bed.

11 Go to page 108 and play a drawing dictation game.

Fun Spot

Exercise 5 ▶ 14 🔊 2.5
- Play the video or recording to find out who was right!

Video/Audio script
Lian: Shhh!
Jen: It's in the kitchen.
Alex: Yes, but where?
Lian: It's in the fridge!
Jen: Yes, it is!
Alex: What …
Lian: Oh, Alex!

Get Grammar! ▶ 15
- Play the Get Grammar! video. If you don't have access to a computer and projector, continue.
- The class repeats the examples after you in chorus.
- Elicit/Tell Ss we use *there's / there is* with singular nouns and *there are* with plurals.
- Tell Ss we can say *some* instead of a number, e.g. *some sweets*.

Language notes
We use *there's* in everyday English.

Exercise 6
- Ss do the exercise individually. Then they compare answers with a partner.

- 👥 Different pairs write answers on the board. One student writes and the other helps. This is a good way of boosting weaker Ss' confidence.

Answers → student page

Exercise 7
- Ss take turns to say sentences about your classroom to a partner.

Exercise 8 🔊 2.6
- Play the recording, pausing for Ss to repeat.
- Ss give you examples using objects in your classroom.

Exercise 9
- Choose Ss to say the answers.

Answers → student page

Exercise 10
- Pairs do the exercise.
- Choose different Ss to write the answers on the board.

Answers → student page

Extra activity
- Pairwork. Student A says a sentence about picture A or B in Exercise 10. (Book closed) Student B says if it is picture A or B. Ss swap and continue.

Exercise 11
- Student A looks at his/her picture on page 108 and describes it for student B to draw it in his/her notebook! Change roles and continue.
- 👥 Invite two Ss who described their picture well to do it for the class.

Finishing the lesson
- 💬 Elicit language learnt in this lesson. E.g.: *Describe photo 1 in the photo story. Where's Alex's phone?* Then ask *Can you use 'there is' / 'there are'? Can you use prepositions of place?* Ss show self-assessment response cards (☺, 😐, ☹).
- 📓 Ss copy the objectives into their notebooks and draw the emoticons that reflect their progress.

⏳ Fast finishers
- Ss write sentences to describe their classroom with *there is/are* and prepositions of place.

3.3

In this lesson

Lesson aims:
- Grammar: *there is / there are* questions and negations

Resources:
- Grammar worksheet 3.3, p. 157
- Tests: Grammar Check 3.3

Homework:
- Workbook Unit 3, p. 28

Assessment for Learning in this lesson
- Setting aims and criteria for success: Warm-up
- Giving feedback: Exercise 3 and 4
- Peer learning: Extra activity and Exercise 6
- Independent learning: Finishing the lesson

Warm-up
- (*Books closed*) Ss make sentences with *there is/are* about the classroom. Student A: *There are some books.* Student B: *There are some books and there's a desk.* Student C: *There are some books, there's a desk and …* Continue until a student can't rememeber and start again.
- Write on the board *There isn't a book. Are there twenty students?* Ask Ss to guess what the sentences mean. Then explain the lesson objectives.

Lead-in
- (*Books open*) Ask the class *Who are the Terrific Two? (Kit and Superdug.) What can you remember about Kit and Superdug? (Superdug's a dog/ superhero. Kit's a cat.)* Ask *Who's Coco?* Ss guess.
- Then ask about each picture in turn. E.g. (Picture 2) *What's this? (A garage.)* (Picture 3 – pointing to Kit's granny) *Who's she?* (Ss guess.) Use the photos to pre-teach *trees, parrot* and *car* as necessary.

Exercise 1
- Use the pictures to teach *walkie-talkie* and *headset* first.

Answer → student page

Exercise 2
- Pairs predict the answer.
- Play the recording. Ss listen, read and circle.

Answer → student page

Exercise 3
- Ss read the sentences, read the dialogue again and complete individually. Before a weak class starts, elicit or tell Ss key words in the sentences to underline. 2 – *blue*, 3 – *two big / garden*, 4 – *bad*, 5 – *Granny / house*.
- Use the Lollipop Stick technique to choose Ss to write the answers on the board.

Answers → student page

Extra activity
- Groups of four act out the cartoon dialogue. (*L1/L2*) The groups discuss what they each did well and what they could improve. (*L1*) Write prompts on the board, e.g. *pronunciation?/hesitation?/expressive?*

Get Grammar!
- Play the Get Grammar! video. If you don't have access to a computer and projector, continue.
- Ss repeat the examples after you in chorus.
- Elicit/Point out word order in questions: *is/are* is positioned before *there*.
- Point out the affirmative and negative short answers.

Language notes
Short answers are usual in everyday English.

3.3 Grammar

I can use the negative and question forms of there is / there are.

The Terrific Two — Dug and Coco

Picture 1
Kit: KIT! HELP! THERE ARE TWO BAD PEOPLE HERE!
Kit: Dug! It's my granny! Go to 10 Paxton Street!
Dug: OK.

Superdug: Kit, there isn't a number on the house.
Kit: Is there a blue car in the garage?
Superdug: Yes, there is.
Kit: Are there two big trees in front of the house?
Superdug: Yes, there are.
Kit: That's Granny's house.

Picture 3
Superdug: Where are the bad people?
Granny: There aren't any bad people here, Dug.
Parrot: Help! Kit! Help!

Picture 4
Superdug: Kit, it's the parrot, not your granny!
Kit: Coco? Oh, he's naughty!
Granny: I'm very sorry, Dug. Coco is a silly boy!
Parrot: Silly boy Coco! Sorry Dug!
Granny: Good boy, Coco!

Picture 5
GOOD BOY, COCO! SILLY BOY, DUG!

---

1 Look at the cartoon. How do Kit and Superdug talk when he is in the air? Circle the correct picture.  
a   b   c

2 🔊 2.7 Listen and read. Who is on the phone in Picture 1? Circle the correct answer.
a Kit's granny   **b Coco, the parrot**
(*Kit thinks it's her Granny.*)

3 Complete the sentences with words from the cartoon.
1 __Kit's__ granny's house is at 10 Paxton Stree
2 Granny's __car__ is blue.
3 There are two big __trees__ in Granny's gard
4 There aren't any bad __people__ in Granny's house.
5 There's only Granny and __Coco__ in the hou __the parrot__

38

Grammar
there is / there are negative and questions

▶ 16 **Get Grammar!**

–	There isn't a red car.	There aren't any people.
?	Is there a red car?	Are there any people?
	Yes, there is. / No, there isn't.	Yes, there are. / No, there aren't.

Yes, there are.
Are there any cupcakes?

4 Circle the correct answer. Then look at the cartoon on page 38 and tick (✔) the true sentences.

1 ✔ *There isn't* / (*There aren't*) any people in Granny's garden.
2 ☐ *There isn't* / (*There aren't*) any cats in the story.
3 ✔ (*There isn't*) / *There aren't* a bike in Granny's garage.
4 ✔ *There isn't* / (*There aren't*) any dogs in Granny's garden.
5 ☐ (*There isn't*) / *There aren't* a phone in Granny's house.
6 ✔ (*There isn't*) / *There aren't* a desk in the living room.

LOOK!
There isn't **a** tree.
There aren't **any** trees.
Is there **a** tree?
Are there **any** trees?

5 Look at the cartoon again. What is missing? Choose from the box.

| TV | photos | table | ~~window~~ | doors |

1 Picture 1 Look behind Dug.
   There isn't a window!
2 Picture 2 Look at Granny's house.
3 Picture 3 Look behind Granny.
4 Picture 4 Look at the books.
5 Picture 5 Look at the wall behind Coco.

6 Look at the picture. In your notebook, write Kit's questions and Dug's answers. Then ask and answer the questions in pairs.

1 a small house next to the big houses?
Kit: *Is there a small house next to the big houses?*
Dug: *Yes, there is.*
2 cars in front of the houses?
3 a dog under the tree?
4 people in the street?
5 chairs in the garden?
6 flowers next to the tree?
7 a cat behind the tree?
8 a parrot in the tree?

7 Go to page 108 and play a memory game.

Fun Spot

39

Exercise 6
- Pairs use the prompts to write questions and answers.
- 🔄 Each pair swaps their books with another pair. They review each other's work.
- Write answers most Ss found difficult on the board and clarify.
- Pairs ask and answer.

Answers
2 Are there any cars in front of the houses? No, there aren't.
3 Is there a dog under the tree? No, there isn't.
4 Are there any people in the street? Yes, there are.
5 Are there any chairs in the garden? No, there aren't.
6 Are there any flowers next to the tree? Yes, there are.
7 Is there a cat behind the tree? No, there isn't.
8 Is there a parrot in the tree? No, there isn't.

Exercise 7
- Pairs look at the pictures on page 108. Student A chooses one but doesn't say which. Student B asks questions with *Is/Are there a/any …?* to find out. They swap.

Finishing the lesson
- 📱 Revise language learnt in this lesson. Open pairs ask each other questions about the cartoon. E.g. *Are there any trees in Granny's garden? (Yes, there are.)* Then ask *Can you ask questions with 'there is' / 'there are'? Can you say negative sentences?* Ss show self-assessment response cards for each (☺, 😐, ☹).
- 📱 Ss copy the objectives into their notebooks and draw the emoticons that reflect their progress.

⏱ Fast finishers
- Ss look at the Vocabulary box on page 35. They write what there is and isn't in the cartoon. E.g. *There isn't a fridge.*
- Ss find and underline examples of *there is/are* in the cartoon.

Exercise 4
- Elicit/Point out the answer in the example is *There aren't* because the noun (*people*) is plural.
- Pairs help each other do the exercise.
- 💬 Check answers using the Thumbs up/down technique.
- Pairs read the sentences again, look at the pictures and tick.

Answers → student page

Look!
- Ss read the examples. Elicit/Explain we use *a* with singular nouns (all forms) and *any* with plural nouns (questions and negatives).
- Encourage Ss to work out the rules by asking prompt questions. E.g. ask *Is 'tree' singular or plural? (Singular.) Is 'trees' singular or plural? (Plural.)*

Exercise 5
- Ask a weak class what's missing from each picture first. Then pairs do the exercise.
- **Critical thinking** Different pairs justify their answers by explaining/pointing.

Answers
2 There aren't any doors! 3 There isn't a TV!
4 There isn't a table! 5 There aren't any photos!

57

3.4

In this lesson

Lesson aims:
- Communication: asking for something and saying where something is

Resources:
- Communication worksheet 3.4, p. 170

Homework:
- Workbook Unit 3, p. 29
- Extra Online Practice Unit 3

Assessment for Learning in this lesson
- Setting aims and criteria for success: Warm-up
- Giving feedback: Exercise 5
- Peer learning: Exercise 4
- Independent learning: Finishing the lesson

Warm-up

- (*Books closed*) Play a game to revise language from this unit. Pairs say true and false sentences about their house for their partner to guess.
- Pairs imagine a guest has arrived. (*L1*) They discuss what they would say in their language. Explain the lesson objectives.

Lead-in

- (*Books open*) Ask Ss questions about the photos to pre-teach *sandwich, ketchup, upstairs, downstairs*.

Exercise 1 ▶17 🔊 2.8
- Ss guess whose house it is. Have a class vote!
- Play the video. If you don't have access to a computer and projector, play the recording.

Answer → student page

Exercise 2 🔊 2.9
- Make sure Ss understand all the expressions in the box before they listen.

Exercise 3
- When pairs act out the dialogues, monitor and refer them to the Communication box.

Answers → student page

3.4 Communication

I can ask for something and ask where something is.

Where's the bathroom?

1
Jen: Hi! Here are your books.
Lucas: Thanks, Jen. Please, come in. Would you like a sandwich?
Jen: Yes, please. I'm really hungry.

2
Jen: This is yummy!
Lucas: Erm … Jen? There's ketchup on your T-shirt.
Jen: Oh, no! Where's the bathroom, please?
Lucas: It's upstairs. Let me show you.

3
Lucas: Is your T-shirt OK?
Jen: Not really. But I'd like another sandwich, please!

1 ▶17 🔊 2.8 Watch or listen and read. Whose house is it? Circle the correct answer.
  a Jen's   b Lian's   **c** Lucas's

2 🔊 2.9 Listen and repeat.

Communication — Having a guest

A: Hello. Please, come in.
B: Thank you.
A: Would you like *a sandwich*?
B: Yes, please. / No, thank you.

A: Where's the *bathroom*, please?
B: It's *upstairs/downstairs*.
   It's *next to* the *living room*.
   Let me show you.

3 Match 1–3 to a–c. Then act out the dialogues in pairs.
1 [c] Would you like a biscuit?
2 [a] Where's the kitchen, please?
3 [b] Where's my jacket, please?

a It's downstairs. Let me show you.
b It's on the chair, next to the sofa.
c Yes, please.

4 Exam Spot Circle the best answer.
1 A: Hello, Maria. Please, come in.
  B: a Yes, please.   **b** Thank you.
    c Let me show you.
2 A: Would you like an ice cream?
  B: a Come in.   b It's downstairs.
    c Yes, please.
3 A: Where's the bathroom?
  B: a Please, come in.   **b** Let me show you.
    c It's next to the bed.

5 Write dialogues. Then act them out in pairs.
1 A: Hi / come in   B: thank
   Hi. Please, come in.   *Thank you.*
2 A: like / a cupcake?   B: no / thank
3 A: like / an apple?   B: yes
4 A: where / the bathroom?   B: It's / Let me show

6 You have a guest from another planet. In pairs, write dialogues in English and in your guest's language. Then act them out in class.
A: *Hello, Xen! Please, come in.*
B: *Nabu midi rona, Tomi.*

Fun Spot

40

Exercise 4
- This is preparation for CYLET Movers, Reading and Writing Part 2.
- Ss check each other's answers.

Answers → student page

Exercise 5
- Ss write dialogues individually.
- Check understanding using the Traffic Lights technique.

Answers
2 A: Would you like a cupcake?
  B: No, thank you.
3 A: Would you like an apple?
  B: Yes, please.
4 A: Where is the bathroom, please?
  B: It's (upstairs). Let me show you.

Exercise 6
- Write two/three planets in English on the board. Pairs decide which their guest is from!

Finishing the lesson

- Ask the class *Can you ask for something and where something is?* Ss show self-assessment response cards for each (☺, 😐, ☹).
- Ss copy the objectives into their notebooks and draw the emoticons that reflect their progress.

⌛ **Fast finishers**
- Ss write sentences to describe the photos in Exercise 1.

I can understand a text about a dream house. **Reading** **3.5**

1 🔊 **2.10** Listen and repeat. Then label pictures 1–6 with the words in the Vocabulary box.

> **Vocabulary** Household objects
>
> carpet   cushion   lamp   plant   poster
> television (TV)

1 television   2 cushion   3 plant
4 poster   5 lamp   6 carpet

2 Which objects in Exercise 1 are in your classroom? Where are they? Tell a partner.

3 **Exam Spot** 🔊 **2.11** Look, read and listen. What is the text about? Circle the correct answer.

a a sport   b a person   (c) a house

4 Read the sentences. Circle *yes*, *no* or *no info*.
1 People skateboard inside the house.
 (yes) / no / no info
2 There's a TV in the living room.
 yes / no / (no info)
3 There are cushions in the living room.
 (yes) / no / no info
4 There are three sofas in the living room.
 yes / (no) / no info
5 There's a carpet in the bedroom.
 yes / (no) / no info
6 There's a big skateboard practice room.
 (yes) / no / no info

5 Read the text again and answer the questions.
1 What rooms are there in the house?
2 What objects are there in the house?
3 What objects in Exercise 1 are **not** in the house?

6 Imagine your dream house. Write five sentences about it in your notebook. Tell your partner.

> There are … rooms. There's a … and there are …
> In my … there is a small/big …

A skateboarder's dream

This house is a perfect house for skateboarders. There aren't any carpets, plants, pictures or posters on the walls in this house. Why? Think about it!

Normally people skateboard in the park or in the garden. In this house people skateboard inside! They skateboard in the living room, in the kitchen, in the bedroom and in the bathroom. They skateboard on the walls too!

Look at the living room. There's a table, some chairs, an armchair and a sofa with some cushions. It looks typical, but people skateboard on the sofa, tables and chairs!

There's a big skateboard practice room too. People train with friends and they have competitions there. It's really cool!

It's a skateboarder's dream house.

41

3.5
In this lesson

Lesson aims:
- Reading: understanding a text about a dream house
- Vocabulary: household objects

Resources:
- Tests: Vocabulary Check 3.5

Homework:
- Workbook Unit 3, p. 30

Assessment for Learning in this lesson
- Setting aims and criteria for success: Warm-up
- Giving feedback: Exercise 4
- Peer learning: Exercise 6
- Independent learning: Finishing the lesson

Warm-up
- (*Books open*) Ss look at page 41. Ask what they expect to learn in this lesson. Explain the lesson objectives.

Exercise 1 🔊 **2.10**
- (*Books closed*) Teach *household objects*. Ask pairs to list the household objects they know in English.
- (*Books open*) After Ss label, pick individuals to write the answers on the board.

Answers → student page

Exercise 2
- Look around the classroom and say *There's a (poster) (on the wall)*.
- Ask Ss to use the objects in Exercise 1 and continue making sentences in pairs.

Exercise 3 🔊 **2.11**
- This is preparation for CYLET Movers, Reading and Writing Part 3.
- Ask Ss to describe the photos. Then say *Have you got a skateboard? Can you skateboard in your house?*

Answer → student page

Exercise 4
- Check answers using response cards. Each time point to one student and make him/her justify the answer.

Answers → student page

Exercise 5
- Divide the class into groups of three. Each student in a group answers one question. Groups race to complete the task. Collect answers on the board.

Answer
1 living room, kitchen, bedroom, bathroom, skateboard practice room 2 table, chairs, armchair, sofa, cushions 3 carpet, plant, poster

Exercise 6
- Write model answers on the board. Ss exchange notebooks and review each other's work in pairs.

Finishing the lesson
- Pointing to the photos, ask Ss *Is this a good dream house for you?* Encourage them to explain why (not) in English.
- Read the lesson objective. Ss show self-assessment response cards (☺, 😐, ☹). Then Ss copy the objective into their notebooks and draw the emoticon that reflects their progress.

⌛ Fast finishers
- Ss list the household objects in their living room.
- Ss write true and false questions about the photos in Exercise 3. They could ask the class at the end of the lesson.

3.6 In this lesson

Lesson aims:
- Listening: understanding a text about beedrooms
- Writing: a text about a bedroom; apostrophes

Resources:
- Tests: Writing Task Unit 3

Homework:
- Workbook Unit 3, p. 31

Assessment for Learning in this lesson
- Setting aims and criteria for success: Warm-up
- Giving feedback: Exercise 4, 6 and 7
- Peer learning: Exercise 3
- Independent learning: Finishing the lesson

Warm-up
- (*Books closed*) Ss play a game with vocabulary from Lesson 3.5. Chosen Ss draw objects on the board, the class guess.
- (*Books open*) Give pairs a minute to look at page 42. Ask *What is this lesson about?* (Bedrooms.) *What do you think you will be able to do at the end of the lesson?* (L1) Explain the lesson objectives.

Exercise 1
- Have a class vote for Ss' favourite bedroom! Choose different Ss to explain their choice.

Exercise 2 🔊 2.12
- This is preparation for PTEYL Springboard, Task Two Listening.
- Before you play the recording, ask Ss to listen for key words.

Answers → student page

Exercise 3 🔊 2.12
- Pairs read the sentences and complete as many as they can, using the photos to help.
- Then play the recording.

Answers → student page

Exercise 4
- Note on the board two things most Ss do well and two common mistakes. Discuss them with the class after.

3.6 Listening and Writing
I can understand and write short texts about bedrooms.

1 Look at photos A–C. Find these objects in the photos. Which is your favourite bedroom? Why?

chair   cushion   desk   plant   wardrobe

A
B
C

2 Exam Spot 🔊 2.12 Listen and match the speakers to their bedrooms. Write A, B or C. There is one extra photo.

C Speaker 1   B Speaker 2

3 🔊 2.12 Complete the sentences with a preposition of place. Then listen again and check.

Speaker 1
1 My bed is <u>next to</u> the window.
2 My school things are <u>on</u> the desk.
3 There's an orange chair <u>in front of</u> my desk.
4 There are orange cushions <u>on</u> the bed.

Speaker 2
5 My clothes are <u>in</u> the wardrobe.
6 There are two beds <u>in</u> my bedroom.
7 The beds are <u>next to</u> the wardrobe.
8 There aren't any posters <u>on</u> the walls.

4 In pairs, describe one of the photos in Exercise 1 for a partner to guess.

42

5 The bedroom in Photo A is Lucas's. Read his blog post about it. What isn't there in the bedroom?

My bedroom
'My bed is next to a green wall. There are two cushions and a toy on my bed. There's a big white desk. It's next to the window. There's a chair too. It's black and it's very cool. There's a computer and a lamp on the desk. My room is great!'

Writing Apostrophes
Remember to use apostrophes with contractions.
there is = there's   is not = isn't   are not = aren't
it is = it's   they are = they're   that is = that's

6 Add apostrophes to these sentences.
1 There isn't a desk in my bedroom.
2 Theres a plant. *There's a plant.*
3 Its under the bed. *It's under the bed.*
4 There arent any books. *There aren't any books.*

7 ✏️ Writing Time Write about your bedroom.

❓ Find ideas
Make a list of objects in your bedroom. Write where they are.

✏️ Draft
Write about your bedroom. Give your text a title.
My bed's …
There's / There isn't a …
There are / There aren't any …

👍 Check and write
Check the apostrophes and write the final version of your text.

Exercise 5
- After Ss read, pairs discuss.
- Different pairs tell the class their ideas.

Possible answers
There isn't a TV / a carpet.
There aren't any posters.

Writing
Write *there is* → *there's* on the board. Check Ss understand *contraction* and *apostrophe*. Ss read the examples.

Exercise 6
- Use the Thumbs up/down technique to find out if the class thinks each apostrophe is right.

Answers → student page

Exercise 7
- Give slower/weaker Ss plenty of time so they can do their best.
- Check Tests Booklet, page 5 for writing tasks marking criteria. Try to indicate the good aspects of Ss' work and list things to improve.

Finishing the lesson
- Ask Ss which exercise was the easiest and which one was the most difficult.
- Ss copy the objectives into their notebooks and draw the emoticons that reflect their progress (☺, 😐, ☹).

⏳ Fast finishers
- Ss draw extra objects in photos A–C and write what/where they are.

Language Revision 3.7

Vocabulary

1 Work in pairs. Student A: Choose a square. Student B: Say where you can find the object. Then swap roles.

A: *3B*
B: *'Wardrobe' … There's a big wardrobe in my bedroom!*

	1	2	3	4
A	bath	bed	desk	door
B	fridge	sofa	wardrobe	chair
C	lamp	window	table	cushion

2 Read the riddles. Write the objects.
1 There are three on my bedroom wall. p*osters*
2 It's on the floor in the living room. c*arpet*
3 It's in the living room. There's a film on it now! T*V*
4 They're green. They are in my garden. p*lants*
5 I sit in it when I read a book. a*rmchair*

3 Look at the picture. Read and complete the sentences with a preposition of place.
1 There are cushions __on__ the beds.
2 There's a sofa __in__ the living room.
3 There's a plant __next to__ the sofa.
4 There's a skateboard __in front of__ the fridge.
5 The cat is __behind__ the door.
6 The trainers are __under__ the bed.

Pronunciation

4 🔊 2.13 Listen and repeat: /ɪ/ or /iː/?
There are s**i**xteen TV**s i**n the l**i**ving room
And thr**ee** b**i**g fr**i**dges **i**n the k**i**tchen!

Grammar

5 Look at the picture in Exercise 3. Complete the text with *there is*, *there isn't*, *there are* or *there aren't*.

¹*There are* five rooms in the house. ²*There is* a living room and there's a kitchen. ³*There is* a bathroom and ⁴*there are* two bedrooms. ⁵*There isn't* a garden but there's a garage. ⁶*There aren't* any windows in the garage.

6 Write questions about the house in Exercise 3. Use *Is there* or *Are there* and the words in brackets.
1 *Is there a table* (a table) in the living room?
2 *Is there* (a TV) in the kitchen?
3 *Are there any* (plants) in the bedroom?
4 *Is there* (a skateboard) in the kitchen?
5 *Are there any* (cushions) in the bathroom?

7 Answer the questions in Exercise 6.
1 *Yes, there is.* 2 *No, there isn't.* 3 *No, there aren't.*
4 *Yes, there is.* 5 *No, there aren't.*

Communication

8 Complete the dialogues with the words in the box.

| please | Where's | show | Hi |
| upstairs | Would | come in | |

1 Mariana: ¹__Hi__ Louise. Please, ²__come in__!
   Louise: Thanks.
   Mariana: ³__Would__ you like a drink?
   Louise: Yes, ⁴__please__.
2 Louise: ⁵__Where's__ your room, Mariana?
   Mariana: It's ⁶__upstairs__. Let me ⁷__show__ you.

Check yourself! ✓
○ I can talk about my house.
○ I can use prepositions of place.
○ I can use *there is / there are*.
○ I can ask for something.
○ I can ask where something is.

43

Possible answers
1A: bathroom 1B: kitchen
1C: different rooms are possible
2A: bedroom 2B: living room
2C: different rooms are possible
3A: bedroom/living room
3B: bedroom 3C: different rooms are possible 4A, 4B, 4C: different rooms are possible

Exercise 2
• Pairs discuss the riddles and write.
Answers → student page

Exercise 3
Answers → student page
• Then Ss say sentences about their room with prepositions of place.

Exercise 4 🔊 2.13
• Tell Ss to smile as they say /iː/!

Exercise 5
• 💬 Use the Basketball technique to check answers.
Answers → student page

Exercise 6
• Ss do the exercise individually. Then pairs compare answers.
Answers → student page

Exercise 7
• 💬 Make a positive comment before correcting.
Answers → student page

Exercise 8
• 💬 Ss work individually. Check understanding using the Traffic Lights technique. Then ask Ss with green and yellow 'lights' to compare answers in pairs. Re-teach the students with red 'lights'.
Answers → student page

Finishing the lesson

• 📖 Read Check yourself! statements. Ss show self-assessment response cards (☺, 😐, ☹).
• ⏳ Give Ss time to read the statements again and to tick.

⏳ Fast finishers
• Pairs write similar riddles to the ones in Exercise 2. They read them for the class to guess.

3.7

In this lesson

Lesson aims:
○ Revising Vocabulary, Grammar and Communication from Unit 3
○ Pronunciation: /ɪ/ and /iː/

Resources:
○ Tests: Language Test Unit 3

Homework:
○ Workbook Unit 3, pp. 32–33
○ Extra Online Practice Unit 3

Assessment for Learning in this lesson
📷 Setting aims and criteria for success: Warm-up
💬 Giving feedback: Exercise 5, 7 and 8
🎓 Independent learning: Finishing the lesson

Warm-up

• (*Books closed*) Play *Noughts and Crosses* with prepositions of place. (See Lesson 5.1, Warm-up.)
• 📷 (*Books open*) Ss look through Unit 3. Pairs tell each other what they found the most challenging and the easiest. (*L1/L2*) Explain the lesson objectives.

Lead-in

• (*Books closed*) Play *Chinese Whispers* with house words. (See Lesson 1.6, Warm-up.)

Exercise 1
• A pair demonstrates the activity.
• Tell Ss sometimes more than one answer is possible.

61

Get Culture

In this lesson

Lesson aims:
- Culture focus: *Houses in the UK*
- BBC video: *Hampton Court Palace* (optional)
- Project: presenting an interesting/unusual house

Resources:
- Project worksheet p. 179

Assessment for Learning in this lesson
- Setting aims and criteria for success: Warm-up
- Giving feedback: Exercise 2 and C.
- Peer learning: Exercise 3, 4 and the Project
- Independent learning: Finishing the lesson

Culture notes
King Henry VIII of England lived from 1491 to 1547 and was king from 1509. Hampton Court was his favourite palace.

Warm-up
- (*Books closed*) Read this riddle to the class. *They're big and they're small. They've got windows. You've all got one. What are they?* Students guess. (*Houses.*)
- (*Books open*) Get Ss to look at pages 44–45 and discuss with the class what they will do in this lesson.

Lead-in
- Critical thinking (*Books open*) Pointing to the photos in Exercise 1, pre-teach the types of houses. Then ask the class *Are these houses like houses in our country?* Challenge Ss to explain their ideas.

Exercise 1
- Elicit/Teach *country*. E.g. point to the photo of the cottage. Say *This house is in the … (country).* Check *city*. Say *(London) is a … (city).*
- After pairs talk, discuss with the class.

Get Culture!
Houses in the UK

1 There are different types of houses in the UK. In pairs, talk about where you can find these types of houses.

a in the city   b in the country
c in the city and in the country

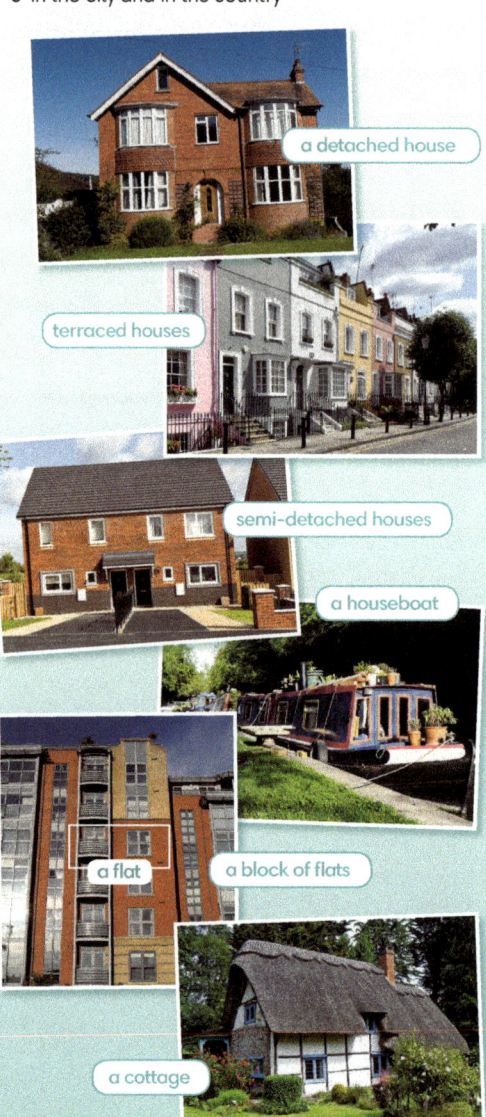

a detached house
terraced houses
semi-detached houses
a houseboat
a flat
a block of flats
a cottage

2 🔊 2.14 Read the texts and circle the type of the house Ian, Lisa and Claire live in. Then listen and check.

Tell me where you live

Ian, 10: I live in a *houseboat* / *semi-detached house*. The boys next door and I are friends. There's a big tree in their garden. In the tree there's a tree-house. We play there all the time!

Lisa, 12: I live in a *block of flats* / *detached house* with twelve floors. Our flat isn't very big. There are two small bedrooms but the living room is nice. The view is fantastic!

Claire, 11: We live in the city, in a street with *terraced houses* / *cottages*. They are all tall and grey but the doors are different colours. Our door is yellow!

3 🔊 2.15 Listen and complete the texts with the words in the box.

> behind   cottage   country   view
> houseboat   small

Martha, 12: My family and I live in the ¹*country*. Our house is a ²*cottage* in Devon, South England. There are lots of trees ³*behind* our house.

Matt, 13: I live in a ⁴*houseboat* on the River Thames. It is very ⁵*small* but I like it. The ⁶*view* is always different!

4 Write a short text about where you live. Use texts in Exercises 2 and 3 to help you.

I live in a block of flats. Our living room is big and the view from it is amazing.

44

Extra activity
- Critical thinking Ask Ss to choose their favourite house and to explain their choice.

Exercise 2 🔊 2.14
- Ask Ss to read the texts quickly and use the context and the photos in Exercise 1 to understand any words they find difficult, e.g.: *next door, tree-house, floor, fantastic, view.*
- Ss read, discuss the answers with a partner and circle. 💬 After Ss listen, use the Lollipop Stick technique to choose different Ss to explain each answer.

Answers → student page

Exercise 3 🔊 2.15
- 🤝 Ss read the texts and predict answers with a partner before they listen. After, pairs stand up and compare their answers with two other pairs.

Answers → student page

Exercise 4
- Ss note key words before they write.
- 🤝 Then they exchange notebooks with a partner and review each other's texts using the Two Stars and a Wish technique.

Hampton Court Palace

A ▶18 Watch the video and answer the presenter's questions. Then circle the correct answer.

Hampton Court was the home of ____ VIII.
a King Charles   b Queen Elizabeth   **c** King Henry

B ▶18 Watch the video again. Complete the sentences with one word from the video.
1 Hampton Court Palace is in _London_.
2 There are _no_ kings or queens in Hampton Court today.
3 There are over 1,000 _rooms_ in Hampton Court.
4 The Great Hall is a big room for _eating_ and parties.
5 The maze in the _garden_ of Hampton Court is very old.

C Discuss in pairs. Which part of Hampton Court Palace is your favourite? Why?

PROJECT

- Work in groups. Make a digital presentation of an unusual or interesting house in your area.
- Take photos of the house or find them on the Internet.
- Write a description of the house. Use these questions to help you.

  Where is the house?   What colour is it?
  What type of house is it?   Is there a garden/garage?
  Is it big/small?

- Put the photos and text together.
- Share your presentation with the class.
  Which is your favourite house? Why?

Houses in my area
- This house is in …
- It's *a detached house* …
- It's *big/small/nice/grey* …
- There is *a tree* …

45

BBC video

Video script → see Teacher's Book p. 139

Presenter's questions
1 (00:30) How old do you think it is?
2 (01:09) There are lots of rooms. Can you guess how many?
3 (01:28) This is the kitchen. Is it like your kitchen at home?
4 (01:49) How many rooms are there in your house?
5 (02:24) How many people can have dinner at Hampton Court Palace at the same time?

Note: if you can't show the video, spend more class time on preparing the Project.

Exercise A ▶18
- Ss look at the photo and the title. Elicit *palace*, *kings* and *queens*.
- Ss read the question. Then play the video.
- First, pause after each of the presenter's questions and ask the class for their ideas.

Answers
Question 1: It's over 500 years old.
Question 2: over 1000
Question 5: 600

- Then check the answer to Exercise A. Ask Ss what they know about King Henry VIII. (See Culture notes.)

Answer → student page

Exercise B ▶18
- Pairs answer any questions they can.
- Ss watch the video and check/complete.

Answers → student page

Exercise C
- 💬 After pairs discuss, use the Lollipop Stick technique to choose different Ss to explain their answer.

Project

Setting the project up
- Allocate at least 10 minutes for setting up the project.
- Choose groups of three/four and ask them to read the instructions.
- Groups choose a house they all know and decide what each student is going to be responsible for (photos, text, design).
- Give Ss the Project worksheets to help them prepare.
- Choose how the presentation will be shared: via the class projector, a file sharing service, email or on the school website.
- If your class can't make digital presentations, ask Ss to prepare posters. Follow the same steps for setting up the project, but ask Ss to draw their houses or print some photos and write by hand.
- Set a date for giving presentations.

Sharing the project
- Before Ss give their presentations, give them some time to practise. Make sure everybody is involved. Take notes. You could comment on: design, interest, accuracy, pronunciation. Remember to praise first.
- Have a class vote for the most popular house!

Finishing the lesson
- The class tells you what they enjoyed most and why.
- Check what Ss have learnt in this lesson using Three Facts and a Fib technique.

⏳ **Fast finishers**
- Students look at the photos in Exercise 1. They choose their favourite and write sentences to describe it.

4.1

In this lesson

Lesson aims:
- Vocabulary: face and hair

Resources:
- Vocabulary worksheet 4.1, p. 149
- Tests: Vocabulary Check 4.1

Homework:
- Workbook Unit 4, p. 34

Assessment for Learning in this lesson
- Setting aims and criteria for success: Warm-up
- Giving feedback: Exercise 4
- Peer learning: Exercise 5 and 8
- Independent learning: Finishing the lesson

Warm-up
- (*Books closed*) Play *Bingo!* Draw a 3 x 3 grid on the board. Ss copy and choose words from the Vocabulary box on page 35 to write in each square. Read the words at random. Ss mark the words in their grids. The student who has marked all squares in a row – vertically, horizontally or diagonally – shouts *Bingo!* and wins the game. Ask Ss to make new grids and repeat the game.
- Write *About me* on the board. Ss predict what they will learn.
- (*L1/L2*) Explain the lesson objective. Then ask Ss to predict what they will be able to say in English at the end of the lesson.

Lead-in
- **Critical thinking** (*Books closed*) Write two column headings *Face* and *Hair* on the board. Ask the class *What face* (point to your face) *and hair* (point to your hair) *words do you know?* Different Ss say a word and write it on the board in the correct column with the class'/your help.

Exercise 1
- Choose one word from the box, point at the corresponding feature of your face and say *I know that!* with a thumbs up gesture. Encourage pairs to continue.
- Then ask different pairs to do it for the class.

4 About me

Vocabulary I can describe someone's face and hair.

In this unit
Vocabulary
- Face and hair
- Parts of the body
- Personality adjectives

Grammar
- *have got* affirmative and negative
- Regular and irregular plural
- *have got* questions and short answers
- Possessive adjectives

▶ 19-20
4.2 Grammar video

▶ 21
4.2 Grammar animation

▶ 22
4.3 Grammar animation

▶ 23
4.4 Communication video

1 Say the words and point at the features of your face.

ears   eyes   hair   mouth   nose

I know that!

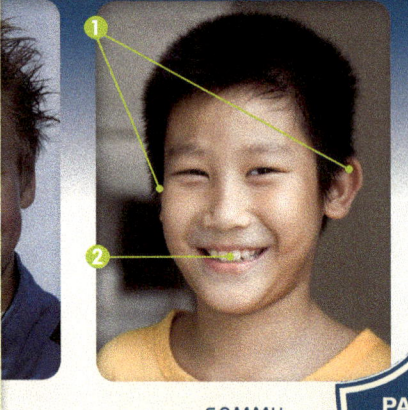

SAMMY   REGAN

PARK HILL PRIMARY SCHOOL

MARIA   ANTEK

46

Exercise 2 🔊 2.16
- Give Ss time to read the words.
- Play the recording. Pause after each word. Ss repeat and find an example in the photos.
- Point out *teeth* is an irregular plural. Challenge a strong student to write the singular (*tooth*) on the board.

Exercise 3
- Different Ss in a weak class look and say each word before they write individually. Then pairs compare their answers.
- Different Ss write the answers on the board.

Answers → student page

Exercise 4
- Pairs race to complete. The first pair to stand up wins!
- Draw the table on the board. Use the Lollipop Stick technique and select individuals to write the words. Tell them the order isn't important. The class says if each word is correct. If it isn't, choose a student to say the correct category/categories.
- Tell Ss that we usually use *grey* to describe an old person's hair. We only use *white* if it is very white.

Answers → student page

4.1

2 🔊 2.16 Listen and repeat. Find the features in the photos on page 46.

Vocabulary Face and hair

Face
ears   eyes   mouth   nose   teeth

Hair
curly   spiky   straight   wavy
blond   dark   red

3 Find the numbers (1–6) in the photos on page 46. Write whose features they are.
1 They're _Sammy's ears_ .   4 It's _Regan's hair_ .
2 They're _Sammy's teeth_ .   5 They're _Maria's eyes_ .
3 It's _Regan's nose_ .   6 It's _Antek's mouth_ .

4 In pairs, write the words in the box in the correct place. You can use them more than once.

| big   blond   blue   brown   curly   dark |
| green   grey   long   red   short   small |
| spiky   straight   wavy   white |

1	eyes	blue big, brown, green, small, dark
2	ears / nose / mouth	big, small
3	hair	blond, brown, curly, grey, long, red, short, spiky, straight, wavy, white
4	teeth	big, small, white

LOOK! Maria's hair **is** brown.

5 Look at the photos on page 46. Circle the correct answer.
1 Regan's eyes are (brown)/ green.
2 Sammy's hair is (straight)/ curly.
3 Maria's hair is (long)/ short.
4 Antek's hair is (spiky)/ wavy.
5 Sammy's hair is blond /(dark).
6 Regan's hair is short /(wavy).
7 Antek's eyes are (blue)/ brown.

6 Look at the children's hair. Complete the words.

a [5] st_ra_ _igh_t
b [3] w_a_ _v_y
c [4] c_u_ r_l_ _y_
d [6] s_p_ik_y_
e [1] lo_ _ng
f [2] sh_or_t

7 🔊 2.17 Listen and number the pictures in Exercise 6.

LOOK!
long/short curly/straight blond/brown/red hair
big/small blue/brown eyes

8 Which words in Exercise 4 describe your hair and eyes? Write them down. Use Look! box to help you. Tell a partner.
_____ _____ _____ hair
_____ _____ eyes

9 In pairs, describe someone in your class. Guess who it is.
A: _Long straight brown hair, brown eyes._
B: _It's Alice!_

10 Do you know a person with …
a green eyes?   _my mum_
b spiky hair?   _____
c grey hair?   _____
d a small nose?   _____

I remember that!

47

Look!
- **Critical thinking** Write on the board *blond straight long hair*. Ask the class *What's wrong?* Challenge Ss to correct the phrase. Then ask Ss to read the information in the Look! box and choose a student to explain the correct order of adjectives.

Exercise 8
- 🎓 Give Ss time to write. They share their description with a partner who makes one positive comment and a suggestion if they have one.

Exercise 9
- Pairs take turns to describe different classmates and to guess. Alternatively, pairs in a weak class write down one description. Different Ss read their descriptions for the class to guess.

Exercise 10
- Give Ss time to think and to write the names of people with characteristics a–d. Then they tell a partner.

Finishing the lesson
- 🎓 Ss look at the predictions they made in the Warm-up and circle the new words in the Vocabulary box they have learnt.
- 🎓 Ask *Can you describe someone's face and hair?* Ss show self-assessment response cards (☺, 😐, ☹).
- 🎓 Ss copy the objective into their notebooks and draw the emoticon that reflects their progress.

⌛ **Fast finishers**
- (*Books closed*) Ss write all the words they know to describe face and hair.
- Ss draw a friend or a family member and label his/her face and hair.

Look!
- Ss read the example. Challenge Ss and ask *Why 'is brown', not 'are brown'?* Then explain that *hair* is singular because we mean hair in general, not one hair.

Exercise 5
- 🌐 Pairs look and circle. Then they stand up and compare answers with two other pairs.

| Answers → student page |

Extra activity
- Pairs write four true/false sentences about the photos on page 46. (*Books closed*) They test another pair.

Exercise 6
- Elicit adjectives that describe the people's hair from a weak class first. Ss write individually. Then pairs compare answers.
- Different Ss spell the answers.

| Answers → student page |

Exercise 7 🔊 2.17
- Play the recording. Pause for pairs to discuss and number the pictures.
- Play the recording again, pausing for different pairs to say and explain each answer by saying the key words.

| Answers → student page |

65

4.2

In this lesson

Lesson aims:
- Grammar: *have got* affirmative and negative
- Vocabulary: parts of the body

Resources:
- Grammar worksheet 4.2, p. 158
- Tests: Grammar Check 4.2, Vocabulary Check 4.2

Homework:
- Workbook Unit 4, p. 35
- Extra Online Practice Unit 4

Assessment for Learning in this lesson
- 🎯 Setting aims and criteria for success: Warm-up
- 💬 Giving feedback: Exercise 2 and 9
- 👥 Peer learning: Exercise 12
- 🎓 Independent learning: Finishing the lesson

Warm-up

- (*Books closed*) Make a 'ball' with a piece of paper. Throw it to a student, who says a face/hair word, points at this feature and then throws the ball at random to another student who continues the game.
- 🎯 (*Books open*) Pairs look at pages 48–49. (*L1/L2*) They discuss what they think they will learn in this lesson. Brainstorm ideas from the class. Then explain the lesson objectives.

Lead-in

- (*Books open*) Ss look at the photos. Ask *Who are they?* (*Mum, Jen, Alex.*) *Are they at home?* (*No, they aren't.*)
- Use the photos to pre-teach words Ss might find difficult, e.g.: *legs, arms, head, tall, high.*

Exercise 1 ▶19 🔊 2.18
- Play the video. If you don't have access to a computer and projector, play the recording.
- Ask a student to answer.

Answer → student page

4.2 Grammar

I can use the affirmative and negative forms of the verb have got.

I haven't got big feet!

At the bookshop.

1
Alex: Ouch, my foot! Be careful!
Jen: It isn't my fault! You've got long legs! And you've got big feet!
Alex: I haven't got big feet! I'm tall!

2
Jen: You've got long arms too! Like this!
Alex: Yeah, but I haven't got a big head, like you!

3
Jen: My head is fine! Mum? Is my head big?
Mum: Stop it, you two! Jen, your brother hasn't got big feet. Alex, your sister hasn't got a big head! Now, hurry up with the books! We haven't got a lot of time.

4
Jen: Oh, they've got *Yummy Cupcakes.* Great! Oh, no! It's too high! Alex? Help me, please!

1 ▶19 🔊 **2.18** Watch or listen and read. Jen needs Alex's help. Why? Finish the sentence.

Because the book is too _high_.

2 Circle the correct answer.
1 (Jen)/ Alex isn't careful.
2 (Alex)/ Jen is tall.
3 Alex's arms are (long)/ short.
4 Jen's head isn't (big)/ fine.
5 Jen's book is about (cupcakes)/ big feet.

3 🔊 **2.19** Listen and read. Find these expressions in the story.

> It isn't my fault! Stop it! Help me, please!

Say it!

4 ▶ Guess! Will Alex help Jen? Have a class vote. *Yes.*

5 ▶20 🔊 **2.20** Now watch or listen and check.

Exercise 2
- Pairs note the answers they know.
- Play the video (stopping it in appropriate places) or refer Ss to the photo story.
- 💬 Check answers using the Basketball technique.

Answers → student page

Exercise 3 🔊 2.19 ▶19
- Play the recording, pausing for Ss to repeat each expression.
- Play the video again. Ss shout *STOP!* when they hear each expression. Alternatively, Ss find and underline the expressions in the dialogue.
- Encourage Ss to think of situations in which they can use these expressions.

Exercise 4
- **Critical thinking** Ss explain their choice. Don't confirm yet!

Answer → student page

Exercise 5 ▶20 🔊 2.20
- Play the video/recording to find out who was right!

Video/Audio script
Jen: That book over there? Please?
Alex: So my long arms are OK, now?
Jen: Come on! Be a good brother!
Alex: Oh, all right!
Jen: Thank you!
Alex: But I want these cupcakes! Ooh, and these! And these too!
Jen: Fine!

4.2

Grammar *have got* affirmative and negative

▶ 21 **Get Grammar!**

I haven't got a hat.

+ Short and long form	− Short and long form
I've (have) got long legs.	I haven't (have not) got long legs.
You've (have) got long legs.	You haven't (have not) got long legs.
He/She/It's (has) got long legs.	He/She/It hasn't (has not) got long legs.
We've (have) got long legs.	We haven't (have not) got long legs.
You've (have) got long legs.	You haven't (have not) got long legs.
They've (have) got long legs.	They haven't (have not) got long legs.

6 Complete the sentences with *'ve got* or *'s got*.
1 Jen: 'Alex, you *'ve got* big feet!'
2 Jen: 'Alex *'s got* long arms.'
3 Alex: 'Jen *'s got* a big head.'
4 Mum: 'We *'ve got* very little time.'
5 Jen: 'They *'ve got* Yummy Cupcakes.'

7 🔊 **2.21** Listen and repeat.

Vocabulary Parts of the body

arm   body   fingers   foot   hand   head
leg   neck   toes

8 Label the parts of the body.

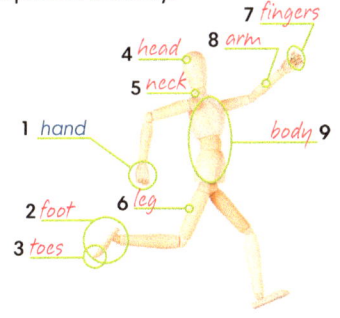

1 hand
2 foot
3 toes
4 head
5 neck
6 leg
7 fingers
8 arm
9 body

9 Write the correct sentences in your notebook.
1 Jen's got blond hair. (brown)
   Jen hasn't got blond hair. She's got brown hair.
2 Alex's got small feet. (big)
3 Jen and Alex have got short legs. (long)
4 Their mum's got blue eyes. (brown)
5 Jen and Alex have got big heads. (small)

LOOK! finger – fingers foot – feet
toe – toes   tooth – teeth

10 **Exam Spot** Look at Ike and Mike. Complete the text with one word in each gap.

big   got   they   has   tall   feet   have

Ike   Mike

Ike and Mike ¹*have* got long spiky hair. ²*They* 've got big mouths but they haven't got ³*big* noses. Mike is ⁴*tall*. He ⁵*has* got green hair. He's ⁶*got* very long arms and very big ⁷*feet*.

11 Write about Ike. Use Exercise 10 to help you.
Ike isn't tall. He's got …

Fun Spot

12 Create a friend for Ike and Mike. Give her a name and describe her.
*Ike and Mike have got a friend.
She's got … and …
She's got … but she hasn't got …*

49

Extra video activity ▶ 19
• Ss memorize the expressions from the Say it! box. (*Books closed*) Play the video. Ss stand up when they hear each expression.

Extra activity
• (*Books open*) Groups act out a scene from the photo story. The class votes for the best actor/actress.

Get Grammar! ▶ 21
• Play the Get Grammar! video. If you don't have access to a computer and projector, continue.
• Ss repeat the examples after you in chorus.
• Point out the contractions. Remind Ss we use them with names too, e.g. *Jen's got …*
• Tell Ss *it's* means *it has (got)* or *it is*, depending on the context.

Exercise 6
• Ss do the exercise individually, referring to the Grammar box for help.

Answers → student page

Exercise 7 🔊 **2.21**
• Play the recording, pausing for Ss to repeat each word in chorus and to touch the corresponding part of their body.

Exercise 8
• Pairs race to label!

Answers → student page

Exercise 9
• 💬 Ss do the exercise individually. Use the Traffic Lights technique to monitor.

Answers
2 Alex hasn't got small feet. He's got big feet. **3** Jen and Alex haven't got short legs. They've got long legs. **4** Their mum hasn't got blue eyes. She's got brown eyes. **5** Jen and Alex haven't got big heads. They've got small heads.

Look!
• Ask Ss to explain how these plurals differ. (*'Feet/teeth'* are irregular.)

Exercise 10
• This is preparation for PTEYL Firstwords Task Six / Springboard Task Five, Reading and Writing.
• First, Ss decide what part of speech is missing in each gap.

Answers → student page

Exercise 11
• Individuals write.
• Pairs swap notebooks and review each other's work.

Possible answer
Ike isn't tall. He's got blue hair. He's got short arms, short legs and a small body. He's got big hands.

Exercise 12
• 👥 Pairs discuss, draw and write about their character. Stick their work up round the classroom. Ss read the descriptions and choose their favourite. Have a class vote for the best new friend!

Finishing the lesson
• Ask Ss for examples of sentences with *have got*. Ask *Can you talk about body parts using 'have got'?* Ss show self-assessment response cards (☺, 😐, ☹).
• Ss copy the objectives into their notebooks and draw the emoticons that reflect their progress.

Fast finishers
• Ss look at the photo story and write the words they know.
• Ss find sentences with *have got* in the photo story.

67

4.3

In this lesson

Lesson aims:
- Grammar: *have got* questions and short answers; *its, our, your, their*

Resources:
- Grammar worksheet 4.3, p. 159
- Tests: Grammar Check 4.3

Homework:
- Workbook Unit 4, p. 36

Assessment for Learning in this lesson
- Setting aims and criteria for success: Warm-up
- Giving feedback: Exercise 2, 4 and 6
- Peer learning: Exercise 5
- Independent learning: Finishing the lesson

Warm-up
- (*Books closed*) Play *Simon Says* with body parts. Ss stand up and follow the instructions, e.g. *Simon says, 'Touch your hair'.* When your instruction is not preceded by the phrase 'Simon says', Ss stand still or else they sit down and stop playing. Continue until there's only one person standing.
- Ask questions with *have got* and *its, our, your, their*. E.g. *Have you got a pet? What's its name?* When Ss answer, ask the class if it's correct. (L1/L2) Explain the lesson objectives.

Lead-in
- (*Books closed*) Write *Superhero of the year* on the board. Pairs guess what it means. (*Books open*) Ss look at the pictures and review their predictions. Challenge a student to explain.
- Use the pictures to pre-teach words Ss might find difficult, e.g.: *car, ears, battery power.*

Exercise 1
- **Critical thinking** Individual Ss race to answer. Challenge a strong student to explain using a complete sentence.

Answer → student page

4.3

Grammar — I can ask questions with the verb *have got* and use *its, our, your* and *their*.

The Terrific Two — My favourite superhero

1 Look at the cartoon. Someone looks like Superdug. Where is this person?
He's next to the tall boy (in a green T-shirt).

2 🔊 2.22 **Listen and read. Who is Wonder Will?** *He's a superhero.*

3 Read the sentences. Circle T (true) or F (false).

1. Superdug is at home. T / **F**
2. Superdug hasn't got a super car. **T** / F
3. X1 and X2 have got super ears. **T** / F
4. Kit's got super eyes. T / **F**
5. X1 and X2 haven't got any battery power now. **T** / F

Exercise 2 🔊 2.22
- After Ss do the exercise, pick an individual to justify the answer and ask Ss what they remember about Will.

Answer → student page

Exercise 3
- To check answers, read the sentences. Ss stand up for *T* and sit down for *F*.
- Individuals justify the answers.

Answers → student page

Extra activity
- Ss pretend to be different characters form the photo story. They describe themselves for the class to guess who they are, e.g. *I've got a green T-shirt.*

Get Grammar! ▶22
- Play the *Get Grammar!* video. If you don't have access to a computer and projector, continue.
- Ss repeat the examples after you in chorus.
- Point out we invert the subject and *have/has* to form a question.

Language notes
People use short answers in everyday English. We don't use contractions for affirmative short answers.

4.3

Grammar *have got* questions and short answers

▶ 22 **Get Grammar!**

?	Short answers
Have I **got** a friend?	Yes, I **have**. / No, I **haven't**.
Have you **got** a friend?	Yes, you **have**. / No, you **haven't**.
Has he/she/it **got** a friend?	Yes, he/she/it **has**. / No, he/she/it **hasn't**.
Have we **got** a friend?	Yes, we **have**. / No, we **haven't**.
Have you **got** a friend?	Yes, you **have**. / No, you **haven't**.
Have they **got** a friend?	Yes, they **have**. / No, they **haven't**.

What **have** you **got**?   I've **got** super powers!

Have you got a brother or a sister?
Yes, I have!

4 Complete the questions with *have … got* or *has … got*.

1 _Has_ Wonder Will _got_ a red suit?
2 _Has_ Ricky _got_ blue hair?
3 _Have_ X1 and X2 _got_ big heads?
4 _Has_ Kit _got_ brown eyes?
5 _Have_ X1 and X2 _got_ long legs?
6 _Has_ Superdug _got_ long ears?

5 Look at the cartoon. Answer the questions in Exercise 4.

1 *No, he hasn't.*

6 In pairs, ask and answer about the superheroes.

	super eyes	super ears	super arms
Wondercat	✓	✓	✗
Iron Girls	✓	✗	✓

A: *Has Wondercat got super eyes?*
B: *Yes, she has.*

LOOK!

it	→	its	The robot hasn't got **its** battery.
we	→	our	Superdug is **our** favourite hero!
you	→	your	They are **your** robots.
they	→	their	Wonder Will is **their** friend.

7 Complete the sentences with *our*, *your* or *their*.

1 They've got green super suits.
   These are _their_ super suits.
2 We've got a super car!
   This is _our_ super car!
3 You've got a new robot!
   This is _your_ new robot.
4 Have they got a super cat?
   Is this _their_ super cat?
5 Has it got a super battery?
   Is this _its_ super battery?

8 Work in pairs. Ask your partner what he/she has got. Answer your partner's questions. Use the words in the box. Then tell the class about your partner.

> a brother or a sister? a pet? a TV in your room?
> a ruler? a friend? a hobby? a bike? a robot?

A: *Have you got a brother or a sister?*

9 🔊 2.23 🔊 2.24
Go to page 107.
Listen and sing Robots' Song.

Fun Spot

51

Look!

- Ss study the information. They repeat the pronouns and adjectives after you in chorus. Point out *its* has no apostrophe and is not a contraction of *it is*. Tell Ss *you/your* is the same for the singular and plural.
- Ss find possessive adjectives in the cartoon. (*Our, their.*)

Exercise 7
- Pairs find and underline the subject pronoun, decide what the corresponding possessive adjective is and write.

Answers → student page

Exercise 8
- Demonstrate the activity in open pairs first. Tell Ss they should take notes to be able to tell the class about their partner.

Exercise 9 🔊 2.23 🔊 2.24
- Play the song and teach Ss appropriate gestures. E.g. *Have you got super ears?* Ss point to their ears.
- When Ss are familiar with the song, play the karaoke version. Ss make the gestures and sing.

Finishing the lesson

- 🎓 Ask different Ss the same questions you asked in the Warm-up. Read the lesson objectives. Ss show self-assessment response cards (☺, 😐, ☹).
- 🎓 Ss copy the objectives into their notebooks and draw the emoticons that reflect their progress.

⏳ **Fast finishers**
- Ss look at the pictures in the cartoon and describe one of the characters.
- Ss write two true/false sentences about the Superdug/Kit using *have got*. They ask the class at the end of the lesson.

Exercise 4
- Ss do the exercise individually, referring to the Grammar box for help.
- 💬 Different individuals write the answers on the board. Involve the class. Ask *Is it correct?* (*Yes, it is. / No, it isn't.*) *Are you sure?* (*Yes, I am. / No, I'm not*).

Answers → student page

Exercise 5
- 🔎 Pairs find the answers in the cartoon and help each other write.

Answers
2 No, he hasn't. **3** Yes, they have. **4** No, she hasn't. **5** No, they haven't. **6** Yes, he has.

Exercise 6
- Remind Ss to use the example to help.
- 💬 Ss in a weak class do this exercise in open pairs. Praise Ss who do well. Encourage them to explain what was good with the class' help. E.g. *(L1) I remembered the word. The grammar was correct. My pronunciation was good.*

Answers
Has Wondercat got super ears? Yes, she has.
Has Wondercat got super arms? No, she hasn't.
Have the Iron Girls got super eyes? Yes, they have.
Have the Iron Girls got super ears? No, they haven't.
Have the Iron Girls got super arms? Yes, they have.

69

4.4

In this lesson

Lesson aims:
- Communication: saying sorry and responding to an apology

Resources:
- Communication worksheet 4.4, p. 171

Homework:
- Workbook Unit 4, p. 37
- Extra Online Practice Unit 4

Assessment for Learning in this lesson
- Setting aims and criteria for success: Warm-up
- Giving feedback: Exercise 3
- Peer learning: Extra activity
- Independent learning: Finishing the lesson

Warm-up
- (*Books closed*) Pairs write two sentences about the characters in Lesson 4.3 for another pair to guess who they are. E.g. *He's got blond hair.* (*Wonder Will.*)
- Take a bag from a student as if by accident and say sorry. Ss predict what the lesson is about. (*Books open*) Then Ss look at page 52 to check. (*L1/L2*) Explain the lesson objectives.

Lead-in
- (*Books open*) Ask *Where are they?* (*At home.*) Use the pictures to pre-teach *keys*. Ask *Is there a problem?* Pairs look and discuss.

Exercise 1 ▶23 🔊 2.25
- Have a class vote!
- Play the video. If you don't have access to a computer and projector, play the recording.

Answer → student page

Exercise 2 🔊 2.26
- First, make sure Ss understand all the phrases in the box.

Extra video activity ▶23
- (*Books closed*) Play the video but with no sound. Pause after each character speaks. Ss say the lines.

Extra activity
- 👥 Pairs practise the dialogue in Exercise 1. Another student listens and takes notes using the Two Stars and a Wish technique.

Exercise 3 🔊 2.27
- 💬 Use the Traffic Lights technique to check how difficult Ss found the exercise.

Answers → student page

Exercise 4
- This is preparation for PTEYL Firstwords/Springboard, Task Four Reading.
- First, ask Ss to predict what the people in the pictures might be saying.

Answers → student page

Exercise 5
- Say *1, 2, 3. Go!* to start the activity!

Finishing the lesson
- 💬 Ask the class *Can you say sorry and respond to an apology?* Ss show self-assessment response cards (☺, 😐, ☹).
- 📓 Ss copy the objectives into their notebooks and draw the emoticons that reflect their progress.

⏳ Fast finishers
- Ss underline the phrases from the Communication box in the dialogue in Exercise 1.

4.4 Communication

I can say sorry and respond to an apology.

Sorry about that!

Dad: Where are my house keys?
Jen: I'm so sorry, Dad. I've got them.
Dad: It's OK. Now, where's my phone? Oops! Sorry, Jen!
Jen: That's all right.
Dad: Are you OK?
Jen: Yes, I'm fine.

Jen: Dad! You've got the phone! It's right there!
Dad: Sorry, my mistake!
Jen: No problem.
Dad: Oh, it's late! Bye, Jen!

Jen: Dad, wait! Your house keys!
Dad: Oh, dear! Sorry about that! Thanks, sweetie! Bye!
Jen: Bye, Dad!

Jen: Come on, really? Erm … Dad?

1 ▶23 🔊 2.25 Watch or listen and read. Who has got Dad's phone? Circle the correct answer.
 a Jen (b) Dad

2 🔊 2.26 Listen and repeat.

Communication — Apologising

A:	B:
I'm so sorry.	It's OK.
Sorry about that!	That's all right.
Sorry, my mistake.	No problem.
Are you OK?	I'm fine.

3 🔊 2.27 Complete the dialogues. Then listen and check. Act out the dialogues in pairs.

1 A: Oops! Sorry about that, Pete!   B: No _problem_.
  A: Are you sure?   B: Yes, I'm _fine_.

2 A: Where's my phone?   B: _Sorry_, I've got it!
  A: That's _all right_.

3 A: This isn't my jacket.   B: Sorry, my _mistake_.
  A: _It's_ OK. Thanks.   Here you are.

4 **Exam Spot** Draw lines from the sentences to the pictures. There is one extra sentence.

1 That's all right.
2 Oh, sorry about that!
3 This isn't my bag.

5 Game! Make dialogues in pairs. Don't stop. The pair that talks the longest wins the game.

A: Where's my bag?
B: I'm so sorry. I've got it. Where are my keys?

I can understand and do a personality quiz. **Reading** 4.5

1 🔊 **2.28** Listen and repeat. Complete the sentences with the words in the Vocabulary box.

Vocabulary Personality adjectives

clever friendly funny helpful nice sporty

1 I speak to everyone. I'm _friendly_.
2 My teacher helps me every day. She's _helpful_.
3 You've got flowers for your mum. You're very _nice_.
4 My friend's jokes are great! He's _funny_.
5 They love football and tennis. They're _sporty_.
6 I've got good marks at school. I'm _clever_.

2 Do the personality quiz! Circle a, b or c.

3 Count how many a, b and c answers you have got and read the key. Do you agree? Tell a friend or the class!

4 🔊 **2.29** Listen to two friends. Are they friendly, funny and sporty? Tick (✔) for *yes* and put a cross (✘) for *no*.

	friendly	funny	sporty
Sam	✔		✔
Sue	✔	✔	

Fun Spot

5 Write about a student from your class. Read the text out. Can the class guess who it is?
A: This student is very friendly and she's sporty. She's very helpful too.
B: Is it Maria?
A: Yes! You're right!

What kind of a person are you? Are you friendly? Are you funny?

QUIZ TIME Do our personality quiz to find out!

1 How many good friends have you got?
  a 3–6 **b** 7–10 **c** 1 or 2
2 Are your jokes funny?
  a Sometimes. **b** Yes! **c** No. My jokes are bad!
3 What's your favourite hobby?
  a Sports. **b** Dancing. **c** Reading.
4 What's your favourite place?
  a School. **b** A party! **c** My room.
5 Are you good at school?
  a I'm OK. **b** Yes, I am!
  c I'm good at my favourite subjects.
6 Your best friend has got a problem. You:
  a help your friend. **b** just say 'I'm sorry'.
  c say 'Speak to your mum'.
7 Your neighbour has got a big bag. You say:
  a 'Hello, I can help!' **b** 'That's big!'
  c 'I'm sorry, I've got homework.'

Key:

A lot of your answers are **a**.
GOOD FRIEND!
You are a good friend. You are very nice! You are helpful and sporty. You are a good student.

A lot of your answers are **b**.
PARTY ANIMAL!
You are very funny and friendly but you aren't always very helpful. Jokes, parties and dancing are your favourite things but you are also a good student.

A lot of your answers are **c**.
HOME LOVER!
You are friendly ... sometimes! You don't like groups. You aren't very sporty but you are usually a good student.

53

4.5

In this lesson

Lesson aims:
○ Reading: understanding a personality quiz
○ Vocabulary: personality adjectives

Resources:
○ Tests: Vocabulary Check 4.5

Homework:
○ Workbook Unit 4, p. 38

Assessment for Learning in this lesson
◎ Setting aims and criteria for success: Warm-up
💬 Giving feedback: Exercise 2
🔄 Peer learning: Exercise 3
🎓 Independent learning: Finishing the lesson

Warm-up
• Critical thinking (*Books closed*) Brainstorm expressions for apologising from Lesson 4.4. (*L1/L2*) Have a class discussion about situations in which it's important to say sorry in your country.
• (*Books open*) (*L1/L2*) Pairs look at page 53, discuss and note what they will do/learn. Don't explain the objectives! Review Ss' predictions at the end of the class.

Lead-in
• (*Books closed*) Ss think of one word to describe them and tell a friend. Brainstorm personality adjectives with the class.

Exercise 1 🔊 **2.28**
• Before Ss do the exercise, they tick any adjectives in the box they know. Challenge Ss to explain the others with your help.

Answers → student page

Exercise 2
• (*Books closed*) Ask different Ss for examples of questions typical of a personality quiz. Challenge strong Ss to suggest questions in English.
• 💬 (*Books open*) Ss do the quiz individually. Use the Traffic Lights technique to monitor.

Exercise 3
• 🔄 Ask Ss to underline anything they disagree with about their personality type in the key and to circle the words that best describe them. Pairs tell each other what they agree/disagree with and why.

Extra activity
• Pairs write an extra quiz question and ask another pair.

Exercise 4 🔊 **2.29**
• Tell Ss Sam and Sue are doing the first three questions of the quiz.
• Pairs predict their answers.
• Then Ss listen and check.

Answers → student page

Exercise 5
• Ss write sentences individually and read them for the class / a group of four to guess.

Finishing the lesson
• 🎓 Pairs refer to the lesson objectives they predicted in the Warm-up. Were they correct?
• 🎓 Ss read the lesson objective and show self-assessment response cards (☺, 😐, ☹).
• 🎓 Ss copy the objective into their notebooks and draw the emoticon that reflects their progress.

⏳ **Fast finishers**
• Ss write sentences about a family member using the adjectives in Exercise 1.

4.6

In this lesson

Lesson aims:
- Listening: understanding texts about cartoon characters
- Writing: a text about a favourite cartoon character; using paragraphs

Resources:
- Tests: Writing Task Unit 4

Homework:
- Workbook Unit 4, p. 39

Assessment for Learning in this lesson
- Setting aims and criteria for success: Warm-up
- Giving feedback: Exercise 4 and 8
- Peer learning: Exercise 6
- Independent learning: Finishing the lesson

Culture notes
The cartoons/characters (left to right): *Penguins of Madagascar* – Skipper, Kowalski, Private, Rico; *Kung Fu Panda 3* – Po; *The Spongebob Movie* – Spongebob Squarepants, Patrick Star; *Minions* – Bob, Kevin, Stuart.

Warm-up
- (*Books closed*) Ss describe a celebrity using personality adjectives.
- (*Books open*) (L1/L2) Pairs discuss what they will do/learn. Explain the lesson objectives.

Lead-in
- (*Books closed*) Pairs race to write a list of cartoon characters.

Exercise 1
- Different Ss say the names.

Answers → Culture notes

Exercise 2 2.30
- Pairs guess before they listen.

Answers → student page

Exercise 3 2.31
- Pairs discuss the characters before they listen.

Answers → student page

Exercise 4 2.31
- Ss write the answers on response cards.

Answers → student page

Exercise 5
- Pairs describe their character to each other. Then Ss stand up and describe their character to three other Ss.

Exercise 6
- Alternatively, pairs read the text aloud and correct each other's pronunciation.

Writing
- Before Ss read the information, challenge them to explain why paragraphs are important.

Exercise 7
- Pairs underline the examples in a different colour before they note them down.

Answers → student page

Exercise 8
- After Ss write their final draft, pairs review each other's work.
- Try to indicate the good aspects of Ss' work and list things to improve.

Finishing the lesson
- Read the lesson objectives. Ss show self-assessment response cards (☺, ☺, ☹).

Fast finishers
- Ss use a dictionary to find more personality adjectives in English.

4.6 Listening and Writing
I can understand and write short texts about cartoon characters.

1 Look at the photos. Can you name the cartoons?

2 🔊 **2.30** Find the characters in the photos. Write the correct number. There is one extra photo. Then listen and check.

- [1] Skipper
- [4] Kevin
- [3] SpongeBob SquarePants

3 🔊 **2.31** Listen to the dialogue and tick (✓) the children's opinion.

	SpongeBob SquarePants	Kevin	Skipper
funny	✓	✓	
helpful	✓		✓
friendly	✓	✓	
clever		✓	✓

4 🔊 **2.31** Complete the sentences with the words in the box. Then listen and check.

> isn't   ~~clever~~   Kevin   cool   ideas

1 SpongeBob SquarePants isn't very _clever_.
2 All Minions are _cool_.
3 _Kevin_ loves bananas and apples.
4 Skipper has got good _ideas_.
5 Sometimes Skipper _isn't_ nice or friendly.

5 Who is your favourite cartoon character? Describe him/her to a friend.

6 Read Lian's web text about her favourite cartoon character. Do you know it?

> **Paragraph 1** Kung Fu Panda's name is Po. He's got a big body and head. He's got big blue eyes and small black ears. They're cool. His legs are short and his arms are long. He's got brown shorts.
>
> **Paragraph 2** I think Po is nice. He's funny and he's friendly. He's got lots of friends. He's clever and he's sporty too. He's very good at kung fu!

Writing — Paragraphs
A paragraph is a part of a text. It's about one main idea. Remember to divide your text into paragraphs!

7 Read Lian's web text again. Write the paragraph numbers. Add examples from Lian's text to each paragraph. *big blue eyes, small black ears, short le...*
- [1] Face and body *big body, big head, ...long ar...*
- [2] Personality *nice, ...funny, friendly, clever*

8 ✏️ **Writing Time** Write about your favourite character from a book or cartoon.

❓ Find ideas
Find a photo of your character. Make a list of words describing his/her face, body and personality.

✏️ Draft
1 Write a paragraph about his/her face and body.
(Your character's name) has got a really friendly face. …
2 Write a paragraph about his/her personality.
He/She isn't very clever but …

👍 Check and write
Check the paragraphs and write the final version of your text.

Language Revision 4.7

Vocabulary

1 Look at Maddy. Write words 1–9 describing her body. Then complete words a–e describing her face.

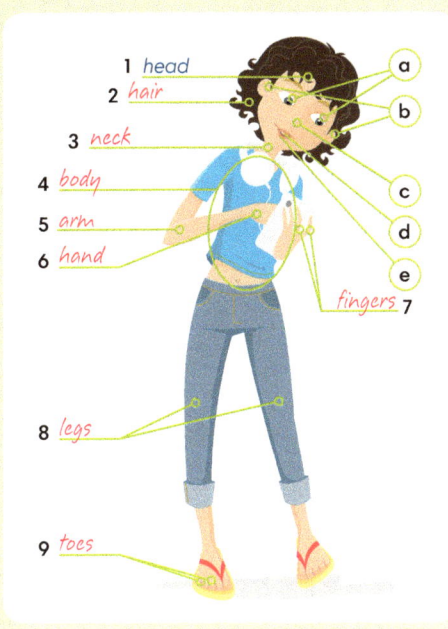

1 head
2 hair
3 neck
4 body
5 arm
6 hand
7 fingers
8 legs
9 toes

a e<u>ye</u>s   b e<u>ar</u>s   c n<u>o</u>se
d t<u>ee</u>th   e m<u>ou</u>th

2 Read sentences 1–3 about Maddy's hair. Tick (✔) the sentence that is true.

1 ☐ She's got long dark straight hair.
2 ☐ She's got short blond curly hair.
3 ✔ She's got short brown wavy hair.

3 Match the word fragments to make five adjectives.

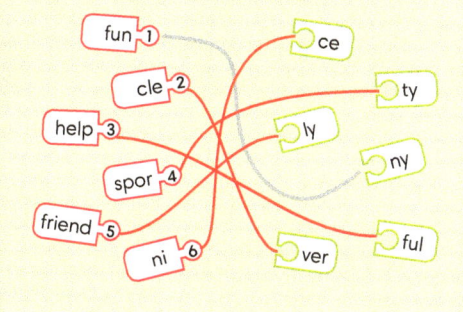

fun – ny
cle – ver
help – ful
spor – ty
friend – ly
(ni, ce also shown)

Pronunciation

4 🔊 2.32 Listen and repeat: /h/.
Her name's **H**elpful **H**elen, **h**er **h**orse's name is Claire. **H**er **h**ome is in **H**astings. She's got white **h**air!

Grammar

5 Write questions in your notebook.

1 Have eyes you brown got ?
   Have you got brown eyes?
2 curly your hair dad Has got ?
3 you and your friends dark hair Have got ?
4 your mum eyes Has got blue ?
5 Have a car your parents got ?
6 a pet got your grandparents Have ?

6 Answer the questions in Exercise 5.

1 Yes, I have. / No, I haven't.

7 Complete the sentences with *its*, *our*, *your* or *their*.

1 _Our_ (we) names are Jo and Alex.
2 This is _their_ (they) new house.
3 Where is _your_ (you) homework?
4 Is it your dog? What's _its_ name?

Communication

8 Complete the dialogues with the words in the box.

| problem | That's | mistake | so | Sorry | It's OK |

1 A: Where's my phone?
   B: I've got it. Sorry, my ¹*mistake*.
   A: ²*That's* all right.
2 B: Ooops! I've got your cap. ³*Sorry* about that.
   A: No ⁴*problem*.
3 A: I haven't got your book today. I'm ⁵*so* sorry.
   B: ⁶*It's OK*.

Check yourself! ✔
○ I can describe someone's face and hair. ☐
○ I can use the verb *have got*. ☐
○ I can use possessive adjectives *its*, *our*, *your* and *their*. ☐
○ I can say sorry and respond to an apology. ☐

Exercise 1
- Answers → student page
- After you check the answers, read the words at random for Ss to point at their body parts.

Exercise 2
- Ss compare answers in pairs.
- Answer → student page

Exercise 3
- Ss do the exercise individually.
- 💬 Use the Lollipop Stick technique to choose different Ss to spell each answer.
- Answers → student page

Exercise 4 🔊 2.32
- Hold a loose piece of paper in front of your mouth and say /h/. The paper should move. Get Ss to do the same!

Exercise 5
- 👥 Pairs review each other's work.

Answers
2 Has your dad got curly hair?
3 Have you and your friends got dark hair? 4 Has your mum got blue eyes? 5 Have your parents got a car? 6 Have your grandparents got a pet?

Exercise 6
- Ss work individually.

Extra activity
- Pairs ask and answer the questions in Exercise 5. Strong Ss close their books!

Exercise 7
- Pairs help each other do the exercise.
- Answers → student page

Exercise 8
- 💬 Ss work individually. Check understanding using the Traffic Lights technique. Then ask Ss with green and yellow 'lights' to compare answers in pairs. Re-teach Ss with red 'lights'.
- Answers → student page

Finishing the lesson
- 📖 Read Check yourself! statements for Ss to tick.

⏳ **Fast finishers**
- Ss write true/false sentences about a classmate's hair.

4.7

In this lesson

Lesson aims:
○ Revising Vocabulary, Grammar and Communication from Unit 4
○ Pronunciation: /h/

Resources:
○ Tests: Language Test Unit 4, Mid-Year Test Units 1–4

Homework:
○ Workbook Unit 4, pp. 40–41
○ Extra Online Practice Unit 4

Assessment for Learning in this lesson
🎯 Setting aims and criteria for success: Warm-up
💬 Giving feedback: Exercise 3 and 8
👥 Peer learning: Exercise 5
📖 Independent learning: Finishing the lesson

Warm-up
- (*Books closed*) Divide the class into two teams. Ask each team in turn these questions: *1 Describe Jen's hair.* (Long and brown.) *2 Name four parts of the body. 3 Spell 'fingers'. 4 What's the plural of 'tooth'?* (Teeth.) *6 You take someone's phone by mistake. What do you say?*
- 🎯 Ask Ss to work in groups and write down what they have learnt in this unit. (L1/L2) Explain the lesson objectives.

Lead-in
- (*Books open*) (L1/L2) Ask *What are your favourite lessons in this unit? Why?* Encourage Ss to explain.

3 & 4

In this lesson

Lesson aims:
- Skills practice: Reading, Writing, Listening and Communication
- Exam practice: CYLET and PTEYL

Resources:
- Tests: Skills Test Units 3&4, Speaking Tasks Units 3&4, Exam Test Units 1–4

Homework:
- Workbook Skills Revision 3&4, pp. 42–43

Assessment for Learning in this lesson
- Setting aims and criteria for success: Warm-up
- Giving feedback: Exercise 2, 3 and 5
- Peer learning: Exercise 4
- Independent learning: Finishing the lesson

Exam Language Bank

This lists the key language from Units 3–4. Here are some ideas to help you make the most of it.
- Encourage Ss to be independent learners. They tick the words they know and check the meaning of the words they can't remember in a dictionary.
- Ss memorize a section, close the book and write down all the words they can remember.
- Make a quick two-minute test. (*Books closed*) Say different words/expressions in English from one section. Ss write or say sentences with them.
- Fast finishers test each other.
  Student A: *What's in the kitchen?*
  Student B: ….
  Student B: *How do you spell 'spiky'?*
  Student A: *S-P-I-K-Y.*

---

3 & 4 Skills Revision

Reading and Writing

What's your favourite place? Write about it!

Bev, 11
1 My favourite place is my granny's house. It's a small cottage in the country. My favourite room is the living room. There are a lot of old things there. There are old books, lamps and some of my old toys!

Jane, 10
2 My favourite place is my classroom! It's very big. There are long, white desks. We've all got our own box for our books and schoolbags. We can play computer games with the teacher on the white board too. It's so cool.

Julieta, 13
3 My favourite place is our home in the country. I go there with my mum, dad and sister at weekends. There are two small bedrooms and a living room. There is a bathroom behind our home. There's a kitchen in the house too but we cook outside. It's fun!

A /
B 2
C 3

1 Work in pairs. Say what you can see in the photos.

2 Read and match texts 1–3 to photos A–C.

3 Read the sentences. Circle *yes*, *no* or *no info*.
1 Bev's house is in the country.   yes / no / **no info**
2 There are toys in the living room. **yes** / no / no info
3 Jane's classroom is small.   yes / **no** / no info
4 All the students in Jane's class have got a computer. yes / no / **no info**
5 Julieta's home in the country has got four rooms. yes / **no** / no info
6 The kitchen is outside.   yes / **no** / no info

4 **Exam Spot** Write about 40–50 words about your favourite place. Use these questions to help you.
1 What is your favourite place?
2 Where is this place?
3 What is inside / next to it?
4 Who is there?
5 What is nice about it?

My favourite place is … It's in … There are … in my favourite place. There is a nice … / There are nice …

5 **Exam Spot** Look and read. Write *yes* or *no*.

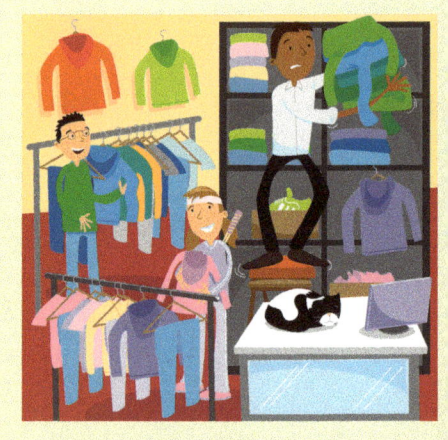

1 The boy has got short, spiky hair.   _yes_
2 There is a brown carpet on the floor. _no_
3 The man has got long arms.   _yes_
4 There aren't any jumpers.   _no_
5 There are six hoodies.   _yes_
6 The girl is sporty.   _yes_

56

Warm-up
- (*Books open*) Pairs choose a character from Units 3–4. They pretend to be a reporter and write five questions to ask the character. Then they roleplay the interview twice, changing roles.
- (*Books closed*) Write *Skills Revision* on the board. Ask a student to remind the class what this means. (*Books open*) Ss look and check. Remind Ss this lesson will help prepare them for CYLET and/or PTEYL too. (See the Introduction.)

Lead-in
- (*Books closed*) Write *places* on the board. Challenge a student to explain. Tell Ss about a place you like and ask Ss to name places they like. Don't ask for details yet.

Exercise 1
- Pairs brainstorm what they can see. Tell them they don't need to write.

Exercise 2
- Remind Ss they don't need to understand details yet, just the key ideas. Give them a time limit to help focus their attention on the general, e.g. 1–2 minutes. Weak classes might need longer.
- Use the Lollipop Stick technique to choose different Ss to justify the answers.

Answers → student page

Skills Revision 3 & 4

Listening

6 **Exam Spot** 🔊 **2.33** Listen and draw lines. There is one extra picture.

Communication

7 **Exam Spot** Read the sentences and circle the best answer.

1 Jane: Hi, come in!
   Peter: a No problem. b Are you OK? (c) Thanks.
2 Jane: Would you like a cupcake?
   Peter: a She's in the kitchen.
         b It's too small.
        (c) No, thanks.
3 Peter: Where's your brother?
   Jane: (a) He's upstairs.
        b He's got a new computer.
        c They're at school.
4 Peter: Oh no! My juice is on the sofa … .
   Jane: a I'm fine, thanks.
        (b) That's all right.
        c It's nice.
5 Peter: Where's the bathroom, please?
   Jane: (a) It's next to the kitchen. Let me show you.
        b This is the living room.
        c All right.

8 **Exam Spot** Work in pairs. Ask and answer the questions.

1 Who is your favourite person in your family?
2 Where do you do your homework?
3 What's in your living room?

Exam Language Bank

Parts of the house		Face
bathroom	garden	ears
bedroom	kitchen	eyes
door	living room	mouth
floor	wall	nose
garage	window	teeth

Inside the house		Hair
armchair	fridge	curly
bath	sofa	spiky
bed	table	straight
chair	wardrobe	wavy
desk		blond
		dark
		red

Prepositions of place		Parts of the body
behind	next to	arm
in	on	body
in front of	under	fingers

Household objects	Parts of the body (cont.)
carpet	foot
cushion	hand
lamp	head
plant	leg
poster	neck
television (TV)	toes

Personality adjectives		
clever	funny	nice
friendly	helpful	sporty

Having a guest	Apologising
Hello. Please, come in.	I'm so sorry.
Thank you.	Sorry about that!
Would you like a *sandwich*?	Sorry, my mistake.
Yes, please. / No, thanks.	Are you OK?
Where's the *bathroom*, please?	It's OK.
It's *upstairs*/*downstairs*.	That's all right.
It's next to the *living room*.	No problem.
Let me show you.	I'm fine.

57

Exercise 3
- 💬 Ss do the exercise individually. Use the Traffic Lights technique to monitor. Then use the Basketball technique to check answers.

Answers → student page

Exercise 4
- This is preparation for PTEYL Springboard, Task Six Writing.
- Ss choose a place, read the questions and make notes. Then they write.
- 👥 Pairs work together to review another pairs' texts using the Two Stars and a Wish technique.

Extra activity
- Choose different Ss to read their texts to the class now or at the end of the lesson. You could ask them to say 'ZZZZ' instead of the name of the place. Ask the class to guess where/what it is.

Exercise 5
- This is preparation for CYLET Starters, Reading and Writing Part 2.
- Ask different Ss to describe the picture first.
- 💬 Use the Thumbs up/down technique to check answers. Choose individuals to justify each answer.

Answers → student page

Extra activity
- Ss draw three extra objects/people in their notebooks. They imagine where they are in the picture in Exercise 5. Then they describe these objects/people and their location for their partner to point at.

Exercise 6 🔊 2.33
- This is preparation for CYLET Starters, Listening Part 1.
- Ask Ss to name the objects outside the picture and to say what there is in the living room.
- Ask Ss to predict which the extra object is.
- Ss listen to the recording twice in the test.
- To check answers, ask different Ss to describe where each object is.

Answers → student page

Exercise 7
- This is preparation for CYLET Movers, Reading and Writing Part 2.
- (*Books closed*) Before Ss start, say each sentence to the class. Ask individuals to respond.
- (*Books open*) Ss do the exercise individually. Then pairs compare answers.
- Choose different individuals to explain the answers.

Answers → student page

Exercise 8
- This is preparation for CYLET/PTEYL Speaking.
- Ss take notes when they speak.

Extra activity
- Ss write three true/false sentences about their partner's answers in Exercise 8 for the class/another pair to guess.

Finishing the lesson
- ✉️ Write the headings *Reading and Writing*, *Listening*, *Communication* on the board. Read each out. Ss show self-assessment response cards (☺, 😐, ☹).
- ✉️ (*L1/L2*) Ss write one sentence about what they did well in each section and one about what they could improve.

⏳ Fast finishers
- Ss study the Exam Language Bank.
- Ss write true/false sentences about the pictures in Exercise 1.

5.1

In this lesson

Lesson aims:
- Vocabulary: action verbs

Resources:
- Vocabulary worksheet 5.1, p. 150
- Tests: Vocabulary Check 5.1

Homework:
- Workbook Unit 5, p. 44

Assessment for Learning in this lesson
- Setting aims and criteria for success: Warm-up
- Giving feedback: Exercise 3 and 5
- Peer learning: Exercise 4
- Independent learning: Finishing the lesson

Warm-up
- (*Books closed*) Play *Noughts and Crosses* with *have got*. Draw a 3 x 3 grid on the board and write a different student's name and an object in each square. E.g. *Tom/computer*. Ss copy the grid into their notebooks and work in pairs. They ask a question using both words to win their 'O' or 'X', e.g. *Has Tom got a computer?* Challenge a strong class to answer the question too!
- Write *Things I can do* on the board. Then ask pairs to predict what they will learn.
- (L1/L2) Explain the lesson objective. Then ask Ss to predict what they will be able to say in English at the end of the lesson.

Lead-in
- (*Books closed*) Challenge the class to tell you what they can do in English. If they don't have enough vocabulary, they can mime.

Exercise 1
- Pairs write the number of each photo next to the corresponding word. Choose one word from the box, mime it and say *I know that!* with a thumbs up gesture. Encourage Ss to continue.

Answers → student page

5 Things I can do

Vocabulary I can understand action verbs.

In this unit

Vocabulary
- Action verbs
- Collocations with *make*, *play* and *ride*

Grammar
- *can* affirmative, negative, questions and short answers

▶ 24–25
5.2 Grammar video

▶ 26
5.2 Grammar animation

▶ 27
5.3 Grammar animation

▶ 28
5.4 Communication video

▶ 29
BBC Culture video

1 Find these actions in the photos.
climb draw jump ride a bike run
skateboard swim

I know that!

Exercise 2 ▶ 2.34
- Play the recording, pausing after each word. Ss repeat it and look for a corresponding photo. Ask a student to say the number of the photo or to mime the word.

Answers
Actions missing in the photos: act, cook, dive, fix, fly, read, sing, write

Exercise 3
- Pairs race to label the pictures.
- Use the Lollipop Stick technique to choose Ss to say and spell each answer.

Answers → student page

Extra activity
- Ss work in pairs. Student A covers the book. Student B says the number of a picture in Exercise 3. Student A says the verb. They swap and continue.

Exercise 4 ▶ 2.35
- Play the recording. Pause after number 1. A student reads the example aloud.
- Play until the end, pausing for pairs to discuss and note their answers.
- Alternatively, do this as a whole class activity. Pause after each sound. Ss tell you their ideas. Vote and check!

Answers → student page

5.1

2 🔊 **2.34** Listen and repeat. Which actions are not in the photos on page 58?

Vocabulary Action verbs

act   climb   cook   dive   draw   fix
fly   jump   read   ride   run   sing
skateboard   swim   write

3 Label the illustrations with words in the Vocabulary box.

1 _cook_   2 _dive_
3 _sing_   4 _write_
5 _fly_   6 _fix_
7 _act_   8 _read_

4 🔊 **2.35** Listen and circle the action you hear.

1 write /(read)   4 write /(skateboard)
2 (swim)/ cook   5 run /(dive)
3 (draw)/ ride   6 (act)/ sing

5 **Exam Spot** Which actions are in the picture? Tick (✓) for *yes* or put a cross (✗) for *no*.

1 ✓ swim   5 ✓ draw
2 ✗ dive   6 ✗ fix
3 ✓ read   7 ✓ ride
4 ✓ jump   8 ✗ fly

6 Work in pairs. Look at the picture in Exercise 5. Mime actions for your partner to guess!

7 In pairs, complete the groups of words.

1 Things we do at school: _read, write, draw_
2 Things actors do: _____
3 Sports: _____
4 Hobbies: _____
5 Things we do at home: _____
6 Things we do in the water: _____
7 Things birds do: _____

8 Make two lists that are true for you. Use the Vocabulary box to help you.

I remember that!

I think it's easy to: _cook,_____.
I think it's difficult to: _____.

59

Exercise 7

- If your class is weak, you could allocate one or two categories per pair. Give weaker pairs the categories with fewer words. If your class is strong, challenge Ss to cover the Vocabulary box. Tell Ss they can use some words more than once.
- Ask each pair to compare their answers with another pair. Ask different Ss to write words in each category on the board.

Answers
2 act, sing 3 swim, dive, jump, run, skateboard, ride, climb
4 sing, read, draw, cook
5 cook, fix, read, write, draw
6 dive, swim 7 sing, fly

Exercise 8

- Alternatively, ask Ss to write their sentences and name on a piece of paper and to give it to you. Read out the sentences to the class. Ss guess whose they are.

Finishing the lesson

- 📖 Ss look at the predictions they made in the Warm-up and circle the new words in the Vocabulary box they have learnt.
- 🎓 Ask *Can you understand action verbs?* Students show self-assessment response cards (☺, ☺, ☹).
- 📖 Ss copy the objective into their notebooks and draw the emoticon that reflects their progress.

⏳ Fast finishers
- (*Books closed*) Ss write all the action verbs they know.

Exercise 5

- This is preparation for CYLET Starters, Reading & Writing Part 2.
- Before pairs do the exercise, ask Ss to cover verbs 1–8. Different Ss name the actions they can see in the picture.
- 💻 To check each answer, use the Thumbs up/down technique. If the answer is 'yes', ask a student to hold up his/her book and point to the action.

Answers → student page

Exercise 6

- Pairs take turns to mime. Alternatively, secretly whisper an action verb to different Ss, who mime it for the class to guess.

Extra activity
- **Critical thinking** Teach/Check *safe* and *dangerous*. Then pairs list the action verbs in the Vocabulary box in the following order: 1 = very safe to 15 = dangerous. They compare their order with another pair and agree on a new order. A spokesperson from each group tells the class their order and justifies it with the help of the group.

5.2

In this lesson

Lesson aims:
- Grammar: *can* affirmative and negative
- Vocabulary: *make, play, ride*

Resources:
- Grammar worksheet 5.2, p. 160
- Tests: Grammar Check 5.2, Vocabulary Check 5.2

Homework:
- Workbook Unit 5, p. 45
- Extra Online Practice Unit 5

Assessment for Learning in this lesson
- Setting aims and criteria for success: Warm-up
- Giving feedback: Exercise 2 and 10
- Peer learning: Exercise 3 and 6
- Independent learning: Finishing the lesson

Culture notes
Shanghai, China, is the biggest city in the world.

Warm-up
- (*Books closed*) Play *Snowman* to revise action verbs. On the board, write a dash for each letter of a word. Ss work in two teams and take turns to guess the letters of the word. Draw a part of the snowman for each wrong guess. (See Lesson 1.1, Warm-up.)
- Using gesture, say one true and one false sentence with *can*. E.g. *I can run fast. I can climb.* Ss say *true/false*. Ask strong Ss to do the same.
- Pairs discuss what they will learn in this lesson. (L1/L2) Explain the lesson objectives.

Lead-in
- (*Books closed*) Write *I can fix it* on the board. Pairs predict what the photo story is about.
- (*Books open*) Pairs review their predictions. Then use the photos to check *(video) camera*. Elicit *talented/genius*. Say *She can do a lot of things. She's very … (talented). A very clever person is a … (genius).*

5.2 Grammar
I can use the verb can *in affirmative and negative sentences.*

I can fix it!

1 Guys, this video is for my granny, in Shanghai. Granny Lin, this is my friend, Lucas.
Lucas: Hello!
Lian: Lucas is very talented! He can play the guitar and he can sing!
Lucas: Well, I can't sing very well but …

2 Lian: Oh no, <u>not again!</u>
Alex: <u>What's wrong?</u>
Lian: It's the camera. I can't see a thing!
Alex: <u>Let me see</u> … Hmm, I can fix it.
Lian: Thanks! Alex is a genius! He can fix things! He can do very clever things with computers too!

3 Jen: Yes, very clever – he can play computer games all day! Cupcake?
Lian: Jen is a fantastic cook! These cupcakes are yummy!

4 Alex: But what about Lian?
Lucas: Yes, what can she do?

---

1 ▶24 🔊 2.36 Watch or listen and read. Finish the sentence.

There's something wrong with Lian's (video) camera .

2 Complete the sentences.
1 The video is for Lian's granny .
2 Lian's granny is in Shanghai .
3 Lucas is very talented.
4 Alex is a genius.
5 Jen is a good cook.

3 🔊 2.37 Listen and repeat. Find these expressions in the story.

Say it!
Not again!   What's wrong?   Let me see …

4 ▶ Guess! Look at the story again. What can Lian do?
Lian can draw , skateboard and eat cupcakes fast

5 ▶25 🔊 2.38 Now watch or listen and check.

60

Exercise 1 ▶24 🔊 2.36
- Play the video. If you don't have access to a computer and projector, play the recording.
- Ask a student to answer. Then check the class' predictions about the story.

Answer → student page

Exercise 2
- First, pairs note the answers they know.
- Play the video again (stopping it in appropriate places) or refer Ss to the photo story to confirm the answers.
- Check answers using the Basketball technique.

Answers → student page

Exercise 3 🔊 2.37 ▶24
- Play the recording, pausing for Ss to repeat each expression.
- Play the video again. Ss shout *STOP!* when they hear each expression. Alternatively, Ss find and underline the expressions in the dialogue.
- Ss use the Think – Pair – Share technique to think of situations in which they can use these expressions.

Exercise 4
- Critical thinking Ss justify their choice. Don't confirm yet!

Answer → student page

5.2

Grammar can affirmative and negative

▶ 26 **Get Grammar!**

+	−
I can jump.	I can't jump.
You can jump.	You can't jump.
He/She/It can jump.	He/She/It can't jump.
We can jump.	We can't jump.
You can jump.	You can't jump.
They can jump.	They can't jump.

I can't dance but I can jump!

6 Write who can do these things. Then look at the photos on page 60 and check.

Lian (x2)   Jen (x2)   Alex (x1)   Lucas (x2)

1 _Lian_ _can_ skateboard.
2 _Lucas_ _can_ sing.
3 _Jen_ _can_ make cupcakes.
4 _Lian_ _can_ draw.
5 _Jen_ _can_ cook.
6 _Alex_ _can_ fix things.
7 _Lucas_ _can_ play the guitar.

7 Follow the lines and write what they can't do. Read the sentences.

1 Lian _can't_ _fix things_ . — draw
2 Jen _can't_ _skateboard_ — cook
3 Alex _can't_ _sing_ — play the guitar
4 Lucas _can't_ _cook_ — fix things
5 Lian _can't_ _play the guitar_ — skateboard
6 Alex _can't_ _draw_ — sing

8 🔊 2.39 Listen and circle can or can't.

1 He can /(can't) swim.
2 She (can)/ can't draw.
3 They (can)/ can't act.
4 He can /(can't) sing.
5 She (can)/ can't run.
6 His brother can /(can't) read.

9 🔊 2.40 Listen and repeat.

Vocabulary make, play, ride

make   a poster / cupcakes
play   computer games / football / the piano
ride   a bike / a horse

LOOK!
play football
play **the** piano

10 Complete Lucas's email with can and make, play or ride.

To: Ben

My family is very talented! My dad ¹_can play_ football very well. My mum ²_can ride_ a horse and she ³_can play_ the piano. My aunt Melina ⁴_can make_ cupcakes. They're yummy! As for me, I ⁵_can play_ the guitar and I ⁶_can ride_ a bike!

11 Work in pairs.
Student A: Write three true and three false sentences.
Student B: Guess which sentences are true. Then swap roles.
A: I can play the guitar.
B: It's true. / It's false.

Fun Spot

61

Exercise 5 ▶ 25 🔊 2.38
- Play the video/recording to check.

Video/Audio script
Lian: I can skateboard and I can draw.
Lucas: But where are the cupcakes?
Lian: And I can eat cupcakes very fast! Sorry, Lucas!

Extra video activity ▶ 24 ▶ 25
- Play the video. Pause when a character says can/can't. Ask Ss to stand up and mime the actions that the characters can/can't do!

Get Grammar! ▶ 26
- Play the Get Grammar! video. If you don't have access to a computer and projector, continue.
- Ss repeat the examples after you in chorus.
- Explain that can't is used in everyday English.

Exercise 6
- 📖 Pairs cover the photo story and complete. Then they swap books with another pair, who check the story and correct their answers.

Answers → student page

Exercise 7
- Ss race to complete.
- Ask individuals to say each sentence.

Answers → student page

Extra activity
- (Books open) Groups of four replace all the people's names and places in the photo story with their own names/ideas. They act out their new dialogue.

Exercise 8 🔊 2.39
- You could pause after each question and get pairs to discuss and note the answer.

Answers → student page

Exercise 9 🔊 2.40
- After Ss listen and repeat, vote for the most popular activity.
- Ask pairs to brainstorm any other collocations they know with make, play and ride and to write them on the board.

Look!
- **Critical thinking** Challenge the class to work out the rule. Explain that we use *the* before a musical instrument.

Exercise 10
- 📱 Ss do the exercise individually. Then they stand up and check their answers with three other Ss. Ask individuals to justify each answer.

Answers → student page

Exercise 11
- Alternatively, Ss read their sentences for the class to guess.

Finishing the lesson
- 📘 Point at the Vocabulary box and ask *Can you use 'can' with these words in questions and negations?* Students show self-assessment response cards (☺, 😐, ☹). Ask Ss to give examples of each.
- 📘 Ss copy the objectives into their notebooks and draw the emoticons that reflect their progress.

⏳ Fast finishers
- Ss look at the photo story and write down the words they know.
- Ss find sentences with can/can't in the photo story.

79

5.3
In this lesson

Lesson aims:
- Grammar: *can* questions and short answers

Resources:
- Grammar worksheet 5.3, p. 161
- Tests: Grammar Check 5.3

Homework:
- Workbook Unit 5, p. 46

Assessment for Learning in this lesson
- Setting aims and criteria for success: Warm-up
- Giving feedback: Exercise 3 and 4
- Peer learning: Exercise 5 and 6
- Independent learning: Finishing the lesson

Warm-up
- (*Books closed*) Play *Memory Chain* with the class. Student A says a sentence with *can*. Student B repeats it and adds another one. Student C repeats both and adds a third, e.g. *He can swim. She can act. I can run.* Continue. Ss who make a mistake or repeat a verb are 'out'!
- Ask Ss if they remember the objectives from Lesson 5.2. Tell them to guess what the objectives for this lesson are. (*Books open*) Ss look at pages 62–63 and check their ideas. (*L1/L2*) Explain the objectives.

Lead-in
- (*Books closed*) Write *Thank you, Superdug!* on the board. Pairs predict what the cartoon is about. (*Books open*) Ss look at the pictures and review their predictions.
- Use the pictures to pre-teach *lovely* and *boat*.

Exercise 1
- Critical thinking Individual Ss race to answer. Challenge a strong student to explain the answers using complete sentences. Accept pointing from a weaker student.

Answers → student page

5.3 Grammar
I can ask and answer questions with the verb *can*.

The Terrific Two Thank you, Superdug

1 Look at the cartoon and answer the questions.
1. What's the title of Dug's book? *Learn to swim.*
2. Who can swim in the cartoon? *The little dog.*

2 🔊 2.41 Listen and read. Finish the sentence.
The woman is Tom and Susan's *mother*.

3 Read the cartoon again and complete the sentences with one word.
1. Dug can *see* the boat over there.
2. Susan and Tom are in the *boat*.
3. Susan and Tom can't *swim*.
4. Kit and Superdug *can* help.
5. Superdug can't swim but he can *fly*.

Exercise 2 🔊 2.41
- After Ss listen and read, pairs agree on the answer. Then ask an individual to justify theirs by referring to the text/Picture 3.

Answer → student page

Exercise 3
- Ss write their answers on response cards.

Answers → student page

Get Grammar! ▶ 27
- Play the *Get Grammar!* video. If you don't have access to a computer and projector, continue.
- Ss repeat the examples after you in chorus.
- Point out we invert the subject and *can* to form a question.

Exercise 4
- Ss work in pairs.
- Each pair swaps their books with another pair. They review each other's work.
- Write answers most Ss found difficult on the board and clarify.

Answers
2 Can Dug fly? No, he can't. 3 Can Tom and Susan fly? No, they can't. 4 Can you see the boat? Yes, I can. 5 Can the little dog swim? Yes, it can.

5.3

Grammar *can* questions and short answers   ▶ 27 Get Grammar!

?	Short answers
Can I swim?	Yes, I can. / No I can't.
Can you swim?	Yes, you can. / No, you can't.
Can he/she/it swim?	Yes, he/she/it can. / No, he/she/it can't.
Can we swim?	Yes, we can. / No, we can't.
Can you swim?	Yes, you can. / No, you can't.
Can they swim?	Yes, they can. / No, they can't.
What can we do?	We can help.

Can he run fast?
No, he can't.

4 In your notebook, write questions and short answers.
1 fly Can Superdug ?
   Can Superdug fly? Yes, he can.
2 Dug fly Can ?
3 Tom and Susan Can fly ?
4 the boat you see Can ?
5 Can swim the little dog ?

5 Look at the cartoon. Ask and answer the questions in pairs.
1 Picture 2 Dug / see the children?
   A: *Can Dug see the children?*
   B: *Yes, he can.*
2 Picture 3 Tom and Susan / swim?
3 Picture 3 What / Kit and Dug / do?
4 Picture 4 Superdug / run fast?
5 Picture 4 Superdug / swim?

6 In pairs, ask and answer about Kit and Dug.

swim?	✔	✘
draw?	✘	✔
cook?	✔	✘

A: *Can Kit swim?* B: *Yes, she can.*

7 Copy the table. Add your idea for number 5. Ask five of your classmates. How many of them *can* or *can't* do these things?

Can you swim?
Yes, I can. / No, I can't.

Can you …	1	2	3	4	5
1 swim?	✔	✔	✘	✘	✘
2 fix a computer?					
3 ride a horse?					
4 draw?					
5 … ?					

8 Write a report of your survey in Exercise 7.
Two people can swim and three people can't swim!

Fun Spot

9 🔊 2.42 🔊 2.43
Go to page 107.
Listen and chant the Activities Rap.

63

Exercise 5
- 🗣 Ss in a weak class do this exercise in open pairs. Praise Ss who do well. Encourage them to explain what was good with the class' help. E.g. *(L1) I remembered the word without looking. The grammar was correct. My pronunciation was good*. Challenge strong Ss by writing the comments on the board so they can explain in English.

Answers
2 Can Tom and Susan swim? No, they can't.
3 What can Kit and Dug do? They can help.
4 Can Superdug run fast? Yes, he can.
5 Can Superdug swim? No, he can't.

Exercise 6
- 🗣 Individuals write questions and answers. Appoint two or three Ss as experts and use the Expert Envoy technique to help weaker Ss. Then pairs act out the dialogues, changing roles.

Answers
Can Dug swim? No, he can't.
Can Kit draw? No, she can't.
Can Dug draw? Yes, he can.
Can Kit cook? Yes, she can.
Can Dug cook? No, he can't.

Exercise 7
- Ss note an extra question. Give all Ss a letter, A or B, so As are sitting next to Bs. Ss A and Ss B interview each other. B's all move round the class in one direction and sit down in the next empty seat next to an A. Ss interview each other again. Continue like this until all Ss have spoken to five classmates Alternatively, ask groups of five to ask and answer if you intend to do the Extra activity below.

Extra activity
- Count and collate the information from Exercise 7 on the board. Then help each group to draw a bar chart to represent the information.

Exercise 8
- Ss do this individually or help each other in the same groups as above.

Exercise 9 🔊 2.42 🔊 2.43
- Play the rap and teach Ss appropriate gestures.
- When Ss are familiar with the rap, play the karaoke version. Ss chant and make the gestures.

Finishing the lesson
- 📖 Read the lesson objectives. Ss show self-assessment response cards (☺, 😐, ☹).
- 📖 Ss copy the objectives into their notebooks and draw the emoticons that reflect their progress.

⌛ **Fast finishers**
- Ss look at the pictures in the cartoon and write down all the words they know.
- *(Books closed)* Ss write two questions they would like to ask Superdug/Kit, using *can*.
- *(After Exercise 4)* Pairs ask and answer the questions in Exercise 4.

5.4

In this lesson

Lesson aims:
- Communication: making suggestions

Resources:
- Communication worksheet 5.4, p. 172

Homework:
- Workbook Unit 5, p. 47
- Extra Online Practice Unit 5

Assessment for Learning in this lesson
- Setting aims and criteria for success: Warm-up
- Giving feedback: Exercise 3
- Peer learning: Extra activity
- Independent learning: Finishing the lesson

Warm-up
- (*Books closed*) Pairs write true and false sentences about what different characters in Unit 5 can/can't do for another pair to guess.
- Write *Let's do something fun!* on the board. Ss predict what the lesson is about. (*L1/L2*) Explain the lesson objective.

Lead-in
- (*Books open*) Ss say what they remember about the characters.
- Pairs look at the photos and predict what the characters are talking about.

Exercise 1 ▶28 🔊 2.44
- Elicit *ice-skate*. Say *Look at Picture 2. She can … (ice-skate).*
- Have a class vote!
- Play the video. If you don't have access to a computer and projector, play the recording.

Answer → student page

Exercise 2 🔊 2.45
- Make sure Ss understand all the phrases in the box before you play the recording.

Extra activity
- Groups of four practise the dialogue in Exercise 1. Then Ss discuss what they did well and what could be improved.

5.4 Communication
I can make suggestions about what to do.

Let's do something fun!

Lucas: Hey, guys, let's do something fun.
Jen: I agree. Any ideas?
Alex: We can go to the park.
Jen: Again? It's not a good idea.
Lian: Let's go ice-skating.
Jen: Great idea!
Lucas: I'm not sure … I can't skate very well.
Lian: No problem. I can teach you.
Lucas: OK, cool! Let's do that!
Alex: Hey, Lucas? You can wear these!
Lucas: Ha, ha! You're so funny!

1 ▶28 🔊 2.44 Watch or listen and read. What do they decide to do? Tick (✓) the correct picture.

1 ☐   2 ✓   3 ☐

2 🔊 2.45 Listen and repeat.

Communication Suggestions

A: Let's *do something fun!* / Let's *go ice-skating!* We can *go to the park!*

B: 🙂 I agree! / Let's do that! / Great idea!
😐 I'm not sure.
☹ It's not a good idea.

3 Complete the sentences with one word.
1 We <u>can</u> go to the cinema!
2 <u>Let's</u> go to the beach!
3 Let's <u>do</u> something fun!
4 <u>We</u> can play football!
5 We <u>can</u> ride our bikes!

4 Exam Spot Circle the best answer.
1 A: Let's do something fun.
  B: a Let me see … **(b)** I agree. Any ideas?
     c What's wrong?
2 A: Let's go to the swimming pool!
  B: a We can go to the park.
     b Let's do something fun.
     (c) I'm not sure … I can't swim very well.
3 A: I can teach you.
  B: a No problem. **(b)** OK. Let's do that!
     c You're so funny.

5 Read and answer. Use expressions in the Communication box.
1 A: We can make cupcakes! B: 🙂 *Great idea!*
2 A: Let's do something fun! B: 🙂 *I agree! / Let's* th
3 A: We can go to the park. B: ☹ *It's not a good*
4 A: Let's go to the zoo. B: 😐 *I'm not sure.*

6 In pairs, make dialogues like those in Exercise 5. Use the ideas in the box and add your own.

> go to the cinema   go to the swimming pool
> make a video   play computer games
> play volleyball   ride our bikes

A: *Let's ride our bikes!*
B: *I agree!*

64

Extra video activity ▶28
- Play the video. Ss stand up when a character makes a suggestion, jump when a character reacts in a positive way or sit down when a character isn't sure or doesn't agree.

Exercise 3
- 💬 Use the Traffic Lights technique to check how difficult Ss found this exercise.

Answers → student page

Exercise 4
- This is preparation for CYLET Movers, Reading and Writing Part 2.
- Ask Ss to cover the answers first and think how they would react in each situation.

Answers → student page

Exercise 5
- Before Ss start, explain that they can choose any expression from the Communication box.

Answers → student page

Exercise 6
- Remind Ss to change roles.

Finishing the lesson
- Ask the class *Can you make suggestions about what to do?* Ss show self-assessment response cards (🙂, 😐, ☹).

⏳ Fast finishers
- Ss write suggestions about things to do after school to ask a friend at the end of the lesson.

I can understand a text about sign language. **Reading** 5.5

1 Look at the photos and the title of the text. Do you know anyone who speaks sign language?

2 🔊 2.46 Read and listen to the text. Match headings a–d to paragraphs 1–4.
a Learn sign language!
b A special language
c Where is sign language important?
d What is sign language?

3 Read the sentences. Circle T (true) or F (false).
1 People who can't hear have got a special language. (T)/ F
2 There is one sign language. T /(F)
3 There is one sign language alphabet. T /(F)
4 Sign language isn't important at home. T /(F)
5 Some TV programmes are in sign language. (T)/ F

4 The pictures show a certain word in British Sign Language alphabet. Go to page 106 and check the word. Can you show it with your hands?

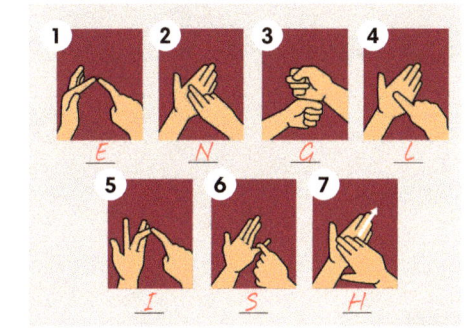

1 E 2 N 3 G 4 L
5 I 6 S 7 H

Sign language

1 [b] At school you can learn different languages, like English, French or Spanish. But there are special schools where teachers and students speak a sign language.

2 [d] In sign language you can make letters and words with your hands. It's for people who can't hear. There are different sign languages and different sign language alphabets.

3 [c] Sign language is important in schools and at home. All the family can learn sign language. They can speak to children who can't hear. Some TV programmes are in sign language too.

4 [a] Are there children at your school who can't hear? You can learn sign language and make friends with them. There are sign language courses!

65

5.5
In this lesson

Lesson aims:
- Reading: understanding a text about sign language

Homework:
- Workbook Unit 5, p. 48

Assessment for Learning in this lesson
- Setting aims and criteria for success: Exercise 1
- Giving feedback: Exercise 2
- Peer learning: Exercise 3
- Independent learning: Finishing the lesson

Culture notes
Sign language is a language based on specific hand movements supported by facial expressions. British Sign Language uses two-hand movements. American Sign Language is a one-handed alphabet.

Warm-up
- (*Books closed*) Groups of four suggest, respond and agree on one activity for them all to do next weekend.

Lead-in
- (*Books closed*) Teach *hear*. Cup one ear with your hand and say *I can hear music*.
- Critical thinking Pairs brainstorm things they do every day that would be difficult if they couldn't hear.

Exercise 1
- Pairs look at the photos and discuss the question. Ask a student to explain what sign language is. Ss tell the class if they know anyone who speaks sign language.
- Ss read the lesson objective. (*L1/L2*) Explain further if necessary.

Exercise 2 🔊 2.46
- After Ss listen and read, pairs discuss the answers.
- Use the Lollipop Stick technique to choose different Ss to justify each answer.

Answers → student page

Exercise 3
- Ask pairs to answer any questions they can. Then they read, underline key words and check. Use the Basketball technique to check answers.

Answers → student page

Exercise 4
- Tell Ss they all know this word. Pairs write their guesses on a response card.

Answer → student page

Extra activity
- Pairs write a question about something they would like to know about sign language. They find the answer on the Internet and tell the class. They either do this at home or in class if possible.

Finishing the lesson
- Read the lesson objective. Ss show self-assessment response cards (☺, 😐, ☹).
- Ss copy the objective into their notebooks and draw the emoticon that reflects their progress.

Fast finishers
- Ss write another true/false sentence about the text.

83

5.6

In this lesson

Lesson aims:
- Listening: understanding texts about after-school clubs
- Writing: an ad for an after-school club; *and, but*

Resources:
- Tests: Writing Task Unit 5

Homework:
- Workbook Unit 5, p. 49

Assessment for Learning in this lesson
- Setting aims and criteria for success: Warm-up
- Giving feedback: Exercise 6
- Peer learning: Exercise 3 and 7
- Independent learning: Finishing the lesson

Warm-up
- (*Books closed*) Ss practise the signs in Lesson 5.5, Exercise 4.
- (*Books open*) (L1/L2) Pairs look at page 66 and discuss what they will learn. Explain the lesson objectives.

Lead-in
- (*Books closed*) Ask the class *What after-school clubs has our school got?* Help with vocabulary.

Exercise 1
- After pairs match and discuss, brainstorm Ss' ideas on the board.

Answers → student page
What you can do:
1 play football 2 paint/draw.
3 act. 4 (learn to) swim/dive

Exercise 2 🔊 2.47
- Pause after each speaker. Pairs discuss before they answer.

Answers → student page

Exercise 3 🔊 2.47
- This is preparation for CYLET Movers, Listening Part 2.
- Pairs try to predict the answers before listening.

Answers → student page

5.6 Listening and Writing
I can understand and write short texts about after-school clubs.

1 Match photos 1–4 to after-school clubs a–d. In pairs, say what you can do in these clubs.

a [4] swimming club   c [3] drama club
b [2] art club   d [1] football club

2 🔊 **2.47** Listen to four children. Match speakers 1–4 to clubs a–d in Exercise 1.

Speaker 1 [b]   Speaker 3 [d]
Speaker 2 [c]   Speaker 4 [a]

3 **Exam Spot** 🔊 **2.47** Listen again. Complete with a number or an action verb.

1 At art club you can learn to paint and _draw_.
2 The number of students in the art club is _twelve_.
3 In drama club they can teach you how to _act_.
4 Football club is for boys and girls from ten to _thirteen_.
5 At swimming club kids can swim and _dive_.

4 Which of the clubs in Exercise 2 do you prefer? Have a class vote!

5 Read the ad for an after-school club. Who is the club for? Circle the correct answer.

It's for students who like *sports* / (*computers*).

Come to Computer Club!
You can make robots and you can play computer games too. How cool is that?
You can write emails but you can't write computer programs? We can teach you.
Where: St Alban's Primary School
When: Monday, 4 o'clock
See you there!
www.U-and-Bot.get

Writing *and, but*
*You **can** make robots **and** you **can** play computer games.*
*You **can** write emails **but** you **can't** write computer programs.*

6 Complete the sentences with *and* or *but*.

1 I can run _and_ I can jump.
2 She can sing _but_ she can't act.
3 They can play computer games _and_ make a robot _but_ they can't write computer programs.

7 **Writing Time** Write an ad for an after-school club.

Find ideas
Make notes about what you can do at the club, and where and when the club is.

Draft
1 Write the title. *Come to … Club!*
2 Write a paragraph about what you can do at the club.
   You can … and …
   You can … but you can't …
3 Write where and when the club is.
   Where: … When: … , … o'clock
4 Write the end. *See you there!*

Check and write
Check all the linkers (*and*, *but*) and write the final version of your text.

Exercise 4
- Ss vote for their favourite. Then encourage Ss to explain their choice.

Exercise 5
- Tell Ss *When* refers to time. Challenge a student to explain *Monday* if necessary.

Answer → student page

Writing
- **Critical thinking** Challenge Ss to explain *and*/*but*. ('And' introduces similar information; 'but' introduces contrasting information.)

Exercise 6
- Use the Traffic Lights technique to monitor.

Answers → student page

Exercise 7
- Pairs follow the steps and write individually. Then they review each other's work using the Two Stars and a Wish technique.

Extra activity
- Display the ads and vote for the most popular club!

Finishing the lesson
- Read the lesson objectives. Ss show self-assessment response cards (☺, 😐, ☹).

Fast finishers
- Ss write what you can do in the after-school clubs at your school.

Language Revision 5.7

Vocabulary

1 Look at the picture and complete the action verbs 1–9. Then write six more action verbs in your notebook.

1 a<u>c</u>t
2 c<u>l</u>im<u>b</u>
3 f<u>i</u>x
4 f<u>l</u>y
5 j<u>u</u>mp
6 r<u>e</u>a<u>d</u>
7 r<u>u</u>n
8 s<u>i</u>ng
9 s<u>w</u>i<u>m</u>

2 Complete the collocations with *make*, *play* or *ride*.

1 <u>make</u> cupcakes
2 <u>ride</u> a bike
3 <u>play</u> the guitar
4 <u>play</u> football
5 <u>ride</u> a horse
6 <u>make</u> a poster

Pronunciation

3 🔊 2.48 Listen and repeat: /ɑː/ or /æ/?

M**a**rk's **A**unt **A**nn can play the guit**a**r
But she c**a**n't sing or **a**ct so she isn't a st**a**r!

Grammar

4 In your notebook, write sentences with *can* (✔) or *can't* (✘) and *and* or *but*.

1 Superdug / fly ✔ / swim ✘
   Superdug can fly but he can't swim.
2 Leo / play the piano ✘ / play football ✔
3 I / make a cake ✘ / make a pizza ✔
4 You / play the guitar ✘ / sing ✘
5 They / skateboard ✔ / run very fast ✔

5 Complete the questions and short answers.

1 <u>Can you swim</u> (you / swim)? No, <u>I can't</u>.
2 <u>Can David sing</u> (David / sing) this song?
  Yes, <u>he can</u>. He's very good.
3 <u>Can the boys act</u> (the boys / act)?
  No, <u>they can't</u>!
4 Mum, <u>can we play</u> (we / play) a computer game?
  No, <u>you can't</u>. It's time for lunch.
5 <u>Can you see</u> (you / see) Mario?
  Yes, <u>I can</u>. He's over there.

Communication

6 Put the dialogue in the correct order. Then act it out in pairs.

a [4] B: I'm not sure … I can't play very well.
b [6] B: OK, cool. Let's do that.
c [2] B: I agree. Any ideas?
d [1] A: Let's do something fun.
e [5] A: No problem. I can teach you.
f [3] A: We can play football.

Check yourself! ✓
- I can understand action verbs.
- I can use collocations with *make*, *play* and *ride*.
- I can use the verb *can* in affirmative and negative sentences.
- I can ask and answer questions with the verb *can*.
- I can make suggestions about what to do.

67

Exercise 1
- Pairs race to do the exercise.

> Answers → student page
> Other action verbs: cook, dive, draw, ride, skateboard, write

Extra activity
- Memory game! Pairs take turns to ask and answer about the picture. Student A: *What's number 1?* Student B: *Act!*

Exercise 2
- Ss do the exercise individually and compare answers.

> Answers → student page

Exercise 3 🔊 2.48
- 💬 After Ss repeat the rhyme, pairs say it to each other. The listener comments on the partner's pronunciation.

Exercise 4
- 💬 Ss work individually. Use the Traffic Lights technique to monitor. Refer Ss to the Writing box on page 66 for help.

> **Answers**
> 2 Leo can't play the piano but he can play football. 3 I can't make a cake but I can make a pizza. 4 You can't play the guitar and you can't sing. 5 They can skateboard and they can run very fast.

Extra activity
- Pairs write a true sentence with *and* and *but* about a classmate. They read it out. The class guesses who it's about.

Exercise 5
- 🔄 Pairs help each other do the exercise.

> Answers → student page

Exercise 6
- 💬 Ss work individually. Before Ss act, check understanding using the Traffic Lights technique. Ss with green and yellow 'lights' compare answers in pairs. Re-teach the students with red 'lights'.

> Answers → student page

Finishing the lesson
- 📖 Read Check yourself! statements for Ss to tick.
- 📖 Discuss how the class can improve, e.g. by reviewing their notes regularly.

> ⏳ **Fast finishers**
> - Ss write more collocations with *make* and *play*.

5.7

In this lesson

Lesson aims:
- Revising Vocabulary, Grammar and Communication from Unit 5
- Pronunciation: /ɑː/ and /æ/

Resources:
- Tests: Language Test Unit 5

Homework:
- Workbook Unit 5, pp. 50–51
- Extra Online Practice Unit 5

Assessment for Learning in this lesson
- 🎯 Setting aims and criteria for success: Warm-up
- 💬 Giving feedback: Exercise 3, 4 and 6
- 🤝 Peer learning: Exercise 5
- 💻 Independent learning: Finishing the lesson

Warm-up
- (*Books closed*) Divide the class into two teams. Ask each team in turn these questions: *1 Say three things you can do in a park. 2 Which character (in the photo story) can fix things?* (Alex.) *3 Can Lucas cook?* (No, he can't.) *4 Say three things we play. 5 Suggest something fun. 6 Respond!*
- 🎯 (L1/L2) Ask Ss to work in groups and write down what they have learnt in this unit. Explain the lesson objectives.

Lead-in
- (*Books open*) (L1/L2) Ask *What are your favourite lessons in this unit? Why?* Encourage Ss to explain.

85

Get Culture

In this lesson

Lesson aims:
- Culture focus: *Kid's London*
- BBC video: *Free time activities* (optional)
- Project: making a leaflet about fun things

Resources:
- Project worksheet p. 180

Assessment for Learning in this lesson
- Setting aims and criteria for success: Warm-up
- Giving feedback: Exercise 3 and C
- Peer learning: Exercise B and the Project
- Independent learning: Finishing the lesson

Culture notes

Hyde Park is one of the biggest parks in London. The lake in the photo is the Serpentine. There are over 4000 trees in the park! You can walk, have a picnic and do sports there.

The river Thames flows through London. The London Eye is a Ferris wheel. It's 135m high. You can take great photos!

You can see dinosaur skeletons in the Natural History Museum.

Warm-up

- (*Books closed*) Write five activities from Unit 5, pages 59 and 61 on the board. Add *have a picnic*, *see a musical* and *see a puppet show*. Challenge the class to explain the new words or do so yourself.
- Pairs order the activities 1–8. (1 = a lot of fun, 8 = not much fun.) Different Ss tell the class and explain.
- (*Books open*) Get pairs to look at pages 68–69 and discuss with the class what they will do in this lesson.

Lead-in

- (*Books closed*) Ask the class *What can people do in London?* Find out what Ss know, if anyone has been there and the places they visited.

Get Culture!
Kids' London

Hyde Park | **The London Eye and the Thames** | **Natural History Museum**

1 Do you know these places in London? What are they? What can you do there?

2 🔊 2.49 Listen and read. Match photos A–D to paragraphs 1–4.

Things to do at the weekend

London is a fun city. There are a lot of things kids can do. Here are some of them.

1 [D] **Go to a museum**
How about the Natural History Museum? There are fun activities for kids: you can make dinosaur T-shirts, see a puppet show or be a scientist for a day!

2 [B] **Family workshops**
Some museums have family workshops. Mums, dads and their kids can draw, paint or make things together. At the Cartoon Museum you can make your own comic!

3 [A] **See a show**
London is famous for its musicals. There are many shows for all the family. You can sing and dance to the songs too.

4 [C] **See the city**
You can see London from the top of the London Eye, or from a boat on the Thames. You can run, play football, skateboard or have a picnic in Hyde Park.

68

3 Read the text again. Circle the correct answer.

Where can you …
1 skateboard?
   in the London Eye capsules / (in Hyde Park)
3 make a comic?
   (at a workshop) / on the Thames
2 sing?
   in the Natural History Museum / (in a musical)
4 go on a boat?
   from the top of the London Eye / (on the Thames)
5 make a T-shirt?
   (at the Natural History Museum) / at the Cartoon Museum

4 🔊 2.50 Listen and write where the people are. Choose from the places in the box.

| A puppet show. | A drawing workshop. |
| ~~The London Eye.~~ | A musical. |

1	*The London Eye.*
2	*A drawing workshop.*
3	*A musical.*
4	*A puppet show.*

5 Work in pairs. What can kids do where you live? Make a list and compare with other students' lists. Whose list is the longest?

Exercise 1
- Collect Ss' ideas on the board. (See Culture notes.)
- Point at the last photo and check whether Ss understand *museum*. Elicit *dinosaur*.

Exercise 2 🔊 2.49
- Ss say what they can see in the photos. Use Photo D to teach *scientist*.
- Ask Ss to deduce the meaning of *activity*, *workshop* and *comic* from the context.

Answers → student page

Exercise 3
- 💬 Use the Basketball technique to check answers.

Answers → student page

Exercise 4 🔊 2.50
- First, pause after each speaker. Pairs discuss and note the answers.

Answers → student page

Extra activity
- Pairs use the Internet at home / in class to find out about another place to visit in London. They make notes and tell the class.

Exercise 5
- Set a time limit, e.g. 2 minutes. Ask Ss to compare their lists with another pair and to agree on one list. Ask Ss to tell the class.

Free time activities

A ▶29 Watch the video and answer the presenter's questions. Which of these activities is not in the video? Circle the correct answer a, b, c or d.

a boxing   b skateboarding   (c) swimming   d ice-skating

B ▶29 Watch the video again and circle T (true) or F (false). Use the information from the video, not what you know.

1 You can ride a BMX bike in Rom Park. (T) / F
2 You can't ride a scooter in Rom Park. T / (F)
3 You can climb without a special hat. T / (F)
4 Boxing isn't a sport. T / (F)
5 Sports can help you make new friends. (T) / F

C Discuss in pairs. Which of the sports or activities in the video can you do? Which would you like to do?

PROJECT

- Work in pairs. Make a leaflet about the fun things visitors can do in your area.
- Take photos of the places or find them on the Internet.
- Write about places with fun activities for kids and their families. Use these questions to help you.
  - What kind of places are they?
  - Where are they?
  - What can people do there?
- Put the photos and text together on the leaflet.
- Share your leaflet with the class.

Fun things to do in ...*

* This is ...
* It is in/near/next to/at ...
* You can play football / skateboard / see a film there.

*Add the name of the place where you live.

69

BBC video

Video script → see Teacher's Book p. 139

Presenter's questions
1 (00:06) What's your favourite weekend activity? Is it skateboarding? Are you a good cook? Or is it playing computer games?
2 (00:42) Can you skateboard?
3 (01:30) Can you name this sport?
4 (1:51) How many sports can you remember from the video?

Note: if you can't show the video, spend more class time on preparing the Project.

Exercise A ▶29
- Point at the photo and ask *Can you do that?*
- Ss read the question. Then play the video.
- First, pause after each of the presenter's questions and ask the class for their ideas.

Answers
Question 3: ice-skating
Question 4: Six (skateboarding, riding a (BMX) bike, riding a scooter, climbing, boxing, ice-skating)

- Then check the answer to Exercise A.

Answer → student page

Exercise B ▶29
- After Ss watch and choose, they compare their answers with three other Ss.

Answers → student page

Exercise C
- Use the Lollipop Stick technique to choose different Ss to explain their answers.

Project

Setting the project up
- Allocate at least 10 minutes for setting up the project.
- Ask Ss to read the instructions.
- Pairs use the list they made in Exercise 5 to help them choose 2–3 fun things for visitors. They note where people do the things.
- Ask pairs to decide how they are going to find photos, when/where they are going to write their text and design the leaflet. Encourage them to work together rather than divide tasks.
- Give Ss the Project worksheets to help them prepare.
- Choose how the leaflet will be shared: via the class projector, a file sharing service, email or on the school website.
- If your class can't make digital leaflets, ask Ss to prepare paper ones. Follow the same steps for setting up the project, but ask Ss to draw pictures, to make their leaflet from paper and to write by hand.
- Set a date for Ss to share their leaflet with the class.

Sharing the project
- Before Ss share their leaflets with the class, give them some time to practise. Make sure everybody is involved. Take notes. You could comment on design, interest, accuracy, pronunciation. Remember to praise first.
- **Critical thinking** Have a class vote for the best designed or most interesting leaflet. Encourage different Ss to explain their choice.

Finishing the lesson
- The class tells you what they enjoyed most and why.
- Check what Ss have learnt in this lesson using Three Facts and a Fib technique.

Fast finishers
- Ss write sentences to describe any of the photos in this lesson.

87

6.1

In this lesson

Lesson aims:
- Vocabulary: daily activities

Resources:
- Vocabulary worksheet 6.1, p. 150
- Tests: Vocabulary Check 6.1

Homework:
- Workbook Unit 6, p. 52

Assessment for Learning in this lesson
- Setting aims and criteria for success: Warm-up
- Giving feedback: Exercise 1 and 3
- Peer learning: Lead-in, Exercise 4 and 5
- Independent learning: Finishing the lesson

Warm-up

- (*Books closed*) Play *Bingo!* Draw a 3 x 3 grid on the board. Ss copy and choose action verbs from page 59 to write in each square. Read the words at random. Ss listen and mark the words they have got in their grids. The student who has marked all squares in a row – vertically, horizontally or diagonally – shouts *Bingo!* and wins the game. You can ask Ss to make new grids and repeat the game.
- Write *My day* on the board. Then ask pairs to predict what they will learn.
- (L1/L2) Explain the lesson objective. Then ask Ss to predict what they will be able to say in English at the end of the lesson.

Lead-in

- (*Books closed*) Challenge the class to use the Think – Pair – Share technique to tell you some things they do every day. Collect the ideas on the board. If Ss don't have enough vocabulary, they can mime. Encourage strong Ss to help.

---

6 My day

In this unit

Vocabulary
- Daily activities
- Days of the week
- Months

Grammar
- Present Simple affirmative
- Adverbs of frequency

▶ 30–31 6.2 Grammar video
▶ 32 6.2 Grammar animation
▶ 33 6.3 Grammar animation
▶ 34 6.4 Communication video

70

Vocabulary I can talk about daily activities.

1 Which of these activities do you do every day?

go to school   have lunch   do (my) homework
watch TV   go to bed

I know that!

get up – go to school – listen to music – hang out with my friends – go to bed – watch TV – tidy my room – do my homework

START → FINISH

Exercise 1
- Draw a clock showing one o'clock on the board. Mime *have lunch* and say *I know that!* with a thumbs up gesture. Encourage Ss to continue. Use the Thumbs up/down technique after each word to check which activities Ss do every day.

Exercise 2 ◀)) 3.1
- Play the recording, pausing after each word. Ss repeat the words and look for the corresponding pictures. Each time ask a student to hold up his/her book and point to the picture or, if there isn't a picture, to mime the word.

Answers → student page

Exercise 3
- Pairs race to do the exercise.
- Use the Lollipop Stick technique to choose different Ss to say each answer.

Answers → student page

Exercise 4
- After individuals do the exercise, they compare answers with a partner. Then ask different Ss to spell each answer.

Answers → student page

6.1

2 🔊 3.1 Listen and repeat. Which expressions can you find in the pictures on page 70?

Vocabulary — Daily activities

do my homework   get up   go to bed
go to school   hang out with my friends
have a shower   have breakfast   have dinner
have lessons   have lunch   listen to music
tidy my room   watch TV

3 Circle the correct answer.
1 get /(go) to bed
2 have /(get) up
3 (tidy)/ listen to my room
4 (have)/ go lessons
5 watch /(listen) to music
6 take /(watch) TV
7 (do)/ have my homework
8 take /(hang out) with my friends

4 Complete the expressions with the words in the box.

lessons   dinner   a shower   breakfast   ~~lunch~~

have:
1 lunch
2 a shower
3 breakfast
4 lessons
5 dinner

LOOK!
have breakfast/lunch/dinner
have **a** shower
have lesson**s**

5 🔊 3.2 Listen and write the activity in your notebook. Use the Vocabulary box to help you.
1 watch TV

6 Number the activities in the order you do them on a typical day. Read your lists in pairs. Are they the same?
☐ have dinner   ☐ get up (1)
☐ have lessons   ☐ have breakfast
☐ go to school   ☐ go to bed
☐ do my homework   ☐ have lunch

7 Look at the pictures. Write the activity. 
1 hang out with my friends 
2 go to school 
3 have a shower 
4 listen to music 
5 get up 
6 tidy my room

8 In pairs, play the board game on page 70.

1 Throw a dice.
2 Go forward.
3 If there's a picture on the square, name the activity.
  • **Correct answer:** stay there.
  • **Wrong answer:** go back two squares.
4 Go to the FINISH first to win!

9 Put the daily activities in the Vocabulary box into groups.

I remember that!

:) My favourite activities: …
:(Activities I don't like: …

71

Look!
• Ask the class *What verb do we use with the words in Exercise 4?* (*Have.*)
• Point out the letters in red in the box.
• Tell Ss we don't use *a* before meals.

Exercise 5 🔊 3.2
• Alternatively, pairs discuss each answer and all Ss write them on response cards.
• Ask different Ss to justify each answer.

Answers
2 go to school 3 have dinner 4 go to bed
5 have a shower 6 get up

Exercise 6
• **Critical thinking** After Ss number individually, they read their lists to each other and discuss any differences. Encourage pairs to explain differences to the class.

Exercise 7
• Challenge strong Ss not to look at the Vocabulary box.
• Ask different Ss to write the answers on the board.

Answers → student page

Exercise 8
• Tell Ss they can earn an extra point if they land on an empty square. They do this by naming an activity that can follow the activity in the preceding picture, e.g. *have breakfast* in the first empty square.
• Challenge a strong class by teaching them *It's my/your turn*.

Exercise 9
• **Critical thinking** Ss write in their notebooks. They explain their ideas to a partner. Tell them to justify their ideas.

Extra activity
• Ss tell a new partner which their favourite activities are and which they don't like. They say two things that aren't true. The partner guesses which.

Finishing the lesson
• 📘 Ss look at the predictions they made in the Warm-up and circle the new words in the Vocabulary box they have learnt.
• 🎓 Ask *Can you say what you do every day?* Students show self-assessment response cards (☺, 😐, ☹).
• 🎓 Ss copy the objective into their notebooks and draw the emoticon that reflects their progress.

⏳ **Fast finishers**
• Ss label the pictures in Exercise 1.
• (*After Exercise 8 or 9*) Pairs play the board game again.
• (*Books closed*) Ss write all the daily activities they can remember in their notebooks.

6.2

In this lesson

Lesson aims:
- Grammar: Present Simple affirmative

Resources:
- Grammar worksheet 6.2, p. 162
- Tests: Grammar Check 6.2

Homework:
- Workbook Unit 6, p. 53
- Extra Online Practice Unit 6

Assessment for Learning in this lesson
- Setting aims and criteria for success: Warm-up
- Giving feedback: Exercise 2, 6 and 9
- Peer learning: Exercise 9
- Independent learning: Finishing the lesson

Warm-up
- (*Books closed*) Play a game to revise daily activities. Divide the class into two teams. Say a verb or a noun from the Vocabulary box on page 71 to each team in turn. One team member completes a collocation. E.g. T: *Hang.* S: *(Hang) out with my friends.* T: *Lunch.* S: *Have (lunch).* If Ss can't answer or get it wrong, the other team has an extra turn.
- (*Books open*) Pairs look at pages 72–73 and discuss what they will learn in this lesson. Brainstorm ideas from the class. Explain the lesson objective.

Lead-in
- (*Books open*) Different Ss name objects, clothes and verbs in the photos. Use them to check vocabulary as necessary, e.g. *get ready, pancakes, walk*.
- Using gesture and appropriate intonation to support meaning, ask the class *Is there anything strange about the photos?* Ss tell you their ideas.

Exercise 1 ▶30 🔊 3.3
- Play the video. If you don't have access to a computer and projector, play the recording.
- Ask a student to answer.

Answer → student page

- Check the class' predictions about the story. Ss should now understand some things aren't true!

Exercise 2
- Pairs read the phrases and note answers they know.
- Play the video again (stopping it in appropriate places) or refer Ss to the photo story to confirm the answers.
- Check answers using the Basketball technique.

Answers → student page

Exercise 3 🔊 3.4 ▶30
- Play the recording, pausing for Ss to repeat each expression.
- Play the video again. Ss shout *STOP!* when they hear each expression. Alternatively, Ss find and underline the expressions in the dialogue.
- Encourage Ss to think of situations in which they can use these expressions. Explain further if necessary.

Exercise 4
- **Critical thinking** Ss justify their choice. Don't confirm yet!

Answers → student page

6.2 Grammar
I can use the Present Simple in affirmative sentences.

I listen to classical music

Lucas asks Jen and Alex about their daily routine for a school survey.

Jen: I get up early. I get ready for school and I have breakfast.
Alex: Me too. Breakfast is very important. Jen makes pancakes.
Jen: Then we walk to school.
Alex: We're never late for school.

Jen: After school we do our homework. In the evening, …
Alex: I listen to classical music and Jen plays the piano.

Lucas: Come on, guys! Alex listens to classical music! Jen plays the piano! Seriously?
Jen: Oh, Alex. Lucas, let me tell you what Alex really does!

1 ▶30 🔊 3.3 Watch or listen and read. Who makes breakfast? Circle the correct answer.

a Lucas   b Alex   **c Jen**

2 Write *A* (Alex), *J* (Jen) or *A and J* (Alex and Jen).

1 get up early   *J*
2 make pancakes   *J*
3 walk to school   *A and J*
4 do homework   *A and J*
5 listen to classical music   *A*
6 play the piano   *J*

3 🔊 3.4 Listen and repeat. Find these expressions in the story.

Me too.   Come on, guys!   Seriously?

Say it!

4 ▶ **Guess!** Circle what you think Alex really does.

1 gets up *early* / **late**
2 has breakfast *at home* / **at school**
3 plays **computer games** / *football*

5 ▶31 🔊 3.5 Now watch or listen and check.

72

Grammar Present Simple affirmative ▶32 **Get Grammar!**

+	
I	listen to music.
You	listen to music.
He/She/It	listens to music.
We	listen to music.
You	listen to music.
They	listen to music.

I go to bed early.
Hammy goes to bed early too.

6 Circle the correct answer.

I ¹(get)/ gets up early. Alex ²get / (gets) up late. Alex ³have /(has) breakfast at school. I ⁴(have)/ has breakfast at home.

Jen and I ⁵(walk)/ walks to school. After school, we ⁶(do)/ does our homework. In the evening, I ⁷(play)/ plays computer games.

LOOK!
get → gets   watch → watches   tidy → tidies
make → makes   go → goes   have → has

7 Read Lucas's blog. Complete the sentences with a verb in the box in the correct form.

go   hang   watch   play   have
have   get   get

Lucas's blog 
My brother and I are very different. Max ¹ _gets_ up early. I ² _get_ up late. I ³ _have_ breakfast at home but Max ⁴ _goes_ to the swimming pool in the morning, so he ⁵ _has_ breakfast at school. Before dinner, I ⁶ _play_ computer games and Max ⁷ _hangs_ out with his friends. But we ⁸ _watch_ the football on TV together!

8 Tick (✔) the things that you do. Tell your partner. Then listen to your partner and tick (✔) the things he/she does.

	Me	Name: _____
1 I get up early.	☐	☐
2 I get up late.	☐	☐
3 I have breakfast at home.	☐	☐
4 I have breakfast at school.	☐	☐
5 I walk to school.	☐	☐
6 I take the bus to school.	☐	☐
7 I watch TV after dinner.	☐	☐
8 I play computer games after dinner.	☐	☐

9 Look at Exercise 8. In your notebook, write what you and your partner do.

I get up early. Nicola gets up early too.
I have breakfast at home. Nicola has …

Fun Spot

10 Play *Who is it?*

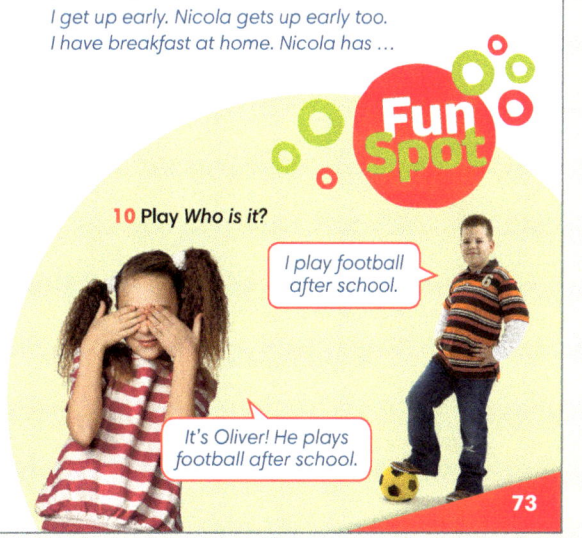

I play football after school.

It's Oliver! He plays football after school.

73

6.2

Look!
- Point out the different third person spellings. Then ask Ss to find and underline all the third person verbs in Exercise 6.

Extra activity
- Pairs predict Lucas' daily routine.

Exercise 7
- Before Ss do the exercise, they read the blog and check their predictions. Explain reading the text before completing will help them understand the context.
- Ask different Ss to write each answer on the board.

Answers → student page

Exercise 8
- After Ss listen and tick, you could use the Thumbs up/down technique to find out how many Ss do each thing.

Exercise 9
- 💬 While monitoring, remember to praise before correcting. Remember you can praise the presentation of written work too. This is a useful way of boosting weak Ss' confidence.
- 🔄 Ask pairs to swap and to review each other's work.

Exercise 10
- Play the game with the class. Challenge the student who guesses by asking the other student to whisper!

Finishing the lesson
- 🎓 Ask different Ss to give examples of Jen/Alex/Lucas' daily routine. Then ask *Can you use the Present Simple in affirmative sentences?* Students show self-assessment response cards (☺, 😐, ☹).
- 🎓 Ss copy the objective into their notebooks and draw the emoticon that reflects their progress.

⌛ Fast finishers
- Ss look at the pictures in the photo story and write down all the words they know.
- (*Books closed*) Ss write down everything they can remember about Jen/Alex/Lucas' daily routine.
- Ss write about a family member's daily routine.

Exercise 5 ▶31 🔊 3.5
- Play the video/recording to check.

Video/Audio script
Jen: Alex gets up late! He hasn't got time for breakfast. We run to school because he's late. In the evening he watches TV and he plays computer games! He never listens to classical music.
Alex: But I'm still your favourite brother!
Jen: That's because I've got only one brother!

Extra video activity ▶30
- Play scene 2. Pause after each character speaks. Hum the intonation he/she uses but don't say the words. Ss imitate you before they practise the scene in pairs.

Get Grammar! ▶32
- Play the Get Grammar! video. If you don't have access to a computer and projector, continue.
- Ss repeat the examples after you in chorus.
- Tell Ss we add *s* to verbs in the third person. Mention spelling is sometimes irregular. (See the Look! box.)

Exercise 6
- 💬 Ss do the exercise individually. Use the Traffic Lights technique to find out how easy/difficult Ss found the exercise. Then ask different Ss to say each answer.

Answers → student page

91

6.3 In this lesson

Lesson aims:
- Grammar: adverbs of frequency
- Vocabulary: days of the week

Resources:
- Grammar worksheet 6.3, p. 163
- Tests: Grammar Check 6.3, Vocabulary Check 6.3

Homework:
- Workbook Unit 6, p. 54

Assessment for Learning in this lesson
- Setting aims and criteria for success: Warm-up
- Giving feedback: Exercise 4 and 5
- Peer learning: Exercise 6
- Independent learning: Finishing the lesson

Warm-up
- (*Books closed*) Pairs say sentences about Alex and Jen's real daily routine. Then they look at Lesson 6.2 to check their ideas.
- (*Books open*) Give pairs time to look at pages 74–75 and to discuss what the lesson will be about. (L1/L2) Then check Ss' ideas and explain the lesson objectives.

Lead-in
- (*Books closed*) Pairs imagine three things Superdug does in the week. Each pair tells another pair. Then different pairs tell the class their ideas. (*Books open*) Ask Ss to look at the pictures in the cartoon to see if any activities are the same as theirs.

Exercise 1
- Ask the first student to find the answer to stand up!

Answer → student page

Exercise 2 3.6
- Before you play the recording, find out which days of the week your Ss know. Explain as necessary and point them out in Superdug's diary in Picture 1. If you wish, use the pictures to teach *a mess*, *free day* and *busy* or encourage Ss to use the pictures and context to understand.
- Ask a student to justify the answer by referring to the text.

Answer → student page

Exercise 3
- Ask Ss to find and underline in the dialogue all the activities Superdug does. Then pairs look at the pictures and decide which activities are not there.

Answers
have dinner with Uncle Roberto, play football, hang out with his friends

Exercise 4
- Ss write their answers on response cards. Ask individuals to justify their answers by referring to the text.

Answers → student page

6.3 Grammar — I can use adverbs of frequency.

The Terrific Two — Dug's busy week

Kit: Dug, your garage is a mess! Can you tidy it, please?
Dug: Sorry, Kit. Today's Monday. On Mondays I always go to the superhero gym.
Kit: How about Tuesday?
Dug: Tuesday isn't a good day. I have swimming lessons on Tuesday.
Kit: OK. Wednesday.
Dug: I usually have dinner with uncle Roberto on Wednesday.
Kit: Thursday? Friday? Saturday?
Dug: I'm often busy on these days. On Thursday I visit my parents. On Friday I play football for the superhero team. And on Saturday we always hang out with our friends.

Kit: How about Sunday?
Dug: But Sunday is my only free day!
Kit: Not this Sunday!

1 Look at the cartoon. Can you see Dug's football shirt? What colour is it? *Orange.*

2 3.6 Listen and read. Which is Dug's free day? *Sunday.*

3 You can't see three activities from Dug's busy week in the cartoon. What are they?

4 Correct the sentences.
1 Dug's ~~kitchen~~ is a mess. *garage*
2 Dug has ~~singing~~ lessons. *swimming*
3 Dug has ~~lunch~~ with his Uncle Roberto. *dinner*
4 Dug visits his ~~granny and grandad~~. *parents*
5 Dug plays ~~basketball~~ for the superhero team. *football*

6.3

Grammar Adverbs of frequency

▶ 33 **Get Grammar!**

■■■■	We always hang out with our friends.
■■■□	He usually goes to the gym.
■■□□	I often visit my grandma.
■□□□	She sometimes has dinner with us.
□□□□	They never get up late.

Adverb + verb	Adverb + *to be*
I always have breakfast.	I am always happy.
They never get up late.	They are never late.

We often watch DVDs
And we always eat popcorn.

5 In your notebook, write how often Dug does these activities.
1 has usually at home breakfast He .
He usually has breakfast at home.
2 sometimes computer games plays He .
3 at home on Tuesday never is He .
4 listens He to music often .
5 gets up He late always .

6 In your notebook, write about Kit's sisters, Lulu and Flo. Use the correct form of the verbs.

1 Lulu and Flo / go to the cinema on Friday. (often)
Lulu and Flo often go to the cinema on Friday.
2 Lulu and Flo / hang out with Kit and Dug. (sometimes)
3 Lulu / go to bed early. (usually)
4 Flo / play computer games. (never)
5 They / be late for school. (sometimes)
6 They / do their homework before dinner. (always)

7 🔊 3.7 Listen and repeat.

Vocabulary Days of the week

Monday Tuesday Wednesday Thursday
Friday Saturday Sunday

8 Complete the words. Tell your partner when Kit does these activities. Which day is missing?
1 watch films — F r i day
2 get up late — S a t u r day
3 cook dinner — W e d n e s day
4 tidy her house — S u n day
5 have a tennis lesson — M o n day
6 go to the gym — T u e s day
Kit watches films on Friday.

9 In your notebook, write sentences that are true for you. When is your free day?
1 always / Monday
I always watch TV on Monday.
2 sometimes / Tuesday
3 often / Thursday
4 usually / Friday
5 never / Saturday
6 always / Sunday

10 Work in pairs. Say one true and one false activity. Can your partner spot the false sentence?
A: *I never get up late. I often cook.*
B: *True, false!*
A: *Correct!*

75

Exercise 7 🔊 3.7
- Tell a strong class this exercise is important to help them with pronunciation. Remind a weak class that repeating the words will help them remember these words better.

Exercise 8
- Make sure Ss realise the days in the column on the right aren't all in the correct order. After Ss write, pairs take it in turns to say sentences about Kit.

> **Answers → student page**
> Missing day is Thursday.

Extra activity
- Ask the class *Who is very busy in your family?* Ss tell a partner about one person and some things he/she does on different days. You may prefer to ask a weak class to first write sentences about the person.
- **Critical thinking** Ask the class *Can we be too busy? Why is free time important?* Have a class discussion.

Exercise 9
- After Ss write, they read their sentences to a partner and tell him/her when their free day is. If you have time, ask some Ss to tell the class.

Exercise 10
- Alternatively, invite different Ss to say true and false sentences to the class. The student who guesses correctly goes next.

Finishing the lesson
- 📖 Read the lesson objective. Ss show self-assessment response cards (☺, 😐, ☹).
- 📓 Ss copy the objective into their notebooks and draw the emoticon that reflects their progress.

> ⏳ **Fast finishers**
> - Ss look at the pictures in the cartoon and write down all the words they know.
> - Ss write more sentences about the cartoon that contain a factual mistake, similar to those in Exercise 4. They read them for the class or another student to correct.

Get Grammar! ▶ 33
- Play the Get Grammar! video. If you don't have access to a computer and projector, continue.
- Ss repeat the examples after you in chorus.
- Draw Ss' attention to the position of adverbs of frequency: after *to be* but before most other verbs.

Exercise 5
- 💬 Ss write individually. Refer them to the Grammar box for help. Use the Traffic Lights technique to monitor. Then ask different Ss to write each answer on the board.

> **Answers**
> 2 He sometimes plays computer games.
> 3 He is never at home on Tuesday. 4 He often listens to music. 5 He always gets up late.

Exercise 6
- 🎨 Pairs use the prompts to write sentences. Remind them to be careful with word order and with third person singular spelling.
- Each pair swaps their books with another pair. They review each other's work.
- Write answers most Ss found difficult on the board and clarify.

> **Answers**
> 2 Lulu and Flo sometimes hang out with Kit and Dug. 3 Lulu usually goes to bed early.
> 4 Flo never plays computer games. 5 They are sometimes late for school. 6 They always do their homework before dinner.

93

6.4

In this lesson

Lesson aims:
- Communication: telling the time

Resources:
- Communication worksheet 6.4, p. 173

Homework:
- Workbook Unit 6, p. 55
- Extra Online Practice Unit 6

Assessment for Learning in this lesson
- Setting aims and criteria for success: Warm-up
- Giving feedback: Exercise 2 and 5
- Peer learning: Exercise 4
- Independent learning: Finishing the lesson

Warm-up
- (*Books closed*) Ss say true sentences about other Ss using adverbs of frequency. The class guess who these classmates are.
- (*Books open*) Pairs look at page 76 and predict what they will learn. (*L1/L2*) Explain the lesson objective.

Lead-in
- (*Books open*) Ss look at the photos and predict what the dialogue is about.

Exercise 1
- Point out Ss just need to find the times, not read all the text.

Answers → student page

Exercise 2 3.8
- Play the video. If you don't have access to a computer and projector, play the recording.
- Use the Lollipop Stick technique to choose a student to explain the answer.

Answer → student page

Extra video activity
- Pairs memorize the dialogue. Then play the video. Pause before each character speaks and elicit his/her lines.

Exercise 3 3.9
- Draw Ss' attention to the use of *at*.

6.4 Communication — I can tell the time.

The film starts at four o'clock

Alex and Lian want to go to the cinema.

1 
Lian: What time is it?
Alex: It's quarter to four. (1)
Lian: What time is the film?
Alex: It's at four o'clock. (2)
Lian: It's too late now.
Alex: Wait, the film is on again at half past four. (3)
Lian: That's better. Let's go.

At the cinema …

2 
Lian: There isn't a film at half past four.
Alex: But it says here there is a film at half past four on Fridays. Oh!
Lian: Exactly! Today's Saturday.

1 Find the times (1–3) in the dialogue. Match them with the clocks (a–c).

a [1]   b [3]   c [2]

2 34   3.8 Watch or listen and read. Why isn't there a show at half past four?
Because the 4:30 show is on Fridays.

3 3.9 Listen and repeat.

Communication — Telling the time

A: What time is it?
B: It's ... four o'clock.

A: What time is the *film/match*?
B: It's at ... ten (minutes) past *four*. 
quarter past *four*. 
half past *four*. 
quarter to *five*. 
ten (minutes) to *five*.

4 Complete the times. Then ask and answer in pairs.

1. 05:40 — It's twenty ___to___ six.
2. 02:30 — It's ___half___ past two.
3. 10:15 — It's quarter ___past___ ten.
4. 03:00 — It's three ___o'clock___.
5. 05:10 — It's ten past ___five___.
6. 07:45 — It's quarter ___to___ eight.

A: What time is it?   B: It's twenty to six.

5 In pairs, make dialogues like those in Exercise 4. Then act them out in class.

1. A: time / the football match?   B: 12:15
   What time is the football match?
   B: time / now?   B: 11:55
2. A: time?   B: 5:40
   B: the party?   B: 6:00

Fun Spot

6 Play *What time is it?* as a class. Ask and answer.
A: What time is it?
B: It's one o'clock. What time is it?
C: It's five past one. What time is it?
D: It's …

76

Exercise 4
- Pairs help each other complete.

Answers → student page

Extra activity
- Ss draw six clock faces with different times. Then in pairs, Ss take turns to ask *What time is it?* and draw the clocks their partner has.

Exercise 5
- Use the Traffic Lights technique to monitor.

Answers
1 B: It's at quarter past twelve. A: What time is it now? B: It's five to twelve.
2 A: What time is it? B: It's twenty to six.
A: What time is the party? B: It's at six o'clock.

Exercise 6
- You can ask Ss to draw big clock faces and hold them up when they speak.

Finishing the lesson
- Ask the class *Can you tell the time?* Ss show self-assessment response cards (☺, 😐, ☹).
- Ss copy the objective into their notebooks and draw the emoticon that reflects their progress.

Fast finishers
- Ss draw clock faces showing different times and write them.

Reading 6.5

I can understand a text about a teenage traveller.

1 Look at the photos and read the first part of the text. Why is this family special? *Because they travel a lot.*

2 🔊 3.10 Read and listen to the text. Circle the correct answer.
1 Réka lives in *Australia* / *(different countries)*.
2 Réka has got a *(brother)* / *sister*.
3 Réka *has got* / *(hasn't got)* a school.
4 Réka hangs out with her friends *in different places* / *(online)*.
5 *Dreamtime Traveler* is Réka's *book* / *(blog)*.
6 Réka's life *is* / *(isn't)* boring.

3 Read the text again and answer the questions.
1 Who is Lalika? *He's Réka's brother.*
2 Who are Réka's teachers?
3 Has Réka got a best friend?
4 What are her two favourite activities?
5 Réka hasn't got a pet. Why?
6 What does Réka watch?

4 What do you like most about Réka's life? Tell a partner.

5 🔊 3.11 Listen and repeat. Find the months in the photos.

Vocabulary Months

January	February²	March²
April	May	June
July	August⁵	September
October⁴	November	December

6 Imagine you travel to different countries like Réka. Plan your journey for a year. Tell the other students about your plan.

Month	Country
January and February	Australia

In January and February I'm in Australia. In March, I'm in …

A day with … Dreamtime Traveler!

Australia – January 2016

1 RÉKA

Réka Kaponay is from Australia, but she lives in different countries! She travels with her parents and brother, Lalika. Today she tells us about her life.

Where's your school?
I haven't got a school! My teachers are my parents and the people we visit.
Who are your friends?
I've got friends in a lot of countries. We hang out online. I haven't got a best friend.
Have you got a pet?
No! I love animals but I can't have a pet. We are always in different places.
What are your favourite hobbies?
Reading and writing! I read a lot and I write my own books. I've got a blog too – *Dreamtime Traveler*. But I also watch TV and films like all teenagers and I love walking and swimming.
Do you like your life?
Yes, I love every day! It's never boring!

2 Machu Picchu, Peru – March 2013 
3 Nazca, Peru – March 2013 
4 Cappadocia, Turkey – October 2014 
5 Paris, France – August 2015

77

Exercise 1
- Pairs discuss. Ask a student to explain the answer.

Answer → student page

Exercise 2 🔊 3.10
- Give Ss time to read the sentences before they listen.
- After Ss listen and read, pairs discuss the answers.
- 💬 Use the Lollipop Stick technique to choose different Ss to justify each answer by referring to the text.

Answers → student page

- You could then ask pairs to find Réka in each photo.

Exercise 3
- ✏️ After Ss write, they swap notebooks with a partner and review each other's work.

Answers
2 Her parents and the people they visit. 3 No, she hasn't. 4 Reading and writing. 5 Because they are always in different places. 6 TV and films.

Exercise 4
- Ss think and note one or two ideas before they speak.

Extra activity
- ⚡ Critical thinking ⚡ Ask *Would you like to live like Réka?* Encourage Ss to explain why (not).

Exercise 5 🔊 3.11
- After Ss do the exercise, they tell a partner their favourite month.

Answers → student page

Exercise 6
- Ss copy the table into their notebooks and plan. Help with vocabulary as necessary.
- Groups of four tell each other about their plans. They choose one plan and tell the class.

Finishing the lesson
- 📘 Read the lesson objective. Ss show self-assessment response cards (☺, 😐, ☹).
- 📘 Ss copy the objective into their notebooks and draw the emoticon that reflects their progress.

⏳ **Fast finishers**
- Ss write true/false sentences about the text.

6.5

In this lesson

Lesson aims:
- Reading: understanding a text about a teenager traveller
- Vocabulary: months

Resources:
- Tests: Vocabulary Check 6.5

Homework:
- Workbook Unit 6, p. 56

Assessment for Learning in this lesson
- 🎯 Setting aims and criteria for success: Warm-up
- 💬 Giving feedback: Exercise 2
- 🔄 Peer learning: Exercise 3
- 🎓 Independent learning: Finishing the lesson

Warm-up
- (*Books closed*) Pairs ask and answer about clubs/subjects at school that they know in English. E.g. Student A: *What time is English on Wednesday?* Student B: *It's at half past ten.*
- 🎯 (*Books open*) (L1/L2) Explain the lesson objectives.

Lead-in
- (*Books closed*) Write *A day with … Dreamtime Traveler!* on the board. Pairs discuss the title and predict what the text is about. Note: *traveler* is American English spelling (*traveller* is British English).

95

6.6

In this lesson

Lesson aims:
- Listening: understanding texts about typical weekends
- Writing: a text about a typical weekend; *before, after*

Resources:
- Tests: Writing Task Unit 6

Homework:
- Workbook Unit 6, p. 57

Assessment for Learning in this lesson
- Setting aims and criteria for success: Warm-up
- Giving feedback: Exercise 2
- Peer learning: Exercise 4 and 7
- Independent learning: Finishing the lesson

Warm-up
- (*Books closed*) Brainstorm questions a journalist would ask Réka. Let weak Ss look at Lesson 6.5. Then pairs roleplay a TV interview with Réka.
- (*Books open*) Pairs look at page 78 and discuss what they will learn. (*L1/L2*) Explain the lesson objectives.

Lead-in
- (*Books closed*) On the board, write W _ _ K _ N _. Ss suggest letters to complete the word. (*Weekend.*)
- Ask different Ss *What's your favourite weekend activity?*

Exercise 1
- Pairs tell the class how their weekends differ.

Exercise 2 🔊 3.12
- This is preparation for PTEYL Firstwords/Springboard, Task Two Listening.
- Before Ss listen, elicit the activities in each picture.
- Ask different Ss to justify their answers.

Answers → student page

Exercise 3 🔊 3.13
- Pairs discuss and complete the sentences before they listen.

Answers → student page

6.6 Listening and Writing
I can understand and write short texts about a typical weekend.

1 Tick (✔) the activities you do at the weekend. Compare with your partner.

1 ☐ tidy my room   6 ☐ sing
2 ☐ play football   7 ☐ play computer games
3 ☐ ride a horse   8 ☐ do my homework
4 ☐ listen to music   9 ☐ have lunch with my family
5 ☐ watch TV

2 **Exam Spot** 🔊 3.12 What is their typical Saturday? Listen and match the names to the pictures. There is one extra picture.

1   2

Brian   Ben   Anna

3   4

3 🔊 3.13 Listen to Ben talking about his weekend. Complete the sentences with the words in the box.

| always   room   ~~usually~~   guitar   bed |

1 Ben *usually* gets up at 7 o'clock on Saturday.
2 Ben tidies his *room* after breakfast.
3 Ben goes to *bed* at 10 o'clock on Saturday.
4 Ben *always* does his homework after breakfast on Sunday.
5 Ben and his best friend play the *guitar* on Sunday.

4 Work in groups. Talk about what you usually do at the weekend. Then tell your class about a student in your group. They guess who it is!

78

---

5 Read Lian's blog. Which is her favourite day? Circle the correct answer.

ⓐ Saturday   b Sunday

My weekend

I usually get up at 8 o'clock on Saturdays. <u>After</u> breakfast I skateboard with my friends. I love my skateboard and I love Saturdays! <u>Before</u> dinner I watch TV or play computer games. I get up at 9 o'clock on Sundays. <u>Before</u> lunch I tidy my room and I do my homework. I always have lunch with my family! <u>After</u> lunch I often draw or listen to music.

Writing *before, after*

lunch
tidy my room   play computer games

Before lunch I tidy my room.
I tidy my room *before* lunch.

After lunch I play computer games.
I play computer games *after* lunch.

6 Underline *before* and *after* in Lian's blog.

7 ✍ **Writing Time** Write about your typical weekend. Use *before* and *after*.

❓ Find ideas
Make a list of what you do.
Saturday: get up late, help Mum, …
Sunday: do my homework, …

✏️ Draft
1 Write a paragraph about Saturday.
 I usually get up at … o'clock on Saturday. I have a shower and I have breakfast. After breakfast I …
2 Write a paragraph about Sunday.
 I always … on Sunday. Before lunch I …

👍 Check and write
Check all *before* and *after* and write the final version of your text.

Exercise 4
- 💬 Before Ss speak to the class, ask them to comment on each other's contributions to the group activity.

Exercise 5
- Ss guess the answer, read and check.

Answer → student page

Writing
- Ss read the information. Challenge them to explain *before* and *after*.

Exercise 6
- Ss do this exercise in pairs.

Answers → student page

Exercise 7
- 💬 Ss write individually. Then they review each other's work using the Two Stars and a Wish technique.

Extra activity
- Display Ss' work. Ss walk round, read the texts and decide who has the most interesting weekend. Vote!

Finishing the lesson
- 🎓 Read the lesson objectives. Ss show self-assessment response cards (☺, 😐, ☹).

Fast finishers
- Ss write sentences about what they do on their favourite weekday.
- Ss write sentences with *before* and *after*.

Language Revision 6.7

Vocabulary

1 Complete the expressions with words in the box. There's one extra word.

> go to   watch   ~~homework~~   listen to   up
> have   my room   friends   school

1. do my _homework_
2. get _up_
3. _watch_ TV
4. go to _school_
5. _go to_ bed
6. _listen_ music
7. tidy _my room_
8. hang out with _friends_

The extra word is _have_.

2 Write three collocations with the extra word in Exercise 1. Do you know any more collocations with this word?

1. _have_ a sh_o_w_e_r
2. _have_ b_r_e_a_k_f_a_s_t
3. _have_ le_ss_on_s_

3 Find and circle the days of the week. Say them in the correct order with your partner. Which day is missing? _Sunday._

jk(Thursday)oi(Tuesday)vb(Saturday)qwe(Monday)op(Friday)mn(Wednesday)klo

4 Answer the questions. Then tell a friend.

1. What month is your birthday? _____
2. What month is Christmas? _December_
3. What month is after February? _March_
4. What month is before August? _July_

Pronunciation

5 🔊 3.14 Listen and repeat: /s/, /z/ or /ɪz/?

Kate get**s** up late and ha**s** breakfast fast,
She watch**es** a film and run**s** for the bus!

Grammar

6 Complete Carla's blog about her typical morning. Use the verbs in the box in the correct form.

> go   get (x3)   hang   have (x3)   listen

I ¹_get_ up at half past seven but my parents ²_get_ up at seven o'clock. My sister, Kate, ³_gets_ up late every day! We ⁴_have_ breakfast together. After breakfast I ⁵_go_ to school with Kate. We go on the bus. Kate ⁶_listens_ to music and I ⁷_hang_ out with my friends. We ⁸_have_ lessons and we ⁹_have_ lunch at one o'clock.

7 In your notebook, write sentences that are true for you.

1. My brother / sister (always)
   My brother always gets up late.
2. My parents (usually)
3. My best friend (often)
4. My granny and grandad (sometimes)
5. My teacher (never)
6. I (always)

Communication

8 Match 1–3 to a–c and make two dialogues.

Dialogue 1
1. _b_ What time is it?   a. OK!
2. _c_ What time is the show?   b. It's five to two.
3. _a_ Let's watch it.   c. At two o'clock.

Dialogue 2
1. _c_ When is the match?   a. It's ten to six.
2. _a_ What time is it now?   b. Yes, let's go!
3. _b_ Let's walk fast then!   c. It's at six o'clock.

Check yourself! ✓
- I can talk about daily activities. ☐
- I can use the Present Simple in affirmative sentences. ☐
- I can use adverbs of frequency. ☐
- I can tell the time. ☐

6.7

In this lesson

Lesson aims:
- Revising Vocabulary, Grammar and Communication from Unit 6
- Pronunciation: /s/ and /z/ or /ɪz/

Resources:
- Tests: Language Test Unit 6

Homework:
- Workbook Unit 6, pp. 58–59
- Extra Online Practice Unit 6

Assessment for Learning in this lesson
- Setting aims and criteria for success: Warm-up
- Giving feedback: Exercise 8
- Peer learning: Exercise 2 and 6
- Independent learning: Finishing the lesson

Warm-up
- (*Books closed*) Divide the class into two teams. Ask each team in turn these questions: *1 Say three daily activities with 'have'. 2 Alex gets up early every day. T/F? (F) 3 Say a sentence with 'She/watch'. 4 Spell 'tidies'. 5 Say what you never do on a Saturday. 6 What time is it now?*
- Ss work in groups and write down what they have learnt in this unit. (L1/L2) Explain the lesson objectives.

Lead-in
- (*Books open*) (L1/L2) Ask *What are your favourite lessons in this unit? Why?* Encourage Ss to explain.

Exercise 1
- Pairs race to do the exercise.

Answers → student page

Exercise 2
- 👥 Ss compare their answers in pairs.

Answers → student page
Other collocations:
have lunch, have dinner

Extra activity
- Play *Chinese Whispers* with daily activities. Ss form lines in front of the board. Whisper a phrase to the students at the end. Each student in both lines whispers the phrase to the person in front of him/her. The Ss at the front write the word on the board!

Exercise 3
- Check the order before Ss speak.

Answers → student page

Exercise 4
- Ask pairs to check who is older.

Answers → student page

Extra activity
- Ss mingle, ask each other *What month is your birthday?* and line up in order of birthday month!

Exercise 5 🔊 3.14
- Challenge Ss to say the rhyme to each other from memory!

Exercise 6
- 👥 Ss work individually. Then they stand up and check their answers with three other Ss.

Answers → student page

Exercise 7
- Alternatively, Ss write their sentences on a piece of paper. Collect them and read for the class to guess who wrote each.

Exercise 8
- 💬 Ss work individually. Use the Traffic Lights technique to monitor.

Answers → student page

Finishing the lesson
- 📖 Read Check yourself! statements for Ss to tick.

⏳ **Fast finishers**
- Ss write sentences about a family member with adverbs of frequency.

5 & 6

In this lesson

Lesson aims:
- Skills practice: Reading, Writing, Listening and Communication
- Exam practice: CYLET and PTEYL

Resources:
- Tests: Skills Test Units 5&6, Speaking Tasks Units 5&6

Homework:
- Workbook Skills Revision 5&6, pp. 60–61

Assessment for Learning in this lesson
- Setting aims and criteria for success: Warm-up
- Giving feedback: Exercise 2 and 3
- Peer learning: Exercise 4 and 5
- Independent learning: Finishing the lesson

Exam Language Bank
- This lists the key language from Units 5–6. Here are some ideas to help you make the most of it.
- Encourage Ss to be independent learners. They tick the words they know and check the meaning of the words they can't remember in a dictionary.
- Ss memorize a section, close the book and write down all the words they can remember.
- Make a quick two-minute test. (*Books closed*) Say different words/expressions in English from one section. Ss write or say sentences with them.
- Fast finishers test each other.
  Student A: *Spell 'Monday'.*
  Student B: *M-O-N-D-A-Y.*
  Student B: *Say two things we make.*
  Student A: *A poster, cupcakes!*

Warm-up
- (*Books open*) Ss imagine they are a celebrity. They tell a partner some things they do every day. The partner guesses who they are!

---

5 & 6 Skills Revision

Reading and Writing

1 Work in pairs. Tell a partner what you and your family can and can't do.
A: *I can play the guitar.*
B: *My granny can't use a mobile phone!*

2 **Exam Spot** Read the ad. What is it about? Circle the correct answer.
(a) A talent contest.   b A London show.

3 Read the ad again. Answer the questions.
1 Who is Meryl? *She's a new star.*
2 What can she do? *She can sing and play the guitar.*
3 How many prizes are there? *There are three prizes.*
4 When is the contest? *It's on Saturday at 10 o'clock.*
5 Where is it? *It's in Town Theatre.*
6 Can dogs come? *No, they can't.*

4 **Exam Spot** Complete Dan's blog with words in the box. There are two extra words.

> can   After   hang   the   get   listen   garden
> room   usually   breakfast   have   ~~house~~

I'm at my cousin Julie's ¹*house* this week. It's in the country. It isn't very big but it's got a fantastic ²*garden* ! My uncle and aunt ³*get* up at half past six. I get up and have ⁴*breakfast* with them and Julie. ⁵*After* breakfast I go to bed again – it's the holidays! Then I tidy my ⁶*room* . Julie and I ⁷*usually* do sports after lunch. Julie ⁸*can* skateboard really well. She's my new teacher! We often ⁹*hang* out with Julie's friends before dinner. Before bed we ¹⁰*listen* to music or watch TV.

5 **Exam Spot** You are at a friend's house for the holidays. Write 40–50 words about what you do. Use these questions to help you.
1 Where is your friend's house?
2 What time do you get up?
3 What do you do before and after lunch?
4 What do you do in the evening?

I'm at my friend's house in (the) …
I get up at … I have breakfast with …
Before lunch I … After lunch we …
In the evening we …

80

'new stars!'
You can be a star too!

This is Meryl. She's a new star! She sings and plays the guitar in a rock band. She can dance too.

What can you do? Show us!
We've got special prizes.

Prize 1 You can be on TV!
Prize 2 Meet a famous band!
Prize 3 Go to a London show!

When: Saturday at 10 o'clock
Where: Town Theatre
Your family and friends can come too!
We're sorry but no cats or dogs.

Listening

6 **Exam Spot** 🔊 3.15 Listen and tick (✓) the correct answer.

1 What can Grace do?
  a ☐   b ✓   c ☐

2 What club is on Thursdays?
  a ☐   b ✓   c ☐

3 What time is the film?
  a ☐ 08:15   b ☐ 07:35   c ✓ 07:45

4 Where is Jill?
  a ✓   b ☐   c ☐

5 What can Uncle Jack do?
  a ☐   b ✓   c ☐

- 🎯 (*Books closed*) Write *Skills Revision* on the board. Ask a student to remind the class what this means. (*Books open*) Ss look through the lesson and tell a partner which activity they are looking forward to most. Remind Ss this lesson will help prepare them for CYLET and/or PTEYL too. (See the Introduction.)

Lead-in
- (*Books closed*) Brainstorm action verbs with the class. Then Ss mime verbs for a partner to guess.

Exercise 1
- When pairs finish Exercise 1, ask the class if they found out anything surprising about their partner and his/her family.

Exercise 2
- This is preparation for CYLET Movers, Reading and Writing Part 3.
- Explain *talent contest* before Ss read.
- 💬 Use the Lollipop Stick technique to choose a student to justify the answer.

Answer → student page

Exercise 3
- 💬 Ss do the exercise individually. Use the Basketball technique to check answers.

Answers → student page

Extra activity
- Pairs make similar posters for a class talent contest! Display them. Ss vote for the best.

Skills Revision 5 & 6

Communication

7 Exam Spot Look at the pictures. Match a–h to 1–6. There are two extra sentences.

1. h
2. b
3. f
4. c
5. d
6. g

a No, it's not a good idea.
b The film's at quarter to five.
c Let's do something fun!
d Let's go skateboarding!
e Swimming? I'm not sure.
f Swimming? Great idea!
g We can ride our bikes!
h What time is it?

8 Exam Spot Work in pairs. Ask and answer the questions.
1 What's your favourite month?
2 Who can sing in your family?
3 What cool things can you do?
4 Have you got a book in English?

Exam Language Bank

Action verbs
act	dive	fly	ride	skateboard
climb	draw	jump	run	swim
cook	fix	read	sing	write

make, play, ride
make a poster
cupcakes
play computer games
football
the piano
ride a bike
a horse

Days of the week
Monday
Tuesday
Wednesday
Thursday
Friday
Saturday
Sunday

Daily activities
do my homework
get up
go to bed
go to school
have lessons
hang out with my friends
have a shower
have breakfast
have dinner
have lunch
listen to music
tidy my room
watch TV

Months
January
February
March
April
May
June
July
August
September
October
November
December

Suggestions
Let's *do something fun*!
Let's *go ice-skating*!
We can *go to the park*.

I agree!
Let's do that!
Great idea!
I'm not sure.
It's not a good idea.

Telling the time
What time is it?
It's *four* o'clock.

What time is the *film/match*?
It's at *ten* (minutes) past *four*.
It's at quarter past *four*.
It's at half past *four*.
It's at quarter to *five*.
It's at *ten* (minutes) to *five*.

81

Exercise 4
- This is preparation for PTEYL Firstwords Task Six / Springboard Task Five, Reading and Writing.
- (*Books closed*) Read the first sentence of the text aloud. The class guesses what the text is about. (*Books open*) Then Ss quickly read and check their ideas. Remind Ss it is important to read the whole text before doing the exercise so they understand the context.
- Ss do the exercise individually. Then they stand up and compare their answers with three other Ss.
- Ask different Ss to explain the answers. E.g. *get* collocates with *up*.

Answers → student page

Extra activity
- Tell pairs to imagine they are now at a crazy friend's house. They imagine and say three things they do. Ask different Ss to tell the class.

Exercise 5
- This is preparation for PTEYL Springboard, Task Six Writing.
- Ss read the questions and make notes. Then they write.
- Pairs work together to review another pairs' texts using the Two Stars and a Wish technique.

Exercise 6 3.15
- This is preparation for CYLET Starters, Listening Part 3 / Movers, Listening Part 4 and PTEYL Firstwords/Springboard, Task One Listening.
- Before you play the recording, ask different Ss to say what they can see in the pictures.
- Ss listen to the recording twice in the test.
- Encourage Ss to justify their answers by referring to key words/ideas they remember.

Answers → student page

Exercise 7
- This is preparation for PTEYL Firstwords/Springboard, Task Four Reading.
- First, ask different Ss to describe each picture in detail.
- Ss do the exercise individually. Then pairs compare answers.
- Choose different individuals to explain the answers.

Answers → student page

Exercise 8
- This is preparation for CYLET/PTEYL Speaking.
- Ss take notes while they speak.
- Then each pair gets together with another pair. Each student tells the other pair about his/her partner.

Finishing the lesson
- Write the headings *Reading and Writing, Listening, Communication* on the board. Read each out. Ss show self-assessment response cards (☺, 😐, ☹).
- Ss write one sentence about what they did well in each section and one about what they could improve.

Fast finishers
- Ss study the Exam Language Bank.

99

7.1

In this lesson

Lesson aims:
- Vocabulary: wild animals

Resources:
- Vocabulary worksheet 7.1, p. 151
- Tests: Vocabulary Check 7.1

Homework:
- Workbook Unit 7, p. 62

Assessment for Learning in this lesson
- Setting aims and criteria for success: Warm-up
- Giving feedback: Exercise 3 and 5
- Peer learning: Exercise 4 and 7
- Independent learning: Finishing the lesson

Warm-up
- (*Books closed*) Ask a student to secretly choose a day of the week and tell the class some things he/she does on it. E.g. *I have two lessons in the afternoon. I often go to Swimming Club.* Ss guess the day. Pairs continue.
- Write *Animals* on the board and ask pairs to predict what they will learn.
- (L1/L2) Explain the lesson objective. Then ask Ss to predict what they will be able to say in English at the end of the lesson.

Lead-in
- (*Books closed*) Brainstorm wild animals with the class. Ss write words they suggest on the board. If Ss suggest a word others don't understand, they can draw it on the board.

Exercise 1
- Pairs write the number of each photo next to the corresponding word. Choose one word from the box, point to the corresponding photo and/or say its number and say *I know that!* with a thumbs up gesture. Encourage Ss to continue.

Answers → student page

7 Animals

Vocabulary I can talk about animals.

In this unit

Vocabulary
- Wild animals
- Pets
- Money
- Adjectives

Grammar
- Present Simple negative, questions and short answers

▶ 35–36 7.2 Grammar video
▶ 37 7.2 Grammar animation
▶ 38 7.3 Grammar animation
▶ 39 7.4 Communication video
▶ 40 BBC Culture video

1 Find the animals in the photos. There is one extra photo.

elephant³   monkey⁵   tiger⁸   giraffe⁴   lion¹
crocodile⁷   kangaroo⁶

Extra photo: 2.

I know that!

Exercise 2 🔊 3.16
- Play the recording, pausing for Ss to repeat each word. Then ask a student to point out the extra photo and to name the animal.
- If your class is weak, ask different Ss to point out all the animals on page 82 and in Exercise 3 as they repeat their names.
- **Critical thinking** Ask the class to say what they think *wild* means and to explain why.

Answer → student page

Exercise 3
- Pairs race to do the exercise.
- Use the Lollipop Stick technique to choose Ss to say and spell each answer.

Answers → student page

Exercise 4 🔊 3.17
- If your class is weak, pause after each sound for Ss to discuss and note the answer. Then ask different Ss to say each answer.

Answers → student page

- Say the names of different animals and ask Ss to produce the corresponding sound.

Exercise 5
- Ss do this exercise individually. Help weak Ss revise action verbs by referring them to the Vocabulary box on page 59, Unit 5.
- Ask different Ss to justify their answers by pointing to the photos in this lesson.

Answers → student page

2 🔊 **3.16 Listen and repeat.** What is the name of the animal in the extra photo on page 82?
Whale.

Vocabulary Wild animals

bird   butterfly   crocodile   elephant   fish
fly   frog   giraffe   kangaroo   lion   monkey
snake   spider   tiger   whale

3 Look at the pictures and complete the words. Use the Vocabulary box to help you.

1. bu_t_ _t_ er _f_ ly
2. b _i_ r _d_
3. _f_ ly
4. s _n_ ak _e_
5. _s_ pid _e_ _r_
6. f _r_ _o_ g
7. _f_ is _h_

4 🔊 **3.17 Listen to the animal sounds. Number the words.** Then check your answers in pairs.

a _5_ bird   d _1_ lion
b _2_ elephant   e _3_ monkey
c _4_ frog   f _6_ snake

5 Read the sentences and circle the correct answer.

1. I can fly!   spider / (bird)
2. I can swim! (whale) / butterfly
3. I'm very tall! frog / (giraffe)
4. I can't jump! kangaroo / (elephant)
5. I've got big teeth! (crocodile) / fly
6. I've got arms and legs. snake / (monkey)

6 The names of the animals got mixed. Write the correct names.

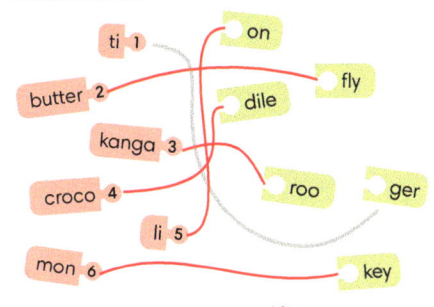

1. _tiger_   4. _crocodile_
2. _butterfly_   5. _lion_
3. _kangaroo_   6. _monkey_

7 Work in pairs. Draw three fantasy animals. Show them to your partner to give them a name.

A: *It's a giraffe and a bird.*
B: *It's a 'giraffird'!*

I remember that!

83

Extra activity
- **Critical thinking** (Books open) Pairs list wild animals they see every day and where they see them. E.g. *Bird – my garden.* They use a dictionary if necessary.
- **Critical thinking** Ss could also use the Internet at school or at home to find out which countries two/three other wild animals live in.

Finishing the lesson
- 📖 Ss look at the predictions they made in the Warm-up and circle the new words in the Vocabulary box they have learnt.
- 📖 Ask *Can you talk about animals?* Students show self-assessment response cards (☺, 😐, ☹).
- 📖 Ss copy the objective into their notebooks and draw the emoticon that reflects their progress.

> ⏳ **Fast finishers**
> - (*Books closed*) Ss write down all the wild animals they can remember.
> - Students work in pairs. (*Book open*) Student A says the number of a photo in Exercise 1. (*Book closed*) Student B says the animal.

Exercise 6
- Challenge strong Ss not to look at the Vocabulary box.
- Ask different Ss to write the answers on the board.

> **Answers → student page**

Extra activity
- Play *Pictionary* with the words in the Vocabulary box. Either play with the class or Ss play in groups of four. If you play with the class, divide Ss into two groups. Ss from each team take turns to come to the board and draw the animal you tell them. They can't write or say anything. The team who guesses first, wins a point. If you play in groups of four, each time a different student draws for the others to guess.

Exercise 7
- The aim of this activity is to stimulate Ss' imagination and to engage them in their learning. It's advisable to set a time limit for this activity, e.g. 4/5 minutes, to focus their attention.
- 🗨 Ask pairs to comment on each other's pictures.
- When Ss finish working in pairs, ask each pair to choose one of their invented creatures and draw it on the board for the class to guess its name.

101

7.2

In this lesson

Lesson aims:
- Grammar: Present Simple negative
- Vocabulary: pets

Resources:
- Grammar worksheet 7.2, p. 164
- Tests: Grammar Check 7.2, Vocabulary Check 7.2

Homework:
- Workbook Unit 7, p. 63
- Extra Online Practice Unit 7

Assessment for Learning in this lesson
- Setting aims and criteria for success: Warm-up
- Giving feedback: Exercise 2 and 7
- Peer learning: Exercise 6 and 7
- Independent learning: Finishing the lesson

Warm-up

- (*Books closed*) Pairs choose an animal and write two or three sentences about it. They use ideas from Exercise 5 in Lesson 7.1. Ss read their sentences to another pair who guess the animal.
- Write *I don't like cats* on the board. Pairs predict what they will learn in this lesson. Brainstorm ideas from the class. Next, Ss look at pages 84–85 and check their ideas. (*L1/L2*) Explain the lesson objectives.

Lead-in

- (*Books open*) Ask pairs to look at the photos and to predict what the story is about. Different pairs tell the class. Don't check *puppy* yet. (See Exercise 1.)

Exercise 1 ▶35 3.18
- Tell Ss they should use the photos and context to understand the photo story.
- Play the video. If you don't have access to a computer and projector, play the recording.
- Ask a student to explain the answer. Then check the class' predictions about the story.

Answer → student page

Exercise 2
- Pairs read the sentences and note the answers they know.
- Play the video again (stopping it in appropriate places) or refer Ss to the photo story to confirm the answers.
- To check answers use the Stand up and Change Places technique.

Answers → student page

Exercise 3 3.19 ▶35
- Play the recording, pausing for Ss to repeat each expression.
- Play the video again. Ss shout *STOP!* when they hear each expression. Alternatively, Ss find and underline the expressions in the dialogue.
- Encourage Ss to think of situations in which they can use these expressions. Explain further if necessary.

Exercise 4
- *Critical thinking* Individuals justify their choice. Don't confirm yet!

Answer → student page

7.2 Grammar

I can use the negative form of the Present Simple and talk about pets.

I don't like cats!

1
- **Alex:** Mum? I want a dog like this! Please?
- **Mum:** Aww … I like dogs but they are hard work, Alex.
- **Alex:** I don't mind!

2
- **Mum:** Can you get up early and take it for a walk? Every day?
- **Jen:** Poor dog! Alex doesn't get up before twelve o'clock at the weekend.
- **Dad:** Big dogs eat a lot.
- **Alex:** But it's small! It doesn't eat a lot.
- **Dad:** Because it's a puppy! These dogs are usually very big!
- **Alex:** Oh, all right.

3
- **Jen:** How about a cat? People don't take cats for a walk.
- **Alex:** I don't like cats! And I'm allergic!
- **Dad:** Look, these are perfect for you! They don't eat a lot and you are not allergic to them.

1 ▶35 3.18 Watch or listen and read. Find a word that means 'baby dog'. — *Puppy.*

2 Read the sentences. Circle T (true) or F (false).
1. Alex wants a pet cat. T /(F)
2. Dad thinks small dogs eat a lot. T /(F)
3. Alex gets up late at the weekend. (T)/ F
4. The puppy in Alex's photo is very big. T /(F)
5. A cat is not a good pet for Alex. (T)/ F

3 3.19 Listen and repeat. Find these expressions in the story.

Say it!
I don't mind!   Poor (dog)!   Oh, all right.

4 ▶Guess! What kind of pet is good for Alex in Dad's opinion? Have a class vote.
a hamster   (b) goldfish   c frog

5 ▶36 3.20 Now watch or listen and check.

84

7.2

Grammar Present Simple negative

I **don't (do not)** get up early.	
You **don't (do not)** get up early.	
He/She/It **doesn't (does not)** get up early.	
We **don't (do not)** get up early.	
You **don't (do not)** get up early.	
They **don't (do not)** get up early.	

▶ 37 **Get Grammar!**

I don't go to school.

6 Circle the correct answer. Then check with the story on page 84.
1. Alex *wants* / (*doesn't want*) a cat.
2. Alex says small dogs *eat* / (*don't eat*) a lot.
3. Alex's mum (*likes*) / *doesn't like* the puppy in the photo.
4. Alex *gets up* / (*doesn't get up*) before twelve o'clock at the weekend.
5. People *take* / (*don't take*) cats for a walk.

7 Complete what Alex says with *don't* or *doesn't*.

1. On weekdays Jen and I go to school but we _don't_ go to school at the weekend.
2. At the weekend Lucas plays computer games but he _doesn't_ play computer games on weekdays.
3. On weekdays Jen gets up early but she _doesn't_ get up early at the weekend.
4. I hang out with my friends at the weekend but I _don't_ hang out with them on weekdays.
5. On weekdays Lian does homework but she _doesn't_ do homework at the weekend.
6. At the weekend my family and I go out for lunch but we _don't_ go out for lunch on weekdays.

8 In pairs, talk about what you do and don't do at the weekend.

I don't go to school at the weekend.

9 🔊 3.21 Listen and repeat. Then label the pictures with the words in the Vocabulary box.

Vocabulary Pets

cat   dog   goldfish   hamster   iguana
parrot   rabbit   tortoise

1. _cat_   2. _parrot_   3. _tortoise_   4. _goldfish_
5. _hamster_   6. _iguana_   7. _rabbit_   8. _dog_    

10 Which pet is good for these people?
Student B: Go to page 108 to help Student A.
Student A: Listen to Student B and decide which pet is good for them.

1. Alex: *goldfish* / (*dog*)?
2. Lucas: *parrot* / *hamster*?
3. Lian: *iguana* / *rabbit*?

B: *Alex wants to play with his pet.*
A: *A dog is a good pet for Alex.*

Student A: Go to page 106 to help Student B.
Student B: Listen to student A and decide which pet is good for them.

4. Granny: *dog* / *hamster*?
5. Aunt Megan: *tortoise* / *parrot*?
6. Jen's friend, Emma: *goldfish* / *big dog*?

85

Exercise 5 ▶ 36 🔊 3.20
- Play the video/recording to check.

Video/Audio script
Alex: A … goldfish? Dad! I can't play with a goldfish!
Jen: Well, it is cute …
Alex: This is not funny …

Extra video activity ▶ 35
- Divide Ss into groups of four and allocate roles: Mum, Dad, Alex and Jen. Play the video. Ss watch their character's actions and body language. Explain that non-verbal communication is very important. After groups act out the story, Ss discuss each other's non-verbal communication.

Get Grammar! ▶ 37
- Play the Get Grammar! video. If you don't have access to a computer and projector, continue.
- Ss repeat the examples after you in chorus.
- Draw Ss' attention to the third person singular auxiliary *does*. Tell them not to add *s* to the main verb in negative sentences.

Exercise 6
- Pairs cover the photo story, discuss each answer and circle. Then they swap books with another pair, who check the photo story and correct their answers.
- Ask different Ss to say each answer.

Answers → student page

Exercise 7
- Ss do the exercise individually, referring to the Grammar box for help. Use the Traffic Lights technique to monitor.
- Ss stand up, discuss and agree the answers with three other Ss. Ask individuals to write the answers on the board.

Answers → student page

Exercise 8
- Give Ss time to think of ideas before they speak.

Exercise 9 🔊 3.21
- (*Books closed*) Brainstorm pets with the class. Ss draw any words that other Ss might not know on the board. (*Books open*) Before you play the recording, ask Ss to tick the words in the box they now know.
- Ask different Ss to say the answers to the matching exercise. After you check the answers, find out what pets Ss have.

Answers → student page

Exercise 10
- Make sure Ss understand that the student who chooses the best pet only does so after listening to his/her partner.

Extra activity
- Ss choose a (new) pet for themselves. They write what it is and why it's a good pet for them. Then they tell a partner/ the class.

Finishing the lesson
- Ask different Ss to remind you of things Jen and Alex don't do on school days / at the weekend. Then ask *Can you use the negative form of the Present Simple?* Students show self-assessment response cards (☺, 😐, ☹).
- Ss copy the objectives into their notebooks and draw the emoticons that reflect their progress.

> **Fast finishers**
> - Ss look at the pictures in the photo story and write down all the words they know.
> - Ss write sentences about what they do and don't do on school days.

103

7.3

In this lesson

Lesson aims:
- Grammar: Present Simple questions and short answers

Resources:
- Grammar worksheet 7.3, p. 165
- Tests: Grammar Check 7.3

Homework:
- Workbook Unit 7, p. 64

Assessment for Learning in this lesson
- Setting aims and criteria for success: Warm-up
- Giving feedback: Exercise 3 and 4
- Peer learning: Exercise 4 and 7
- Independent learning: Finishing the lesson

Warm-up
- (*Books closed*) Ss write three sentences about what a family member doesn't do on a weekday or at the weekend. Then groups of four tell each other.
- (*Books open*) Give pairs time to look at pages 86–87 and to discuss the lesson objectives. (*L1/L2*) Explain.

Lead-in
- (*Books open*) Ask the class questions about the pictures to recycle vocabulary and generate interest. E.g. *Where are they?* (At Dug's house.) *What has Kit got in Picture 2?* (A newspaper/magazine.) *Is Dug happy in Picture 5?* (No!)
- Elicit/Teach *reporter* and *interview*. Point at the reporter and ask *Who is the man?* S: *He's a … (reporter).* T: *Reporters ask people questions. They … (interview) people.* Check Ss understand *foreign (language)* by giving examples.

Exercise 1
- First, pairs predict what magazine Kit is reading.
- Ask the first student to find the answer to stand up!

Answer → student page

Exercise 2 3.22
- Before you play the recording, ask pairs to guess the answer.
- Remind Ss to use the pictures and context to understand.

Answer → student page

Exercise 3
- Ss find each answer in the text before they circle. Then pairs compare answers.
- Ask individuals to justify their answers by referring to the text. Point to relevant pictures to help weak Ss.

Answers → student page

Get Grammar! 38
- Play the Get Grammar! video. If you don't have access to a computer and projector, continue.
- Ss repeat the examples after you in chorus.
- Draw Ss' attention to third person singular questions. Point out the main verb has no *s*.
- Point out question words (*What* in the example) are placed before *do/does*.

Exercise 4
- Pairs help each other complete, referring to the Grammar box for help.
- Use the Traffic Lights technique to monitor. Then ask different Ss to say each answer.

Answers → student page

7.3

Grammar
Present Simple questions and short answers

▶ 38 **Get Grammar!**

?	Short answers
Do I **sing**?	Yes, I **do**. / No, I **don't**.
Do you **sing**?	Yes, you **do**. / No, you **don't**.
Does he/she/it **sing**?	Yes, he/she/it **does**. / No, he/she/it **doesn't**.
Do we **sing**?	Yes, we **do**. / No, we **don't**.
Do you **sing**?	Yes, you **do**. / No, you **don't**.
Do they **sing**?	Yes, they **do**. / No, they **don't**.
What **do** you **do** to relax?	I play computer games.

Does Max watch DVDs to relax?
Yes, he does.

4 Complete the reporter's questions to Superdug with *Do* or *Does*.
1 _Do_ you know Superman? ✗
2 _Do_ you hang out with friends? ✔
3 _Does_ Kit help you? ✔
4 _Do_ you go to the gym? ✔
5 _Do_ you and Kit listen to music? ✗
6 _Does_ Kit visit you at the weekend? ✗

5 In your notebook, write Superdug's answers to the questions in Exercise 4.
1 ✗ No, I don't.

6 In pairs, roleplay the questions and answers in Exercises 4 and 5.
A: *Do you know Superman?*
B: *No, I don't.*

7 In your notebook, write the questions to Kit.
1 you / play the guitar?
   Do you play the guitar?
2 you / listen to pop music?
3 Superdug / eat superhero food?
4 Superdug / watch TV?
5 you and Superdug / hang out every day?
6 Superdug / have swimming lessons?

8 🔊 3.23 Listen to Kit's answers to the questions in Exercise 7. Write them in your notebook.
1 *No, I don't.*

9 Game! Complete the questions. In pairs, ask the questions and mime the answers. Get a point for each correct guess.
1 What _do you do_ (do) to relax?
2 What _do you have_ (have) for breakfast?
3 Where _do you do_ (do) your homework?
4 What _do you do_ (do) after school?
5 What _do you do_ (do) on Friday after dinner?
6 Where _do you hang out_ (hang out) with your friends?

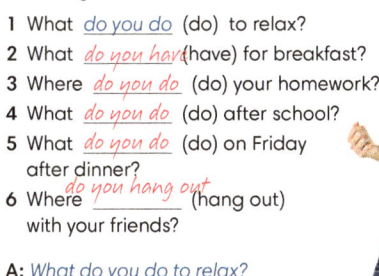

A: *What do you do to relax?*
B: (mimes the answer)
A: *I know! You play the guitar!*

Fun Spot

10 🔊 3.24 🔊 3.25
Go to page 107.
Listen and sing the Questions Song.

87

Exercise 8 🔊 3.23
• Before you play the recording, ask the class to predict the answers.

Answers
2 Yes, I do. 3 No, he doesn't.
4 Yes, he does. 5 No, we don't.
6 No, he doesn't.

Exercise 9
• Check Ss have completed the questions correctly before they ask and mime.
• Alternatively, the class asks different Ss a question. They mime the answer.

Answers → student page

Extra activity
• Ss use the information from Exercise 9 to write a paragraph about their partner on a sheet of loose paper. They write the partner's name on the paper and give you their text. Read out as many texts as you have time for. Ss guess who each is about.

Exercise 10 🔊 3.24 🔊 3.25
• Play the song. Teach Ss some appropriate gestures as they sing.
• When Ss are familiar with the song, play the karaoke version. Ss make the gestures and say the words.

Finishing the lesson
• 🎓 Read the lesson objective. Ss show self-assessment response cards (☺, 😐, ☹).
• 📓 Ss copy the objective into their notebooks and draw the emoticon that reflects their progress.

⏳ Fast finishers
• Ss look at the pictures in the cartoon and write down all the words they know.
• Ss write extra interview questions for Kit/Dug. They could ask the class at the end of the lesson.

Exercise 5
• Ss write their answers individually. Then they compare them with a partner.

Answers
2 Yes, I do. 3 Yes, she does. 4 Yes, I do.
5 No, we don't. 6 No, she doesn't.

Exercise 6
• You could suggest Ss use props, e.g. a notebook and a pen for the reporter and a jacket/jumper over their shoulders for Superdug. If they have time, they could cut two holes in a piece of A4 and make simple head bands like Dug's to hold up as they speak.

Exercise 7
• Pairs use the prompts to write questions.
• 🔄 Each pair swaps their books with another pair. They review each other's work.
• Write the answers most Ss found difficult on the board and clarify.

Answers
2 Do you listen to pop music?
3 Does Superdug eat superhero food?
4 Does Superdug watch TV?
5 Do you and Superdug hang out every day?
6 Does Superdug have swimming lessons?

105

7.4 In this lesson

Lesson aims:
- Communication: buying a ticket

Resources:
- Communication worksheet 7.4, p. 174

Homework:
- Workbook Unit 7, p. 65
- Extra Online Practice Unit 7

Assessment for Learning in this lesson
- Setting aims and criteria for success: Warm-up
- Giving feedback: Exercise 1 and 6
- Peer learning: Exercise 3
- Independent learning: Finishing the lesson

Warm-up
- (*Books closed*) Different Ss imagine something unusual they do after school. The class asks yes/no questions to find out what. E.g. *Do you go to the zoo?* (*Yes, I do. / No, I don't.*)
- (*Books open*) (L1/L2) Explain the lesson objective.

Lead-in
- (*Books open*) Pairs predict where the characters are. Don't answer yet!
- Pre-teach *ticket* if necessary.

Exercise 1 ▶39 3.26
- Tell Ss to use the context to help them understand *guide*.
- Play the video. If you don't have access to a computer and projector, play the recording.
- Ask Ss where the characters are. (*At the zoo.*) Then use the Lollipop Stick technique to check the answer.

Answer → student page

Exercise 2 3.27
- Make sure Ss understand all the expressions in the box before you play the recording.

Extra video activity ▶39
- Play the video. Ask Ss to beep or buzz when they hear *please* or *thank you*.

7.4 Communication I can buy a ticket.

One ticket, please

Dad:	Get a ticket, Lucas. Jen and I have got passes.
Attendant:	Can I help you?
Lucas:	Can I have a ticket to the zoo, please?
Attendant:	That's eighteen pounds fifty, please.
Lucas:	Here you are.
Attendant:	Thank you. Here's your ticket. Would you like a guide?
Lucas:	No, thank you. Just the ticket, please. I've got all the information on my phone.
Lucas:	Where do we start?
Jen:	At the café. I'm so hungry I could eat a horse!
Lucas:	Shh! We are at the zoo.

1 ▶39 3.26 Watch or listen and read. Why don't they need a guide? *Because Lucas has got all the information on his phone.*

2 3.27 Listen and repeat.

Communication Buying a ticket
A: Can I help you?
B: Can I have *one ticket / two tickets* to *the zoo*, please?
A: That's *eighteen pounds fifty*.
B: Here you are.
A: Here's your ticket. / Here are your tickets.
B: Thanks.

3 3.28 Put the sentences in the dialogue in the correct order. Then listen and check.
a [6] Thanks.
b [5] Here are your tickets.
c [2] Can I have three tickets to the aquarium, please?
d [4] Here you are.
e [3] That's twelve pounds sixty, please.
f [1] Can I help you?

LOOK! £ = pound
£4.20 = four (pounds) twenty

4 Write how much it is.

ZOO £ 18.50 — 1 *eighteen pounds fifty* 
MUSEUM £ 8.20 — 2 *eight pounds twenty* 
CINEMA £ 9.30 — 3 *nine pounds thirty* 
CONCERT £ 21.50 — 4 *twenty-one pounds fifty*

5 In pairs, roleplay buying a ticket to the museum. Use the prompts.
A: help / you? *Can I help you?*
B: three tickets *Can I have three tickets, please?*
A: £ 24.60 *That's £24.60.*
B: here *Here you are.*
A: your tickets *Here are your tickets.*
B: thanks *Thanks.*

6 In pairs, act out three more dialogues. Use the tickets in Exercise 4 and the expressions in the Communication box.

88

Exercise 3 3.28
- Pairs help each other to order the sentences.

Answers → student page

Language notes
£1 = 100p (pence). We don't usually say 'pence' when we say the price.

Extra activity
- Play *Noughts and Crosses*. Draw a 3 x 3 grid on the board and write different amounts in each square. Teams need to say the correct amounts to win their 'O' or 'X'.

Exercise 4
- Different Ss write the answers on the board.

Answers → student page

Exercise 5
- Ss use the Communication box to help.

Answers → student page

Exercise 6
- Use the Traffic Lights technique to monitor.

Finishing the lesson
- Say *Can you buy a ticket?* Ss show self-assessment response cards (☺, 😐, ☹).

Fast finishers
- Ss find the phrases from the Communication box in the dialogue in Exercise 1.

I can understand a text about amazing animals. **Reading** **7.5**

1 In your notebook, write names of animals which …
  a swim very well.   b eat a lot.   c can sing.
  a Fish, whale. b Elephant, lion. c Bird.

2 **Exam Spot** 🔊 3.29 Read and listen to the web page about amazing animals. Match texts 1–3 to photos A–C.

Amazing animals!

A — an elephant
B — a giraffe
C — a humpback whale

1 [B] These animals are very <u>fast.</u> They can run at 55 kilometres an hour! They only sleep one or two hours every night. They've got <u>cute</u> faces. They don't drink much water but they like eating. They can eat leaves from tall trees. They eat 45 kilos of food every day!

2 [A] These animals are big but they can run very fast. They love water and they can swim too. They love their families. They are very <u>clever</u> and <u>friendly</u> but sometimes they can be <u>dangerous!</u> They eat plants. They eat up to 270 kilos of food and they drink about 75 litres of water every day!

3 [C] These animals eat a lot of very small fish and are very <u>strong</u>. They can jump out of the water. They like having fun! We can't hear them but they sing and they 'write' songs! Some people think they are <u>ugly</u> but in fact they are <u>cute</u>.

3 Read the text again and complete the table.

	giraffes	elephants	humpback whales
What do they eat/drink?	leaves, water	plants, water	fish
What can they do?	run, eat leaves from tall trees	run, swim	jump, sing, 'write' songs
What do they like/love?	eating	their families	having fun

4 🔊 3.30 Listen and repeat. Then label pictures 1–6 with the adjectives in the Vocabulary box.

Vocabulary Adjectives
cute dangerous fast slow
strong ugly

1 dangerous 2 slow
3 ugly   4 cute
5 fast   6 strong

5 Read the text again. Find and underline adjectives used to describe each animal.

6 🔊 3.31 Listen to two children. Write the animals they speak about.
Speaker 1: kangaroos
Speaker 2: butterflies

Fun Spot

7 Game! Work in teams of four. Your teacher says an adjective. Write as many animals with that quality as you can in one minute. Compare your animals with other teams.
Teacher: *fast*
Team: *giraffe, elephant, …*

89

Exercise 1
- Brainstorm ideas on the board.

Answers → student page

Exercise 2 🔊 3.29
- This task checks reading for gist – a skill tested in CYLET Movers, Reading and Writing Part 3.
- 💬 After pairs match, use the Lollipop Stick technique to choose different Ss to justify each answer.

Answers → student page

Exercise 3
- 🔄 When pairs complete, they compare answers with two other pairs.

Answers → student page

Exercise 4 🔊 3.30
- Ss repeat and point to the corresponding animals.

Answers → student page

Exercise 5
- Ss do the exercise individually.

Answers → student page

- **Critical thinking** Ss say which of the three animals is their favourite and explain why.

Exercise 6 🔊 3.31
- After you check answers, pairs discuss what they remember about the animals.

Answers → student page

Extra activity
- Pairs write two sentences about an animal, similar to those in Exercise 6. They read them to another pair/the class, who can ask just one question about it before they guess what it is.

Exercise 7
- The group with the longest list reads it out to the class.

Finishing the lesson
- 📖 Read the lesson objective. Ss show self-assessment response cards (☺, 😐, ☹).
- 📓 Ss copy the objective into their notebooks and draw the emoticon that reflects their progress.

⏳ **Fast finishers**
- Ss label the animals in Exercise 4.

7.5

In this lesson

Lesson aims:
- Reading: understanding a text about amazing animals
- Vocabulary: adjectives

Resources:
- Tests: Vocabulary Check 7.5

Homework:
- Workbook Unit 7, p. 66

Assessment for Learning in this lesson
- 🎯 Setting aims and criteria for success: Warm-up
- 💬 Giving feedback: Exercise 2
- 🔄 Peer learning: Exercise 3
- 🎓 Independent learning: Finishing the lesson

Warm-up
- (*Books closed*) Throw a paper ball to a student. He/She names a wild animal and throws the ball to a classmate who names another. Continue like this. Ss can't repeat the animal.
- 🎯 (*Books open*) (*L1/L2*) Explain the lesson objectives.

Lead-in
- (*Books closed*) Pairs list the wild animals they saw last time they went to a zoo.

107

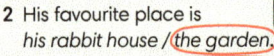

7.6

In this lesson

Lesson aims:
- Listening: understanding texts about pets
- Writing: an email asking a friend to look after a pet

Resources:
- Tests: Writing Task Unit 7

Homework:
- Workbook Unit 7, p. 67

Assessment for Learning in this lesson
- Setting aims and criteria for success: Warm-up
- Giving feedback: Exercise 3
- Peer learning: Exercise 4 and 8
- Independent learning: Finishing the lesson

Warm-up
- (*Books closed*) Pairs mime the adjectives from Lesson 7.5 for the class to guess.
- (*Books open*) (L1/L2) Explain the lesson objectives.

Lead-in
- (*Books closed*) Play *Snowman* using the names of pets from Lesson 7.2. On the board, write a dash for each letter of a word. Ss work in two teams and take turns to guess the letters of the word. Draw a part of the snowman for each wrong guess. (See Lesson 1.1, Warm-up.)

Exercise 1
- Pre-teach *look after*.

Exercise 2 3.32
- Check if any pair had all the animals on their list.

Answers
Pets in the recording: dogs, hamsters, rabbits, goldfish, iguanas, snakes, tortoises

Exercise 3 3.32
- This is preparation for CYLET Starters, Listening Part 3 / Movers, Listening Part 4 and PTEYL Firstwords/Springboard, Task One Listening.
- Ask different Ss to justify their answers.

Answers → student page

Exercise 4 3.33
- Pairs read the sentences and predict the answers before they listen. Tell Ss we often use *he/she* to refer to pets, not *it*.

Answers → student page

Exercise 5
- Ss think and note their ideas before they speak to a partner.

Extra activity
- Ss make a poster about the pet they chose in Exercise 5 and present it to the class.

Exercise 6
- Refer Ss to the text to justify the answer.

Answer → student page

Writing
- Ss read the Writing box and analyse the email.

Exercise 7
- Ss use the Writing the box to help them order.

Answers → student page

Exercise 8
- Ss follow the steps and write individually. Then pairs review each other's work using the Two Stars and a Wish technique.

Finishing the lesson
- Read the lesson objectives. Ss show self-assessment response cards (☺, 😐, ☹).

Fast finishers
- Ss list pets they don't want and explain why.

Language Revision 7.7

Vocabulary

1 Circle the odd one out. Why is it different?
1 a bird   b butterfly   c fly   (d) kangaroo
2 a crocodile (b) snake   c tiger   d elephant
3 (a) monkey   b fish   c frog   d whale
4 a giraffe   b lion   (c) spider   d tiger

2 Write how many of these pets you can see.
1 cats _one_   4 goldfish _six_   7 dogs _two_
2 rabbits _four_   5 tortoises _three_   8 hamsters _five_
3 parrots _two_   6 iguanas _one_

3 Complete the adjectives.
1 stro_ng_   3 danger_o u s_   5 fa_s t_
2 sl_o w_   4 ug_l y_   6 cu_t e_

Pronunciation

4 🔊 3.34 Listen and repeat: /s/.
Sue's snake Simon just eats,
eats and eats.
He sits on the sofa and
steals all the sweets!

Grammar

5 Read the text and write negative sentences in your notebook.

Jason and his family are very different!
Jason wants an iguana. His sister, Jackie, wants a rabbit and their parents want a parrot!
They all watch TV. Jackie and their parents like films and Jason likes cartoons!
At the weekends Jason goes to the park with his friends, Jackie hangs out with her best friend and their parents visit the neighbours.

1 Jackie and Jason / want / a parrot
   Jackie and Jason don't want a parrot.
2 Their parents / want / an iguana
3 Jackie / like / cartoons
4 Jason / go to the park / with parents
5 Their parents / go to / the park

6 In your notebook, write questions and short answers.

1 Jason / want / a rabbit
   A: *Does Jason want a rabbit?*
   B: *No, he doesn't.*
2 their parents / want / an iguana?
3 they all / watch TV?
4 What / Jackie / do / at the weekend?
5 Where / Jason / go / at the weekend?

Communication

7 Read the mini-dialogues and circle a or b.
1 Can I help you?
   (a) Can I have a ticket, please?
   b Would you like a ticket?
2 That's ten pounds ninety.
   a The money's here.   (b) Here you are.
3 Here are your tickets.
   (a) Thanks.   b No, they aren't.

Check yourself! ✓
○ I can talk about pets.
○ I can use the negative form of the Present Simple.
○ I can ask questions in the Present Simple.
○ I can buy a ticket.

91

7.7

In this lesson

Lesson aims:
○ Revising Vocabulary, Grammar and Communication from Unit 7
○ Pronunciation: /s/

Resources:
○ Tests: Language Test Unit 7

Homework:
○ Workbook Unit 7, pp. 68–69
○ Extra Online Practice Unit 7

Assessment for Learning in this lesson
🎯 Setting aims and criteria for success: Warm-up
💬 Giving feedback: Exercise 6
🤝 Peer learning: Exercise 5
📖 Independent learning: Finishing the lesson

Warm-up
• (*Books closed*) Ask different Ss questions about this unit, e.g.: *1 Spell 'kangaroo'. 2 Say something Lucas doesn't do on weekdays.* (E.g. *play computer games.*) *3 Does Superdug have piano lessons?* (*Yes, he does.*) *4 What do you do to relax?*
• 🎯 Ss work in groups and write down what they have learnt in this unit. (L1/L2) Explain the lesson objective.

Lead-in
• (*Books open*) (L1/L2) Ask *What are your favourite lessons in this unit? Why?* Encourage Ss to explain.

Exercise 1
• Pairs race to answer.

Answers → student page
Explanations:
1 Kangaroos can't fly.
2 Snakes haven't got legs.
3 The other three animals live in/near water. 4 Spiders have got eight legs.

Exercise 2
• Ss compare answers in pairs.

Answers → student page

Extra activity
• (*Books closed*) Say true/false sentences about the picture in Exercise 2 for Ss to guess.

Exercise 3
• Ask Ss to spell the answers.

Answers → student page

Exercise 4 🔊 3.34
• After, get pairs to say the rhyme to each other as fast as possible!

Exercise 5
• 🤝 Ss check their answers with three other Ss.

Answers
2 Their parents don't want an iguana. 3 Jackie doesn't like cartoons. 4 Jason doesn't go to the park with his parents. 5 Their parents don't go to the park.

Exercise 6
• 💬 Use the Traffic Lights technique to find out how easy/difficult Ss found this exercise.

Answers
2 Do their parents want an iguana? No, they don't.
3 Do they all watch TV? Yes, they do. 4 What does Jackie do at the weekend? She hangs out with her best friend. 5 Where does Jason go at the weekend? He goes to the park with his friends.

Exercise 7
• First, have a class vote.

Answers → student page

Finishing the lesson
• 📖 Read Check yourself! statements for Ss to tick.

⏳ **Fast finishers**
• Ss write more questions for Exercise 1.

109

Get Culture

In this lesson

Lesson aims:
- Culture focus: *Pets in the UK*
- BBC video: *London Zoo* (optional)
- Project: making a digital photo album of the class'/ your ideal pets

Resources:
- Project worksheet p. 180

Assessment for Learning in this lesson
- Setting aims and criteria for success: Warm-up
- Giving feedback: Exercise 1
- Peer learning: Exercise 3, B and the Project
- Independent learning: Finishing the lesson

Warm-up
- (Books closed) Play *Hot seat* with pet names from Lesson 7.2. Ask a student to sit on a chair at the front with his/her back to the board. Write a pet on the board. Different Ss say individual words associated with the pet to help the student guess it. Allow a maximum of, e.g. 10 words. Ss can't mime, say sentences or make noises. If the student guesses the word, he/she has another turn. If he/she can't, choose another student.
- (Books open) Get pairs to look at pages 92–93 and discuss with the class what they will do in this lesson.

Lead-in
- **Critical thinking** (Books closed) Ask the class *Why do people have pets?* Have a class discussion! (*A pet is a friend; pets help us relax.*)
- (Books open) Pointing at each photo above Exercise 1, ask the class *Is this a good pet for you?* Ss explain why (not).
- Use the photos to explain *unusual* and *exotic*.

Exercise 1
- Use the Lollipop Stick technique to choose different Ss to tell the class their ideas. Encourage Ss to explain.

Get Culture!
Pets in the UK

1 Discuss these questions in class.
1. Which pets are popular in your country?
2. Do you know any unusual pets? What are they?
3. Would you like to have an exotic animal as a pet?

2 🔊 3.35 Listen and read. Match photos A–D to texts 1–3. There is one extra photo.

Pets in the UK
Some people in the UK want an unusual pet. This is why they choose exotic animals. Here are three unusual pets that you can have in the UK.

1 [B] **Tarantulas**
Spiders are scary but some people think tarantulas are pretty. They are quiet animals and they don't need a lot of space or food, so they aren't hard work.

2 [D] **Pygmy hedgehogs**
People like pygmy hedgehogs because they are small and cute. They eat cat food and they eat a lot! This is why they need a lot of space to run and play.

3 [A] **Axolotls**
They've got a funny name and they look funny too. They live in the water. They can be brown, black, yellow, white or other colours. And here's an amazing fact: if they lose a part of their body, they can make a new one!

92

3 Read the texts again and answer the questions.
1. Which pet eats a lot?
   The pygmy hedgehog.
2. Which pet can make new body parts?
3. Which pet needs a lot of space?
4. Which pet doesn't need a lot of food?
5. Which pet can be different colours?
6. Which pet can be scary?

4 🔊 3.36 Listen and circle the correct answer.
1. Which is the number one pet in the UK?
   a Cats.   (b) Dogs.
2. Which animal is number 3 in the list?
   a Rabbit.   (b) Fish.
3. Which are two top names for pets in the UK?
   (a) Alfie and Bella.   b Cookie and Dolly.
4. What's their dog's name?
   (a) George.   b Mrs C.

5 Work in pairs. Imagine you can have one of the animals in photos A–D.
1. Which of the animals do you choose? Why?
2. Think of a name for your animal.

Exercise 2 🔊 3.35
- Tell Ss they should use the photos and context to help them understand the text.
- After Ss listen and read, check whether they can deduce the meaning of any new words, e.g. *lose, need, scary, space*.
- Then pairs do the matching exercise.

Answers → student page

- Elicit/Tell Ss the pet in Photo C is a snail.

Exercise 3
- 📱 Ss answer individually. Then they stand up and check their answers with three other Ss.

Answers
2 The axolotls. 3 The pygmy hedgehog.
4 The tarantula. 5 The axolotls. 6 The tarantula.

Exercise 4 🔊 3.36
- The class predicts the answers first.
- Pause after each speaker. Pairs discuss and note the answer.

Answers → student page

Extra activity
- Pairs use the Internet at home / in class to find out about another unusual pet.

Exercise 5
- Explain each pair must choose just one animal. After, different pairs explain their choice to the class.

The London Zoo

A ▶40 Watch the video and answer the presenter's questions. What do the animals do after breakfast?

After breakfast the animals like to play.

B ▶40 Watch the video again. Write the animals in the box next to the correct sentence. Use the information from the video, not what you know.

| penguins | stick insects | tigers | monkeys | tortoises | lions |

1 They're fast. *tigers*
2 They're slow. *tortoises*
3 They're green. *stick insects*
4 They eat fish. *penguins*
5 They eat meat. *tigers*
6 They love toys. *monkeys*

C Discuss in groups. Which animals in the London Zoo would you like to see? Why?

PROJECT

- Make a class digital photo album of the class pets and/or your ideal pets.
- Create a digital poster about your pet and/or your ideal pet. Write short descriptions. Use these questions to help you.
    - What are they?
    - What are their names?
    - What do they look like?
    - What do they eat?
    - What can they do?
    - What is a fun fact about them?
- Add photos to your descriptions.
- Collect all the posters to make a digital class album.

My pet
- This is my pet *rabbit*. His/Her name's …
- He/She's *cute/clever*.
- He/She eats …
- He/She can …
- Here's a fun fact about *rabbits*: …

93

BBC video

Video script → see Teacher's Book p. 139

Presenter's questions
1 (00:06) Do you like animals?
2 (01:16) Which is your favourite (animal)?
3 (02:05) How many legs does the millipede have? Does it have a) 200 legs or b) 300 legs?

Note: if you can't show the video, spend more class time on preparing the Project.

Exercise A ▶40
- Pointing to the photo, ask the class *What are these animals?* (*Monkeys*.) *Do you like them?*
- Ss predict the answer. Then play the video.
- First, pause after each of the presenter's questions and ask the class for their ideas.

Answers
Question 3: b

- Then check the answer to Exercise A.

Answer → student page

Exercise B ▶40
- Ss write any answers they can. Then they watch and check. Use the Expert Envoy technique to help Ss if necessary.

Answers → student page

Extra video activity ▶40
- Play the video. Ss stand up when they see an animal and try to mimic its posture.

Exercise C
- Ss explain their choices to the class.

Project

Setting the project up
- Allocate at least 10 minutes for setting up the project.
- Ask Ss to read the instructions.
- Explain that each student should make a digital poster about a pet. It could be a pet they own or a pet they'd like to have.
- Give Ss the Project worksheets to help them prepare.
- Ask three or four volunteers to be coordinators. Their job is to collect the digital posters, create the photo album and share it with the class, e.g. upload it onto the school website, share it via a file sharing service or create a DVD.
- Agree with the class how they will give their work to the coordinators. (E.g. a memory stick / email.)
- If your class can't make digital posters, ask Ss to prepare paper ones. Follow the same steps for setting up the project, but ask Ss to draw their pets and to write by hand. Volunteers collate all the pages together to make a photo album or you could make a classroom display.
- Set a date for creating the posters and the photo album.

Sharing the project
- Project the album or give Ss time to look at the display. You could ask Ss to note two questions as they watch/look to ask the pet owners afterwards. Have a class vote for the most informative text!

Finishing the lesson
- The class tells you what they enjoyed most and why.
- Check what Ss have learnt in this lesson using Three Facts and a Fib technique.

Fast finishers
- Ss check any new words in a dictionary.

8.1

In this lesson

Lesson aims:
- Vocabulary: sports

Resources:
- Vocabulary worksheet 8.1, p. 151
- Tests: Vocabulary Check 8.1

Homework:
- Workbook Unit 8, p. 70

Assessment for Learning in this lesson
- Setting aims and criteria for success: Warm-up
- Giving feedback: Exercise 1, 3 and 4
- Peer learning: Exercise 3 and 7
- Independent learning: Finishing the lesson

Warm-up
- (*Books closed*) Ask Ss to imagine they are one of the characters in Unit 7. Ss work in pairs. They ask each other questions to find out their partner's identity. E.g. Student A: *Do you have piano lessons?* Student B: *No, I don't.* Student A: *Are you Kit?*
- Write *I like that!* on the board and mime a few sports. Ss predict what they will learn.
- (L1/L2) Explain the lesson objective. Then write on the board: 1 *I play football.* 2 *He's got long legs.* 3 *Windsurfing is exciting.* Ask Ss to decide which sentence doesn't fit in with the lesson objective.

Lead-in
- (*Books closed*) Brainstorm sports with the class. Ss write words they suggest on the board. If Ss suggest a word others don't understand, they can draw it on the board.

Exercise 1
- Choose one word from the box, mime it and say *I know that!* with a thumbs up gesture. Encourage Ss to continue. Observe whether there are any Ss who find this activity difficult.

8 I like that!

Vocabulary I can talk about sports.

In this unit

Vocabulary
- Sports
- Seasons and weather
- Healthy lifestyle

Grammar
- love/like/don't like/hate + -ing
- Object pronouns
- Question words

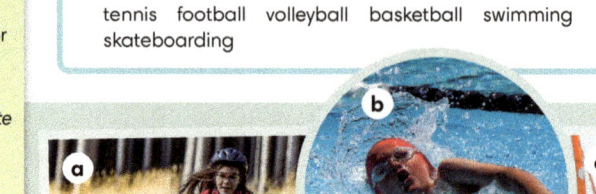

1 Read these words. What do they mean?
tennis   football   volleyball   basketball   swimming   skateboarding

I know that!

94

Exercise 2 3.37
- Play the recording, pausing for Ss to repeat each word and to say the letter of the corresponding photo. Then ask a student to name the sport that appears twice.

Answers → student page

Exercise 3
- This is preparation for CYLET Starters, Reading and Writing Part 3.
- Pairs race to do the exercise.
- Use the Lollipop Stick technique to choose Ss to say and spell each answer.

Answers → student page

- (*Books closed*) Spell five sports and ask Ss to write them on a piece of paper. Ss compare in pairs and correct each other.

Extra activity
- Groups of four play a game! (*Book open*) One student in a group chooses someone in the photos on page 94 and mimics their posture. (*Books closed*) The other students guess the sport to win a point. The person who guesses first, mimics another posture. The game continues until all the photos are used.

2 🔊 **3.37** Listen and repeat. Find the sports in the photos on page 94. One sport appears twice. What is it? *Roller skating.*

Vocabulary: Sports

badminton basketball cycling
football hockey ice-skating roller skating
sailing skateboarding skiing
swimming table tennis taekwondo
tennis volleyball windsurfing

3 **Exam Spot** Write the words. Use the Vocabulary box to help you.

1 tekaodnwo t a e k w o n d o
2 siilang s a i l i n g
3 rloerl kasitng r o l l e r s k a t i n g
4 sktbraoadenig s k a t e b o a r d i n g
5 siknig s k i i n g
6 hoecky h o c k e y
7 bsktbaelal b a s k e t b a l l
8 bdatinmon b a d m i n t o n

4 Work in pairs. Put the sports in the Vocabulary box in groups. A sport can be in more than one group.

Indoor sports: *basketball,* _____
Outdoor sports: *football,* _____
Team sports: _____
Winter sports: _____
Water sports: _____

LOOK!
I **do** taekwondo.
I **go** swimming.
I **play** tennis.

5 🔊 **3.38** Write *go* or *play*. Compare in pairs. Then listen and check.

1	_go_	cycling	7	_go_	windsurfing
2	_play_	basketball	8	_play_	badminton
3	_play_	hockey	9	_play_	table tennis
4	_go_	skiing	10	_go_	sailing
5	_go_	skateboarding	11	_play_	football
6	_go_	roller skating	12	_go_	ice-skating

6 What sports do they do? Complete the sentences with *do*, *go* and *play* and the words in the box.

badminton hockey roller skating sailing
skiing swimming table tennis taekwondo

1 Mario 2 (Sue labeled 3, 4) 5 Peter 6 7 Fran 8

Mario ¹ *plays badminton* at school.
He ² *goes roller skating* at the weekend.
Sue ³ *plays table tennis* at school.
She also ⁴ *goes sailing* with her dad.
Peter ⁵ *plays hockey* .
He ⁶ *does taekwondo* every week.
Fran ⁷ *goes skiing* in winter.
She always ⁸ *goes swimming* in the morning.

7 Complete the sentences with the names of sports. Add *do*, *go* or *play* where necessary.

I remember that!

I never _____ .
I watch _____ on TV.
I think _____ is boring.
I think _____ is great!
I _____ with friends.
I _____ every day.
I often _____ at school.

95

Exercise 4
• 💬 After pairs do the exercise, collect Ss' answers on the board. Ss explain why some sports are in more than one group.

Possible answers
Indoor sports: badminton, ice-skating, swimming, table tennis, taekwondo, volleyball.
Outdoor sports: badminton, basketball, cycling, football, hockey, ice-skating, roller skating, sailing, skateboarding, skiing, swimming, tennis, volleyball, windsurfing.
Team sports: basketball, football, hockey, sailing, volleyball.
Winter sports: hockey, ice-skating, skiing.
Water sports: sailing, swimming, windsurfing.

Look!
• **Critical thinking** Ask pairs if they can suggest a rule for using *go*, *do* and *play* + sports.

Language notes
We usually use *play* with team sports involving a ball and a competitive element; *go* with activities ending –*ing* where we actually go somewhere to do it; and *do* with individual activities such as martial arts.

Exercise 5 🔊 3.38
• After Ss listen and check, they look at the phrases once again. Ask them whether everything is clear and explain further if necessary.

Answers → student page

• (*Books closed*) Read sports and ask Ss to say the corresponding verbs in chorus.

Exercise 6
• Make sure Ss understand that each person is wearing clothes that represent two sports.
• Remind Ss they will need to use the Present Simple in the third person singular.
• Ask different Ss to write the answers on the board and to justify them.

Answers → student page

Exercise 7
• 🔄 Each student swaps books with another student. They review each other's work. Next, pairs get together. Groups of four tell each other their ideas. Encourage strong Ss to agree, disagree and to express surprise. You could write relevant 'Say it' expressions on the board to help, e.g. Unit 6: *Me too. / Seriously?*

Finishing the lesson
• 📖 Ss look at the predictions they made in the Warm-up and circle the new words in the Vocabulary box they have learnt.
• 🗣 Ask *Can you talk about sports?* Students show self-assessment response cards (☺, 😐, ☹).
• 📖 Ss copy the objective into their notebooks and draw the emoticon that reflects their progress.

⏳ Fast finishers
• (*Books closed*) Ss draw a character wearing clothes for two different sports and write two sentences about him/her, using Exercise 6 as a model.

113

8.2
In this lesson

Lesson aims:
- Grammar: *love/like/don't like/hate + -ing*; object pronouns

Resources:
- Grammar worksheet 8.2, p. 166
- Tests: Grammar Check 8.2

Homework:
- Workbook Unit 8, p. 71
- Extra Online Practice Unit 8

Assessment for Learning in this lesson
- Setting aims and criteria for success: Warm-up
- Giving feedback: Exercise 2, 8 and 9
- Peer learning: Exercise 6 and 10
- Independent learning: Finishing the lesson

Warm-up
- (*Books closed*) Ss write two sentences like those in Lesson 8.1, Exercise 7 on a slip of paper. Collect and read the sentences for the class to guess who they are about.
- (*Books open*) Ss discuss what they will learn. (*L1/L2*) Explain the lesson objectives.

Lead-in
- (*Books open*) Ask pairs to look at the photos and to predict what the story is about. (*Choosing a summer camp.*)

Exercise 1 ▶41 🔊 3.39
- Play the video. If you don't have access to a computer and projector, play the recording.
- Ask Ss to explain/mime the answers. Elicit *getting wet* too.

Answer → student page

Exercise 2
- Ss note the answers they know.
- Play the video again (stopping it in appropriate places) or refer Ss to the photo story to confirm the answers.
- Ss write their answers on response cards.

Answers → student page

8.2 Grammar
I can use verbs *love/like/don't like/hate + -ing* and use object pronouns.

Let's go to summer camp!

Lian: Hey guys, do you want to go to summer camp with me?
Alex: Maybe. What do you do there?
Lian: Horse-riding, rock climbing … I like rock climbing.
Jen: I don't like it!
Lian: How about water sports? There's sailing, windsurfing …
Alex: No, thanks. I don't like getting wet.
Jen: That's true. Lian, you like sports. We like them, but we want to do other things too. Cooking, for example?
Lian: There's a cooking camp in …
Alex: No, thanks. I love eating but I hate cooking!
Lian: Let's find a camp we all like.

1 ▶41 🔊 3.39 Watch or listen and read. Find two sports in the dialogue that are not in the Vocabulary box on p. 95.
Horse-riding and rock-climbing.

2 Read the dialogue again. Complete the sentences with one word.
1 Lian wants to go to <u>summer</u> camp.
2 <u>Jen</u> doesn't like rock climbing.
3 Sailing and windsurfing are <u>water</u> sports.
4 Windsurfing is not a good sport for <u>Alex</u>.
5 Jen wants to go to a <u>cooking</u> camp but Alex doesn't.

3 🔊 3.40 Listen and repeat. Find these expressions in the dialogue.

> Maybe.   That's true.   **Say it!**

4 ▶ **Guess!** Look at the summer camp brochures. Which camp is good for all three of them? Circle a, b or c.
a tech camp   **b** fun camp   c sports camp

5 ▶42 🔊 3.41 Now watch or listen and check.

96

Exercise 3 🔊 3.40 ▶41
- Play the recording, pausing for Ss to repeat each expression.
- Play the video again. Ss shout *STOP!* when they hear each expression. Alternatively, Ss find and underline the expressions in the dialogue.
- Encourage Ss to think of situations in which they can use these expressions.

Exercise 4
- **Critical thinking** Individuals justify their choice. Don't confirm yet!

Answer → student page

Exercise 5 ▶42 🔊 3.41
- Play the video/recording to check.

Video/Audio script
Alex: How about tech camp? It sounds good!
Jen: No …
Lian: Look here!
Jen: Not another sports camp!
Lian: No, not the sports camp. The fun camp. There are lots of different activities.
Jen: That's good!
Alex: Hang on! What time do you get up at summer camp?
Lian: Early?
Alex: No, thanks! But you can go. Have fun!
Jen: Oh, Alex!

8.2

Grammar
love/like/don't like/hate + -ing

| I **love** eat**ing**. |
| I **don't like** gett**ing** wet. |
| I **hate** cook**ing**. |
| **Do** you **like** cycl**ing**? Yes, I do. / No, I don't. |
| What **do** you **like** do**ing**? I **like** cook**ing**. |

▶ 43 **Get Grammar!**

Hammy hates getting wet!

6 Read the dialogue on page 96 again. Complete the sentences with *likes, doesn't like, loves* or *hates*.

1 Jen _doesn't like_ rock climbing.
2 Lian _likes_ rock climbing.
3 Alex _doesn't like_ getting wet.
4 Alex _loves_ eating but he _hates_ cooking.

7 Look at the photos. Write true sentences in your notebook. Use *love, like, don't like* or *hate + -ing*.

| get up   draw   play   swim |
| cook   do homework |

1 *I like playing computer games.*

8 🔊 3.42 What do these people like or don't like doing? Listen and circle T (true) or F (false).

1 She doesn't like playing volleyball.   T /**F**
2 Brian likes swimming.   T /**F**
3 She hates getting up early.   **T**/ F
4 They love skateboarding.   **T**/ F
5 Jake doesn't like playing football.   T /**F**

Grammar Object pronouns

I → me	he → him	we → us
you → you	she → her	you → you
	it → it	they → them

She is a good friend. I like **her**.
You don't like **sports**. We love **them**.

9 Read Lian's email. Circle the correct answer.

My friend, Alex, loves fixing computers. ¹(**He**)/ Him knows a lot of things about ²they /(**them**) I don't, so I usually ask ³he /(**him**) for help. ⁴(**We**)/ Us often hang out with his sister, Jen. I like ⁵she /(**her**) a lot. Jen loves making cupcakes. ⁶(**They**)/ Them are amazing! Alex and I love chocolate so ⁷(**she**)/ her often makes chocolate cupcakes for ⁸we /(**us**).

10 Write about your friends or family. What do they *love/like/don't like/hate doing*? Use Lian's email in Exercise 9 to help you.

My friend, …, likes … He/She knows a lot of things about …

97

Exercise 8 🔊 3.42
- Play the recording once and ask Ss to do the activity individually.
- 💬 Play the recording again, but stop it after each dialogue. Use the Stand up and Change Places technique to check answers.

Answers → student page

Grammar
- Ask Ss to analyse the Grammar box in pairs.
- Point out *you* and *it* are the same form as the object pronouns they correspond to.
- **Critical thinking** Ask the class to tell you why we use object pronouns. (*To avoid repetition / to be clear.*) Point out we must use them. Write on the board: A: *You don't like sports.* B: *We love.* ✗ *We love them.* ✓

Exercise 9
- Pairs help each other answer.
- 💬 Use the Traffic Lights technique to find out how easy/difficult Ss found the exercise. Re-teach/Explain as necessary. E.g. write Lian's email on the board with the correct answers. Then ask different Ss to draw a line between each object pronoun and the object it replaces. E.g. link *computers* in the first sentence to *them* in sentence two.

Answers → student page

Exercise 10
- Ss review each other's work, using the Two Stars and a Wish technique.

Finishing the lesson
- Ask the class *Can you use 'love'/'like'/'don't like'/'hate'? Can you use object pronouns?* Ss show self-assessment response cards (☺, ☺, ☹).
- Ss copy the objectives into their notebooks and draw the emoticons that reflect their progress.

⌛ Fast finishers
- Ss find and underline the object pronouns in the photo story. (*Me, it, them.*)

Get Grammar! ▶ 43
- Play the Get Grammar! video. If you don't have access to a computer and projector, continue.
- Ss repeat the examples after you in chorus.
- Ask Ss to read the Grammar box and elicit what verb form is used after activity verbs expressing general likes/dislikes, e.g.: *love, like, don't like, hate.* (Verb + *-ing*.)

Exercise 6
- Pairs cover the photo story, discuss each answer and write. Then they swap books with another pair, who check the photo story and correct their answers.

Answers → student page

Exercise 7
- Ss do the exercise individually, referring to the Grammar box for help.

Possible answers
I love/like/don't like/hate (2) cooking / (3) doing homework / (4) getting up / (5) swimming / (6) drawing.

Extra video activity ▶ 42
- Play the ending of the story. Pairs watch, then write an alternative ending and act it out for the class. Vote for the most creative!

Extra activity
- Groups of four invent a summer camp, list the activities it offers and make a leaflet.

115

8.3

In this lesson

Lesson aims:
- Grammar: question words

Resources:
- Grammar worksheet 8.3, p. 167
- Tests: Grammar Check 8.3

Homework:
- Workbook Unit 8, p. 72

Assessment for Learning in this lesson
- 🎯 Setting aims and criteria for success: Warm-up
- 💬 Giving feedback: Exercise 3 and 5
- 🌐 Peer learning: Exercise 4 and 7
- 💻 Independent learning: Finishing the lesson

Warm-up
- (*Books closed*) Ss write true and false sentences about themselves with *love/like/don't like/hate* and read them to a partner who says *True* or *False*.
- 🎯 (*Books open*) Pairs look at pages 98–99 and discuss what they will learn. (*L1/L2*) Explain the lesson objective.

Lead-in
- (*Books open*) Ask the class questions about the pictures to recycle vocabulary and generate interest. E.g. *Describe the woman and her clothes.* (*She's got sports clothes.*) *What sport does she like?* (*Tennis.*) *Are they happy in Picture 2?* (*Yes.*) *Is Dug happy in picture 5?* (*No!*) Ss predict why Dug isn't happy.
- Use the photo to check *(ask for an) autograph*, or encourage Ss to guess from the context after they listen and read.

Exercise 1
- Ask the first student to find the answer to stand up!

Answer → student page

8.3 Grammar — I can ask detailed questions.

The Terrific Two — Dug's sports hero

1 Look at the cartoon. Who has got a mobile phone in the story? *Superdug and Irina.*

2 🔊 3.43 Listen and read. Who is Irina Peters? *She's a tennis champion.*

3 Read the sentences. Circle T (true) or F (false).
1. Irina wants Dug's autograph. T / **F**
2. Irina is Superdug's fan. **T** / F
3. Kit doesn't know who Irina Peters is. T / **F**
4. Dug's got the wrong phone. **T** / F
5. Dug doesn't know where his phone is. **T** / F

Exercise 2 🔊 3.43
- Before you play the recording, ask pairs to guess the answer.
- After, ask a student to refer to the text to justify the answer.

Answer → student page

Exercise 3
- Ss work individually, referring to the text.
- 🏀 Use the Basketball technique to check answers.

Answers → student page

Extra activity
- Pairs imagine what happens next in the cartoon story. They write a dialogue together, e.g. between Irina Peters, Dug and Kit. Pairs act it out for a different pair and/or the class.

Get Grammar! ▶44
- Play the Get Grammar! video. If you don't have access to a computer and projector, continue.
- Ss repeat the examples after you in chorus.
- Write these words on the board in this order: *numbers/time/place/possession/people/objects or information*. Then challenge the class to match the words to the question words in the Grammar box. (Numbers – *how many*, time – *when*, place – *where*, possession – *whose*, people – *who*, objects or information – *what*.)

8.3

Grammar Question words

▶ 44 **Get Grammar!**

Who is Dug's sports hero?	It's **Irina Peters**.
What have you got there?	I've got **Irina's autograph**.
When is the game?	It's **on Tuesday**.
Where does she live?	She lives **in London**.
Whose phone is it?	It's **Irina's** phone.
How many photos have you got?	I've got **80** photos.

Where does she live? — *She lives in Hong Kong.*

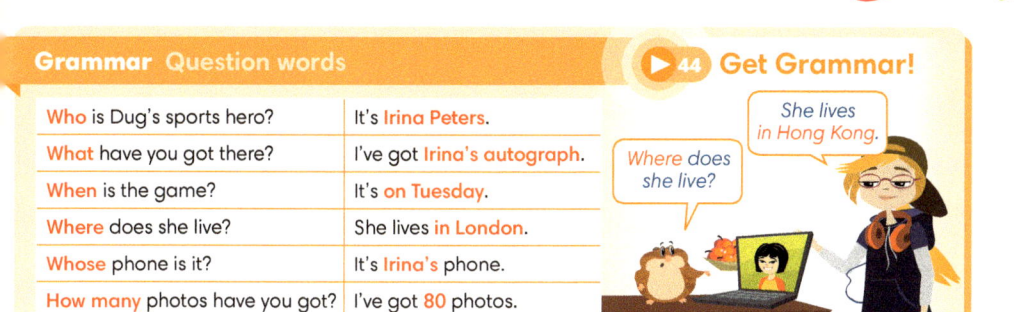

4 Match the questions to the answers.
1. [d] Where do Superdug and Kit live?
2. [c] Who is a tennis champion?
3. [a] How many sisters has Kit got?
4. [f] When is Dug's birthday?
5. [b] What is Kit's favourite dinner?
6. [e] Whose bike is red and white?

a Two.
b Fish and chips.
c Irina.
d In the UK.
e Superdug's.
f On 5th July.

5 Do you know the Tefific Two? Write questions in your notebook. Then answer the questions in pairs.
1 (look at page 14)
 A: Who is uncle Roberto?
 B: He's Superdug's uncle.
2 (look at page 26)
3 (look at page 38)
4 (look at page 50)
5 (look at page 62)
6 (look at page 74)

6 🔊 3.44 Listen to Superdug's questions. Then circle Kit's answers. 
1 (On Wednesdays.) / At her house.
2 (Two cars.) / I've got them.
3 In Spain. / (You are.)
4 (It's my sister's.) / Two sisters.
5 They're Wonder Will's. / (I think there are four.)
6 (It's in your room.) / It's nice.

7 **Exam Spot** Write questions about the underlined sentence fragments.
1 A: What is your favourite sport ?
 B: My favourite sport is rock climbing.
2 A: Who is your favourite sportsperson ?
 B: My favourite sportsperson is Andy Murray.
3 A: Where do you live ?
 B: I live at 6 Rose Street.
4 A: When is your birthday ?
 B: My birthday is on August 26.
5 A: Whose phone is this ?
 B: This is my phone.
6 A: How many brothers and sisters have you got ?
 B: I've got one brother and one sister.

8 In pairs, ask questions in Exercise 7 and give true answers.
 A: What is your favourite sport?
 B: It's ... .

Fun Spot

9 Game! Make as many questions as you can in three minutes. Use only the words in the box! Who is the winner?

where	Jack	swim	is
does	can	when	what
whose	who	he	like

Where is Jack? Can Jack swim? ...

99

Exercise 4
- 🏁 Pairs race to write their answers on response cards.

Answers → student page

- After you check the answers, ask Ss to cover the second column. Read the questions and check how many correct answers Ss remember.

Exercise 5
- 💬 Ss write their questions individually. Use the Traffic Lights technique to monitor.
- 💬 Before pairs ask and answer, use the Lollipop Stick technique to choose different Ss to write the questions on the board.
- Instead of pairwork, you could divide the class into two teams. Teams take turns to choose a question in any order to ask the other team, who answer to win a point.

Answers
2 What is in the box? Superdug's new superhero suit. **3** Where is Granny's house? 10, Paxton Street. **4** Whose eyes are green? Kit's eyes are green. **5** How many children are in the boat? Two children are in the boat. **6** When does Superdug play football? He plays football on Fridays.

Exercise 6 🔊 3.44
- Give Ss time to read the answer options before you play the recording.

Answers → student page

Exercise 7
- This is preparation for PTEYL Springboard, Task Three Reading and Writing.
- Before Ss write, elicit what kind of information is underlined. E.g. say *Andy Murray – this is a question about a … (person)*.
- Pairs help each other write the questions.
- 🔄 Each pair swaps their books with another pair. They review each other's work. Then different pairs write the answers on the board.

Answers → student page

Exercise 8
- Depending on how much time you have, you could ask some Ss to tell the class about their partner.

Exercise 9
- You could do this exercise in pairs or groups of four.

Possible answers
Where is Jack?
Where does Jack swim?
Where can Jack swim?
When does Jack swim?
When can Jack swim?
Who is Jack?
Who does Jack like?
Who can swim?
What does Jack like?
Whose friend is Jack?
Whose friend can swim?
Whose friend is like Jack?
Does Jack swim?
Can Jack swim?

Finishing the lesson
- 📖 Read the lesson objective. Ss show self-assessment response cards (☺, 😐, ☹).
- 📓 Ss copy the objective into their notebooks and draw the emoticon that reflects their progress.

⏳ Fast finishers
- Ss look at the pictures in the cartoon and write down the words they know, e.g. clothes, body parts, emotions.
- Ss write more questions about the cartoon characters. They could ask another fast finisher or the class at the end of the lesson.

117

8.4

In this lesson

Lesson aims:
- Communication: talking about the weather

Resources:
- Communication worksheet 8.4, p. 175

Homework:
- Workbook Unit 8, p. 73
- Extra Online Practice Unit 8

Assessment for Learning in this lesson
- Setting aims and criteria for success: Warm-up
- Peer learning: Exercise 5 and 6
- Independent learning: Finishing the lesson

Warm-up
- (*Books closed*) Divide the class into two teams and play *Noughts and Crosses*. Fill in the 3 x 3 grid with the question words from Lesson 8.3 and other prompts. Teams need to make questions to win their 'O' or 'X'. E.g. *(Whose/phone) Whose phone is it?*
- (*Books open*) Pairs discuss what they will learn. (*L1/L2*) Explain the lesson objective.

Lead-in
- (*Books open*) Pairs look at the photos and predict where each character is. Don't confirm yet.
- Elicit *rainy* and *cold*. Point to Jen's umbrella and then shiver. Say *It's … (rainy) and … (cold)!*

Exercise 1 ▶45 🔊 3.45
- Play the video. If you don't have access to a computer and projector, play the recording.
- Ask *Where's Jen?* (*In London.*) *Where's Lucas?* (*In Spain.*)
- Ss refer to the text and answer.

Answer → student page

- Ask Ss to explain *dentist's appointment*. Ask *Does Jen want to go?* (*No.*)

Exercise 2 🔊 3.46
- Pause for Ss to repeat each weather word and to mime or draw a picture on the board.

8.4 Communication — I can talk about the weather.

What's the weather like?

Lucas is on holiday in Spain but it's rainy in London.

Jen: Hi Lucas! Why aren't you at the beach? Isn't it hot and sunny?
Lucas: It's three o'clock. It's too hot and too sunny. What's the weather like in the UK?
Jen: It's cold and rainy. We can't go swimming.
Lucas: That's a pity.
Jen: Yes, but it's OK. It often rains in summer.
Lucas: Well, I hope it's sunny tomorrow.
Jen: Ouch! Me too, but I still can't go swimming.
Lucas: Why?
Jen: I have a dentist's appointment!
Lucas: Eurgh! I hate going to the dentist.
Jen: Me too!
Lucas: See you soon! Bye!

1 ▶45 🔊 3.45 Watch or listen and read. Complete the sentence.

Jen can't go swimming today because *it's cold and rainy*.

2 🔊 3.46 Listen and repeat.

Communication
Talking about the weather

A: What's the weather like?
B: It's *cloudy/cold/hot/rainy/snowy/sunny/warm/windy*.
It's *cold/hot/rainy/sunny* in *winter/summer/autumn/spring*.

3 What's the weather like? Complete the sentences.

1 It's ___*rainy*___  .   2 It's ___*windy*___ .
3 It's ___*cloudy*___ .   4 It's ___*sunny*___ . 

4 Which months are in each season?
1 Summer: _____
2 Spring: _____
3 Winter: _____
4 Autumn: _____

5 Exam Spot Circle the best answer.
1 A: What's the weather like in autumn in Spain?
   B: **a** It is warm and sunny.   b I hope it's warm.
      c I like sunny weather.
2 A: I want to go windsurfing tomorrow.
   B: a Yes, it's cold.
      b It's usually warm and windy.
      c I hope it's warm and windy.
3 A: What's the weather like today?
   B: a It's often cold and cloudy.
      b It's cold and cloudy.
      c Yes, it is.

Fun Spot

6 Game! Sports and weather.
Student A: Say what the weather is like.
Student B: Suggest a sport you can do.
Then swap roles.
A: *It's windy.*   B: *Let's go windsurfing!*

100

Extra video activity ▶45
- (*Books closed*) Play the video, pausing to elicit weather words from the class.

Exercise 3
- Ss complete individually, using the Communication box to help.

Answers → student page

Exercise 4
- Point out the answers depend on geographical location and discuss with the class.

Exercise 5
- This is preparation for CYLET Movers, Reading and Writing Part 2.
- Pairs help each other do the exercise.

Answers → student page

Extra activity
- **Critical thinking** Ss tell a partner what their favourite season is and why.

Exercise 6
- When pairs finish, ask them to discuss how well each other used the weather words.

Finishing the lesson
- Ask the class *Can you talk about the weather?* Ss show self-assessment response cards (☺, 😐, ☹).
- They copy the objective into their notebooks and draw the emoticon that reflects their progress.

Fast finishers
- Ss find the words from the Communication box in the dialogue in Exercise 1.

I can understand short texts about healthy habits. **Reading** 8.5

1 🔊 **3.47** Listen and repeat. Then match the phrases in the Vocabulary box to photos a–f in the magazine article.

Vocabulary Healthy lifestyle

brush your teeth   do exercise
drink a lot of water   eat fruit and vegetables
go to bed early   have friends

1 Photo a: _drink a lot of water_
2 Photo b: _go to bed early_
3 Photo c: _eat fruit and vegetables_
4 Photo d: _brush your teeth_
5 Photo e: _do exercise_
6 Photo f: _have friends_

2 Tell a partner two healthy things that you do.

Teen health
Read our top tips!

1 **C** A healthy teenager sleeps from ten to six o'clock. Go to bed early and get up at the same time every day! And don't play on your phone for a long time before bed.

3 🔊 **3.48** Read and listen to the text. Match headings A–F to tips 1–6.

A Healthy teeth   D People you like
B Be sporty   E Healthy food
C Sleep well   F Water is great!

4 **Exam Spot** Read the text again. Complete the sentences with one word.

1 It's a good idea to _get_ up at the same time every day.
2 Healthy teenagers eat fruit and _vegetables_ five times a day.
3 Healthy teenagers drink _water_, not cola.
4 It's good to brush your _teeth_ after every meal.
5 When you want to be active, you can walk or ride _ride_ your bike to school.
6 _Friends_ can help us with our problems.

5 Read the sentences. Decide if these things are healthy (✔) or not healthy (✘).

1 I sleep five hours every night, from 1 to 6 o'clock. ✘
2 I never eat vegetables. ✘
3 I often brush my teeth after dinner but never after breakfast. ✘
4 I go swimming at the weekend. ✔
5 I meet my friends two or three times every week. ✔

2 **E** Don't say 'I hate vegetables!' Find fruit and vegetables you like and eat them … five times a day! And don't eat a lot of chocolate.

3 **F** Healthy teenagers drink a lot of water. Have water in your schoolbag, not cola!

4 **A** How often do you brush your teeth? Just after breakfast? Brush them after every meal every day! You can brush them after lunch at school too!

5 **B** Do you like football, swimming or volleyball? No? No problem! You can ride your bike to school or walk to be active every day.

6 **D** Do you play computer games or watch TV after school? Hang out with your friends sometimes. Friends are fun and they help us with our problems.

101

Exercise 1 🔊 **3.47**
- Give Ss time to read the expressions before you play the recording.
- Ss do the matching exercise and compare answers with a partner.

Answers → student page

Exercise 2
- After pairs speak, ask different Ss to tell the class.

Exercise 3 🔊 **3.48**
- 💬 Give Ss time to read the headings before you play the recording. Then Ss do the matching exercise individually. Use the Basketball technique to check answers.

Answers → student page

Exercise 4
- This is preparation for CYLET Movers, Reading and Writing Part 5.
- 🔄 Ss complete individually. Then Ss stand up and compare their answers with three other Ss. Ask different Ss to justify each answer.

Answers → student page

Exercise 5
- Ss do the exercise individually. Then groups of four compare their answers.

Answers → student page

Extra activity
- Critical thinking Ss use Exercise 5 to help them write four true sentences about themselves. E.g. *I sleep eight hours a night, from eleven o'clock to seven o'clock.* Next, they read each sentence to the partner, who decides if it is a healthy habit or not.

Finishing the lesson
- 📖 Read the lesson objective. Ss show self-assessment response cards (☺, 😐, ☹).
- 📝 Ss copy the objective into their notebooks and draw the emoticon that reflects their progress.

⏳ **Fast finishers**
- Ss write sentences about a family member's healthy habits.

8.5
In this lesson

Lesson aims:
○ Reading: understanding a text about healthy habits
○ Vocabulary: healthy lifestyle

Resources:
○ Tests: Vocabulary Check 8.5

Homework:
○ Workbook Unit 8, p. 74

Assessment for Learning in this lesson
🎯 Setting aims and criteria for success: Warm-up
💬 Giving feedback: Exercise 3
🔄 Peer learning: Exercise 4
🎓 Independent learning: Finishing the lesson

Warm-up
- (*Books closed*) Pairs discuss and note two things they like and two they don't like about each season. They tell another pair. E.g. *In summer it's often sunny so you can play outside.*
- 🎯 (*Books open*) (L1/L2) Explain the lesson objectives.

Lead-in
- (*Books closed*) Ask the class *Who has got a healthy snack in the bag? What is it?* Any Ss who have a healthy snack show or tell the class. Ask further questions, e.g. *How many apples do you eat every day?*

119

8.6

In this lesson

Lesson aims:
- Listening: understanding texts about healthy lifestyles
- Writing: a text about a healthy lifestyle; grammar mistakes

Resources:
- Tests: Writing Task Unit 8

Homework:
- Workbook Unit 8, p. 75

Assessment for Learning in this lesson
- 🎯 Setting aims and criteria for success: Warm-up
- 💬 Giving feedback: Exercise 6
- 👥 Peer learning: Exercise 7
- 🎓 Independent learning: Finishing the lesson

Warm-up
- (*Books closed*) Pairwork. Student A imagines and describes Student B's lifestyle. Student B takes notes and then says *True* or *False*. Students swap and continue.
- 🎯 (*Books open*) (L1/L2) Explain the lesson objectives.

Lead-in
- (*Books closed*) The class names favourite sports champions.
- **Critical thinking** Ask *Is it easy to be a champion? Why (not)?*

Exercise 1
- Ask Ss if the sentences are true for the champions they named.

> Answers → student page

Exercise 2 🔊 3.49
- Ss use the photos in Exercise 3 to predict the answers.

> Answers → student page

Exercise 3 🔊 3.49
- This is preparation for CYLET Starters, Listening Part 2.
- Ss answer any questions they can before they listen.

> Answers → student page

Exercise 4
- Pairs discuss the question.
- Monitor and help if necessary.

8.6 Listening and Writing
I can understand and write short texts about healthy lifestyle.

1 Complete the sentences about sports champions with *train*, *good* and *healthy*.
- a Champions are _good_ at their sport.
- b They _train_ a lot.
- c They have got a _healthy_ lifestyle.

2 🔊 3.49 Listen to the interviews with Denise and Gary. What are their sports?
Denise – volleyball.   Gary – taekwondo.

3 **Exam Spot** 🔊 3.49 Listen again. Read the questions and complete the interviewer's notes about Denise and Gary.

Denise
1. Where does she play volleyball?
   At _City_ Club.
2. When does she train?
   At _seven_ o'clock in the morning.
3. How often does she eat fruit and vegetables?
   Every day.
4. Has she got time for homework?
   Yes, she does

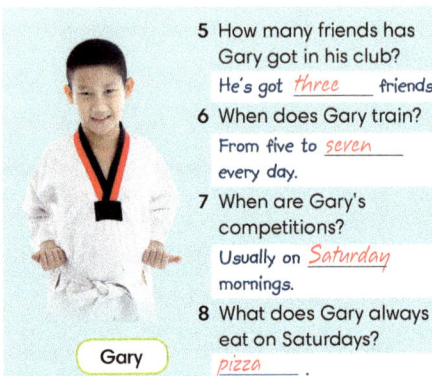

Gary
5. How many friends has Gary got in his club?
   He's got _three_ friends.
6. When does Gary train?
   From five to _seven_ every day.
7. When are Gary's competitions?
   Usually on _Saturday_ mornings.
8. What does Gary always eat on Saturdays?
   pizza.

4 Have Denise and Gary got a healthy lifestyle? Tell a partner.

Extra activity
- **Critical thinking** Discuss with the class why some people have unhealthy lifestyles.

Exercise 5
- Ss circle Lucas' healthy habits and underline less healthy ones.

Answers
Yes: Lucas loves sleeping. He drinks water, plays the guitar every day and he meets his friends. No: He doesn't like healthy food and he isn't sporty.

Writing
- Draw Ss' attention to the example. Remind them to use *-ing* forms after *love, like, don't like* and *hate*. You could also remind them to be careful with third person singular forms.

---

5 Has Lucas got a healthy lifestyle? Read his blog and find out.

My lifestyle!

Sleep: I go to bed at half past nine on school days and I get up at eight o'clock. I *love* sleeping!

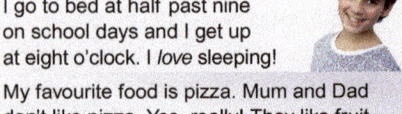

Food: My favourite food is pizza. Mum and Dad don't like pizza. Yes, really! They like fruit and vegetables … . I drink a lot of water.

Sports and friends: I'm not very sporty but I like watching football on TV. I love music and I play the guitar every day after school from 5 to 6. I often hang out with Jen, Alex and Lian too!

Writing
Checking for grammar mistakes

Read through the first draft of your text to check for grammar mistakes. Check your final draft too.
I love ~~sleep~~ sleeping.

6 Correct the underlined mistakes.
1. I like <u>eat</u> chocolate. _eating_
2. I hate swimming but my friends like <u>him</u>. _it_
3. He <u>eat</u> a healthy breakfast. _eats_
4. We like <u>do</u> sports. _doing_

7 **Writing Time** Write about your lifestyle.

❓ **Find ideas**
Make notes under these headings.
- Sleep: *I go to bed at … / I get up at …*
- Food: *My favourite food is …*
- Sports and friends: *I'm / I'm not very sporty. I love/like/don't like/ hate … I often/sometimes hang out with …*

✏️ **Draft**
Write about your lifestyle.

👍 **Check and write**
Check your grammar and write the final version of your text.

Exercise 6
- 💬 Use the Lollipop Stick technique to check answers.

> Answers → student page

Exercise 7
- 👥 Remind Ss to check both drafts. Pairs use the Two Stars and a Wish technique to review each other's work.

Finishing the lesson
- 🎓 Read the lesson objectives. Ss show self-assessment response cards (☺, 😐, ☹).

⏳ **Fast finishers**
- Ss write sentences about another character's lifestyle.

Language Revision 8.7

Vocabulary

1 Read sentences 1–5. Then complete the words to find the names of sports.

1 You play these sports with a ball.
- a b<u>asketball</u>
- b t<u>able</u>   t<u>ennis</u>
- c t<u>ennis</u>

2 You don't usually play these sports in a team.
- a r<u>oller</u>   s<u>kating</u>
- b sk<u>ateboarding</u>
- c t<u>aekwondo</u>

3 You do these sports inside and outside.
- a f<u>ootball</u>
- b h<u>ockey</u>
- c v<u>olleyball</u>
- d c<u>ycling</u>
- e b<u>adminton</u>
- f s<u>wimming</u>

4 You do these sports in the winter.
- a s<u>kiing</u>
- b i<u>ce</u>-s<u>kating</u>

5 You need windy weather for these sports.
- a w<u>indsurfing</u>
- b s<u>ailing</u>

2 Jamie's lifestyle isn't healthy. Help him! Complete the sentences with the words in the box.

> teeth
> friends
> water
> vegetables
> ~~Do~~
> early

1 <u>Do</u> exercise every day.
2 Eat fruit and <u>vegetables</u>.
3 Drink a lot of <u>water</u>.
4 Brush your <u>teeth</u> after you eat.
5 Hang out with your <u>friends</u>.
6 Go to bed <u>early</u>.

Grammar

3 Read again about Jamie. Put the verbs in the correct form.

Jamie isn't very sporty. He doesn't like ¹<u>doing</u> (do) sports at school and he doesn't like ²<u>playing</u> (play) football with his friends. He ³<u>hates</u> (hate) cycling too. He sometimes ⁴<u>goes</u> (go) roller skating with his sister. They like ⁵<u>going</u> (go) to the park but not when it's cold and rainy. Jamie loves ⁶<u>watching</u> (watch) sports on TV at home!

4 Write questions. Then ask and answer in pairs.

1 sport your What's favourite ? <u>What's your favourite sport?</u>
2 many sports you How do train ? <u>How many sports do you train?</u>
3 is Who teacher your ? <u>Who is your teacher?</u>
4 you When train do ? <u>When do you train?</u>
5 do you Where train ? <u>Where do you train?</u>
6 you got a sports hero Have ? <u>Have you got a sports hero?</u>

5 Read the sentences. Replace the underlined object pronouns with the words in the box.

> winter sports   your sister   chocolate   ~~your mum~~   Mr Smith

1 I like her. <u>your mum</u>
2 I don't like them. <u>winter sports</u>
3 I love it! <u>chocolate</u>
4 They like him. <u>Mr Smith</u>
5 I can help her. <u>your sister</u>

Pronunciation

6 🔊 3.50 Listen and repeat: /r/.

Rosema**r**y and Jane
Love **r**unning in the **r**ain!

Communication

7 Match the sentence halves 1–4 to a–d.

1 What's the weather — d like in the UK today?
2 It's sunny but it's — a in summer in the UK.
3 It's often rainy — c windy.
4 It's sometimes cold in — b the UK in the winter.

Check yourself! ✓

- I can talk about sports.
- I can use verbs love/like/don't like/hate + -ing.
- I can use object pronouns.
- I can ask detailed questions.
- I can talk about the weather.

8.7

In this lesson

Lesson aims:
- Revising Vocabulary, Grammar and Communication from Unit 8
- Pronunciation: /r/

Resources:
- Tests: Language Test Unit 8, End-of-Year Test Units 1–8

Homework:
- Workbook Unit 8, pp. 76–77
- Extra Online Practice Unit 8

Assessment for Learning in this lesson
- Setting aims and criteria for success: Warm-up
- Giving feedback: Exercise 3
- Peer learning: Exercise 3 and 4
- Independent learning: Finishing the lesson

Warm-up
- (Books closed) Ask different Ss questions about this unit, e.g.: *1 Name four outdoor sports. 2 Spell 'taekwondo'. 3 Say three sports and ask Ss to say play, do or go. 4 What's the weather like in spring?*
- (L1/L2) Ss work in groups and write down what they have learnt in this unit. Explain the lesson objectives.

Lead-in
- (Books open) (L1/L2) Ask *What are your favourite lessons in this unit? Why?* Encourage Ss to explain.

Exercise 1
- Pairs race to answer.
- Then ask Ss to cover the answers with a small piece of paper and check whether they remember the answers.

Answers → student page

Extra activity
- (Books closed) Divide Ss into two teams. Ask teams in turn to spell sports from this unit.

Exercise 2
- Ss compare answers in pairs.

Answers → student page

Extra activity
- **Critical thinking** Pairs discuss the advice in Exercise 2 and choose the three most important ideas.

Exercise 3
- Use the Traffic Lights technique to monitor.
- Ss compare their answers with three other Ss.

Answers → student page

Exercise 4
- Ss work individually. Then they swap notebooks with their partner and review each other's work. Check answers before Ss speak.

Answers → student page

Exercise 5
- If your Ss are weak, do this exercise with the whole class.

Answers → student page

Exercise 6 🔊 3.50
- Get pairs to say the rhyme to each other as fast as possible.

Exercise 7
- Have a class vote for each answer. Ss justify their choice.

Answers → student page

Finishing the lesson
- Read Check yourself! statements for Ss to tick.

Fast finishers
- Ss write questions about their lifestyle with question words. E.g. *How often do you brush your teeth?* They ask another fast finisher or the class when appropriate.

7 & 8

In this lesson

Lesson aims:
- Skills practice: Reading, Writing, Listening and Communication
- Exam practice: CYLET and PTEYL

Resources:
- Tests: Skills Test Units 7&8, Speaking Tasks Units 7&8, Exam Test Units 5–8

Homework:
- Workbook Skills Revision 7&8, pp. 78–79

Assessment for Learning in this lesson

- Setting aims and criteria for success: Warm-up
- Giving feedback: Exercise 3 and 4
- Peer learning: Exercise 3 and 5
- Independent learning: Finishing the lesson

Exam Language Bank

This lists the key language from Units 7–8. Here are some ideas to help you make the most of it.

- Encourage Ss to be independent learners. They tick the words they know and check the meaning of the words they can't remember in a dictionary.
- Ss memorize a section, close the book and write down all the words they can remember.
- Make a quick two-minute test. (*Books closed*) Say different words/expressions in English from one section. Ss write or say sentences with them.
- Fast finishers test each other.
  Student A: *Spell 'hockey'*.
  Student B: *H-O-C-K-E-Y*.
  Student B: *Say four indoor sports*.
  Student A: *volleyball, basketball, …*

---

7 & 8 Skills Revision

Reading and Writing

SPORTS WEEK
What sports do you like? What's your favourite sport? Write and tell us!

1 I'm not usually very sporty. I hate team sports and I don't like water sports. But there is one sport I love. It's table tennis! I'm really good at it. It's my favourite.
I play every day at school with my school friends in summer and in winter. I play in school competitions too. I usually win!
Jill, 11

2 I'm in a football club and I play hockey but my favourite sport isn't a ball sport. It's skiing.
There are some great places to ski in my country, Argentina. I always go skiing in August with my family. Yes, August! It's winter here in August.
Rod, 12

3 My best friend's got a boat and I go sailing in the summer. That's cool but my number one sport is swimming.
I go to my town's swimming pool on Mondays and Fridays after school with my swimming club. I don't often swim in the sea. The water is very cold in Scotland!
Alistair, 13

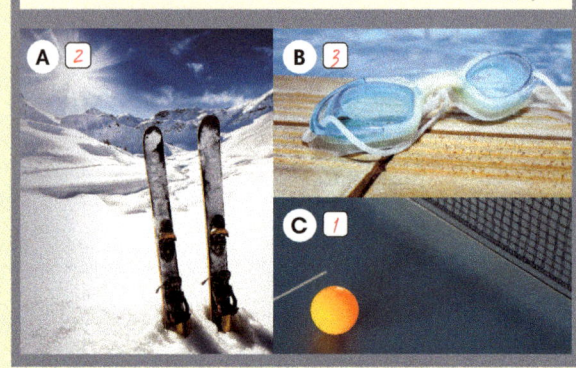

A 2 B 3 C 1

1 Work in pairs. Look at photos A–C. What sports do you use the objects in?

2 Read texts 1–3 and match them to photos A–C.

3 Read the questions and complete the table.

	What's his/her favourite sport?	Where does he/she do it?	Who does he/she do it with?
Jill	table tennis	at school	friends
Rod	skiing	in Argentina	family
Alistair	swimming	swimming pool	swimming club

4 **Exam Spot** Complete the text with words in the box. There are two extra words.

My ¹body and head are orange and black. I see with my two yellow ²eyes. My four ³legs are very strong. I've got big teeth and I'm dangerous. I can run very fast. I don't eat fruit and ⁴vegetables. I usually eat meat. I like the ⁵sun but I don't like very hot weather. Do I like ⁶swimming? Yes, I like water! What am I? I am a tiger.

a body   b sun
c man   d swimming
e eyes   f vegetables
g teeth h legs

5 **Exam Spot** Write 40-50 words about your favourite sport. Use these questions to help you.

1 What's your favourite sport?
2 When do you do it?
3 Where do you do it?
4 Who do you do it with?
5 Are you a champion?

My favourite sport is …
I do/go/play … at … / on … /with
I'm / I'm not a champion and/but I always/sometimes/never win.

Warm-up

- (*Books open*) Read this riddle. Ss guess the sport. *Two teams play this game. There are usually six people in a team. People play it indoors or on the beach.* (Volleyball.)
- (*Books closed*) Write *Skills Revision* on the board. Ask a student to remind the class what this means. (*Books open*) Ss look through the lesson and tell a partner which activity they are looking forward to most. Remind Ss this lesson will help prepare them for CYLET and/or PTEYL too. (See the Introduction.)

Lead-in

- **Critical thinking** (*Books closed*) Ask the class *Is it OK to not like sport?* (*Yes. You can do exercise without doing sports.*)

Exercise 1

- Pairs race to answer.

Answers
A skiing B swimming C table tennis

Exercise 2

- Ss compare answers with a partner.

Answers → student page

Exercise 3

- Ss find the answers in the text and fill in the table. Then Ss compare answers in pairs.
- Check answers by drawing the table on the board. Use the Lollipop Stick technique to choose different Ss to complete it.

Answers → student page

Skills Revision 7 & 8

Listening

6 Exam Spot 🔊 3.51 Listen and match names 1–4 to pictures a–f. There are two extra pictures.

1 _e_ Beatrice 2 _b_ Charlie 3 _f_ Mel 4 _d_ Jeff

a b  c  d  e  f

Communication

7 Exam Spot Read the answers and complete the questions.

1 A: Have _you got any tickets for the concert_?
   B: Yes, we have. There are a lot of tickets.
2 A: Can _I have three tickets_____?
   B: Yes, sure. Three tickets are twenty-seven pounds, please.
3 A: Where _is the concert_____?
   B: It's June so the concert is in the park.
4 A: Can _I buy CDs at the concert_____?
   B: Yes. You can buy CDs at the concert.
5 A: What time _does it start_____?
   B: At 8 o'clock.

8 Exam Spot Work in pairs. Ask and answer the questions.

1 What do you do to relax?
2 Where do you go for your holidays?
3 What's the weather like in winter in your country?
4 Have you got an apple in your schoolbag?

Exam Language Bank

Wild animals
bird
butterfly
crocodile
elephant
fish
fly
frog
giraffe
kangaroo
lion
monkey
snake
spider
tiger
whale

Sports
badminton
basketball
cycling
football
hockey
ice-skating
roller skating
sailing
skateboarding
skiing
swimming
table tennis
taekwondo
tennis
volleyball
windsurfing

Pets
cat
dog
goldfish
hamster
iguana
parrot
rabbit
tortoise

Healthy lifestyle
brush your teeth
do exercise
drink a lot of water
eat fruit and vegetables
go to bed early
have friends

Adjectives

| cute | fast | strong |
| dangerous | slow | ugly |

Buying a ticket
Can I help you?
Can I have _a ticket/two tickets to the zoo_, please?
That's _eighteen pounds fifty_.
Here you are.
Here is your ticket. / Here are are your tickets.
Thanks.

Talking about the weather
What's the weather like?
It's _cloudy/cold/hot/rainy/snowy/ sunny/warm/ windy_.
It's _cold/hot/rainy/sunny_ in _winter/summer/ autumn/spring_.

105

Exercise 6 🔊 3.51
- This is preparation for PTEYL Firstwords/Springboard, Task Two Listening.
- Pairs describe the pictures to each other before they listen.
- Ss listen to the recording twice in the test.
- Encourage Ss to justify their answers by referring to key words/ideas they remember.

Answers → student page

Exercise 7
- This is preparation for PTEYL Springboard, Task Three Reading and Writing.
- Help a weak class underline key words in the answers to help them write the questions. (2 Three tickets. 3 The park. 4 Buy. 5 Eight o'clock.)
- Pairs help each other write.
- Choose different individuals to write each question on the board.

Answers → student page

Exercise 8
- This is preparation for CYLET/ PTEYL Speaking.
- Ss take notes while they speak.
- Then each pair gets together with another pair. Each student tells the other pair about his/her partner.

Finishing the lesson
- 💻 Write the headings _Reading and Writing_, _Listening_, _Communication_ on the board. Read each out. Ss show self-assessment response cards (☺, 😐, ☹). Then they write one sentence about what they did well in each section and one about what they could improve.

⌛ **Fast finishers**
- Ss study the Exam Language Bank.

Extra activity
- Ask different Ss to come to the front and to mime doing a sport for the class to guess.

Exercise 4
- This is preparation for CYLET Starters, Reading and Writing Part 4.
- (_Books open_) Tell Ss to look carefully at the pictures and words. Explain it's a good idea to read all of the text before they choose answers. Challenge them to explain why. (_Then they will know what it is about._)
- Ss do the exercise individually. Then ask pairs to compare answers.
- 💬 Use the Traffic Lights technique to find out how easy/difficult Ss found the exercise.

Answers → student page

Extra activity
- Pairs write two or three sentences about another animal, using ideas in Exercise 4 to help. E.g. _I'm not dangerous. I'm very slow. I'm a pet._ (_A tortoise._) Ss read their sentences for the class to guess the animal.

Exercise 5
- This is preparation for PTEYL Springboard, Task Six Writing.
- Ss make notes before they write.
- 🔄 Pairs work together to review each other's texts using the Two Stars and a Wish technique.

123

Extra reference

Answers

Unit 0 Lesson 0.3, Page 9, Exercise 6

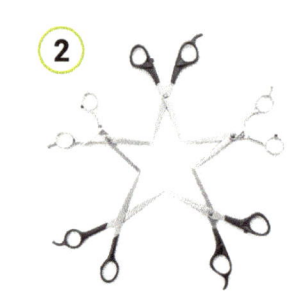

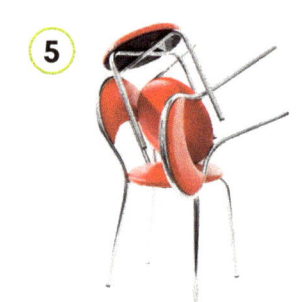

1
2
3
4
5
6

Unit 5 Lesson 5.5, Page 65, Exercise 4

1 E
2 N
3 G
4 L
5 I
6 S
7 H

Student A activities

Unit 1 Lesson 1.5, Page 17, exercise 7

Describe the photos. Use the example to help you.

A: *'It's mum, dad, and three sons. They are on holiday'.*
B: *It's photo A.*

A
B
C
D

Unit 7 Lesson 7.2, page 85, Exercise 10

4 Granny wants to go for walks with her pet.
5 Aunt Megan loves birds.
6 Emma doesn't want a big pet.

Songs and raps

Unit 0   Lesson 0.1, Page 5, Exercise 4

🔊 1.3 🔊 1.4 Alphabet Rap

A, B, C, D,
E, F, G,
Say the alphabet, say it with me!
H, I, J, K, L, M, N, O, P,
is funny as you can see. 
R, S, T, U and V
four more letters and we're free.
W, X, Y and
Shh …  is sleepy, so are we!

Unit 2   Lesson 2.3, Page 27, Exercise 9

🔊 1.42 🔊 1.43 Kit's Rap

Is she clever?   Yes, she is.
Is she fun?   She's all that!
Is she the best?   Her name's Kit
Is she the one?   and she's a cool cat!

Now you rap. You can rap about a friend!

Unit 4   Lesson 4.3, Page 51, Exercise 9

🔊 2.23 🔊 2.24 Robots' Song

Unit 5   Lesson 5.3, Page 63, Exercise 9

🔊 2.42 🔊 2.43 Activities Rap

I can act, I can sing, I can draw a cat
I can dive, I can swim – Can you do all that?
I can act, I can sing, I can draw a cat.
I can dive, I can swim – I can do all that!

Now you rap. Use different activities you know.

Unit 7   Lesson 7.3, Page 87, Exercise 10

🔊 3.24 🔊 3.25 Questions Song

Do you play computer games?
Do you watch TV?
Do you hang out with your friends?
Then you're just like me!
Yes, you're just like me!

Does your mum say 'Get up now!'?
Does she count to three?
Do you say 'Oh, it's not fair!'?
Then you're just like me!
Yes, you're just like me!

Do you have your breakfast?
Do you go to school?
Do you like your English class?
Then you're really cool!
Yes, you're really cool!

Have you got super ears,
Have you got super eyes?

  Yes, we've got superpowers,
  We are super guys!

Have you got super arms,
or maybe a super nose?

  We have got super feet
  And twenty super toes!

Have you got a super boat,
Have you got a bike?

  No, we've got a super car,
  And its name is Mike!

Extra reference

Pairwork activities

Unit 3   Lesson 3.2, Page 37, Exercise 11

Play a drawing dictation game. Describe one of the pictures for your partner to draw.

Unit 3   Lesson 3.3, Page 39, Exercise 7

Play a memory game.
Student A: Choose one of the pictures above.
Close your book.
Student B: Ask Student A questions.
Then swap roles.   A: *Picture 1.*
B: *Chairs?*
A: *There are four chairs.*

Student B activities

Unit 1   Lesson 1.5, Page 17, exercise 7

Describe the photos. Use the example to help you.

A: *'It's mum, dad, and three sons. They are on holiday'.*
B: *It's photo A.*

Unit 7   Lesson 7.2, page 85, Exercise 10

1 Alex wants to play with his pet.
2 Lucas doesn't like birds.
3 Lian's mum is allergic to cats and rabbits.

1 & 2 Get more on Geometry!

Shapes

1 🔊 **25 Listen and repeat. Look at the pictures and number the words in the Vocabulary box.**

Vocabulary Shapes

circle [2] line [1] rectangle [5]
square [3] triangle [4]

1 ～ 2 ● 3 ■ 4 ▲ 5 ▬

2 Read and match texts 1–3 to pictures A–D. There is one extra picture.

A   B   C   D

1 [B] Look! This is my new top. It's cool. It's blue with squares, triangles and orange and yellow lines. A small circle is on my top too.

2 [C] My favourite top is old but it isn't boring. It's yellow with red squares, green lines and triangles. No rectangles and no circles!

3 [A] My T-shirts are one colour. My favourite T-shirt is blue with one big rectangle, small triangles and a circle. No squares or lines!

3 Read the texts in Exercise 2 again. Complete the table.

	Clothes	Colours	Shapes
1	top	blue, orange, yellow	squares, triangles, lines, circle
2	top	yellow, red, green	squares, lines, triangles
3	T-shirt	blue	rectangle, triangles, circle

4 Read the sentences and circle T (true) or F (false).

1 The rectangle on T-shirt A is small. T / (F)
2 T-shirt A is one colour. (T) / F
3 Top C is yellow with one square and one triangle. T / (F)
4 The squares on top C are black. T / (F)
5 The circle on top B is blue. (T) / F
6 The lines on top B are black and blue. T / (F)

5 Design a T-shirt or a top with shapes. Then complete the sentences.

This is my _____ .
The shapes are _____ .

- Alternatively, say the number of each shape yourself.

Answers → student page

Extra activity
- (*Books closed*) Say a shape and ask Ss to draw it in their notebooks. Ask them to compare their drawing with a partner's. Then ask a student to draw the correct shape on the board. Continue with different shapes and Ss. Challenge a strong class by giving them extra information. E.g. say *Draw three small triangles and one big triangle.*

Exercise 2
- Ask the class to describe each item of clothing as best they can.
- Ss do the matching exercise individually.
- Use the Lollipop Stick technique to choose different Ss to say and justify each answer.

Answers → student page

Exercise 3
- After pairs help each other complete the table, collect Ss' answers on the board.

Answers → student page

Exercise 4
- Pairs race to answer. The first pair to finish stands up!
- To check answers use the Stand up and Change Places technique.

Answers → student page

Exercise 5
- Give Ss time to draw and write. Then ask groups of four to look at each others' work. They choose their favourite design and tell the class. Encourage them to explain why.

Finishing the lesson
- Ask different Ss to draw the different shapes from this lesson on the board.
- Ask *Can you describe shapes?* Students show self-assessment response cards (☺, 😐, ☹).

Fast finishers
- Ss draw and write about a favourite T-shirt/top.

---

1 & 2

In this lesson

Lesson aims:
○ Vocabulary: shapes

Assessment for Learning in this lesson
- Setting aims and criteria for success: Warm-up
- Giving feedback: Exercise 2
- Peer learning: Exercise 3
- Independent learning: Finishing the lesson

Warm-up
- (*Books closed*) Ask different Ss about a favourite item of clothing. E.g. T: *What are your favourite clothes?* S: *My jeans, my hoodie and my old T-shirt.* T: *What colour is your T-shirt?* S: *It's (blue and white).*
- Ss look at page 90 in the Workbook. (L1/L2) Explain that the objective of this lesson is to learn the names of basic geometrical shapes. Then write on the board: *1 My T-shirt is yellow with blue circles. 2 My jacket is red. No lines or squares! 3 My dog is brown.* Ask Ss to read out the sentence which doesn't fit in with the lesson objective.

Lead-in
- (*Books closed*) Draw the different shapes in Exercise 1 on the board and teach *shapes*.

Exercise 1 🔊 **25**
- Play the recording, pausing for Ss to repeat each word and say the number of the corresponding shape.

127

3 & 4

In this lesson

Lesson aims:
- Vocabulary: materials

Assessment for Learning in this lesson
- Setting aims and criteria for success: Warm-up
- Giving feedback: Exercise 5
- Peer learning: Exercise 6
- Independent learning: Finishing the lesson

Warm-up

- (*Books closed*) (*L1*) Brainstorm materials you can see in your classroom.
- Ss look at page 91 in the Workbook. (*L1/L2*) Explain that they are going to learn the names of basic materials. Then write on the board:
1 A glass window. 2 A blue pen. 3 A cardboard box. Say each sentence and ask Ss to predict which sentence doesn't fit in with the lesson objective.

Lead-in

- (*Books open*) Ss name the objects in the photos in Exercise 4.

Exercise 1 26

- Play the recording, pausing for Ss to repeat each word. Ss/You say the number of the corresponding photo.
- Tell Ss all the words are both nouns and adjectives except for *wooden* (adjective). Noun: *wood*.

Answers → student page

Extra activity

- (*Books closed*) Choose different objects made of/from the materials in the Vocabulary box and play *Touch and Guess* with materials. (See Lesson 2.1, Warm-up.)

Exercise 2

- Ask Ss to read the definition of *recycled*. Teach strong Ss *newspaper* and *(coffee) cup*.

Extra activity

- (*L1/L2*) Pairs list any objects they know that can be recycled.
- Critical thinking (*L1*) Discuss with Ss why recycling is important.

Get more on Science!
Materials

1 🔊 **26** Listen and repeat. Find the materials in photos 1–6.

Vocabulary Materials
cardboard   glass   metal   paper   wooden
    6   3   1,5   2   4,1

2 Look at the picture. What is 'recycled'?

Recycled = a new thing from an old thing.

3 Look at the photos in Exercise 4 again. Which household objects are recycled?
Recycled objects: photos 1, 2, 4, 6.

4 Find these words in the text. Which household object is missing? *Cardboard wardrobe.*

paper lamp	cardboard wardrobe
metal bath	wooden table	glass window
metal sofa		

Is your house eco-friendly?

We've got a very nice house. There are many recycled household objects in it. This <u>wooden coffee table</u> is in our living room and it's recycled. This <u>lamp</u> is in my bedroom. It's my mum's idea. It's from paper. In the bathroom we've got a <u>metal bath</u>. It's eco-friendly but it isn't recycled. It's very old. This beautiful <u>glass window</u> is very old too.

My favourite object is the <u>metal sofa</u> in our living room. It's my dad's idea. It's grey and brown. Our house is great!

5 Read the text again. Circle *Yes* or *No*.
1 Is the house nice? **Yes** / No
2 Is the bath old? **Yes** / No
3 Is the lamp metal? Yes / **No**
4 Is the window recycled glass? Yes / **No**
5 Is the sofa in the bedroom? Yes / **No**
6 Is the table wooden? **Yes** / No

6 Think of three materials for each object.

Beds	Lamps	Doors	Desks
wooden, metal, cardboard	paper, glass, metal	wooden, glass, metal	metal, wooden, glass

7 What is there in your house? Complete the sentences.

There's a/an _____ in my _____.
It's *cardboard / glass / metal / paper / wooden*.

There are _____ in my _____.
They're *cardboard / glass / metal / paper / wooden*.

Exercise 3

- Ss guess which objects are recycled. Don't confirm yet.

Answer → student page

Exercise 4

- After Ss underline the words in the text, they compare answers with a partner.

Answer → student page

- Check Ss' predictions from Exercise 3.

Exercise 5

- Ss do the exercise individually. Use the Basketball technique to check answers.

Answers → student page

Exercise 6

- Groups of four help each other complete the table. There is no right or wrong answer.

Possible answers → student page

Exercise 7

- Alternatively, ask Ss to write on a piece of paper. Collect the answers and read them out for the class to guess who wrote each.

Finishing the lesson

- Ask *What materials words can you use?* Different Ss say a word and point to or describe an example in the classroom. Then Ss show self-assessment response cards (☺, 😐, ☹).

Fast finishers
- Ss write sentences describing different household objects in their house.

5 & 6 Get more on Music!

Musical instruments

1 🔊 27 Listen and repeat. Label photos 1–6.

Vocabulary Musical instruments

acoustic guitar   drums   electric guitar
keyboard   melodica   violin

1 *electric guitar*
2 *melodica*
3 *acoustic guitar*
4 *violin*
5 *drums*
6 *keyboard*

2 Read the quiz. Circle T (true) or F (false). Check your answers on page 95. What's your score?

My score is ___ / 10

QUIZ TIME!

1. The acoustic guitar is from France. — T /**F**
2. The guitar has got a head, a neck and a body. — **T**/ F
3. When you play the guitar, its head is on your legs. — T /**F**
4. You play the melodica with your mouth and toes. — T /**F**
5. You play the drums with your fingers and feet. — **T**/ F
6. The violin is a glass instrument. — T /**F**
7. The keyboard is an electric instrument. — **T**/ F
8. The body of the electric guitar is usually wooden. — **T**/ F
9. The violin and the acoustic guitar are in the same family of instruments. — **T**/ F
10. The drums are from the USA. — T /**F**

3 Look at the false sentences in the quiz. Correct them using the words in the box.

body   China   fingers   ~~Spain~~   wooden

1 The acoustic guitar is from   *Spain*   .
2 When you play the guitar, its   *body*   is on your legs.
3 You play the melodica with your mouth and   *fingers*   .
4 The violin is a   *wooden*   instrument.
5 The drums are from   *China*   .

4 What can Jane play? Look at the quiz again. Read and complete the text.

My name's Jane. I can play the   *acoustic guitar* . It's wooden and it's big. You play this instrument with your fingers. And I love its colours: brown and black.

5 Imagine you can play one of the instruments from the quiz and complete. Use Exercise 4 to help.

I can play the _____ . It's _____ and _____ . You play this instrument with your _____ .

---

5 & 6

In this lesson

Lesson aims:
- Vocabulary: musical instruments

Assessment for Learning in this lesson
- Setting aims and criteria for success: Warm-up
- Peer learning: Exercise 3
- Independent learning: Finishing the lesson

Warm-up
- (*Books closed*) Draw appropriate number of dashes for *musical instrument* on the board. Ss suggest the letters to guess these words.
- Ss look at page 92 in the Workbook. (*L1/L2*) Ask the class to tell you what they expect to do in this lesson. Explain that they are going to learn the names of musical instruments and practise describing them.

Lead-in
- (*Books closed*) Ask Ss to name any musical instruments they can.

Exercise 1 🔊 27
- Play the recording, pausing for Ss to repeat each word. Ss/You say the number of the corresponding photo.
- Ss label individually. Then pairs compare answers.

Answers → student page

Extra activity
- (*Books closed*) Play the class a short track from any song in which you can hear two or more musical instruments in the Vocabulary box. They tell you instruments they think they can hear.
- Alternatively, ask different Ss to mime playing a musical instrument for the class to guess.

Exercise 2
- Ask Ss to do the Quiz individually. You may like to give them a time limit as Ss work at different speeds.
- Encourage them to help each other if they can't remember vocabulary.
- Find out who did well. E.g. ask *Who has 10/10? Who has 9/10?* Remember to praise them!

Answers → student page

Exercise 3
- 👥 Pairs complete the sentences. Then they stand up and compare their answers with another two pairs.

Answers → student page

Exercise 4
- Pairs predict the answer before they read and check. Point out they need to read all of the text in order to find the answer.
- Pairs tell each other which musical instruments from the Vocabulary box they can play and which they'd like to play. Ask different Ss to tell the class about their partner.

Answer → student page

Exercise 5
- Ss write individually.
- You could then ask Ss to work in groups of four. Each student reads his/her text but doesn't name the instrument. The group guesses what it is.

Finishing the lesson
- Ask *Can you name and describe some musical instruments?* Students show self-assessment response cards (☺, 😐, ☹).

Fast finishers
- Ss write another true or false sentence about a musical instrument in the Vocabulary box.

129

7 & 8

In this lesson

Lesson aims:
- Vocabulary: sports equipment

Assessment for Learning in this lesson
- 🎯 Setting aims and criteria for success: Warm-up
- 💬 Giving feedback: Exercise 2
- 🌐 Peer learning: Exercise 4
- 🎓 Independent learning: Finishing the lesson

Warm-up
- (*Books closed*) **Critical thinking** Pairs list sports boys usually like and girls usually like. Ask different Ss to help write each list on the board. Encourage them to justify their ideas.
- 🎯 Ss look at page 93 in the Workbook. (*L1/L2*) Ask the class to tell you what they expect to do in this lesson. Explain that the lesson objective is to learn sports equipment vocabulary and to use it to write about a sport they like.

Lead-in
- (*Books closed*) If possible bring in some simple realia, e.g. a ping pong ball or a football and a helmet. See if Ss can name the object(s).
- Ss tell you any sports equipment words they know.

Exercise 1 🔊 28
- Play the recording, pausing for Ss to repeat each word. Ss/You say the letter of the corresponding photo. Give Ss time to note each answer before you continue.

> Answers → student page

Exercise 2
- Ask Ss in a weak class to name the sports in the photos before they read.
- 💬 Use the Lollipop Stick technique to choose different Ss to say answers 1–5. You could then ask Ss to number the sports in the box in order of preference and to explain their decisions to a partner.

> Answers → student page

Get more on Sports!
Sports equipment

1 🔊 **28** Listen and repeat. Find these objects in the photos in Exercise 2.

Vocabulary Sports equipment

bat *b*   goggles *d*   helmet *a*   net *c*   racket *e*   stick *f*

2 What sports do these teens like? Complete the texts with the words in the box. There are four extra sports.

badminton   cycling   football   hockey   roller skating
table tennis   tennis   swimming   volleyball

1. I love *cycling* because I can hang out with my friends outside and be active. We ride our *bikes* at the weekend. I always wear a helmet.

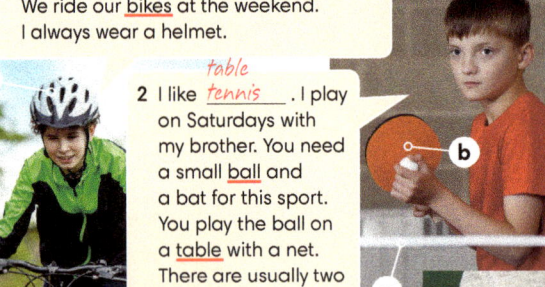

2. I like *table tennis*. I play on Saturdays with my brother. You need a small *ball* and a bat for this sport. You play the ball on a *table* with a net. There are usually two or four players.

3. I love playing *tennis*. I often play with my sister. We play on Wednesdays and Fridays. I have a new racket. It's a birthday present.

4. I like *swimming* I'm in a club. I train every day and I think I'm good at it. I wear goggles because I hate getting water in my eyes. I wear a *swimming cap* too because I've got long hair.

5. I love *hockey*. I like playing on ice but you can play this sport on grass too. You need a long stick to play. And it's also good to wear a helmet.

3 Look at the texts again and underline four more pieces of equipment.

4 Complete the table with equipment words from the texts.

Tennis	racket, net, ball
Hockey	helmet, stick, net
Volleyball	net, ball
Football	net, ball
Swimming	goggles, swimming c...
Table tennis	bat, net, table
Cycling	helmet, bike

5 Do you like sport? Complete the sentences for you.

I like _____ . I play / go / do _____ with _____ .
To do this sport I need _____ .

Exercise 3
- Ss do the exercise individually. Then they compare their answers with a partner.

> Answers → student page

Exercise 4
- 🌐 Pairs help each other complete the table. Then collect the answers on the board.

> Answers → student page

Extra activity
- Divide Ss into four teams and give each a piece of paper. Each team chooses a writer. Say a sports equipment word. The teams race to write down as many sports as they can in which you need it. If any team says *STOP* at any time, everyone must stop writing.
- Then teams count their words. The team with the longest list reads it out. If it's correct, they win a point. If it isn't, ask the team with the second longest list to read theirs for a point, etc. Continue with a new word.

Exercise 5
- Give Ss time to write. Remind Ss to refer to the words in the Vocabulary box to help.
- Ask different Ss to read their texts to the class.

Finishing the lesson
- 🎓 Ask *Can you use sports equipment words to talk about sports?* Students show self-assessment response cards (☺, 😐, ☹).

⏳ Fast finishers
- Ss list equipment you need for other sports they know.

Word list

Unit 0
Get started!
Vocabulary
Numbers 1-20
1 one /wʌn/
2 two /tuː/
3 three /θriː/
4 four /fɔː/
5 five /faɪv/
6 six /sɪks/
7 seven /ˈsevən/
8 eight /eɪt/
9 nine /naɪn/
10 ten /ten/
11 eleven /ɪˈlevən/
12 twelve /twelv/
13 thirteen /ˌθɜːˈtiːn/
14 fourteen /ˌfɔːˈtiːn/
15 fifteen /ˌfɪfˈtiːn/
16 sixteen /ˌsɪkˈstiːn/
17 seventeen /ˌsevənˈtiːn/
18 eighteen /ˌeɪˈtiːn/
19 nineteen /ˌnaɪnˈtiːn/
20 twenty /ˈtwenti/

Numbers 10-100
10 ten /ten/
20 twenty /ˈtwenti/
30 thirty /ˈθɜːti/
40 forty /ˈfɔːti/
50 fifty /ˈfɪfti/
60 sixty /ˈsɪksti/
70 seventy /ˈsevənti/
80 eighty /ˈeɪti/
90 ninety /ˈnaɪnti/
100 a hundred /ə ˈhʌndrəd/

Colours
black /blæk/
blue /bluː/
brown /braʊn/
green /griːn/
grey /greɪ/
orange /ˈɒrəndʒ/
pink /pɪŋk/
purple /ˈpɜːpəl/
red /red/
white /waɪt/
yellow /ˈjeləʊ/

In my bag
book /bʊk/
coloured pencil /ˌkʌləd ˈpensəl/
notebook /ˈnəʊtbʊk/
pen /pen/
pencil /ˈpensəl/
pencil case /ˈpensəl keɪs/
pencil sharpener /ˈpensəl ˌʃɑːpənə/
rubber /ˈrʌbə/
ruler /ˈruːlə/
sandwich /ˈsæn(d)wɪdʒ/
scissors /ˈsɪzəz/

Classroom objects
bin /bɪn/
board /bɔːd/
chair /tʃeə/
clock /klɒk/
desk /desk/

Classroom language
Close your books.
Listen (to the story).
Look (at the photo).
Open your books.
Read (the text).
Sit down.
Stand up.
Work in pairs.
Write (your name), please.
***
Can you help me?
Can you repeat (that)?
I'm ready.
What's *kredka* in English?
Other
cupcake /ˈkʌpkeɪk/
double /ˈdʌbəl/

Unit 1
Family and friends
1.1

Vocabulary Family
aunt /ɑːnt/
brother /ˈbrʌðə/
cousin /ˈkʌzən/
dad /dæd/
daughter /ˈdɔːtə/
father /ˈfɑːðə/
grandfather/grandad /ˈɡrændˌfɑːðə/ /ˈɡrændæd/
grandmother/granny /ˈɡrænˌmʌðə/ /ˈɡræni/
mother /ˈmʌðə/
mum /mʌm/
parents /ˈpeərənts/
sister /ˈsɪstə/
son /sʌn/
uncle /ˈʌŋkəl/

1.2
Say it!
Be careful! /ˌbi ˈkeəfəl/
Hold this, please! /ˈhəʊld ðɪs ˌpliːz/
I've got it! /ˌaɪv ˈɡɒt ɪt/
Other
best friend /ˌbest ˈfrend/
birthday /ˈbɜːθdeɪ/
birthday cake /ˈbɜːθdeɪ keɪk/
card /kɑːd/
class /klɑːs/
classmate /ˈklɑːsmeɪt/
eat /iːt/
friend /frend/
from /frɒm/
happy /ˈhæpi/
Happy birthday! /ˌhæpi ˈbɜːθdeɪ/
Let's have a break. /ˌlets v eɪ breɪk/
lovely /ˈlʌvli/
my darling /ˌmaɪ ˈdɑːlɪŋ/
present /ˈprezənt/
school trip /ˈskuːl trɪp/
She is 70 years old. /ʃi ɪz ˌsevənti ˌjɪəz ˈəʊld/
The cake is a mess. /ðə keɪk s eɪ mes/
We're ready for the cake. /wɪə ˈredi fə ðə keɪk/
yummy /ˈjʌmi/

1.3

Vocabulary Countries and nationalities
American /əˈmerəkən/
British /ˈbrɪtɪʃ/
China /ˈtʃaɪn ə/
Chinese /ˌtʃaɪˈniːz/
France /frɑːns/
French /frentʃ/
Italian /ɪˈtæliən/
Italy /ˈɪtəli/
Poland /ˈpəʊlənd/
Polish /ˈpəʊlɪʃ/
Spain /speɪn/
Spanish /ˈspænɪʃ/
the UK /ðə ˌjuː ˈkeɪ/
the USA /ðə ˌjuː es ˈeɪ/
Other
Bye now! /ˈbaɪ naʊ/
family album /ˈfæməli ˌælbəm/
Help! /help/
hungry /ˈhʌŋgri/
in the photo /ɪn ðə ˈfəʊtəʊ/
name /neɪm/
No idea. /ˌnəʊ aɪˈdɪə/
Sorry. /ˈsɒri/
superhero /ˈsuːpəˌhɪərəʊ/
What about you? /wɒt əˈbaʊt jə/
You're right. /ˌjɔː ˈraɪt/

1.4
Communication
Introductions
He is my classmate.
He is my friend.
Hello, Lucas.
Lucas, this is my mum.
Mum, this is Lucas.
Nice to meet you.
Nice to meet you too.
Other
bag /bæg/
famous /ˈfeɪməs/
film star /ˈfɪlm stɑː/
kids /kɪdz/
Let's go. /ˌlets ˈgəʊ/
neighbour /ˈneɪbə/
pop star /ˈpɒp stɑː/
sports person /ˈspɔːts ˌpɜːsən/

1.5

Vocabulary Places
at a party /ˌæt ə ˈpɑːti/
at home /ət ˈhəʊm/
at school /ət ˈskuːl/
in the garden /ɪn ðə ˈgɑːdn/
in the park /ɪn ðə ˈpɑːk/
on holiday /ɒn ˈhɒlədeɪ/
Other
favourite /ˈfeɪvərət/
great /greɪt/
I'm four. /ˌaɪm ˈfɔː/
near /nɪə/
She's fun! /ʃiz ˈfʌn/
too /tuː/

1.6
Other
interesting /ˈɪntrəstɪŋ/
International Friendship Day /ˌɪntəˌnæʃənəl ˈfrendʃɪp deɪ/
spell /spel/

Get Culture
English around the world
biggest /ˈbɪg ɪst/
capital city /ˌkæpɪtl ˈsɪti/
different /ˈdɪfərənt/
flag /flæg/
live /lɪv/
most people /ˌməʊst ˈpiːpəl/
speak /spiːk/
summer /ˈsʌmə/
winter /ˈwɪntə/

Unit 2
My things
2.1

Vocabulary Clothes
boots /buːts/
cap /kæp/
coat /kəʊt/
dress /dres/
hoodie /ˈhʊdi/
jacket /ˈdʒækət/
jeans /dʒiːnz/
jumper /ˈdʒʌmpə/
shirt /ʃɜːt/
shoes /ʃuːz/
skirt /skɜːt/
T-shirt /ˈtiː ʃɜːt/
top /tɒp/
tracksuit /ˈtræksuːt/
trainers /ˈtreɪnəz/
trousers /ˈtraʊzəz/
Other
at the weekend /ət ðə ˌwiːkˈend, ˈwiːkend/

2.2

Vocabulary Adjectives
big /bɪg/
boring /ˈbɔːrɪŋ/
cool /kuːl/
long /lɒŋ/
new /njuː/
old /əʊld/
short /ʃɔːt/
small /smɔːl/

Word list

Say it!
Hang on! /ˌhæŋ 'ɒn/
Here you are. /'hɪə jə ˌɑː/
Over there. /ˌəʊvə 'ðeə/
What's up? /ˌwɒts 'ʌp/
Other
put away /ˌpʊt ə'weɪ/
too (small) /tuː (smɔːl)/

2.3
Other
Are you sure? /ˌɑː jə 'ʃɔː/
box /bɒks/
boy /bɔɪ/
clever cat /ˈklevə ˈkæt/
cool /ˌkuːl/
girl /gɜːl/
size /saɪz/
suit /suːt/

2.4
Communication
Asking for personal information
How old are you?
What's your favourite film?
What's your favourite music?
What's your favourite sport?
What's your name?
Where are you from?
Who's your favourite actor?
Who's your favourite singer?
Who's your favourite sports person?
Other
Good question. /gʊd ˈkwestʃ(ə)n/
High five! /ˌhaɪ 'faɪv/
rock /rɒk/
school band /ˌskuːl 'bænd/

2.5
Vocabulary My things
backpack /ˈbækpæk/
games console /ˈgeɪmz kənˌsəʊl/
laptop computer /ˌlæptɒp kəm'pjuːtə/
mobile phone /ˌməʊbaɪl 'fəʊn/
mountain bike /ˈmaʊntən baɪk/
skateboard /ˈskeɪtbɔːd/
Other
Congratulations! /kənˌgrætʃəˈleɪʃənz/
Don't worry! /ˌdəʊnt 'wʌri/
even /ˈiːvən/
fantastic /fænˈtæstɪk/
favourites /ˈfeɪvrəts/
gadget /ˈgædʒət/
How cool is that? /haʊ ˌkuːl ɪz 'ðæt/
No problem. /ˌnəʊ 'prɒbləm/
pet /pet/
pocket /ˈpɒkət/

right size /raɪt saɪz/
That's easy. /ˌðæts 'iːzi/
That's not all. /ˌðæts nɒt 'ɔːl/
That's right. /ˌðæts 'raɪt/
You're cold. /ˌjɔː 'kəʊld/

Unit 3
In the house

3.1
Vocabulary In the house
Parts of the house
bathroom /ˈbɑːθrʊm/
bedroom /ˈbedrʊm/
door /dɔː/
floor /flɔː/
garage /ˈgærɪdʒ/
garden /ˈgɑːdn/
kitchen /ˈkɪtʃən/
living room /ˈlɪvɪŋ ruːm/
wall /wɔːl/
window /ˈwɪndəʊ/
Inside the house
armchair /ˈɑːmtʃeə/
bath /bɑːθ/
bed /bed/
chair /tʃeə/
desk /desk/
fridge /frɪdʒ/
sofa /ˈsəʊfə/
table /ˈteɪbəl/
wardrobe /ˈwɔːdrəʊb/

3.2
Vocabulary
Prepositions of place
behind /bɪˈhaɪnd/
in /ɪn/
in front of /ɪn ˈfrʌnt əv/
next to /ˈnekst tə/
on /ɒn/
under /ˈʌndə/
Say it!
Right there! /ˌraɪt 'ðeə/
There it is! /ˈðeər ɪt ɪz/
Wait! /weɪt/
Yuk! /jʌk/
Other
carton /ˈkɑːtn/
DVD /ˌdiː viː 'diː/
maybe /ˈmeɪbi/
milk /mɪlk/
orange juice /ˈɒrəndʒ dʒuːs/
some /səm/
sweets /swiːts/

3.3
Other
bad people /ˌbæd 'piːpəl/
car /kɑː/
go /gəʊ/
naughty /ˈnɔːti/
number /ˈnʌmbə/
parrot /ˈpærət/
silly /ˈsɪli/
tree /triː/

3.4
Communication
Having a guest
Hello.
It's downstairs.
It's next to the living room.
It's upstairs.
Let me show you.
No, thank you.
Please, come in.
Thank you.
Where's the bathroom, please?
Would you like a sandwich?
Yes, please.
Other
another /əˈnʌðə(r)/
I'd like … /ˌaɪd 'laɪk/
Not really. /ˌnɒt 'rɪəli/

3.5
Vocabulary
Household objects
carpet /ˈkɑːpət/
cushion /ˈkʊʃən/
lamp /læmp/
plant /plɑːnt/
poster /ˈpəʊstə/
television (TV) /ˈteləˌvɪʒən (ˌtiː 'viː)/
Other
competition /ˌkɒmpəˈtɪʃən/
dream /driːm/
inside /ɪnˈsaɪd/
It looks typical. /ɪt ˌlʊks 'tɪpɪkəl/
look at /ˈlʊk ət/
perfect /ˈpɜːfɪkt/
picture /ˈpɪktʃə/
skateboarder /ˈskeɪtbɔːdə/
something /ˈsʌmθɪŋ/
Think about it! /ˈθɪŋk əˌbaʊt ɪt/
train /treɪn/
Why? /waɪ/

Get Culture
Houses in the UK
Types of houses
block of flats /ˌblɒk əv 'flæts/
cottage /ˈkɒtɪdʒ/
detached house /dɪˈtætʃt haʊs/
houseboat /ˈhaʊsbəʊt/
semi-detached house /ˈsemi dɪˈtætʃt haʊs/
terraced houses /ˈterəst ˌhaʊz ɪz/
Other
country /ˈkʌntri/
fantastic /fænˈtæstɪk/
floor /flɔː/
next door /ˌnekst 'dɔː/
tree-house /ˈtriː haʊs/
view /vjuː/

Unit 4
About me

4.1
Vocabulary
Face and hair
Face
ears /ɪəz/
eyes /aɪz/
mouth /maʊθ/
nose /nəʊz/
teeth /tiːθ/
Hair
blond /blɒnd/
curly /ˈkɜːli/
dark /dɑːk/
red /red/
spiky /ˈspaɪki/
straight /streɪt/
wavy /ˈweɪvi/

4.2
Vocabulary
Parts of the body
arm /ɑːm/
body /ˈbɒdi/
fingers /ˈfɪŋgəz/
foot /fʊt/
hand /hænd/
head /hed/
leg /leg/
neck /nek/
toes /təʊz/
Say it!
Help me, please! /ˈhelp mi pliːz/
It isn't my fault! /ɪt ˌɪzənt maɪ 'fɔːlt/
Stop it! /ˈstɒp ɪt/
Other
a lot of /ə 'lɒt əv/
fine /faɪn/
high /ˌhaɪ/
Hurry up! /ˌhʌri 'ʌp/
Ouch! /aʊtʃ/
tall /tɔːl/
time /taɪm/

4.3
Other
battery power /ˈbætəri ˌpaʊə/
hero /ˈhɪərəʊ/
like /laɪk/
super power /ˈsuːpə ˌpaʊə/

4.4
Communication
Apologising
Are you OK?
I'm so sorry.
Sorry about that!
Sorry, my mistake.
***
I'm fine.
It's OK.
No problem.
That's all right.

132

Word list

Other
house keys /haʊs kiːz/
Oh, dear. /əʊ dɪə/
sweetie /ˈswiːti/

4.5
Vocabulary
Personality adjectives
clever /ˈklevə/
friendly /ˈfrendli/
funny /ˈfʌni/
helpful /ˈhelpfəl/
nice /naɪs/
sporty /ˈspɔːti/

Other
always /ˈɔːlwəz/
answer /ˈɑːnsə/
dancing /ˈdɑːnsɪŋ/
do a quiz /ˌduː ə ˈkwɪz/
good at /ˈɡʊd ət/
good student /ˌɡʊd ˈstjuːdənt/
group /ɡruːp/
hobby /ˈhɒbi/
home lover /ˈhəʊm ˌlʌvə/
homework /ˈhəʊmwɜːk/
How many? /ˌhaʊ ˈmeni/
joke /dʒəʊk/
kind /kaɪnd/
party animal /ˈpɑːti ˌænəməl/
person /ˈpɜːsən/
personality /ˌpɜːsəˈnæləti/
place /pleɪs/
reading /ˈriːdɪŋ/
room /ruːm/
say /seɪ/
sometimes /ˈsʌmtaɪmz/
speak to /ˈspiːk tə/
subject /ˈsʌbdʒɪkt/
usually /ˈjuːʒuəli/

Unit 5
Things I can do

5.1
Vocabulary
Action verbs
act /ækt/
climb /klaɪm/
cook /kʊk/
dive /daɪv/
draw /drɔː/
fix /fɪks/
fly /flaɪ/
jump /dʒʌmp/
read /riːd/
ride /raɪd/
run /rʌn/
sing /sɪŋ/
skateboard /ˈskeɪtbɔːd/
swim /swɪm/
write /raɪt/

5.2
Vocabulary
make, play, ride
make a poster /ˌmeɪk ə ˈpəʊstə/
make cupcakes /ˌmeɪk ˈkʌpkeɪks/
play computer games /ˌpleɪ kəmˈpjuːtə ɡeɪmz/
play football /ˌpleɪ ˈfʊtbɔːl/
play the piano /ˌpleɪ ðə piˈænəʊ/
ride a bike /ˌraɪd ə ˈbaɪk/
ride a horse /ˌraɪd ə ˈhɔːs/

Say it!
Let me see … /ˌlet mi ˈsiː/
Not again! /ˌnɒt əˈɡen/
What's wrong? /ˌwɒts ˈrɒŋ/

Other
all day /ˌɔːl ˈdeɪ/
camera /ˈkæmərə/
can /kæn/
I can't see a thing. /aɪ ˌkɑːnt ˌsiː ə ˈθɪŋ/
talented /ˈtæləntəd/
video /ˈvɪdiəʊ/
well /wel/

5.3
Other
boat /bəʊt/
fast /fɑːst/
lovely day /ˌlʌvli ˈdeɪ/
One minute, please. /ˌwʌn ˈmɪnət ˌpliːz/
who /huː/

5.4
Communication
Suggestions
Let's do something fun!
Let's go ice skating!
We can go to the park!
***
Great idea!
I agree!
I'm not sure.
It's not a good idea.
Let's do that!

Other
guys /ɡaɪz/
teach /tiːtʃ/
wear /weə/

5.5
Other
alphabet /ˈælfəbet/
course /kɔːs/
hear /hɪə/
important /ɪmˈpɔːtənt/
language /ˈlæŋɡwɪdʒ/
learn /lɜːn/
letter /ˈletə/
make friends with /ˌmeɪk ˈfrendz wɪð/
sign language /ˈsaɪn ˌlæŋɡwɪdʒ/
teacher /ˈtiːtʃə/
TV programme /ˌtiː ˈviː ˌprəʊɡræm/
word /wɜːd/

5.6
Other
after school /ˌɑːftə ˈskuːl/
ball /bɔːl/
class /klɑːs/
club /klʌb/
come /kʌm/
game /ɡeɪm/
now /naʊ/
paint /peɪnt/
star /stɑː/
today /təˈdeɪ/

Get Culture
Kid's London
activity /ækˈtɪvəti, əkˈtɪvɪti/
comic /ˈkɒmɪk/
dinosaur /ˈdaɪnəsɔː/
from the top of /frəm ðə ˈtɒp əv/
kid /kɪd/
museum /mjuːˈziəm/
musical /ˈmjuːzɪkəl/
puppet /ˈpʌpət, ˈpʌpɪt/
scientist /ˈsaɪəntəst, ˈsaɪəntɪst/
show /ʃəʊ/
together /təˈɡeðə/
workshop /ˈwɜːkʃɒp/

Unit 6
My day

6.1
Vocabulary
Daily activities
do my homework /ˌduː maɪ ˈhəʊmwɜːk/
get up /ˌɡet ˈʌp/
go to bed /ˌɡəʊ tə ˈbed/
go to school /ˌɡəʊ tə ˈskuːl/
hang out with my friends /ˌhæŋ ˌaʊt wɪð maɪ ˈfrendz/
have a shower /ˌhæv ə ˈʃaʊə/
have breakfast /ˌhæv ˈbrekfəst/
have dinner /ˌhæv ˈdɪnə/
have lessons /ˌhæv ˈlesənz/
have lunch /ˌhæv ˈlʌntʃ/
listen to music /ˌlɪsən tə ˈmjuːzɪk/
tidy my room /ˌtaɪdi maɪ ˈruːm/
watch TV /ˌwɒtʃ ˌtiː ˈviː/

6.2
Say it!
Come on, guys! /ˌkʌm ˈɒn ɡaɪz/
Me too. /mi ˈtuː/
Seriously? /ˈsɪəriəsli/

Other
classical music /ˌklæsɪkəl ˈmjuːzɪk/
daily routine /ˌdeɪli ruːˈtiːn/
early /ˈɜːli/
get ready for school /ˌɡet ˌredi fə ˈskuːl/
in the evening /ɪn ði ˈiːvnɪŋ/
late for school /ˌleɪt fə ˈskuːl/
never /ˈnevə/
pancakes /ˈpænkeɪks/
really /ˈrɪəli/
school survey /ˈskuːl ˌsɜːveɪ/
walk /wɔːk/

6.3
Vocabulary
Days of the week
Monday /ˈmʌndi/
Tuesday /ˈtjuːzdi/
Wednesday /ˈwenzdi/
Thursday /ˈθɜːzdi/
Friday /ˈfraɪdi/
Saturday /ˈsætədi/
Sunday /ˈsʌndi/

Other
busy /ˈbɪzi/
busy week /ˌbɪzi ˈwiːk/
free day /ˌfriː ˈdeɪ/
gym /dʒɪm/
How about Tuesday? /ˌhaʊ əˌbaʊt ˈtjuːzdi/
mess /mes/
often /ˈɒfən/
swimming lesson /ˈswɪmɪŋ ˌlesən/
team /tiːm/
visit /ˈvɪzət/

6.4
Communication
Telling the time
What time is it?
It's four o'clock.
***
What time is the film?
What time is the match?
It's at ten (minutes) past four.
It's at quarter past four.
It's at half past four.
It's at quarter to five.
It's at ten (minutes) to five.

Other
That's better. /ˌðæts ˈbetə/
The film is on again at … /ðə ˌfɪlm s ɒn əˈɡen ət/
too late /ˌtuː ˈleɪt/

6.5
Vocabulary *Months*
January /ˈdʒænjuəri/
February /ˈfebruəri/
March /mɑːtʃ/
April /ˈeɪprəl/
May /meɪ/
June /dʒuːn/
July /dʒʊˈlaɪ/
August /ˈɔːɡəst/
September /sepˈtembə/
October /ɒkˈtəʊbə/

Word list

November /nəʊˈvembə/
December /dɪˈsembə/

Other
animal /ˈænɪm(ə)l/
blog /blɒg/
every /ˈevri/
life /laɪf/
live /lɪv/
love /lʌv/
my own /maɪ əʊn/
online /ˈɒnlaɪn/
teenagers /ˈtiːnˌeɪdʒə(r)z/
travel /ˈtræv(ə)l/
walking /ˈwɔːkɪŋ/
writing /ˈraɪtɪŋ/

6.6

Other
grandparents /ˈgrændˌpeərənts/
meet my friend /ˌmiːt maɪ ˈfrend/
take the bus /ˌteɪk ðə ˈbʌs/

Unit 7
Animals

7.1

Vocabulary
Wild animals
bird /bɜːd/
butterfly /ˈbʌtəflaɪ/
crocodile /ˈkrɒkədaɪl/
elephant /ˈeləfənt/
fish /fɪʃ/
fly /flaɪ/
frog /frɒg/
giraffe /dʒəˈrɑːf/
kangaroo /ˌkæŋgəˈruː/
lion /ˈlaɪən/
monkey /ˈmʌŋki/
snake /sneɪk/
spider /ˈspaɪdə/
tiger /ˈtaɪgə/
whale /weɪl/

7.2

Vocabulary **Pets**
cat /kæt/
dog /dɒg/
goldfish /ˈgəʊldˌfɪʃ/
hamster /ˈhæmstə/
iguana /ɪˈgwɑːnə/
parrot /ˈpærət/
rabbit /ˈræbət/
tortoise /ˈtɔːtəs/

Say it!
I don't mind! /aɪ ˌdəʊnt ˈmaɪnd/
Oh, all right! /əʊ ˌɔːl ˈraɪt/
Poor (dog)! /ˌpɔː (ˈdɒg)/

Other
at the weekend /ət ðəˌwiːkˈend/
because /bɪˈkɒz/
before /bɪˈfɔː/
every day /ˌevri ˈdeɪ/
hard work /ˌhɑːd ˈwɜːk/
I'm allergic (to) /aɪm əˈlɜːdʒɪk (tə)/
puppy /ˈpʌpi/
take the dog for a walk /ˌteɪk ðə ˌdɒg fər ə ˈwɔːk/

7.3

Other
at all /ət ˈɔːl/
foreign language /ˌfɒrən ˈlæŋgwɪdʒ/
interview /ˈɪntəvjuː/
magazine /ˌmægəˈziːn/
player /ˈpleɪə/
relax /rɪˈlæks/
reporter /rɪˈpɔːtə/
together /təˈgeðə/
win /wɪn/
work /wɜːk/

7.4

Communication
Buying a ticket
Can I have one ticket to the zoo, please?
Can I have two tickets to the zoo, please?
Can I help you?
Here are your tickets.
Here is your ticket.
Here you are.
Thanks.
That's eighteen pounds fifty.

Other
guide /gaɪd/
I could eat a horse. /aɪ kəd iːt eɪ hɔːs/
pass /pɑːs/
start /stɑːt/

7.5

Vocabulary
Adjectives
cute /kjuːt/
dangerous /ˈdeɪndʒərəs/
fast /fɑːst/
slow /sləʊ/
strong /strɒŋ/
ugly /ˈʌgli/

Other
amazing /əˈmeɪzɪŋ/
at 55 kilometres an hour /ət ˌfɪfti faɪv ˌkɪləmiːtəz ən ˈaʊə/
drink /drɪŋk/
food /fuːd/
having fun /ˌhævɪŋ ˈfʌn/
hour /aʊə/
jump out /ˌdʒʌmp ˈaʊt/
kilo /ˈkiːləʊ/
leaves /liːvz/
litre /ˈliːtə/
night /naɪt/
plants /plɑːnts/
sleep /sliːp/
think /θɪŋk/
water /ˈwɔːtə/

7.6

Other
at night /ət ˈnaɪt/
children /ˈtʃɪldrən/
dog food /ˈdɒg fuːd/
easy /ˈiːzi/
in the day /ɪn ðə ˈdeɪ/
it's cold /ˌɪts ˈkəʊld/
look after a pet /ˌlʊk ˌɑːftər ə ˈpet/
number one /ˌnʌmbə ˈwʌn/
pet shop /ˈpet ʃɒp/
play /pleɪ/

Get Culture
Pets in the UK
exotic /ɪgˈzɒtɪk/
lose /luːz/
need /niːd/
quiet /ˈkwaɪət/
scary /ˈskeəri/
space /speɪs/
unusual /ʌnˈjuːʒuəl, -ʒəl/

Unit 8
I like that!

8.1

Vocabulary **Sports**
badminton /ˈbædmɪntən/
basketball /ˈbɑːskɪtbɔːl/
cycling /ˈsaɪklɪŋ/
football /ˈfʊtbɔːl/
hockey /ˈhɒki/
ice-skating /ˈaɪs ˌskeɪtɪŋ/
roller skating /ˈrəʊlə ˌskeɪtɪŋ/
sailing /ˈseɪlɪŋ/
skateboarding /ˈskeɪtbɔːdɪŋ/
skiing /ˈskiːɪŋ/
swimming /ˈswɪmɪŋ/
table tennis /ˈteɪbəl ˌtenəs/
taekwondo /taɪˈkwɒndəʊ/
tennis /ˈtenəs/
volleyball /ˈvɒlibɔːl/
windsurfing /ˈwɪnd sɜːfɪŋ/

8.2

Say it!
Maybe. /ˈmeɪbi/
That's true. /ˌðæts ˈtruː/

Other
find /faɪnd/
for example /fər ɪgˈzɑːmpəl/
get wet /ˌget ˈwet/
hate /heɪt/
horse-riding /ˈhɔːs ˌraɪdɪŋ/
rock climbing /ˈrɒk ˌklaɪmɪŋ/
summer camp /ˌsʌmə ˈkæmp/
want /wɒnt/
water sports /ˈwɔːtə spɔːts/

8.3

Other
autograph /ˈɔːtəgrɑːf/
fan /fæn/
right now /ˌraɪt ˈnaʊ/
the same /ðə ˈseɪm/
Well done! /ˌwel ˈdʌn/
whose /huːz/

8.4

Communication
Talking about the weather
What's the weather like?
It's cloudy.
It's cold.
It's hot.
It's rainy.
It's snowy.
It's sunny.
It's warm.
It's windy.
***
It's cold in winter.
It's hot in summer.
It's rainy in autumn.
It's sunny in spring.

Other
appointment /əˈpɔɪntmənt/
at the beach /ət ðə ˈbiːtʃ/
I hope … /aɪ ˈhəʊp/
That's a pity. /ˌðæts ə ˈpɪti/

8.5

Vocabulary
Healthy lifestyle
brush your teeth /ˌbrʌʃ jə ˈtiːθ/
do exercise /ˌduː ˈeksəsaɪz/
drink a lot of water /ˌdrɪŋk ə lɒt əv ˈwɔːtə/
eat fruit and vegetables /ˌiːt ˌfruːt ənd ˈvedʒtəbəlz/
go to bed early /ˌgəʊ tə ˌbed ˈɜːli/
have friends /ˌhæv ˈfrendz/

Other
active /ˈæktɪv/
chocolate /ˈtʃɒklət/
five times a day /ˌfaɪv ˌtaɪmz ə ˈdeɪ/
for a long time /fər ə ˌlɒŋ ˈtaɪm/
from … to … /frɒm … tuː …/
health /helθ/
healthy /ˈhelθi/
meal /miːl/
school bag /ˈskuːlbæg/
tip /tɪp/

8.6

Other
champion /ˈtʃæmpiən/
competitions /ˌkɒmpəˈtɪʃənz/
in the morning /ɪn ðə ˈmɔːnɪŋ/
pizza /ˈpiːtsə/

Audio and video scripts

Students' Book audio scripts

🔊 **1.5** Unit 0, 0.1, Exercise 6
1 A, E   3 W, U   5 M, N
2 G, C   4 B, P   6 I, Y

🔊 **1.6** Unit 0, 0.1, Exercise 8
W = Woman M = Man
1
W: She's Jen Newman.
M: Newman. How do you spell that?
W: N-E-W-M-A-N.
2
W: He's Lucas Ortiz.
M: How do you spell Ortiz?
W: O-R-T-I-Z.
3
W: She's Lian Cavendish.
M: How do you spell that?
W: C-A-V-E-N-D-I-S-H.
4
W: My name's Megan Higgins.
M: How do you spell that?
W: H-I-double G-I-N-S.

🔊 **1.10** Unit 0, 0.2, Exercise 7
a Twenty.   d Forty.   g Eight.
b Seven.   e Twelve.   h Nineteen.
c Thirteen.   f Fifty.

🔊 **1.15** Unit 0, 0.3, Exercise 9
B = Boy T = Teacher G = Girl
1
B: Can you repeat that, please?
T: Yes, Tomas. Giraffe. Giraffe. OK?
2
G: Can you help me, Miss?
T: Yes, Maria. How can I help you?
3
B: How do we say *elefante* in English?
T: We say *elephant*.
4
G: I'm ready!
T: Good. Class, are you ready too?
5
B: What does *amazing* mean?
T: It means *really good*.

🔊 **1.17** Unit 1, 1.1, Exercise 7
W = Woman M = Man
1
W: John is Julia's son.
M: No, he isn't. He's Julia's father.
2
M: Anna is Peter's daughter.
W: Yes, that's right. Anna is Peter's daughter.
3
W: Julia is Agatha's mother.
M: No, that's not right. Agatha is Julia's mother. Julia is Agatha's daughter.
4
M: Agatha is Tom's aunt.
W: Erm … no. She's his grandmother.
5
W: Paul is John's son.
M: Yes. Well done!
6
M: Mark is Anna's cousin.
W: Mark? Yes. Correct.

🔊 **1.21** Unit 1, 1.2, Exercise 10
1 Lucas is Jen's new friend. He's eleven years old.
2 Alex is in Lian's class. They are classmates. They're twelve.
3 Lucas's brother is in Spain now. He's sixteen years old.
4 Jen is ten years old. She's Alex's sister!

🔊 **1.26** Unit 1, 1.4, Exercise 3
A = Adam L = Lisa D = Desi
A: Lisa, this is Desi. He's my best friend. Desi, this is my cousin, Lisa.
L: Hello, Desi. Nice to meet you.
D: Nice to meet you too, Lisa.

🔊 **1.29** Unit 1, 1.5, Exercise 6
B = Boy I = Isabel
1
B: Hey, that's a nice photo.
I: It's my favourite. I'm at a party with Tommy. He's my cousin.
2
I: I'm with you and your mum in this photo.
B: We're in the park.
I: No, we aren't. We're in your garden!
3
I: Look! It's you!
B: Oh, yes! I'm at school.
4
I: It's a photo of my uncle and aunt. They're at home with their dog Vincent.
B: Cool!

🔊 **1.30** Unit 1, 1.6, Exercise 2 and 3
P = Presenter T = Tom M = Maria J = Juan
P: It's International Friendship Day! Phone 005468976 and tell me about your best friends.
1
P: Hello, caller one!
T: Hi! I'm Tom. My best friend is my cousin Monica. She's eleven. Monica's from France. Now she's in the UK with her family.
P: Thank you, Tom!
2
P: Our next caller is Maria from Argentina.
M: Hello. My best friend's name is Jack.
P: How do you spell Jack?
M: J-A-C-K. He isn't from Argentina. He's Chinese. Oh, and he's two years old!
P: That's interesting! Thank you, Maria!
3
P: Caller three is Juan. Hello, Juan!
J: Hi! My two best friends aren't my classmates. They're my neighbours, Giorgia and Toni! They're from Italy. Hello, Giorgia and Toni!
P: Thanks, Juan! Happy Friendship Day everyone!

🔊 **1.33** Get Culture! English around the world, Exercise 4
1 Hiya! I'm Erin. I live in Leeds. It is a big city in the north of England, in the UK.
2 Hi! I'm Peter. My family and I are from the USA. At my school we speak English and Spanish.
3 Hello! My name's Ollie and I'm Australian. My country's very, very big and beautiful.
4 Hello there! My name's Mary and I'm from London, UK. I'm in New York with my aunt and uncle now. They live here.

🔊 **1.35** Unit 2, 2.1, Exercise 3
1 Now, where's my T-shirt? Ah, here it is!
2 Hm … This isn't my jumper. It's Lisa's.
3 … my tracksuit … and my football trainers … and done!
4 Nice skirt, Mum! I love the colour.
5 Oh! It's chilly today. I need a coat!
6 The brown boots or the blue shoes with this dress?

🔊 **1.41** Unit 2, 2.3, Exercise 7
1 Is Superdug's old suit small?
2 Are the puppies white?
3 Are you in class?
4 Is he twelve years old?
5 Are these your shoes?
6 Are we friends?

🔊 **1.46** Unit 2, 2.4, Exercise 3
B = Boy G = Girl
1
B: What's your favourite film?
G: It's *Superman*.
2
G: What's your name?
B: It's Carl Neal. That's N-E-A-L.
3
B: Where are you from?
G: I'm from Paris, France.
4
G: How old are you?
B: I'm twelve.
5
B: Who's your favourite singer?
G: It's Taylor Swift.

🔊 **1.49** Unit 2, 2.6, Exercise 2 and 3
B = Boy G = Girl
1
B: Are these your classmates?
G: Yes, they are. That's my best friend, Sam.
B: His cap's cool.
G: It's cool but it's too big!
2
B: Is she Sam's sister?
G: Yes, she is. Her name's Janet.
B: Is that her skateboard?
G: Yes, it is. It's her favourite thing.
3
B: Are those your new friends?
G: Yes, they are. That's Ben. His backpack's blue.
B: Ah, yes. And his trainers are green.
G: No, they aren't. Ben's trainers are red.
B: His mountain bike's cool!
4
B: Look. That's Monica.
G: Who?
B: Monica. That's her new mobile phone.
G: Her skirt's too long.
B: Yes, it is!

🔊 **1.51** Skills Revision 1&2, Exercise 6
S = Shaun B = Brian
1
S: Is this the sports club?
B: Yes, it is. I'm the sports teacher. I'm Brian Smith.
S: Pardon?
B: My name's Brian Smith. S-M-I-T-H.
S: Nice to meet you!
2
B: Nice to meet you too! What's your name?
S: I'm Shaun.
B: Can you spell that?
S: S-H-A-U-N.
3
S: Cool! Can my best friend come too?
B: Great! What's your best friend's name?
S: David. D-A-V-I-D.
4
B: How old are you Shaun?
S: I'm twelve.
B: Is David twelve too?
S: No, he isn't. He's thirteen.
5
B: What's your address, Shaun?
S: 13 Bristol Road.
B: 30 Bristol Road?
S: No, number 13.

135

2.12 Unit 3, 3.6, Exercise 2 and 3

1. My bedroom is upstairs. My bed is next to the window. It's white and it's very cool. There are two plants in the window. My school things are on my desk. The chair in front of my desk is orange and the cushions on my bed are orange too.
2. My bedroom is downstairs. There's a small white desk and a blue chair. There's a big wardrobe too. My clothes are in the wardrobe. There are two beds next to the wardrobe – one for me and one for my brother. My bedroom isn't very big. There aren't any posters on the walls and there isn't a computer.

2.15 Get Culture! Houses in the UK, Exercise 3

M1 = Martha M2 = Matt

M1: My family and I live in the country. Our house is a cottage in Devon, South England. There are lots of trees behind our house.
M2: I live in a houseboat on the River Thames. It is very small but I like it. The view is always different!

2.17 Unit 4, 4.1, Exercise 7

1. Long straight red hair, green eyes.
2. Short curly brown hair, blue eyes.
3. Long wavy blond hair, brown eyes.
4. Short curly red hair, blue eyes.
5. Short straight brown hair, green eyes.
6. Short spiky black hair, brown eyes.

2.27 Unit 4, 4.4, Exercise 3

G = Girl B = Boy

1
G: Oops! Sorry about that, Pete!
B: No problem.
G: Are you sure?
B: Yes, I'm fine.
2
B: Where's my phone?
G: Sorry, I've got it.
B: That's all right.
3
G: This isn't my jacket.
B: Sorry, my mistake. Here you are.
G: It's OK. Thanks.

2.29 Unit 4, 4.5, Exercise 4

S1 = Sam S2 = Sue

S1: What's that?
S2: It's a quiz. Let's do it. Question one is 'How many good friends have you got?'
S1: I've got ten friends, maybe.
S2: Yes, you're very friendly. My answer is five friends. I think I'm friendly too.
S1: What's question two?
S2: The question is 'Are your jokes funny?' Sorry, Sam. Your jokes are bad!
S1: OK, OK, you're right. But I think your jokes are funny.
S2: Thanks, Sam. You're very nice.
S1: Question three is 'What's your favourite hobby?' That's easy! I *love* sports!
S2: I'm *not* sporty. My answer is 'reading'.
S1: What's question four?

2.30 Unit 4, 4.6, Exercise 2

Kevin is tall. He's got two brown eyes and black hair. He's with his friends Stuart and Bob. His body is yellow.
Spongebob has got a big yellow face and body and short, thin legs. He's with his best friend Patrick Star.
Skipper's got very blue eyes and some 'Cheezy Dibbles'! He's with his friends Rico, Kowalski and Private.

2.31 Unit 4, 4.6, Exercise 3 and 4

G = Girl B = Boy

G: Spongebob Squarepants is very funny and very nice. He's friendly and helpful but he isn't very clever.
B: All Minions are cool but my favourite is Kevin. He's got a friendly face. He's very sporty and he's very funny! He's clever. Oh, and he loves bananas and apples!
G: I like Skipper from *Penguins of Madagascar*. He's helpful and he's got good ideas. He's clever. He isn't usually nice or friendly, but that's OK.

2.33 Skills Revision 3&4, Exercise 6

W = Woman B = Boy

1
W: Put the plant next to the window.
B: Pardon? Where do I put the plant?
W: Next to the window.
B: OK.
2
W: Now, put the books in the schoolbag.
B: Sorry? Put the books where?
W: In the schoolbag.
B: Oh, right.
3
W: Now, please put the cushion on the sofa.
B: The cushion?
W: Yes.
B: OK. It's on the sofa.
4
W: And now, put the armchair in front of the TV.
B: Pardon? Where do I put the armchair?
W: In front of the TV.
B: Right. I can do that.
5
W: Put the lamp behind the sofa.
B: Sorry? The lamp?
W: Yes. Put it behind the sofa.
B: OK.
6
W: Now, please put the computer games under the chair.
B: The computer games?
W: Yes.
B: OK. They're under the chair.

2.39 Unit 5, 5.2, Exercise 8

B1 = Boy 1 B2 = Boy 2

1. Something I can't do … erm … I can't swim.
2. I can draw cartoons.
3.
B1: We can act.
B2: Yes, we can!
4. No, he can't sing at all!
5. I can run fast!
6. My baby brother can't read.

2.47 Unit 5, 5.6, Exercise 2 and 3

1. Come to my club. It's great! Look at my picture! You can learn how to draw and paint. There are twelve students in the club. It isn't boring.
2. I can't act but that's OK. They can teach you how to act. The teacher says we can all be stars. The class is today. Let's go!
3. It's my favourite club. It's for boys and girls from ten to thirteen. I can't run with the ball very fast but that's OK. It's fun and there are games with other schools.
4. My club is cool. It's on Fridays after school. I'm not very sporty but the teacher is very good. There are eighteen kids. We can all swim now and we can dive too.

2.50 Get Culture! Kid's London, Exercise 4

B = Boy G = Girl M = Mum D = Dad

1
B: Hey! I can see our house!
G: Where?
B: There! Behind the park. Can you see it?
G: Yes, I can! It looks so small!
2
M: This is really bad. That's it! I can't draw!
B: No, Mum. It's a very nice … erm … dog.
M: It isn't a dog. It's a horse.
B: You're right. It *is* bad …
M: Oh, well.
3
G: Can we sit here, Dad?
D: Let me see … We've got numbers 15 and 16. There they are.
G: I'm so happy! This is my favourite musical!
D: Good. I'm happy you're happy!
4. This is Mork. Mork is a big dinosaur. He can't fly.
This is Peta. Peta is a small dinosaur. He can fly.

3.2 Unit 6, 6.1, Exercise 5

B = Boy M = Man W = Woman G = Girl

1
B: Can we watch the cartoons? Please?
M: Yeah, OK.
2 Oops!
3
M: Dinner's ready.
G: Mmm! Yummy!
4
B: Night, Mum!
W: Goodnight, sweetie!
5
W: Nicki?
G: Can't hear you! I'm in the shower!
6 All right!

3.12 Unit 6, 6.6, Exercise 2

B = Ben J = Jules

B: Hi, Jules.
J: Hello, Ben. Where's Anna?
B: She's at school.
J: But it's Saturday! She hasn't got lessons today.
B: Anna always goes to Dance Club on Saturday. Dance Club is at school.
J: Oh. And where's your brother Brian? Is he at Football Club?
B: No, he isn't. Brian's at home. He usually does his homework on Saturday.
J: So, what's your typical Saturday, Ben?
B: I often hang out with my friends. We ride our bikes and skateboard in the park.

3.13 Unit 6, 6.6, Exercise 3

I usually get up at 7 o'clock on Saturday. After breakfast I tidy my room. Then I take the bus to school and I play football. I'm in the school football team. I often hang out with my friends after lunch on Saturday. We ride our bikes or skateboard in the park. I usually play computer games before dinner. I go to bed at 10 o'clock on Saturday.
I get up at half past nine on Sunday. I always do my homework after breakfast. I have lunch at home on Sunday with my mum, dad, sister and grandparents. I sometimes meet my best friend after lunch on Sunday. We're in a band! We play our guitars and we sing.

3.15 Skills Revision 5&6, Exercise 6
B = Boy G = Girl G1 = Grace M = Man
W = Woman

1 What can Grace do?
B: Can you skateboard, Grace?
G1: No, I can't. And I can't swim.
B: What can you do?
G1: I can climb. Look!

2 What club is on Thursday?
B: Is Football Club on Tuesday?
G: No, it isn't. Running Club is on Tuesday. Football Club is on Friday.
B: And when's Computer Club?
G: It's on Thursday.

3 What time is the film?
G: What time is it?
W: It's twenty-five past seven.
G: We're late! The film is at quarter to eight!
W: Oh, no. Let's run!

4 Where is Jill?
G: Mr Parker, is Jill at home?
M: No, she isn't. She always has piano lessons on Thursday.
G: But it's Wednesday today!
M: Oh, yes. I'm sorry! Jill has a singing lesson today.

5 What can Uncle Jack do?
G: Look at this photo. It's Uncle Jack and his horse.
B: Wow! Can Uncle Jack ride a horse?
G: Yes, he can, but he can't ride a bike!
B: I can't ride a horse but I can ride a scooter.

3.23 Unit 7, 7.3, Exercise 8
R = Reporter K = Kit

1
R: Do you play the guitar?
K: No, I don't. I just play the piano.

2
R: Do you listen to pop music?
K: Yes, I do. I like pop music!

3
R: Does Superdug eat superhero food?
K: No, he doesn't, but he eats a lot.

4
R: Does Superdug watch TV?
K: Yes, he does. He likes the cartoons and funny films.

5
R: Do you and Superdug hang out every day?
K: No, we don't. But we do a lot of things together.

6
R: Does Superdug have swimming lessons?
K: No, he doesn't. He can swim very well now.

3.28 Unit 7, 7.4, Exercise 3
A = Attendant G = Girl
A: Can I help you?
G: Can I have three tickets to the aquarium, please?
A: That's twelve pounds sixty, please.
G: Here you are.
A: Here are your tickets.
G: Thanks.

3.31 Unit 7, 7.5, Exercise 6
B = Boy G = Girl

1
B: What is it?
G: You can guess. They've got two big strong legs and two short legs. They run fast and they can jump nine metres!
B: Are they tall?
G: Yes, but their babies are very small and cute.
B: They're kangaroos!

2
B: Now you guess my animal. They can fly. They can't hear and they can't eat.
G: Poor things!
B: … but they can drink! They drink from flowers. They are different colours …
G: They're butterflies!

3.32 Unit 7, 7.6, Exercise 2 and 3
I = Interviewer J = Jo
I: Welcome to *Pet Special*. Today I'm in Jo's pet shop. Good morning, Jo!
J: Hi, Michael.
I: Jo, in your shop, what is the favourite pet for children?
J: Hmmm. Children love hamsters and rabbits, but the number one pet in my shop is goldfish.
I: What animal is in that box, Jo? Is it an iguana?
J: No. It's a snake! Careful. It's dangerous!
I: I don't like snakes … Have you got a pet?
J: Yes, a dog. He's here with me. Look.
I: It's cute! What does it eat?
J: It eats dog food and it drinks water. It likes walks too. Dogs like a walk every day. I also have a tortoise.
I: Are tortoises easy to look after?
J: No, they aren't. They sleep when it's cold and they like a garden! Hamsters are easy to look after. They sleep in the day and play at night.
I: Thank you, Jo! Next week we …

3.33 Unit 7, 7.6, Exercise 4
I've got a new pet. It's a baby rabbit! He's white and his ears are black. He's clever and he's very friendly. He likes his rabbit house but his favourite place is the garden. He can run fast and he can jump! He eats grass and red and green vegetables, and he drinks water. I want another rabbit so he has a friend.

3.36 Get Culture! Pets in the UK, Exercise 4
D = Dad L = Liz

1
D: What's the most popular pet in the UK? Can you guess?
L: Cat?
D: No, guess again.
L: Rabbit?
D: Come on, Liz!
L: Dog.
D: That's right!

2
D: Cat is number two.
L: And after that?
D: Erm … Fish? Really?

3
D: There's a list with the top names for pets.
L: What are they?
D: Alfie, Bella …

4
D: I don't see our cat's name in the list.
L: Because 'Mrs C' is an unusual name.
D: The dog's name is in the list: 'George' – number 10.
L: Aww!

3.38 Unit 8, 8.1, Exercise 5
1 I go cycling at the weekend.
2 Do you play basketball?
3 My brother plays hockey!
4 Let's go skiing!
5 Where do you go skateboarding?
6 I go roller skating with my friends.
7 He often goes windsurfing.
8 Can you play badminton?
9 They play table tennis to relax.
10 We can't go sailing today!
11 She plays football!
12 Let's go ice-skating!

3.42 Unit 8, 8.2, Exercise 8
G = Girl M = Man B = Boy

1
G: I like sports but I don't like playing basketball.
M: How about volleyball?
G: Volleyball is OK. I like it.

2
G: I love swimming. What about you, Brian?
B: No, I don't like water sports. I like roller skating.

3
M: Let's go cycling tomorrow. Around seven?
G: What, in the morning?
M: Yes.
G: No way, Dad. I like cycling but I hate getting up early.

4
B: I can play hockey but I don't like it.
G: I like it. What's your favourite sport?
B: Skateboarding. I love it!
G: Me too!

5
G: Jake, why do you like playing football so much?
B: I don't know. I just … do. It's a great sport.
G: I don't like it. It's so boring!

3.44 Unit 8, 8.3, Exercise 6
1 When do you visit your granny?
2 What can you see in the picture?
3 Who is your favourite superhero?
4 Whose phone is this?
5 How many sandwiches are there?
6 Where's my new suit?

3.49 Unit 8, 8.6, Exercise 2 and 3
D = Denise I = Interviewer G = Gary

1 Denise
I: Denise is in Year 7. She's a volleyball champion! Denise, is it easy to be a champion?
D: No, it isn't! But I really love it.
I: Where do you play volleyball?
D: I play at City Club.
I: When do you train?
D: At seven o'clock in the morning.
I: That's early! What time do you get up?
D: At six o'clock, in winter too.
I: Wow! Do you eat special food?
D: I eat fruit and vegetables every day. And I drink a lot of water.
I: Have you got time for your homework?
D: Yes, I always do my homework!
I: Thanks, Denise!

2 Gary
I: Gary is a taekwondo champion. Gary, why taekwondo?
G: It's fun! And three of my friends are in my taekwondo club.
I: When do you train?
G: After school from five to seven o'clock every day.
I: And when are your competitions?
G: They're usually on Saturday mornings.
I: What's your favourite food?
G: I like eating healthy food but I love pizza! We always eat pizza at home on Saturdays.
I: Thank you, Gary!

🔊 **3.51 Skills Revision 7&8, Exercise 6**
Z = Zak B = Belinda
- **Z:** Hi, Belinda. I've got my photos from summer camp.
- **B:** Great! Can I see?
- **Z:** Yes. These are my new friends! Here's the first photo – Beatrice from France. She's got short black hair.
- **B:** Oh, I see. Does Beatrice like tennis?
- **Z:** Yes, she does. She loves it! She plays every day.
- **B:** And who is that boy?
- **Z:** That's Charlie. Look. He's with Bobby.
- **B:** Who's Bobby?
- **Z:** Bobby isn't a boy. He's a dog! He lives at the camp. Hey, Belinda, look at this photo! It's Mel's birthday party.
- **B:** Has Mel got long curly brown hair?
- **Z:** Yes, that's right. And in this photo we're at the zoo. Look at Jeff!
- **B:** Ugh! Jeff's got a snake! It's ugly.
- **Z:** It isn't ugly. It's cute!
- **B:** Your summer photos are lovely, Zak. How often do you speak to your new friends?

Get Grammar! video scripts
M = Max A = Anna H = Hammy

▶ **4 Unit 1, 1.2**
- **M:** Hello. I'm Max.
- **A:** Hi. I'm Anna.
- **M and A:** We're friends!
- **H:** Hi! I'm Hammy.
- **M:** Hammy is my pet hamster.
- **A:** It's Max's birthday today. He's eleven! Hammy, the present! Oh, no!
- **M:** Oh, thank you, Anna! They're … erm … very nice! You're great!
- **H:** I'm sorry.

▶ **5 Unit 1, 1.3**
- **A:** Nice … erm … cat!
- **M:** It isn't a cat. It's Hammy!
- **A:** But Hammy isn't orange.
- **H:** No, I'm not orange and I'm not fat! Look at my ears! They aren't big!
- **M:** I'm not good at this.
- **A:** No, you aren't.
- **H:** But I am! Ta-da!

▶ **10 Unit 2, 2.2**
- **M:** Hey, this isn't my T-shirt!
- **A:** That's my T-shirt! These aren't my trainers!
- **M:** Hey, those are my trainers! This is Anna's too! This isn't my rucksack. It's Anna's! Anna, that is my rucksack!
- **A:** Oh, dear! Yes, it is! Hammy?

▶ **11 Unit 2, 2.3**
- **A:** Max! We're late for the wedding. Are you ready?
- **M:** Yes, I am. What's wrong? Is this shirt OK?
- **H:** No, it isn't.
- **M:** Are my trousers OK?
- **A:** No, they aren't!
- **M:** But these are my only good clothes.
- **H:** Wait!
- **M:** My T-shirt and jeans? Are they OK for the wedding?
- **H:** Yes, they are. Now hurry up!
- **M:** OK, I'm ready now!
- **H:** No, you aren't! Now you're ready!

▶ **15 Unit 3, 3.2**
- **M:** Anna? There's a rat under the sofa.
- **A:** A rat? Help!
- **M:** There are two rats under the table, too!
- **A:** Oh, no! There's one behind the TV.
- **H:** It's OK. They're my friends. Mikey, Momo, Missie and Molly. Oh, right. Would you like some cheese? There is cheese in the fridge, right?
- **A:** Oh, Hammy!
- **M:** Let me see …

▶ **16 Unit 3, 3.3**
- **A:** There isn't a tree.
- **M:** No problem! Is there any orange juice?
- **A:** Yes, there is.
- **M:** Are there any cupcakes?
- **A:** Yes, there are.
- **H:** Yummy!
- **A:** Oh, no! There aren't any glasses.
- **M:** Hold on!

▶ **21 Unit 4, 4.2**
- **M:** Hammy! I've got a hat! Anna's got a hat! We've got sunglasses too! Where are your sunglasses and hat?
- **H:** I haven't got a hat. I haven't got sunglasses!
- **M:** Anna?
- **A:** Mhh?
- **M:** Hammy hasn't got sunglasses or a hat!
- **A:** Hang on … Here you are!
- **H:** What?

▶ **22 Unit 4, 4.3**
- **H:** Max, have you got a brother or a sister?
- **M:** No, I haven't.
- **H:** Has Anna got a brother or a sister?
- **M:** Yes, she has. She's got a sister.
- **H:** Have you got a photo of your sister, Anna?
- **A:** Yes, I have. Here it is. How about you, Hammy? Have you got a brother or a sister?
- **H:** Yes, I have. Look!
- **A:** Wow! That's a lot of brothers and sisters! Have all hamsters got big families?
- **H:** Yes, they have!

▶ **26 Unit 5, 5.2**
- **M:** We can dance!
- **H:** I can't dance …
- **M:** No, you can dance, Hammy! It's very … interesting …
- **H:** And I can't sing!
- **A:** Oh, Hammy… Well, you can't sing very well but you can jump!
- **H:** Oh, yes! I can jump!
- **A:** Oh, no!

▶ **27 Unit 5, 5.3**
- **A:** Hammy, this is Spot. Spot, this is Hammy. Spot is Granny's dog.
- **H:** Hi, Spot! Can you talk?
- **A:** No, he can't talk.
- **M:** What can he do?
- **H:** Can he … erm climb a tree?
- **A:** No, he can't. He's a dog, not a cat. Can dogs climb trees? No, they can't!
- **H:** OK. Can he jump?
- **A:** Yes, he can. Spot, jump! Jump, boy!
- **H:** Can he run fast?
- **M:** Can you run fast, Spot?
- **A:** Come on. Run! Spot!

▶ **32 Unit 6, 6.2**
- **M:** Hammy always sleeps in my bedroom. We go to bed early. Hammy! We read in bed. It's very relaxing. I read a book. Hammy reads his comic. I listen to music. Music is very relaxing. Hammy listens to music too. Hammy! I watch films. Hammy watches films too!
- **H:** Aaaargh!

▶ **33 Unit 6, 6.3**
- **M:** I usually hang out with Anna and Hammy at the weekend.
- **A:** Max and I sometimes play computer games.
- **M:** Hammy doesn't like games. He never plays with us. He is usually in the kitchen. He makes popcorn.
- **M:** We often watch DVDs.
- **H:** And we always eat popcorn!
- **M:** Hammy usually eats all of the popcorn!
- **H:** Sorry!

▶ **37 Unit 7, 7.2**
- **M:** Come on, Hammy. Let's go to school.
- **H:** School? I'm not a student. I don't go to school.
- **M:** It's Pet Day today. We take our pets to class and we talk about them.
- **H:** Oh! I can talk about myself! How about: 'Hello, I'm Hammy the hamster. I don't eat a lot and I exercise every day. Max doesn't take me for a walk. I run a lot … Max doesn't like cats or dogs – he likes me!'
- **A:** Hammy, I don't think it's a good idea. Hamsters don't talk. Only Max and I can understand you!
- **H:** Oh …

▶ **38 Unit 7, 7.3**
- **H:** Hey, there's a quiz here … 'Do you know your friend?' You answer questions about Max and Max – about you.
- **A and M:** That's fun! Let's do it!
- **H:** OK, Anna, Does Max watch DVDs to relax?
- **A:** Yes, he does.
- **H:** Max, do you watch DVDs to relax?
- **M:** Yes, I do!
- **H:** Well done, Anna! OK … Max. Do you and Anna listen to the same music?
- **M:** Yes, we do. We listen to hard rock.
- **H:** Anna, do you listen to hard rock?
- **A:** No, I don't! Max listens to hard rock. I don't like it!
- **H:** Ooops … No point for you, Max. Well done, Anna! You've got 100 correct answers! Max's got only four.
- **A:** Only four? Max!

▶ **43 Unit 8, 8.2**
- **H:** We love sports! Max and Anna like skating.
- **M:** Hammy loves climbing.
- **H:** I like flying too! Yipee! But I hate getting wet!

▶ **44 Unit 8, 8.3**
- **H:** Who is this girl?
- **A:** This is Kimi. She's my new friend. She's Chinese.
- **H:** Where does she live?
- **A:** In Hong Kong.
- **H:** How old is she?
- **A:** I don't know.
- **H:** What does she do? Is she a student?
- **A:** I'm not sure.
- **H:** I don't understand. What's the problem?
- **A:** She doesn't speak English very well and I don't speak Chinese …
- **H:** One moment, please! Nǐhǎo Kimi! Wǒ shī Hammy. Nǐ hǎo ma? (Translation: Hello, Kimi! I'm Hammy. How are you?)
- **A:** Does Hammy speak Chinese?
- **M:** Yes, of course! He's a Chinese hamster!

Get Culture! video scripts

▶ **7 This is the UK**
Hi there! I'm Maddie. Welcome to *Get Culture!* Let's find out about … the United Kingdom! This is the United Kingdom of Great Britain and Northern Ireland. Or, the UK, for short.

There are four countries in the UK: England, Wales, Northern Ireland and Scotland.
This is the UK flag. Its name is the Union Jack. The UK is a very green country. There are also towns and big cities. There are 64 million people in the UK. People from the UK are British. But there are also people from countries like China, France, Poland, Spain and the USA. Wow! 64 million! That's a lot of people! What about your country?
This is London. London is the capital of the UK. It's a big and busy city. 9 million people live here. What's the name of the capital of your country? London is the home of the Royal family. Look! There they are! That's Queen Elizabeth. Those are her grandsons, William and Harry. Prince William has two children, a son and a daughter. That's their mum, Princess Kate.
Are you ready for a question? OK, let's go. What is the name of the UK flag? Is it a) The Union John or b) The Union Jack? That's right, it's 'b', the Union Jack! Well done! See you next time. Bye!

18 Hampton Court Palace

Hi, everyone! It's time for *Get Culture!* Are you ready to find out more about the UK? Let's find out about a famous palace. It's called Hampton Court Palace.
Hampton Court Palace is here, in London. It's a very old palace. How old do you think it is? It's over 500 years old! It's very big.
This is King Henry VIII. He was a very famous king in British history. Hampton Court Palace was his home. There are no kings or queens in Hampton Court Palace today.
Let's have a look inside! There are lots of rooms. Can you guess how many? There are over one thousand! Look at all the paintings on the walls. This is the kitchen. Is it like your kitchen at home? This is the Great Hall. It's a big room for eating and for parties. That's a lot of rooms! How many rooms are there in your house?
Now, let's have a look outside. These are the gardens. They're very big and beautiful. Look at this maze. It's over 300 years old. It's easy to get into the maze but it's very difficult to get out! Hampton Court Palace is a great place to visit.
Now, for a question. How many people can have dinner at Hampton Court Palace at the same time? The answer is 600 people! That's a lot of washing up! Bye for now and see you next time!

29 Free time activities

Hello! And welcome back to *Get Culture!* What's your favourite weekend activity? Is it skateboarding? Are you a good cook? Or is it playing computer games? Let's find out what kids in the UK like to do at the weekend.
This is Rom Park in London. Look at those children on their BMX bikes. They can do clever things on their bikes. They can jump too! Look! He's on a skateboard. Can you skateboard? Wow! Look at that! He can skate on his hands! You can ride a scooter at Rom Park too. Rom Park looks like great fun! Let's check out another great outdoor sport. They've got special hats for climbing. Look how high they can climb. They can climb down the wall too. Skating and climbing are fun! Other sports are fun too. Let's have a look at them.
This sport is called boxing. These children are very good. Can you name this sport? Yes, it's ice-skating! These girls can go very fast! It's a good idea to do sports. They help you to stay fit and you can make new friends too!
Now, time for a question. How many sports can you remember from the clip/video? See you next time! Bye for now.

40 London Zoo

Hi there and welcome to *Get Culture!* Do you like animals? Yes? Great! Then let's find out about a fun and busy place in London, with lots of different animals.
This is London Zoo. It's a very big zoo with nearly 20,000 animals. There are beautiful, tall giraffes. And cute, funny penguins. There are fast animals, like this tiger. And slow animals, like this very old tortoise. There are strange and interesting animals, like this monkey … or this long, black millipede. It has 300 legs. That's a lot of legs! Or this big, green stick insect! Look, it's 22 cm long.
It's great to find out about all these different animals. Which is your favourite?
Let's find out some more about the animals at London Zoo. The animals wake up very early and have their breakfast. The zookeeper gives the penguins fish. This tiger likes to eat meat. The llamas like to have fruit for breakfast. After breakfast the animals like to play. This tiger likes playing with a ball. These monkeys love toys. The penguins like swimming.
Wow, what a busy place London zoo is! Are you ready for a question? How many legs does the millipede have? Can you remember? Does it have a) 200 legs or b) 300 legs? The answer is 'b', 300 legs. I hope you enjoyed finding out about London Zoo. Bye!

Workbook audio scripts

4 Unit 1, 1.6, Exercise 1 and 2
Photo 1
Hi. I'm Rob and I'm ten. I'm from the UK. My best friend is Victor. He's ten too. He isn't British, he's from France. In this photo, we're at Victor's house. My mum and Victor's mum are best friends too.
Photo 2
In this photo, I'm on holiday in the USA. I'm with my cousin Mel. She's twelve. Mel is American. We're good friends.

6 Unit 2, 2.6, Exercise 2 and 3
R = Rose L = Luke
R: Hey, Luke. That's a cool mountain bike. Is it new?
L: Hi, Rosa. Yes, it is. But it's my brother's! My bike is old … but my skateboard is new! Look!
R: Oh, it's great! And red's my favourite colour. Is it your favourite colour too?
L: No, it isn't. My favourite colour is blue, like my new trainers – look! They're my favourite things.
R: Oh, yes. They're cool.
L: So, what's your favourite thing? Is it your games console?
R: Hmm … No! It's my mobile phone. Look!

7 Skills Revision 1&2, Exercise 5
G = Girl M = Man B = Boy L = Lily D = Dad MS = Mrs Smith
Example
G: Is Uncle Tom in the garden?
M: No, he isn't.
G: Is he in the park with his friends?
M: No, he isn't. He's at a party with Aunt Kate.
1
B: What's your favourite birthday present, Lily?
L: This blue jacket is cool, but my new mobile phone is my favourite.
B: Wow! Are those books presents too?
L: No, they aren't.
2
B: What's in that bag, Dad?
D: My new trainers.
B: Your new trousers?
D: No. My new *trainers*.
3
G: Who's your best friend?
B: Jo.
G: Jo? It's his birthday today. He's eleven!
B: No, he isn't. He's *twelve*.
4
B: Mrs Smith, is that your dog?
MS: No, it isn't. My dog is small.
B: Is it brown?
MS: No. It's black and brown.

9 Unit 3, 3.6, Exercise 1, 2 and 3
B = Boy N = Nancy
B: How many rooms are there in your new house, Nancy?
N: Umm, let me think … four, five, no, six. Yes, there are six and a garage.
B: Oh, is it a big house?
N: Well, there are six rooms, but they are small. There's a living room and a kitchen downstairs, and the bathroom isn't upstairs – it's downstairs too. Upstairs there are three bedrooms: my parents' room, my sister's room and my room. I like my bedroom, it's cool.
B: Is there a television in it?
N: No, there isn't. The TV is in the living room.

11 Unit 4, 4.6, Exercise 1 and 2
T = Teacher B = Boy
1
T: Dolphins have got small eyes, long noses and very big mouths. They've got lots of teeth, but it's OK – dolphins are very friendly.
B: Yes, and they're funny too. Are they clever?
T: Yes, they are. They're very clever.
2
T: Pandas have got big black eyes and their bodies are black and white.
B: Are they clever?
T: Yes, they are. But they aren't very friendly.
B: Oh. But I like them! They're funny.
3
T: Ostriches have got long necks and long legs. They're very funny. And they're clever too. But be careful – they aren't friendly.

12 Skills Revision 3&4, Exercise 4
C = Charlie A = Anne
C: Hi, Anne. Come in!
A: Thanks.
C: Have you got your new skateboard?
A: Sorry. It's at home.
C: What about your bike?
A: It's at home too. But I've got a good computer game we can play. Look!
C: That's cool.
A: Where's your computer?
C: It's on the table in the living room. Come on. … Oh, no! It isn't here.
A: Is it in your bedroom?
C: No. I know! It's in the kitchen.
A: Are your parents at home?
C: Mum's in the garden and Dad's in the garage. Come on. Here's my computer.
A: That's a cool photo. Who are they?
C: They're my brother and my cousin. My brother is the boy with short curly blond hair. My cousin Bob's got short dark spiky hair.
A: Charlie, what's that under the table next to the brown box? Look! It's black and white.
C: Where?
A: It's under the table next to that brown box!
C: Oh, that's Mimi, my cat! Come on, Anne. Have you got the computer game?

139

🔊 14 Unit 5, 5.6, Exercise 2, 3 and 4
S = Sarah T = Tommy E = Erin

- **S:** Hi, welcome to the Fix It Club! I'm Sarah. What's your name?
- **T:** I'm Tommy and this is my sister, Erin.
- **S:** Can I help you?
- **T:** Can you fix this? It's Erin's special teddy bear. Look.
- **S:** Let me see … Oh, dear! It hasn't got any eyes!
- **E:** My teddy can't see! And he's only got one ear.
- **S:** Don't worry, I can help your teddy bear. I can make two new eyes. What colour? Black or blue?
- **T:** Blue, please. Can you make an ear too?
- **S:** Yes, I can. One big ear.
- **E:** Thank you.

🔊 16 Unit 6, 6.6, Exercise 1 and 2
I love our holidays in Italy. We always go in August. My aunt lives there. She's British but she lives in Italy. She's a teacher in an Italian school. After breakfast, we usually go to the beach. It's my favourite place. We play games. My favourite game is 'Catch'. That's C-A-T-C-H. We stand in the sea and throw and catch a beach ball. It's fun. We often have a picnic lunch. After lunch, we often go to bed! It's always very hot! After that I have a shower and then we go for a walk. We often walk on the beach. We usually go to bed late, but I always get up early.

🔊 17 Skills Revision 5&6, Exercise 5
G = Girl MW = Mrs Williams

- **G:** This is a nice photo, Mrs Williams. Is this boy your son? He's very tall!
- **M:** Yes, that's Rob. He's at his basketball club in this photo. Can you play basketball?
- **G:** No, I can't! I'm too short. But I can swim. I'm in the school team.
- **M:** My daughter, Ann, can swim too. Here's a photo of her at the swimming pool. She always goes swimming on Saturday mornings.
- **G:** What time is her swimming lesson? I swim on Saturdays too.
- **M:** At eight o'clock.
- **G:** I go at ten o'clock.
- **M:** Ann's cousin Barny goes swimming at ten o'clock.
- **G:** Barny! Has he got long curly black hair?
- **M:** Yes, he has! He's twelve.
- **G:** Barny is in my class at school.
- **M:** He's in this photo. He isn't at the swimming pool. He's on a climbing wall!
- **G:** I like that photo. Who's the girl with the cupcakes?
- **M:** That's Karen. She's Ann's best friend. She can cook great cupcakes.
- **G:** Karen isn't in my class but I think she goes to my school.
- **M:** This is Barny and his friend May. Is May in your class?
- **G:** Yes, she is! She's really nice! I like their bikes. They're cool!
- **M:** They often ride their bikes in the park on Sundays.

🔊 19 Unit 7, 7.6, Exercise 1, 2 and 3
E = Emma T = Ted

- **E:** Hi, Ted. Come and see my new pets.
- **T:** Oh, right. Where are they, Emma? In the garden?
- **E:** No, they're upstairs, in my bedroom. Look!
- **T:** Ooh … Emma, are they hamsters?
- **E:** Yes, they are. Do you like them?
- **T:** Yes, I do. They're cute. I like that brown one – with the white nose! And the other one is brown too. Are they brothers?
- **E:** No, they're sisters! There's another one. She's brown and white. Look, here she comes now.
- **T:** Oh yes. *[to the animals]* Hello! … Oh, she's my favourite! Are they easy to look after?
- **E:** Well, no, not really. It's important to keep them clean and warm. And they need new food every day.
- **T:** What do they eat?
- **E:** They love fruit, but they don't like oranges. And I give them special hamster food from the pet shop.
- **T:** You're so lucky. I like my rabbits, but I want some hamsters too!

🔊 21 Unit 8, 8.6, Exercise 2 and 3
W = Woman T = Tom

- **W:** So, Tom, what's your favourite food?
- **T:** Oh! I love chips. I don't usually eat them because I know they aren't good for me. I eat a lot of fruit and vegetables. And I drink a lot of water every day.
- **W:** What about exercise? Do you like sport?
- **T:** Well, hmmm, I'm not very sporty, but I like cycling. I always walk to school. I sometimes go swimming too.
- **W:** What time do you go to sleep?
- **T:** I usually go to bed at about half past nine, but I don't go to sleep then. I read a book till 10 o'clock.

🔊 22 Skills Revision 7&8, Exercise 4
M = Mum B = Boy
Example

- **M:** What's your homework today?
- **B:** To write about sports in our town.
- **M:** You can write about Hillside Sports Centre.
- **B:** Good idea! Um, how do you spell *Hillside*?
- **M:** H-I-double L-S-I-D-E.

1
- **B:** Where is Hillside Sports Centre?
- **M:** It's next to the cinema.
- **B:** Next to the cinema? Is it new?
- **M:** Yes, it is.

2
- **B:** How many sports can you do there?
- **M:** That's difficult.
- **B:** Nine? Ten?
- **M:** Fifteen, I think.
- **B:** Fifteen?! That's a lot!

3
- **B:** What team sports are there?
- **M:** Football, volleyball and basketball.
- **B:** Great. I love basketball. Can you play hockey there?
- **M:** No, you can't.

4
- **B:** Is there a café where people can speak to their friends?
- **M:** Yes, there is.
- **B:** What type of food has it got?
- **M:** Healthy food. The healthy snacks and fruit juices are great!

🔊 23 Exam Practice 1–4, Part 4
M = Man G = Girl
Look at the picture. Listen and look. There is one example.

- **M:** Look at this picture.
- **G:** There are some monkeys in the garden!
- **M:** Now. Can you see the monkey with the cat?
- **G:** The monkey with the cat? Yes, I can see it. Can I colour its cap purple?
- **M:** Yes, please.

Can you see the monkey with the purple cap? This is an example. Now you listen and colour.

1
- **M:** There's a monkey on a bike. Can you see it?
- **G:** Yes, I can.
- **M:** Can you colour that monkey's cap green?
- **G:** OK. The monkey on the bike has got a cool cap now!

2
- **G:** Look at that monkey! It's got a mobile phone!
- **M:** Oh, yes, I like its phone.
- **G:** Can I colour its cap blue?
- **M:** Yes, that's a good colour for its cap.

3
- **G:** What now?
- **M:** Can you see the monkey in the tree?
- **G:** Oh yes, I can. It's got long arms!
- **M:** Colour that monkey's cap red.
- **G:** Right. The monkey in the tree has got a nice cap now.

4
- **G:** Look at that monkey with the plant.
- **M:** Yes, the plant is very nice!
- **G:** Can I colour that monkey's cap pink?
- **M:** Yes, please.

5
- **G:** The monkey under the tree has got a book. Can I colour its cap?
- **M:** Yes. What colour?
- **G:** My favourite colour is orange.
- **M:** OK. Colour it orange.
- **G:** It's a great picture now!

🔊 24 Exam Practice 5–8, Part 3
G = Grace M = Man
Look at the picture. Listen and write a name or a number. There are two examples.

- **G:** Hello! This is my dog.
- **M:** What's the dog's name?
- **G:** It's Tom.
- **M:** Oh. Can you spell that, please?
- **G:** Yes! T-O-M.
- **M:** Thanks. How old is Tom?
- **G:** He's four.
- **M:** Four?
- **G:** That's right.

Can you see the answers? Now you listen and write a name or a number.

1
- **M:** And what's your name?
- **G:** My name's Grace.
- **M:** Can you spell it, please?
- **G:** Yes, it's G-R-A-C-E.
- **M:** Good!

2
- **M:** Do you go to school?
- **G:** Yes. I go to Bird House school.
- **M:** Oh. How do you spell that?
- **G:** It's B-I-R-D.

3
- **M:** Who sits next to you in class?
- **G:** My friend Alex.
- **M:** Is that a boy or a girl?
- **G:** It's a girl. She spells it A-L-E-X.

4
- **M:** Has Alex got a dog too?
- **G:** No, she hasn't but she has got two parrots!
- **M:** Two parrots?
- **G:** Yes. They live in a small house in the garden.

5
- **G:** Look. This is my favourite book. There's a family of lions in it.
- **M:** Oh. How many lions are there?
- **G:** Eight!
- **M:** Eight!?!
- **G:** Yes, it's a big family. The story is very funny!

Workbook answer key

Unit 0

0.1
Exercise 1
2 Alex 3 Lucas 4 Lian
Exercise 2
2 cupcakes 3 twelve 4 skateboarding
5 Spain 6 Maths
Exercise 3
2 m 3 s 4 a 5 h 6 n
Exercise 4
1 apple 3 hobby 4 music 5 name
6 sport
Exercise 5
2 How do you spell your surname?
3 I'm in the UK now. 4 My hobby is music. 5 I'm twelve years old.

0.2
Exercise 1
2 He is a superhero. 3 Kit is Dug's best friend. 4 She is very clever.
Exercise 2

16	12	1	10
8	4	11	17	6
3	20	14	18	7
19	9	13	2	15

Exercise 3
2 twelve 3 sixteen 4 twenty 5 five
6 nine 7 thirteen 8 seventeen
Exercise 4
2 23 3 71 4 13 5 68 6 19 7 30 8 86
9 42 10 100
Exercise 5
2 black 3 yellow 4 white 5 pink
6 purple 7 green 8 brown 9 grey
10 orange 11 red
Exercise 6
2 blue 3 yellow 4 brown 5 red 6 grey
7 pink 8 black 9 white 10 green

0.3
Exercise 1
2 rubber 3 ruler 4 scissors 5 book
6 coloured pencil
Exercise 2
2 a 3 a 4 a 5 an 6 a
Exercise 3
2 pencils 3 sandwiches 4 notebooks
5 eggs 6 boxes
Exercise 4
desk, chair, board, clock
Exercise 5
2 They're 3 It's 4 It's 5 They're
6 They're
Exercise 6
2 S 3 T 4 T 5 S 6 T
Exercise 7
a 5 b 3 c 4 e 2 f 6

Check yourself!
Exercise 1
1 sixty 2 thirty-two 3 blue 4 yellow
5 black
Exercise 2
1 pencil case 2 notebook 3 chair
4 sandwich 5 clock
Exercise 3
1 They're 2 a 3 It's 4 an 5 They're
Exercise 4
1 oranges 2 boxes 3 bins 4 umbrellas
5 rubbers
Exercise 5
1 please 2 down 3 books 4 pairs
5 up

Unit 1

1.1
Exercise 1
2 e 3 f 4 g 5 b 6 c 7 a
Exercise 2
2 cousin 3 uncle 4 grandad 5 aunt
6 granny 7 son
Exercise 3
2 grandfather/grandad 3 aunt
4 cousins 5 daughter 6 sister 7 son
Exercise 4
2 son 3 cousins 4 grandmother/granny 5 uncle

1.2
Exercise 1
2 is 3 am 4 is 5 is 6 are 7 are
Exercise 2
2 's 3 'm 4 's 5 's 6 're 7 're
Exercise 3
2 am 3 are 4 is 5 are 6 are
Exercise 4
2 His 3 Her 4 your
Exercise 5
2 my 3 are 4 They 5 is 6 Her

1.3
Exercise 1
2 You aren't right. 3 I'm not a superhero. 4 Ben isn't my friend.
5 She isn't my aunt. 6 They aren't my cousins.
Exercise 2
1 isn't at school 2 aren't happy, They aren't at home. 3 isn't a teacher, He isn't ready for school.
Exercise 3
2 France, French 3 the UK, British
4 Italy, Italian 5 China, Chinese 6 the USA, American 7 Spain, Spanish
Exercise 4
1 is/isn't 2 is/isn't 3 are/aren't 4 are/aren't 5 'm/'m not 6 'm/'m not
2 are/'re 3 'm not 4 are/'re 5 is/'s 6 is not/isn't 7 is/'s 8 is not/isn't 9 is/'s

1.4
Exercise 1
2 a 3 b 4 b
Exercise 2
2 He's 3 Hi 4 to meet you 5 Nice
Exercise 3
2 a 3 c 4 d
Exercise 4
Students' own answers.

1.5
Exercise 1
1 B 2 C 3 A
Exercise 2
2 d 3 f 4 a 5 b 6 e
Exercise 3
2 British 3 Spanish 4 Spanish 5 Italian
6 British
Exercise 4
1 party 2 school 3 garden 4 park

1.6
Exercise 1
2 F 3 T 4 T 5 F 6 T
Exercise 2
Rob: British Victor: 10, French
Mel: 12, American
Exercise 3
Clara and Bianca are best friends. Clara is nine and Bianca is ten. Clara is from the UK. She's British. Bianca is from Italy. She's Italian.
Exercise 4
Clara: UK, British
Bianca: Italy, Italian
Exercise 5
Suggested answer:
Pierre and Pedro are best friends. Pierre is 12 and Pedro is 11. Pierre is from France. He' French. Pedro is from Spain. He's Spanish.

1.7
Exercise 1
1 aunt 2 father 3 brother 4 daughter
5 granny
Exercise 2
1 garden 2 American 3 school
4 France 5 home
Exercise 3
1 are 2 is/'s 3 are not/aren't 4 are/'re
5 am not/'m not
Exercise 4
1 His 2 Freddie's 3 her 4 Nadia's
5 Clara's
Exercise 5
1 is 2 Hi/Hello 3 Nice 4 meet 5 too

Word blog
Exercise 1
1 uncle 2 sister 3 granny 4 cousins
Exercise 2
2 e 3 b 4 f 5 c 6 a
Exercise 3
1 present 2 cake 3 balloon 4 party

Fun Spot!
2 A 3 D 5 D 6 A 7 B 8 C 9 B 11 A
12 B
Extra sentences: 4, 10

Unit 2

2.1
Exercise 1
2 jeans 3 hoodie 4 skirt 5 jumper
6 dress
Exercise 2

T	R	A	C	K	S	U	I	T
E	H	B	W	Q	L	W	T	F	D
L	T	V	I	H	S	H	O	E	S
R	R	B	U	E	S	Y	P	U	S
Y	O	I	Y	R	C	L	T	B	H
B	U	T	F	F	A	E	U	X	I
O	S	M	V	C	P	C	G	Q	R
O	E	I	J	A	C	K	E	T	T
T	R	M	Q	W	S	N	Q	D	P
S	S	C	O	A	T	F	I	S	Y

2 trousers 3 boots 4 jacket 5 shoes
6 cap 7 top 8 shirt 9 coat
Exercise 3
2 jumper 3 jeans/trousers 4 boots
5 cap 6 hoodie 7 trousers/jeans
8 shoes/trainers
Exercise 4
2 hoodie 3 shirt 4 tracksuit 5 boots
6 jeans/trousers

2.2
Exercise 1
2 This 3 These 4 Those 5 This
6 That
Exercise 2
1 cool 2 new, old 3 short, long
4 small, big
Exercise 3
2 are too short 3 is too long
4 are too old
Exercise 4
2 These are boring shoes. 3 This is a small shirt. 4 That is an old boot.
5 Those are new trousers.

2.3
Exercise 1
2 . 3 ? 4 ? 5 . 6 ?
Exercise 2
2 Is 3 Are 4 Are 5 Is 6 Is
Exercise 3
a 5 b 3 d 6 e 4 f 2
Exercise 4
1 Yes, they are. / No, they aren't.
2 Yes, he is. / No, he isn't. 3 Yes, she is. / No, she isn't. 4 Yes, it is. / No, it isn't. 5 Yes, I am. / No, I'm not.

Exercise 5
2 I am 3 Is Ben 4 he isn't 5 Are you
6 we are 7 Is he 8 he is
Exercise 6
2 Are you at school? 3 Are you eleven? 4 Is your best friend ten?
5 What is your best friend's name?
6 Are your friends happy?
Exercise 7
Students' own answers.

2.4
Exercise 1
2 b 3 d 4 a 5 c
Exercise 2
2 Where 3 How 4 Who 5 What
Exercise 3
a 2 c 4 d 5 e 3
Exercise 4
2 are you from 3 's your favourite sport
4 's your favourite book 5 's your favourite singer
Exercise 5
Students' own answers.

2.5
Exercise 1
1 B 2 C 3 A
Exercise 2
1 Luke 2 Anna 3 Becky
Exercise 3
2 T 3 F 4 F 5 T 6 T

2.6
Exercise 1
2 mountain bike 3 mobile phone
4 backpack 5 hoodie 6 games console
Exercise 2
1, 2, 3, 6
Exercise 3
1 b 2 a 3 a 4 b
Exercise 4
Suggested answers:
2 . 3 . 4 . 5 ? 6 ! 7 .
Exercise 5
Students' own answers.

2.7
Exercise 1
1 boring 2 backpack 3 cap 4 top
5 skirt
Exercise 2
1 mobile phone 2 shirt 3 jeans
4 trainers 5 skateboard
Exercise 3
1 a 2 b 3 b 4 a 5 b
Exercise 4
1 Yes, it is. 2 No, they aren't. 3 Yes, we are. 4 No, he isn't. 5 Yes, she is.
Exercise 5
a 3 b 5 d 1 e 2 f 4

Word blog
Exercise 1
1 hoodie 2 dress 3 boots
Exercise 2
1 singer 2 actor 3 guitarist
4 superhero
Exercise 3
1 mobile phone 2 backpack 3 skirt
4 jumper 5 cap

Fun Spot!
Suggested answers:
1 In Picture A, the dog is small. It is big in Picture B. 2 In Picture A, the car is boring/old. It is cool/new in Picture B.
3 In Picture A, the dress is long. It is short in Picture B. 4 In Picture A, the boy's tracksuit is green. It is grey in Picture B. 5 In Picture A, the girl's T-shirt/top is white. It is orange in Picture B.

Skills Revision 1&2
Exercise 1
b
Exercise 2
1 cake 2 friends 3 isn't 4 are 5 new
6 top
Exercise 3
1 no 2 no 3 yes 4 no 5 yes
Exercise 4
1 is from the UK / is British 2 is 11/ eleven (years old) 3 is Katia 4 are purple and white 5 is her jacket
Exercise 5
1 C 2 B 3 C 4 A
Exercise 6
1 f 2 e 3 a 4 b

Unit 3
3.1
Exercise 1
2 an armchair 3 a sofa 4 a chair
5 a table 6 a fridge 7 a window
Exercise 2
2 desk 3 wardrobe 4 floor 5 bed
6 wall
Exercise 3
2 bathroom 3 living room 4 bedroom
5 garage 6 garden
Exercise 4
2 c 3 a 4 d 5 b
3.2
Exercise 1
2 There are, A 3 There is, A 4 There is, A 5 There are, B 6 There are, B
Exercise 2
2 in front of 3 on 4 under 5 next to
6 behind
Exercise 3
1 in 2 is, under 3 are, in front of
4 is, behind 5 is, next to
Exercise 4
2 in 3 are 4 on 5 a 6 next to 7 are
8 There
Exercise 5
Students' own answers.
3.3
Exercise 1
2 Are 3 Is 4 isn't 5 Are 6 aren't
Exercise 2
2 There isn't a phone on the table. F
3 There isn't a TV in the room. T
4 There aren't any parrots in the picture. F
5 There aren't any books in the picture. T
Exercise 3
2 Are they any 3 Is there a 4 Are there any 5 Is there a 6 Are there any
Exercise 4
a 2 b 4 c 5 d 6 f 3
Exercise 5
2 Is there a garage next to your house? No, there isn't. 3 Are there any armchairs in your living room? Yes, there are. 4 Are there any pencils on your desk? No, there aren't. 5 Is there a desk in your bedroom? Yes, there is.
Exercise 6
2 an 3 are 4 any 5 are 6 a
3.4
Exercise 1
2 f 3 b 4 e 5 d 6 a
Exercise 2
2 a, c 3 a, b 4 a, c 5 b, c
Exercise 3
2 Thank 3 like 4 Yes 5 Where
6 show
3.5
Exercise 1
1, 2, 4, 5, 8

Exercise 2
1 five 2 two 3 four
Exercise 3
2 carpet 3 lamp 4 poster 5 cushion
6 plant
3.6
Exercise 1
a
Exercise 2
1 In Nancy's house there are six rooms.
2 The bathroom is downstairs. 3 There are three bedrooms. 4 There isn't a TV in Nancy's bedroom. / There's a TV in the living room.
Exercise 3
C
Exercise 4
My dream bedroom by Jack
In my dream bedroom <u>there's</u> a big bed. <u>It's</u> blue. Next to the bed <u>there's</u> a table with a lamp. On the floor <u>there's</u> a big carpet. <u>It's</u> red, yellow and orange. There <u>aren't</u> any plants in the room but there are lots of posters and photos of my friends. There <u>isn't</u> a TV but <u>there's</u> a computer.
Exercise 5
Students' own answers.
3.7
Exercise 1
1 armchair 2 wardrobe 3 window
4 cushion 5 table
Exercise 2
1 bedroom 2 under 3 kitchen
4 in front of 5 fridge
Exercise 3
1 are 2 a pen 3 aren't 4 is 5 aren't
Exercise 4
1 isn't 2 Are 3 any 4 aren't 5 a
Exercise 5
a 4 b 3 c 5 e 1 f 2
Word blog
Exercise 1
1 kitchen 2 bathroom 3 living room
Exercise 2
1 cushions 2 bed 3 armchair 4 wall
5 sofa 6 TV
Exercise 3
1 C 2 D 3 F 4 E 5 A 6 B
Fun Spot!
Suggested answers:
Bedroom:
There's a bath next to the desk.
There's a TV under the desk.
Kitchen:
There's a cat in the fridge.
There's a bed in front of the fridge.
There's a plant on the bed.
Garden:
There's a wardrobe in the garden.
There aren't any plants in the garden.

Unit 4
4.1
Exercise 1
2 hair 3 eye 4 nose 5 teeth 6 mouth
Exercise 2
2 D 3 A 4 C
Exercise 3
1 blond 2 spiky, red 3 curly, black
4 long, black
Exercise 4
1 spiky 2 long, straight 3 curly, black
4 wavy, blond
Exercise 5
2 big blue eyes 3 long curly brown hair
4 short wavy red hair 5 small brown eyes
Exercise 6
2 E 3 H 4 H 5 H 6 E

4.2
Exercise 1
2 has got / 's got 3 have not got / haven't got 4 have got / 've got
5 has not got / hasn't got
6 have got / 've got
Exercise 2
2 He hasn't got a new skateboard.
3 Jen hasn't got a new coat. 4 She's got a new skirt. 5 Alex and Jen haven't got a cat. 6 They've got a games console.
Exercise 3
2 neck 3 arm 4 feet, toes
5 hands, fingers
Exercise 4
2 feet 3 eyes 4 teeth 5 legs 6 feet
7 eyes 8 ears
1 B 2 A
Exercise 5
2 haven't got 3 've got 4 hasn't got
5 've got 6 has got
4.3
Exercise 1
2 Have 3 Has 4 Have
Exercise 2
a 4 b 2 c 3
Exercise 3
2 Have your classmates got super powers? 3 Has your best friend got any brothers? 4 Have you got a sister?
5 Have your parents got a computer?
Exercise 4
2 Yes, they have. / No, they haven't.
3 Yes, he/she has. / No, he/she hasn't.
4 Yes, I have. / No, I haven't.
5 Yes, they have. / No, they haven't.
Exercise 5
1 Their 2 Its 3 Your 4 Our
Exercise 6
2 Has 3 got 4 its 5 Have 6 any 7 've
8 Their 9 haven't
4.4
Exercise 1
1 a 3 b 2 d 4
2 a 2 b 3 c 1 d 4
3 a 2 b 4 c 1 d 3
Exercise 2
2 a 3 b 4 a 5 b
Exercise 3
2 That's 3 sorry 4 OK 5 fine
6 mistake 7 problem
Exercise 4
Jason: Sorry, my mistake. / Sorry about that! / I'm so sorry.
Matt: It's OK. / That's all right. / No problem.
4.5
Exercise 1
1, 2, 3, 4, 5
Exercise 2
2 F 3 T 4 T 5 F
Exercise 3
2 helpful 3 clever 4 friendly 5 funny
4.6
Exercise 1
a panda 2 a dolphin 1 an ostrich 3
Exercise 2

	dolphins	pandas	ostriches
friendly	✓	✗	✗
funny	✓	✓	✓
clever	✓	✓	✓

Exercise 3
Paragraph 1: Elephants are very big! They've got big grey bodies, big ears and very long trunks.
Paragraph 2: Elephants aren't very friendly but sometimes they are helpful. They're clever too.

Exercise 4
Paragraph 2
Exercise 5
Suggested answer:
Giraffes are very tall. They've got long necks and long legs. They are orange and brown.
Giraffes are clever and friendly.
4.7
Exercise 1
1 long 2 big 3 nose 4 legs 5 helpful
Exercise 2
1 funny 2 straight 3 curly 4 friendly
5 clever
Exercise 3
1 Has 2 got 3 Have 4 haven't
5 hasn't
Exercise 4
1 Their 2 your 3 Its 4 Our 5 its
Exercise 5
1 problem 2 mistake 3 all right
4 you OK 5 I'm fine
Word blog
Exercise 1
1 nose, B 2 head, A 3 eyes, A
4 ears, B 5 teeth, A
Exercise 2
1 blond 2 blue 3 subject 4 good
5 sporty 6 funny
Exercise 3
1 house keys 2 batteries
3 good marks
Fun Spot
body: hand, finger, toe, foot, mouth
personality: clever, nice, funny, friendly

Skills Revision 3&4
Exercise 1
1 F 2 T 3 F 4 T 5 F
Exercise 2
1 are 2 sister 3 kitchen 4 small 5 got
6 old 7 behind
Exercise 3
1 He's American. / He's from the USA.
2 He's got short brown hair. 3 He's got blue eyes. 4 He is friendly and funny.
5 He's got two sisters.
Exercise 4
1 A 2 B 3 A 4 C
Exercise 5
1 c 2 e 3 a 4 g

Unit 5
5.1
Exercise 1
2 e 3 a 4 c 5 b 6 g 7 h 8 d
Exercise 2
2 act 3 sing 4 cook 5 write
Exercise 3
2 Fly 3 Climb 4 Read 5 Write 6 Ride
Exercise 4
2 fix 3 write 4 run 5 swim
5.2
Exercise 1
2 can't 3 can't 4 can't 5 can 6 can
Exercise 2
2 Sam can't run fast. 3 Grandad can play football. 4 Mum can't skateboard.
5 Sally can't cook very well.
Exercise 3
2 Lucas can't sing well. 3 Alex can fix computers. 4 Granny can't play the guitar. 5 Jen can make cupcakes.
Exercise 4
Suggested answers:
2 ✓ 3 ✗, I can't fly. 4 ✗, Dogs can't read. 5 ✓ / ✗, My friend can cook.
6 ✓ / ✗, I can read Chinese.
Exercise 5
2 make 3 ride 4 ride 5 play 6 make
Student's own answers.

Exercise 6
Suggested answers:
2 can/can't play **3** can/can't make
4 can/can't fix **5** can/can't ride
6 can/can't run
5.3
Exercise 1
2 Can I/you draw? **3** Can Tom run fast? **4** Can May sing well? **5** Can we/you help? **6** Can the cat climb?
Exercise 2
2 No, they can't. **3** No, she can't.
4 No, he can't. **5** No, it can't.
6 Yes, he can.
Exercise 3
2 Can you play volleyball? **3** Can your mum speak English? **4** Can your classmates speak Spanish? **5** Can you ride a horse? **6** Can your best friend play the piano?
Exercise 4
Suggested answers:
1 Yes, I can. / No, I can't. **2** Yes, I can. / No, I can't. **3** Yes, she can. / No, she can't. **4** Yes, they can. / No, they can't.
5 Yes, I can. / No, I can't. **6** Yes, he/she can. / No, he/she can't.
Exercise 5
2 see **3** can **4** Can **5** help **6** Can **7** dance **8** can **9** Can **10** play
11 can't
5.4
Exercise 1
2 f **3** b **4** d **5** a **6** c
Exercise 2
2 good ☹ **3** idea ☺ **4** sure ☺ **5** agree ☺
Exercise 3
a 6 **b** 2 **c** 5 **e** 4 **f** 3
Exercise 4
2 a **3** a **4** b **5** a
Exercise 5
Suggested answers:
1 B: I agree! / Let's do that! / Great idea!
2 A: Let's watch that! / We can watch that!
B: I'm not sure.
3 A: Let's go there! / We can go there!
B: It's not a good idea.
5.5
Exercise 1
1 eyes **2** ears **3** nose
Exercise 2
2 hear **3** hands **4** friends
Exercise 3
a
Exercise 4
2 Jasmine **3** lots of friends **4** can
5 aren't
Exercise 5
2 e **3** a **4** f **5** c **6** d
5.6
Exercise 1
teddy bear
Exercise 2
fix an old teddy bear
Exercise 3
C
Exercise 4
1 Erin **2** his sister's **3** Yes, she can.
4 They're blue.
Exercise 5
2 and **3** but **4** and **5** but
Exercise 6
Student's own answers.
5.7
Exercise 1
1 jump **2** write **3** climb **4** cook
5 skateboard

Exercise 2
1 play **2** make **3** read **4** ride **5** play
Exercise 3
1 can **2** and **3** but **4** can't **5** can
Exercise 4
1 Yes, she can. **2** Can the dogs sing?
3 No, they can't. **4** Can the boy ride his bike? **5** Yes, he can.
Exercise 5
1 can **2** sure **3** can't **4** problem
5 Great/Good
Word blog
Exercise 1
1 play football **2** run **3** swim
4 ride a horse **5** jump
Exercise 2
1 ride **2** wrong **3** Can **4** pool **5** idea
6 play
Exercise 3
1 alphabet **2** letters **3** words
Fun Spot
1 can **2** can **3** can't **4** can **5** can't
6 can't **7** can **8** can

Unit 6
6.1
Exercise 1
1 ✗ have a shower, ✓ listen to music, ✓ do my homework, ✓ hang out with my friends
2 ✗ have lessons, ✓ have lunch, ✓ watch TV, ✗ get up, ✓ have breakfast
Exercise 2

F	D	R	R	E	W	O	R	Y	T	C	S
R	I	H	O	M	E	W	O	R	K	A	H
I	N	O	L	U	Y	F	O	P	P	O	O
E	N	T	V	S	G	E	M	X	I	W	W
N	E	E	Q	I	E	C	K	D	S	S	E
D	R	R	S	C	H	O	O	L	O	M	R

2 room **3** dinner **4** shower **5** music
6 school **7** TV **8** friend
Exercise 3
2 get up **3** do **4** go **5** go **6** have
Exercise 4
1 I get up in the morning. **2** I have breakfast. **3** I go to school. **5** I do my homework. **6** I go to bed.
Exercise 5
in the living room: get up
in the kitchen: tidy my room
in the bedroom: have a shower
6.2
Exercise 1
2 does **3** play **4** get up **5** listens
6 goes
Exercise 2
2 do **3** draws **4** drink **5** look
6 washes **7** carry
Exercise 3
2 He goes to school with his sister.
3 He does his homework before dinner.
4 He watches TV after dinner.
5 He plays football with his friends.
Exercise 4
1 drinks **2** watch, play **3** tidies, helps
4 has, eats **5** hang out, have
6 does, watches
Exercise 5
Suggested answers:
1 I have lunch (at school too).
2 Laura does her homework in the kitchen. I do my homework (in my room). **3** Laura plays the piano. I play (the guitar). **4** Laura likes apples. I like (cupcakes).

6.3
Exercise 1
2 always **3** usually **4** sometimes
5 never **6** sometimes
Exercise 2
2 Kit often helps me at home.
3 Uncle Roberto sometimes visits me.
4 I never cook dinner. **5** Kit is always happy. **6** Kit and I usually have fun.
Exercise 3
3 Wednesday **2** Tuesday **6** Saturday
7 Sunday **4** Thursday **5** Friday
Exercise 4
2 usually gets up late on Sunday
3 is usually happy **4** often plays football on Saturday **5** sometimes plays computer games
Exercise 5
Student's own answers.
6.4
Exercise 1
2 a **3** g **4** h **5** e **6** d **7** f **8** c
Exercise 2
2 twenty (minutes) past twelve
3 half past twelve **4** twenty-five (minutes) to three **5** ten (minutes) to three **6** five (minutes) to three
Exercise 3
2 It's at quarter past seven. **3** What time is *Happy Days*? **4** What time is *Super Girl*? **5** It's at ten (minutes) to eight. **6** What time is it now?
Exercise 4
b 4 **c** 6 **d** 2 **e** 3 **f** 5
Exercise 5
Student's own answers.
6.5
Exercise 1
1 Mike E, F **2** Dasha A, C, D
Exercise 2
2 T **3** F **4** T **5** F **6** F
Exercise 3
1 big **2** his friends **3** has lessons
4 busy
Exercise 4
2 February **3** June **4** October **5** April
6 August
Exercise 5
1 February **2** April **3** June **4** August
5 October
6.6
Exercise 1
2 British **3** teacher **4** beach **5** catch
Exercise 2
2 usually **3** often **4** often **5** always
Exercise 3
We never go to school in August. It's a holiday! I get up late. I often play computer games <u>before</u> breakfast. I never have breakfast in bed. I have it in the kitchen. <u>After</u> breakfast I often hang out with friends. <u>Before</u> dinner I sometimes help my parents. I usually watch TV <u>after</u> dinner. I often go to bed late.
Exercise 4
1 play computer games **3** have breakfast **4** hang out with friends
5 help my parents **6** have dinner
7 watch TV **8** go to bed
Exercise 5
Student's own answers.
6.7
Exercise 1
1 have **2** hang **3** play **4** watch **5** go
Exercise 2
1 August **2** Saturday **3** November
4 April **5** Wednesday

Exercise 3
1 go **2** likes **3** tidies **4** do **5** have
Exercise 4
1 I am always busy. **2** We often play tennis. **3** Mum never watches TV.
4 I sometimes tidy my room.
5 Jess is usually late.
Exercise 5
1 past **2** is **3** minutes **4** at **5** clock
Word blog
Exercise 1
1 past **2** shower, o'clock
3 lunch, quarter **4** do, five
Exercise 2
2 Friday **3** Wednesday **4** before
5 June **6** February
Exercise 3
1 b **2** d **3** c **4** a
Fun Spot
Suggested answers:
She always goes swimming / has swimming lessons.
She usually listens to music.
She usually plays computer games.
She never does her homework.
She always watches TV.
She never plays football.
She sometimes reads.

Skills Revision 5&6
Exercise 1
a
Exercise 2
1 T **2** T **3** F **4** F **5** T **6** F
Exercise 3
1 pancakes **2** homework **3** bedroom
4 television **5** friends
Exercise 4
1 She has breakfast at eight (o'clock).
2 She goes to school at half past eight.
3 She has lessons all day! **4** She does her homework at five (o'clock). **5** She has dinner at granny's house at quarter to seven.
Exercise 5
1 E **2** A **3** C **4** B
Exercise 6
1 C **2** B **3** A **4** A

Unit 7
7.1
Exercise 1
2 e **3** c **4** g **5** h **6** f **7** b **8** a
Exercise 2
2 spider, d **3** fish, a **4** fly, b **5** tiger, e
Exercise 3
2 Whales **3** Snakes **4** Birds **5** Frogs
6 Spiders
Exercise 4
1 kangaroo **2** tiger **3** frog **4** whale
5 fly **6** fish **7** monkey
Exercise 5
Suggested answers:
swim: fish, whale
run: giraffe, tiger, lion
fly: fly, butterfly
7.2
Exercise 1
2 I don't get up early on Saturdays.
3 Lucy does not like cats.
4 Josh doesn't go to school by bike.
5 We do not hang out on Mondays.
Exercise 2
2 don't tidy **3** don't watch **4** doesn't go **5** don't like **6** doesn't speak
Exercise 3
3 My friend plays in the garden.
4 My sister doesn't tidy her bedroom.
5 Joe and Adam hang out after school.
6 We don't go to school on Sundays.

Exercise 4
2 Dad doesn't get up early. 3 Jen and Alex play computer games. 4 Mum and Dad don't play computer games. 5 Mum listens to classical music. 6 Jen doesn't listen to classical music.
Exercise 5
2 c 3 e 4 d 5 f 6 b 7 h 8 g
Exercise 6
Student's own answers.

7.3
Exercise 1
2 Does 3 Do 4 Does 5 Do 6 Do
Exercise 2
a 4 b 5 d 6 e 3 f 2
Exercise 3
2 don't 3 Does 4 does 5 Do 6 do
Exercise 4
2 Do you like chocolate? 3 Does your teacher ride a bike to school? 4 Do your friends play football on Saturdays? 5 Do you tidy your room at the weekend? 6 Does your dad go to the gym?
Exercise 5
Student's own answers.
2 Yes, I do. / No, I don't. 3 Yes, he/she does. / No, he/she doesn't. 4 Yes, they do. / No, they don't. 5 Yes, I do. / No, I don't. 6 Yes, he does. / No, he doesn't.
Exercise 6
1 do 2 does, have 3 do, play 4 does, drink 5 do, go 6 Does, speak

7.4
Exercise 1
2 Would 3 thanks 4 you are 5 Here are
Exercise 2
a 5 b 7 d 3 e 8 f 4 g 6 h 2
Exercise 3
2 2.50 3 eight pounds ninety 4 5.30 5 one pound twenty
Exercise 4
2 have 3 please 4 like 5 Yes 6 That's 7 Here 8 are 9 here

7.5
Exercise 1
2 F 3 T 4 F 5 T 6 F
Exercise 2
Suggested answers:
fast ✓ strong ✓ lots of teeth ✓ long body ✓ cute face ✗ big ears ✗
Exercise 3
2 are 3 other sharks 4 have got 5 can
Exercise 4
1 They usually eat fish and other sea animals. 2 No, they don't. 3 Yes, they can. 4 They can hear fish.

7.6
Exercise 1
B
Exercise 2
2 They are sisters. 3 It's brown and white. 4 They need new food every day. 5 It comes from a pet shop.
Exercise 3
1 three 2 aren't 3 don't like 4 rabbits
Exercise 4
2 There are six. 3 No, they haven't. 4 No, they don't. 5 We don't know.
Exercise 5
Student's own answers.

7.7
Exercise 1
1 hamster 2 iguana 3 parrot 4 goldfish 5 rabbit

Exercise 2
1 fast bird 2 dangerous lion 3 slow tortoise 4 ugly frog 5 strong elephant
Exercise 3
1 doesn't sing 2 don't live 3 doesn't like 4 don't speak 5 don't want
Exercise 4
1 Does Tom wear jeans to school? 2 No, he doesn't. 3 Do your friends like football? 4 Yes, they do. 5 Does your granny visit you every week?
Exercise 5
1 you 2 have 3 please 4 that's 5 are
Word blog
Exercise 1
1 hamsters 2 iguanas 3 dog 4 birds
Exercise 2
2 eat 3 are 4 are 5 can 6 can't 7 are 8 aren't
Exercise 3
1 plants, F 2 flies, T 3 sweets, F 4 leaves, T 5 small fish, T
Fun Spot
giraffe, frog, crocodile, lion, parrot/bird, elephant, snake, iguana

Unit 8
8.1
Exercise 1
2 hockey 3 windsurfing 4 volleyball 5 table tennis 6 ice-skating
Exercise 2
2 basketball 3 taekwondo 4 sailing 5 roller skating 6 tennis
Exercise 3
2 go 3 do 4 play 5 play 6 go 7 go 8 play 9 go 10 play
Exercise 4
2 f 3 c 4 a 5 b 6 e
Exercise 5

skiing	badminton	basketball
swimming	table tennis	hockey
	taekwondo	volleyball

8.2
Exercise 1
2 making, Jen 3 getting up, cooking, Alex 4 skateboarding, climbing, Lian
Exercise 2
2 What does Monica like doing? 3 Janet isn't going to bed early. 4 Mark loves watching funny films. 5 Wendy likes sailing and windsurfing. 6 Does Tim like doing taekwondo?
Exercise 3
2 like 3 hates 4 loves 5 don't like 6 love 7 likes 8 doesn't like
Exercise 4
2 it 3 you 4 them 5 him 6 us
Exercise 5
2 she 3 plays 4 her 5 hate 6 playing 7 me

8.3
Exercise 1
2 It's on the table. 3 It's my mum's bike. 4 Five. 5 There's a notebook. 6 It's Mr Evans.
Exercise 2
2 Who 3 What 4 What 5 How many
Exercise 3
2 Where 3 How many 4 Who 5 Whose 6 When
Exercise 4
2 When do you go to bed on Mondays? 3 Where do your friends hang out? 4 What is your favourite food? 5 Who is your favourite singer?
Exercise 5
Students' own answers.

8.4
Exercise 1
a 3 b 5 c 6 e 2 f 4
Exercise 2
2 cloudy 3 windy 4 rainy 5 snowy 6 cold 7 warm 8 hot
Exercise 3
2 a 3 d 4 b 5 a 6 b
Exercise 4
1 spring 2 summer 3 autumn 4 winter
Exercise 5
2 often 3 winter 4 cloudy 5 summer
Exercise 6
2 like 3 rainy 4 wet 5 hope 6 hot

8.5
Exercise 1

	Sam	Tammy
do exercise	often	never
eat healthy food	no	yes

Exercise 2
2 She never does exercise. 3 She likes reading and cooking. 4 He likes eating cakes, chocolate, pizza and chips. 5 Yes, she does. 6 He usually drinks cola.
Exercise 3
2 f 3 b 4 a 5 c 6 e
Exercise 4
2 teeth 3 fruit 4 vegetables 5 do 6 exercise 7 go 8 bed

8.6
Exercise 1
food C sleep A exercise B
Exercise 2
Question 1: food Question 2: exercise Question 3: sleep
Exercise 3
2 fruit 3 water 4 cycling 5 walks 6 swimming 7 half past nine 8 ten (o'clock)
Exercise 4
2 doesn't 3 always has 4 reading 5 like 6 is 7 at 8 sleeping
Exercise 5
Suggested answer:
May doesn't like fruit, but she loves vegetables. She usually drinks a lot of water.
May always walks to school. She likes doing taekwondo and she plays badminton at the weekend. She usually goes to bed at 10 o'clock. She gets up at 7.30 every day.

8.7
Exercise 1
1 taekwondo 2 ice-skating 3 January 4 autumn 5 early
Exercise 2
1 brush 2 play 3 go 4 drink 5 fruit
Exercise 3
1 My sister doesn't like roller skating. 2 Do you like swimming? 3 I love singing. 4 We don't like getting up early. 5 Do your friends like eating pizza?
Exercise 4
1 Where 2 How 3 them 4 her 5 it
Exercise 5
1 like 2 It's 3 it 4 is 5 Me
Word blog
Exercise 1
1 rainy 2 cloudy 3 cold
Exercise 2
1 cold 2 winter 3 skiing 4 hot 5 windsurfing 6 dangerous

Exercise 3
1 American football 2 water skiing 3 horse riding
Fun Spot
Suggested answers:
Tina likes roller skating / playing volleyball / playing badminton / playing the piano / eating pizza.
Dale likes reading books / playing basketball / playing tennis / playing the guitar / eating fruit.

Skills Revision 7 & 8
Exercise 1
1 T 2 F 3 T 4 T 5 F 6 F
Exercise 2
1 sunny 2 roller 3 three 4 man 5 sandwich 6 tree
Exercise 3
1 It's yellow and blue. 2 It eats parrot food and bananas. 3 It can speak! 4 It's clever and funny. 5 It likes playing with a ball.
Exercise 4
1 next to 2 15/fifteen 3 volleyball 4 healthy
Exercise 5
1 d 2 e 3 a 4 g

Exam Practice 1–4
Part 1
1 ✗ 2 ✗ 3 ✗ 4 ✓ 5 ✓
Part 2
1 desk 2 window 3 bedroom 4 armchair 5 bathroom
Part 3
1 yes 2 yes 3 no 4 no 5 no
Part 4
1 monkey on bike – green 2 monkey with mobile phone – blue 3 monkey in tree – red 4 monkey with plant – pink 5 monkey with book – orange
Part 5
1 Would you like some orange juice? 2 I'm so sorry! 3 Let me show you the bathroom. 4 Don't worry! I'm fine! 5 Who's your favourite singer?

Exam Practice 5–8
Part 1
1 Children 2 bikes 3 birds 4 shop 5 morning
Part 2
1 wall 2 kangaroo 3 monkey 4 tree 5 fish
Part 3
1 Grace 2 Bird 3 Alex 4 two/2 5 eight/8
Part 4
1 A 2 C 3 C 4 A 5 C 6 B

Get more on Geometry!
See Teacher's Book p. 127
Get more on Science!
See Teacher's Book p. 128
Get more on Music!
See Teacher's Book p. 129
Get more on Sports!
See Teacher's Book p. 130

Photocopiable resources – teaching notes

1.1 Vocabulary
- Ss look at the picture and complete the family words individually. They compare answers in pairs.
- Ss analyse the picture in pairs and try to guess who's missing. Then they order the letters and check their guesses.

> **Answers**
> parents, sister, brother, uncle, aunt, father, mother, grandmother, grandfather, cousin; son, daughter

- Ask Ss what diminutives of the family words they can remember. Get them to work in pairs and race to make a list. (*Mum, dad, granny, granddad*.)

2.1 Vocabulary
- Ss complete the words individually.

> **Answers**
> (from left to right) boots, cap, coat, dress, hoodie, jacket, jeans, jumper, shirt, skirt, shoes, top, tracksuit, trainers, trousers, T-shirt

- Ask Ss to work in pairs. They cut out two sets of cards, shuffle and put them face down on the desk. Then they take turns to uncover two cards at a time and say what they can see, e.g. *coat*. If the cards match a student can keep them. If the cards don't match, a student puts them back face down. The student with the most cards at the end of the game is the winner.

3.1 Vocabulary
- Revise *bed*, *table*, *wall* and *floor* by pointing to the picture. Explain that in the old ghost's house objects are in unusual places.
- Each student draws objects 1–10 in the house and numbers them accordingly. Then in pairs, Ss take turns to say where their objects are.

4.1 Vocabulary
- Ask Ss to work in pairs. They follow the maze, discuss and decide whether the collocations are correct.
- Ask Ss what's wrong with the incorrect collocations and whether they can correct them. Brainstorm ideas on the board.

> **Answers**
> **1** short spiky blond hair (✓)
> **2** small red face (✓)
> **3** straight grey mouth (✗; straight hair; grey eyes/hair)
> **4** long curly brown hair (✓)
> **5** white teeth (✓)
> **6** small blue eyes (✓)
> **7** big wavy ears (✗; big ears/eyes/face/mouth/nose/teeth; wavy hair)
> **8** curly dark nose (✗; curly hair; dark hair/eyes)

5.1 Vocabulary
- Ss work in pairs. They cut out and mix up one set of cards and put them face down on the desk. Ss take turns to take a card and mime the activity for their partner to guess.
- Alternatively, Ss cut out two sets of cards, mix them up and put them face down on the desk. Each student picks two cards at a time. He/She can keep the cards if they match or if the activities on the cards can be done at the same time, e.g. *cook* and *sing*.

6.1 Vocabulary

> **Answers**
> **Across: 1** lunch **5** TV **6** have **8** go
> **9** dinner **10** homework **11** bed **12** get
> **Down: 1** listen **2** breakfast **3** shower
> **4** tidy **7** friends

- After Ss complete the crossword, ask them to play a game. One student chooses a word from the crossword and his/her partner makes a collocation with this word. Student A: *Lunch*. Student B: *Have lunch*.

7.1 Vocabulary
- Ss work individually and then compare answers in pairs.

> **Answers**
> **1** lion **2** butterfly **3** spider **4** elephant
> **5** whale **6** fly **7** frog **8** giraffe
> **9** kangaroo **10** bird **11** monkey
> **12** snake **13** crocodile **14** tiger **15** fish

- Ss play a game in pairs. They take turns to read the clues for their partner to guess the animals.

8.1 Vocabulary
- Ss complete the words individually and compare answers in pairs.

> **Answers**
> (from left to right) football, table tennis, badminton, windsurfing, basketball, skiing, cycling, swimming, ice-skating, roller skating, sailing, skateboarding, taekwondo, tennis, volleyball, hockey

- Divide Ss into groups of three. Each student cuts out one set of cards. Two students place their cards face up in any order they want but in a 4 x 4 grid. The third student reads the phrases in any order until one of the two students puts four cards face down horizontally, vertically or diagonally. Ss change roles and play two more times.

1.2 Grammar

> **Answers**
> **Exercise 1** **2** We are at school. **3** Jason is Sofia's son. **4** Alex and Jen are happy. **5** Bobby is my dog. **6** You are my friend.
> **Exercise 2** **2** d **3** b **4** f **5** a **6** c
> **Exercise 3** **2** He is at a party. **3** I am eleven. **4** She is my sister. **5** You are in this photo! **6** They are lovely presents!
> **Exercise 4** Students' own answers.

1.3 Grammar

> **Answers**
> **Exercise 1** **2** aren't **3** isn't **4** isn't **5** aren't **6** 'm not
> **Exercise 2** **2** They are not George's friends. **3** She is not your cousin. **4** It is not your pet cat. **5** We are not ready. **6** I am not good at English.
> **Exercise 3** **2** is **3** aren't **4** are **5** isn't **6** isn't

2.2 Grammar

> **Answers**
> **Exercise 1** **2** Those are my brother's **3** isn't his **4** my trainers **5** Those aren't my mum's **6** your hoodie
> **Exercise 2** **2** Those are **3** This isn't **4** That is **5** These are **6** This isn't
> **Exercise 3** **2** too short **3** too small **4** too long **5** too old
> **Exercise 4** **2** Those aren't **3** That is **4** This isn't **5** This is **6** That isn't **7** Those are **8** These aren't

2.3 Grammar

> **Answers**
> **Exercise 1** **2** e **3** d **4** f **5** b **6** a
> **Exercise 2** **3** Is **4** it isn't **5** Are **6** we are **7** Are **8** they aren't **9** Is **10** he/she is **11** Are **12** I am
> **Exercise 3** **2** Are you cool? **3** Are your shoes brown? **4** Is your favourite music hip hop? **5** Is it your birthday today? **6** Is your best friend in this class?
> **Exercise 4** Students' own answers.

3.2 Grammar

> **Answers**
> **Exercise 1** **2** is **3** are **4** is **5** are **6** are The text is about picture B.
> **Exercise 2** **2** There's **3** There are **4** There's **5** There are **6** There are
> **Exercise 3** **2** There are two mobile phones on the sofa. **3** There's a door next to the window. **4** There are three books on the table.
> **Exercise 4** **2** T **3** T **4** F (the apples are on the table)

3.3 Grammar

Answers
Exercise 1 2 aren't 3 isn't 4 isn't 5 aren't 6 aren't
Exercise 2 2 Is there a computer on the desk? 3 Are there any clothes on the floor? 4 Is there an armchair? 5 Are there two beds? 6 Is there a big wardrobe?
Exercise 3 b 4 c 6 d 5 e 2 f 1
Exercise 4 2 Are there any bikes in the garden? (✗) 3 Are there any chairs in the kitchen? (✗) 4 Is there a TV in the living room? (✓) 5 Are there any trees in the garden? (✓) 6 Is there a fridge in the garage? (✓)

4.2 Grammar

Answers
Exercise 1 2 c 3 b 4 b 5 a
Exercise 2 2 His teacher hasn't got a car. 3 Her cousins have got three dogs. 4 Jorge has got blue eyes. 5 We've got a big classroom. 6 I haven't got a cool phone.
Exercise 3 2 My best friend hasn't got a bike. 3 We've got a new English teacher. 4 My parents haven't got a skateboard. 5 I haven't got long hair.
Exercise 4 2 's got short 3 's got big (white) 4 head 5 's got short blond spiky

4.3 Grammar

Answers
Exercise 1 2 Have we got 3 Has your brother got 4 Have they got 5 Have I got 6 Has your granny got
Exercise 2 2 Have, Yes, I have. 3 Have, No, they haven't. 4 Has, No, it hasn't. 5 Has, Yes, she has. 6 Has, No, he hasn't.
Exercise 3 2 c 3 e 4 d 5 b 6 a
Exercise 4 2 Have you got a parrot? 3 Have you got long fingers? 4 Have your parents got blue eyes? 5 Has your granny got long hair? 6 Have you got a robot? Students' own answers.

5.2 Grammar

Answers
Exercise 1 2 can't 3 can 4 can 5 can 6 can't
Exercise 2 2 She can't dive. 3 I can speak English. 4 We can't ride a horse. 5 You can run fast. 6 He can't swim.
Exercise 3 Students' own answers.
2 I can/can't dive 3 I can/can't speak English. 4 I can/can't ride a horse. 5 I can/can't run fast. 6 I can/can't swim.
Exercise 5 Students' own answers.

5.3 Grammar

Answers
Exercise 1 2 e 3 f 4 b 5 a 6 d
Exercise 2 2 ✓ 3 ✓ 4 ✗ What can we do? 5 ✓ 6 ✗ Can she speak English?
Exercise 3 2A: Can we dive? 2B: Yes, we can. 3A: Can they speak Chinese? 3B: Yes, they can. 4A: Can I act? 4B: No, you/I can't. 5A: Can your cat jump? 5B: Yes, it /he/she can. 6A: Can you draw a cartoon? 6B: No, I can't.
Exercise 4 2 Can he run fast? (✓) 3 Can they skateboard? (✗) 4 Can he fix things? (✗) 5 Can she play the guitar? (✓) 6 Can it fly? (✓)

6.2 Grammar

Answers
Exercise 1 2 have 3 go 4 do 5 tidy 6 watch
Exercise 2 2 has 3 goes 4 does 5 tidies 6 watches
Exercise 3 1 make 2 have, go 3 have, has 4 listen, does 5 tidy, plays 6 hang out, watches
Exercise 4 1 gets up 2 goes, goes, her mum 3 Katy, Jackie 4 watch TV

6.3 Grammar

Answers
Exercise 1 2 I often hang out with my friends at the weekend. 3 My parents never play computer games. 4 My sister is usually late. 5 We sometimes go to the cinema. 6 You always do your homework.
Exercise 2 2 usually makes 3 sometimes hang out 4 always do 5 often play 6 never watches
Exercise 3 Students' own answers.
Exercise 4 2 hangs out with his friends 3 usually, Sundays 4 Students' own answers.

7.2 Grammar

Answers
Exercise 1 2 e 3 d 4 a 5 f 6 b
Exercise 2 2 don't walk 3 doesn't play 4 don't eat 5 don't do 6 doesn't work
Exercise 3 2 doesn't tidy 3 like 4 don't listen 5 doesn't speak 6 eats
Exercise 4 Students' own answers.

7.3 Grammar

Answers
Exercise 1 2 Does your granny speak English? 3 Do we have music lessons? 4 Do I speak English well? 5 Does your brother tidy his room? 6 Do our parents go to the gym?
Exercise 2 b 4 c 6 d 1 e 3 f 2
Exercise 3 2 Yes, I do. 3 Yes, they do. 4 Does your sister want 5 Does she like
Exercise 4 2 Do you hang out with friends every day? 3 Do you listen to music before breakfast? 4 Do your parents do sport? 5 Does your best friend speak English? 6 What do you do on Sundays?
Exercise 5 Students' own answers.

8.2 Grammar

Answers
Exercise 1 2 cooking 3 skateboarding 4 doing 5 eating 6 getting
Exercise 2 2 Does your mum like spiders? 3 Do your parents like Justin Bieber? 4 Does our teacher like our class? 5 Do you like skateboarding? 6 Do I like ice-creams?
Exercise 3 2 doesn't, spiders 3 don't, Justin Bieber 4 does, our class 5 do, skateboarding 6 do, ice-creams
Exercise 4 Students' own answers.

8.3 Grammar

Answers
Exercise 1 2 a, D 3 b, B 4 a, E 5 b, A
Exercise 2 2 What 3 When 4 Where 5 Who
Exercise 3 2 What are 3 How old 4 Who is your 6 When do you
Exercise 4 Students' own answers.

1.4 Communication

- Ss work in pairs to find the best place for the extra sentences.

Answers
Exercise 1 Dialogue 1: after 'Dad, this is Jonas.' **Dialogue 2:** before or after 'I'm Robbie's classmate.'

- After Ss roleplay all scenarios in Exercise 2, ask them to change groups and act out the dialogues once again.

2.4 Communication

Answers
1 What's your name? 2 How old are you? 3 Where are you from? 4 What's your favourite music? 5 Who's your favourite singer? 6 What's your favourite sport? 7 Who's your favourite sports person? 8 What's your favourite film? 9 Who's your favourite actor?

3.4 Communication

Answers
Dialogue 1
A: Hello. Please, come in.
B: Thank you.
A: Would you like a sandwich?
B: No, thanks.
A: Would you like a biscuit?
B: Yes, please! I love chocolate biscuits!
Dialogue 2
A: Oh, no! Where's my phone?
B: It's on the sofa.
A: Thanks! Where's the bathroom, please?
B: It's upstairs. Let me show you.

4.4 Communication

Answers
Dialogue 1 The order is: 3, 2, 4, 1
Dialogue 2 The order is: 2, 1, 3
Dialogue 3 The order is: 3, 2, 1

- After Ss order the dialogues and practise them in pairs, ask them to stand up and act out each dialogue once again with a different partner, but replace the underlined words with their own ideas. They can also use the prompts in the pictures.

5.4 Communication

- Ss complete the dialogue in pairs. Draw their attention to the smilies. Tell them that each smily represents a reaction.

Answers
2 agree 3 can 4 go 5 beach

- Ss cut out one set of cards and put them face down on the desk. One student turns over a card and makes a suggestion. His/Her partner reacts using the sentence represented by the smily on the card. They swap and continue.

6.4 Communication

- Ss use the example dialogue to ask and answer questions about the events on their cards. Ask them not to look at each other's cards.
- After Ss complete the times of the events and the current times, they check their answers in pairs.

7.4 Communication

- Ss work in pairs and correct the dialogue.

Answers
Bill: Can I have three tickets to the concert, ~~thanks~~ please?
Bill: ~~Please~~ Thanks.

- Divide the class into group A and group B. Ask Ss to stand up and roleplay each scenario with a different partner.

8.4 Communication

- Ask Ss to look at the pictures and make sure they know what weather words they represent.
- When Ss complete their cards, ask them to check answers in pairs.

Answers
Student A
Spain: hot and sunny
The UK: cold and windy
Poland: cold and cloudy
Italy: warm and sunny
Australia: cloudy and rainy
Student B
The USA: cold and sunny
Scotland: sunny and rainy
France: cloudy and rainy
China: cold and cloudy
Spain: cold and windy

Play – *Where's the chocolate?*
About the play

Where's the chocolate? is a play all your students can get involved in. It's about the mysterious theft of anything made of chocolate from the Jones family's kitchen!

- How many characters are there?
There are nineteen characters. If you have more students, add more aliens!

- When is the best time for the play?
Where's the chocolate? is a fun, motivating way of finishing the school year. It's ideal for showing parents what their children have learnt in their English lessons and is a great way to help students revise.

- Do I need a proper stage?
No! Use your classroom, the school gym, hall or playground!

- What about preparation?
There is only one setting. We've provided a basic stage plan to help you (please see below). Your students will have fun making the scenery and choosing their props and costumes.

- Language to pre-teach
fence (draw one on the board), *shout* (demonstrate), *hide* (demonstrate)

Where is the play?
The play is in the Jones family's garden and Mr Grim's garden. There's a fence between the two gardens.

- The Jones' garden
It's big! There's a table and two or three chairs. Ask students to draw or make a tree and some flowers. Students draw the door to their house and a window. Put a football in the garden.

- The fence
Ask students to make a fence. They can use cardboard and draw a fence on it.

- Mr Grim's garden
It's small. There's a small table and one chair. Students draw or make one tree. Students make a house of cardboard or paper and draw the door to Mr Grim's house and a window.

Props
- Scene 1
a book, a mobile phone, a laptop, a box with a small chocolate cake, some chocolates and chocolate cupcakes

- Scene 2
the box from Scene 1, a football, the aliens' spaceship*

- Scene 3
the spaceship

- Scene 4
a football, a chocolate cake, the spaceship

*Students cut cardboard or card into the shape of a spaceship. The aliens carry it when they arrive and leave.

1.1 Vocabulary

Look at the picture of Martin's family and complete the words. Then order the letters to find two family words that are missing in the picture.

par _____   sis _____   bro _____   un _____   au _____

fat _____   mot _____   gra _____   gra _____   co _____

s n o _____   d u a r h t g e _____

2.1 Vocabulary

Complete the words. Then play the memory game in pairs.

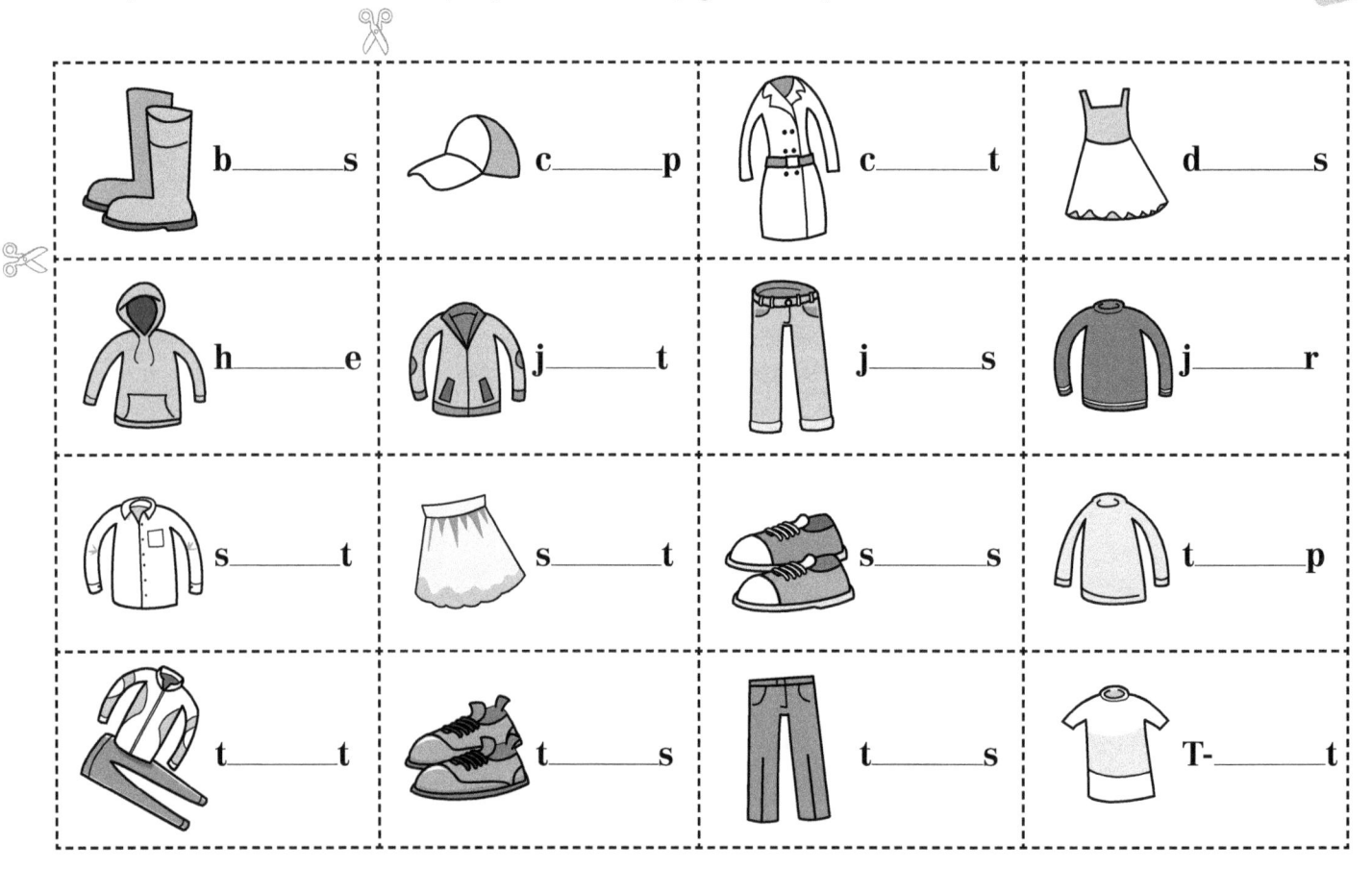

b___s	c___p	c___t	d___s
h___e	j___t	j___s	j___r
s___t	s___t	s___s	t___p
t___t	t___s	t___s	T-___t

3.1 Vocabulary

Draw objects 1–10 in the old ghost house! Number your drawings and say where they are.

1. armchair
2. bath
3. fridge
4. desk
5. sofa
6. door
7. wardrobe
8. garage
9. chair
10. window

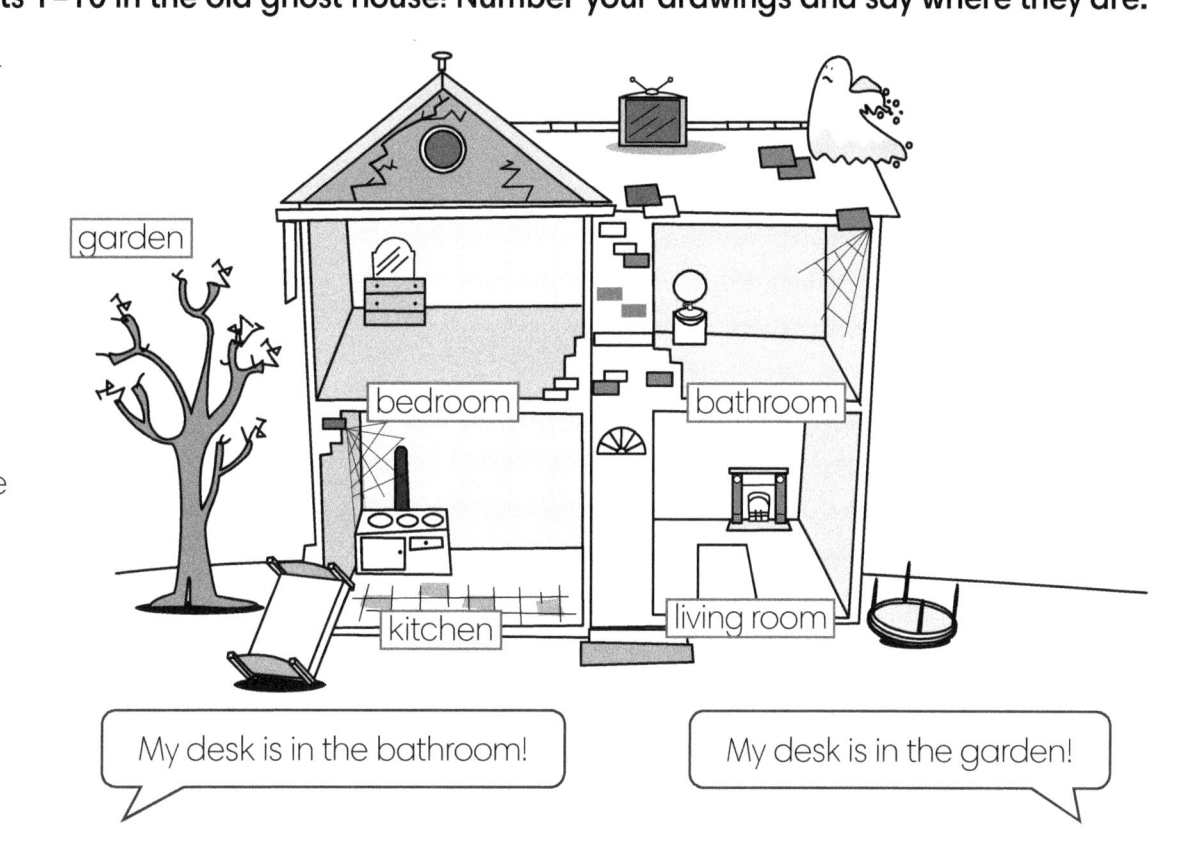

garden
bedroom
bathroom
kitchen
living room

My desk is in the bathroom!

My desk is in the garden!

4.1 Vocabulary

Follow the maze! Are the collocations correct? Tick (✓) or cross (✗).

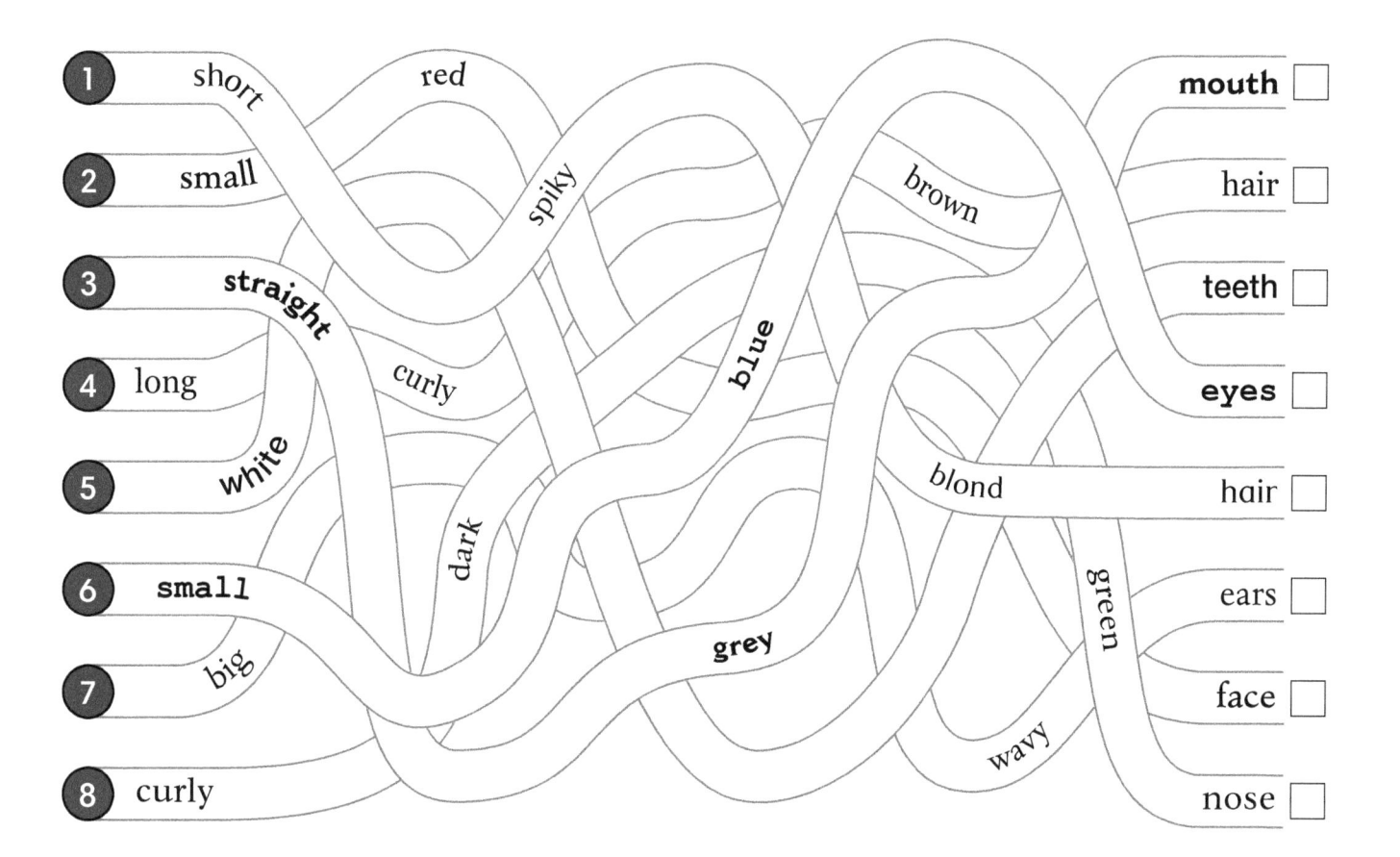

1. short
2. small
3. **straight**
4. long
5. white
6. **small**
7. big
8. curly

red, spiky, curly, dark, brown, blue, blond, grey, green, wavy

mouth ☐
hair ☐
teeth ☐
eyes ☐
hair ☐
ears ☐
face ☐
nose ☐

© Pearson Education Limited 2017 PHOTOCOPIABLE

149

5.1 Vocabulary

Work in pairs. Play the miming game.

run	cook	act	climb	read
draw	dive	jump	sing	write
skateboard	ride	swim	fix	fly

6.1 Vocabulary

Read the clues and complete the crossword.

Across
1 have _____
5 watch _____
6 _____ lessons
8 _____ to school
9 have _____
10 do my _____
11 go to _____
12 _____ up

Down
1 _____ to music
2 have _____
3 have a _____
4 _____ my room
7 hang out with my _____

7.1 Vocabulary

Order the letters and write animals. Use the clues to help.

1. n l i o — l_____ I'm yellow-brown.
2. e u t y t r b f l — b_____ I'm different colours.
3. p i e d r s — s_____ I've got eight legs.
4. l e n p t e h a — e_____ I'm very big.
5. w a e h l — w_____ I live in water.
6. y l f — f_____ I'm small.
7. r g o f — f_____ I'm green.
8. i r f a f g e — g_____ I've got a long neck.
9. n a g r a o k o — k_____ I can jump.
10. i d r b — b_____ I can fly.
11. o m y e n k — m_____ I'm funny.
12. n s a e k — s_____ I'm long and thin.
13. d c e o r o i c l — c_____ My teeth are big.
14. g r e t i — t_____ I can run fast.
15. h s f i — f_____ I can swim but I can't run.

8.1 Vocabulary

Complete the sports words. Then work in groups of three and play *Bingo!*

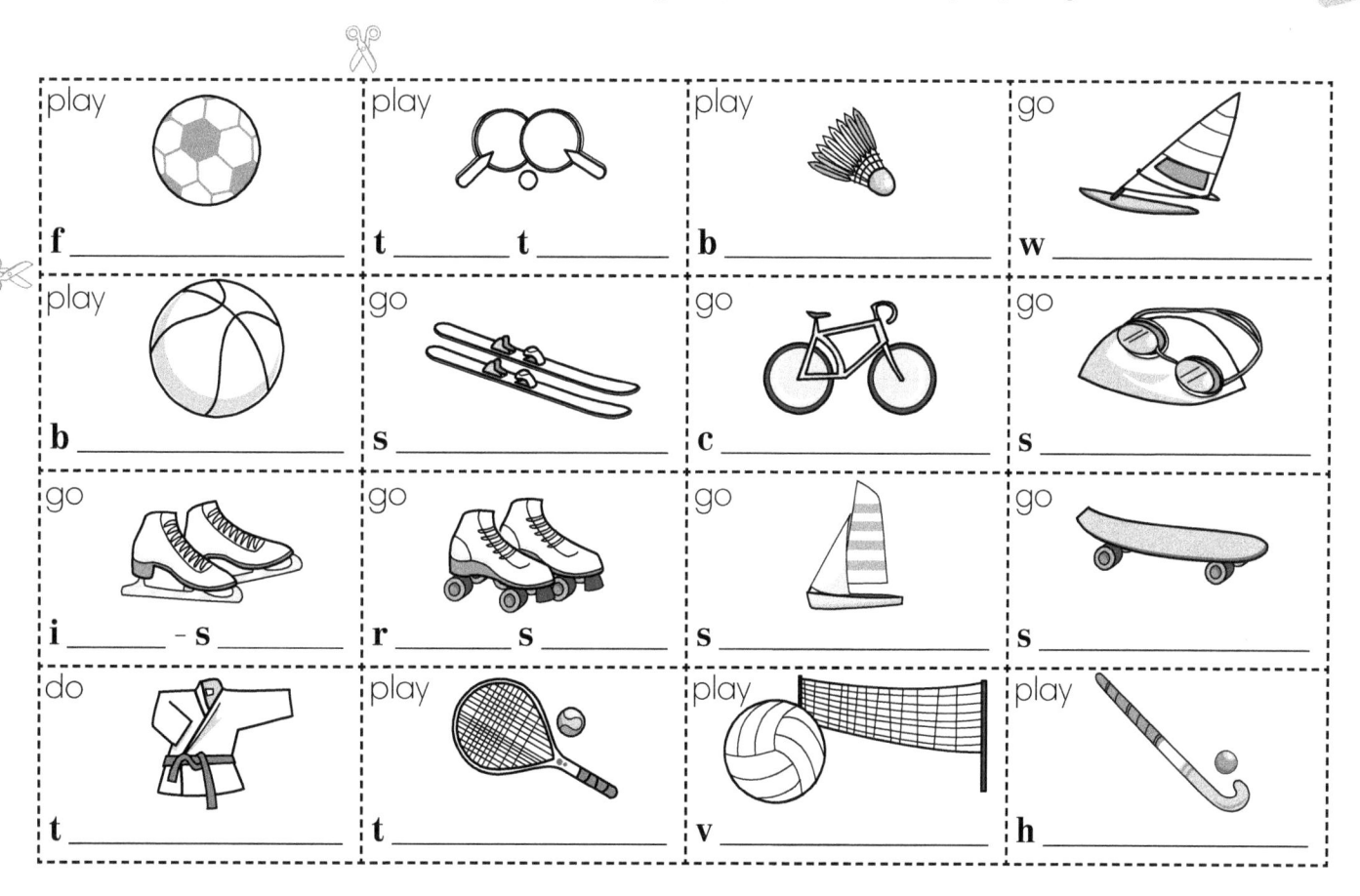

play [football] f____	play [table tennis] t____ t____	play [badminton] b____	go [windsurfing] w____
play [basketball] b____	go [skiing] s____	go [cycling] c____	go [swimming] s____
go [ice-skating] i____ - s____	go [roller skating] r____ s____	go [sailing] s____	go [skateboarding] s____
do [taekwondo/judo] t____	play [tennis] t____	play [volleyball] v____	play [hockey] h____

© Pearson Education Limited 2017 PHOTOCOPIABLE

1.2 Grammar

1 Correct the underlined words. Then write the correct sentences.

1 I <u>are</u> Jake.　　　　　　　　I am Jake.
2 We <u>am</u> at school.　　　　　_____
3 Jason <u>are</u> Sofia's son.　　　_____
4 Alex and Jen <u>is</u> happy.　　_____
5 Bobby <u>are</u> my dog.　　　　_____
6 You <u>is</u> my friend.　　　　　_____

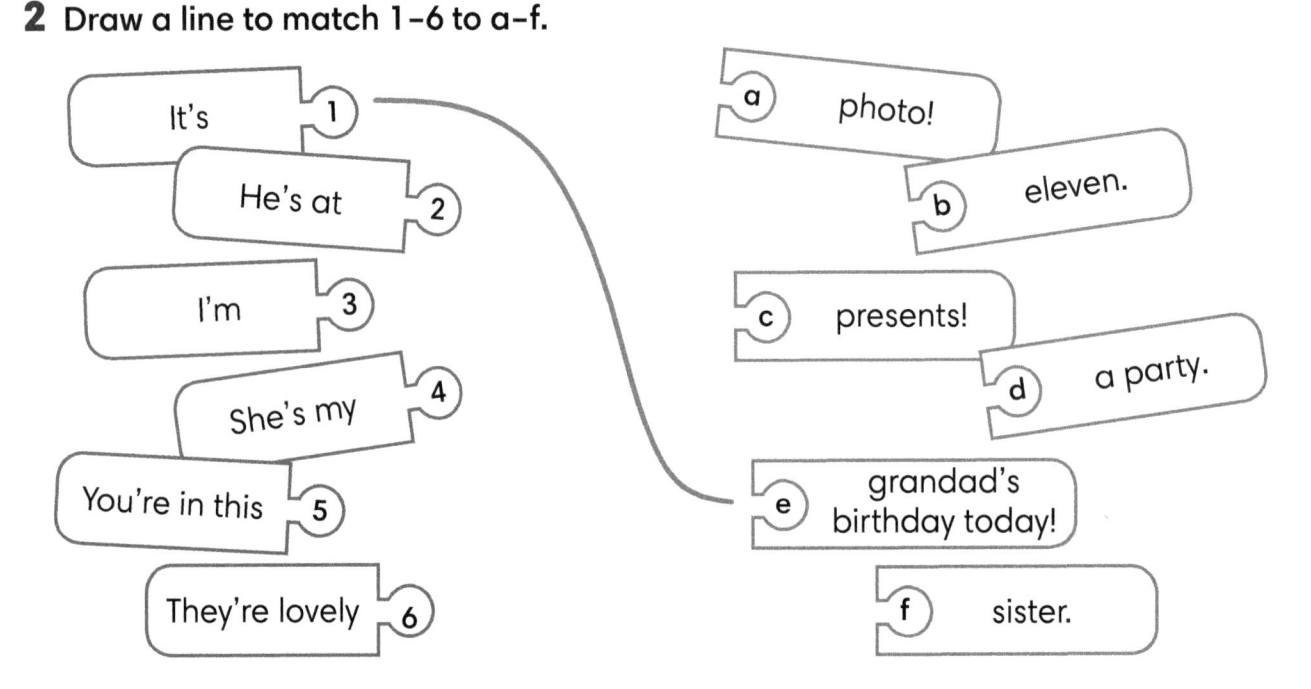

2 Draw a line to match 1–6 to a–f.

1 It's
2 He's at
3 I'm
4 She's my
5 You're in this
6 They're lovely

a photo!
b eleven.
c presents!
d a party.
e grandad's birthday today!
f sister.

3 Rewrite the sentences in Exercise 2 using the long form of *to be*.

1 *It is grandad's birthday today!*
2 _____
3 _____
4 _____
5 _____
6 _____

4 Complete and circle to make the sentences true for you. Make two sentences false! Then in pairs, take turns to read the sentences for your partner to say *true/false*.

1 My mum's name is _____ .
2 My dad's from _____ .
3 My *brother / sister* is _____ years old.
   His / Her favourite colour is _____ .
4 My favourite teacher is *Ms / Mr* _____ .
5 My best friend is a *boy / girl*. *He's / She's* at *school / home* now.
6 _____ is my best classmate.

My mum's name is Jane.

True?

© Pearson Education Limited 2017　PHOTOCOPIABLE

1.3 Grammar

1 Moody Michael never says 'yes'! Complete the sentences with the negative form of *to be*. Use the short form.

Nice Nicole / *Moody Michael*

1 I'm good at football. — You <u>aren't</u> good at football.
2 They're George's friends. — They _____ George's friends.
3 She's my cousin. — She _____ your cousin.
4 It's my pet cat. — It _____ your pet cat.
5 We're ready. — We _____ ready.
6 You're good at English. — I _____ good at English.

2 Rewrite Moody Michael's sentences in Exercise 1 using the long form of *to be*.

1 <u>You are not good at football.</u>
2 _____
3 _____
4 _____
5 _____
6 _____

3 Complete the text with the correct form of *to be*.

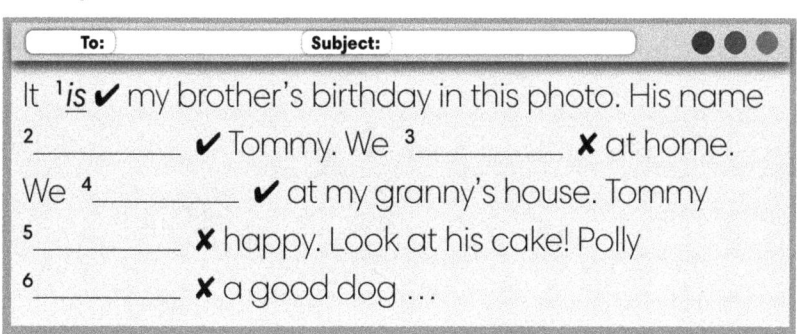

To: _____ Subject: _____

It ¹<u>is</u> ✔ my brother's birthday in this photo. His name ² _____ ✔ Tommy. We ³ _____ ✘ at home. We ⁴ _____ ✔ at my granny's house. Tommy ⁵ _____ ✘ happy. Look at his cake! Polly ⁶ _____ ✘ a good dog …

4 Work in pairs. Take turns to describe a person for your partner to guess his name.

	Don	Carl	Mark	James
teenager	✔	✘	✔	✘
teacher	✘	✔	✘	✔
superhero	✔	✘	✘	✔
British	✘	✔	✔	✘
Polish	✔	✘	✘	✔
happy	✔	✔	✔	✔

He isn't a teenager and he isn't British …

He's James!

© Pearson Education Limited 2017 PHOTOCOPIABLE

2.2 Grammar

1 Put the words in the correct order to complete the sentences.

1. her is This
   This is her cap.
2. brother's are my Those
   _____ shoes.
3. his isn't
   That jacket _____ .
4. trainers my
   These are _____ .
5. Those mum's aren't my
   _____ tops.
6. hoodie your
   This is _____ .

2 Complete the sentences with _this_ / _these_ (→) or _that_ / _those_ (⟶) and the correct form of _to be_.

1. → _This is_ my jacket. ✓
2. ⟶ _____ her boots. ✓
3. → _____ your coat. ✗
4. ⟶ _____ my mum's cap. ✓
5. → _____ my dad's jeans. ✓
6. → _____ his tracksuit. ✗

3 Look at the pictures. Complete the sentences with _too_ and _long, short, big, small, old_.

1. He's _too big_.
2. They're _____ .
3. It's _____ .
4. It's _____ .
5. They're _____ .

4 Complete the sentences for Mary. Use _this, that, these_ or _those_ and the correct form of _to be_. Then in pairs, take turns to point at the clothes and say.

1. _These are_ my boots.
2. _____ my trousers. They're too long.
3. _____ my dress.
4. _____ my dress. It's too small.
5. _____ my coat.
6. _____ my jacket. It's too big.
7. _____ my shoes.
8. _____ my jeans. They're too short.

> These are Mary's boots.

2.3 Grammar

1 Draw a line to match 1–6 to a–f.

1 Is this present for me?
2 Are you from China?
3 Are we happy?
4 Are they cool?
5 Is she your cousin?
6 Is he your brother?

a Yes, he is.
b No, she isn't.
c Yes, it is.
d Yes, we are.
e No, I'm not.
f No, they aren't.

2 Complete the questions with *am*, *is* or *are*. Then complete the short answers.

¹*Is* this class 7B?

Yes, ²*it is*.

³_____ this your desk?

No, ⁴_____.

⁵_____ we classmates?

Yes, ⁶_____.

⁷_____ those your books?

No, ⁸_____.

⁹_____ the teacher cool?

Yes, ¹⁰_____.

¹¹_____ you good at English?

Yes, ¹²_____.

3 Use the sentences to write questions.

1 That is your schoolbag.
   Is that your schoolbag?
2 You are cool.
   _____
3 Your shoes are brown.
   _____
4 Your favourite music is hip hop.
   _____
5 It's your birthday today.
   _____
6 Your best friend is in this class.
   _____

4 Work in groups of four. Ask and answer the questions in Exercise 3. Use short answers. Tick (✓) for *yes* and cross (✗) for *no*.

Question	Partner 1	Partner 2	Partner 3
1			
2			
3			
4			
5			

Is that your schoolbag?

No, it isn't.

3.2 Grammar

1 Read and circle the correct answer. Which picture is the text about?

There ¹(is)/ are a big sofa in my living room and there ² is / are a big table. It's behind the sofa. There ³ is / are four chairs next to the table. There ⁴ is / are an armchair in front of the TV. It's my cat's favourite place! There ⁵ is / are two big windows and there ⁶ is / are three pictures.

2 Complete the sentences about Picture A. Use *There's* or *There are.*

1 <u>There's</u> a big sofa.
2 _____ a table in front of the sofa.
3 _____ two armchairs.
4 _____ a dog on one armchair.
5 _____ two small windows.
6 _____ four pictures.

3 Write two more sentences about Picture A and Picture B.

1 (A) big table / behind the sofa   <u>There's a big table behind the sofa.</u>
2 (A) two mobile phones / on the sofa   _____
3 (B) a door / next to the window   _____
4 (B) three books / on the table   _____

4 Look and circle T (true) or F (false). Then in pairs, take turns to say true or false sentences about the picture for your partner to guess. Use the ideas in the box.

1 There are two big fridges.   T /(F)
2 There's one table.   T / F
3 There's orange juice in one fridge.   T / F
4 There are five apples under the table. T / F

1 schoolbag / table
2 cat / table
3 boys / kitchen
4 bike / garden
5 phone / schoolbag
6 phone / table

There's a schoolbag under the table.

False! It's on the table.

© Pearson Education Limited 2017 **PHOTOCOPIABLE**

3.3 Grammar

1 Complete the sentences with isn't or aren't.

1 There **aren't** any sweets in my schoolbag.
2 There _____ any DVDs in the living room.
3 There _____ a desk in my bedroom.
4 There _____ a computer in my classroom.
5 There _____ any people in the garden.
6 There _____ any books on the table.

2 Put the words in the correct order to make questions about a bedroom.

1 any photos there Are on the wall ?   _Are there any photos on the wall?_
2 there on the desk Is a computer ?   _____
3 on the floor there any clothes Are ?   _____
4 there an armchair Is ?   _____
5 Are two beds there ?   _____
6 Is a big wardrobe there ?   _____

3 Match the answers to the questions in Exercise 2.

a [3] Yes, there are! There's a jacket and jeans.
b [ ] Yes, there is. The armchair is next to the bed.
c [ ] Yes, there is. It's very big!
d [ ] No, there aren't. There's just one.
e [ ] No, there isn't. The computer is on the bed!
f [ ] No, there aren't. There's a photo on the desk.

4 Write questions using _Is there a_ or _Are there any_. Look and tick (✓) or cross (✗). Then in pairs, take turns to ask and answer. Use short answers.

1 bath / bathroom?   ✗   _Is there a bath in the bathroom?_
2 bikes / garden?   [ ]   _____
3 chairs / kitchen?   [ ]   _____
4 TV / living room?   [ ]   _____
5 trees / garden?   [ ]   _____
6 fridge / garage?   [ ]   _____

Is there a bath in the bathroom?

No, there isn't!

4.2 Grammar

1 Circle the correct answer.

1 My brother _____ got big feet!
   a is   b have   (c) has

2 I _____ a dog but I've got a cat.
   a 've got   b have got   c haven't got

3 They _____ blond hair.
   a got   b 've got   c has got

4 My granny _____ curly hair.
   a have got   b 's got   c got

5 We _____ a very big house.
   a haven't got   b hasn't got   c not got

2 Correct the underlined words. Then write the correct sentences.

1 My aunt have got curly hair.
My aunt has got curly hair.

2 His teacher haven't got a car.
_____

3 Her cousins has got three dogs.
_____

4 Jorge is got blue eyes.
_____

5 We're got a big classroom.
_____

6 I hasn't got a cool phone.
_____

3 Put the words in the correct order to make sentences.

1 a cat hasn't Jane got .   *Jane hasn't got a cat.*
2 friend hasn't got My best a bike . _____
3 teacher a new got We've English . _____
4 a skateboard haven't My parents got . _____
5 hair haven't got I long . _____

4 Look at the aliens and complete the sentences. Then in pairs, take turns to describe an alien for your partner to say the number.

She's got a very long neck and …

Number one.

1 She 's got long straight hair.
2 He _____ legs.
3 She _____ teeth.
4 He's got a very small _____ .
5 She _____ hair.

4.3 Grammar

1 Use the words in the box to complete the dialogues.

| Has your brother got | Has your granny got | Have I got |
| ~~Have you got~~ | Have they got | Have we got |

1 A: *Have you got* my book? — B: No, I haven't.
2 A: _____ homework today? — B: Yes, we have.
3 A: _____ your schoolbag? — B: Yes, he has.
4 A: _____ cool hair? — B: Yes, they have.
5 A: _____ long legs? — B: No, you haven't.
6 A: _____ a dog? — B: No, she hasn't.

2 Complete the questions with *have* or *has*. Write short answers.

1 A: *Have* we got an English lesson today?
   B: *Yes, we have.* ✓
2 A: _____ you got my DVD?
   B: _____ ✓
3 A: _____ they got big eyes?
   B: _____ ✗
4 A: _____ your phone got a new battery?
   B: _____ ✗
5 A: _____ mum got my top?
   B: _____ ✓
6 A: _____ he got my book?
   B: _____ ✗

3 Draw a line to match 1–6 to a–f.

1 My school is small.
2 These are my cats.
3 We've got an English lesson today.
4 My classroom is 5A.
5 My neighbour's dog is black.
6 My grandparents have got three dogs.

a Their cat isn't happy!
b Its name is Terry.
c Their names are Jan and Jay.
d Your classroom is 5B.
e Our teacher is cool.
f Your school is big.

4 Write questions. Then in pairs, take turns to ask and answer. Circle your partner's answers.

1 you / a cat? *Have you got a cat?* Yes / No
2 you / a parrot? _____ Yes / No
3 you / long fingers? _____ Yes / No
4 parents / blue eyes? _____ Yes / No
5 granny / long hair? _____ Yes / No
6 you / a robot? _____ Yes / No

> Have you got a cat?

> Yes, I have. I've got three cats!

5.2 Grammar

1 Look at the picture. Complete the sentences with *can* or *can't*.

1 He <u>can</u> fly.
2 They _____ sing.
3 He _____ fix things.
4 We _____ act.
5 You _____ draw.
6 She _____ climb.

2 Write sentences with *can* (✓) or *can't* (✗).

1 They / cook ✓ — <u>They can cook.</u>
2 She / dive ✗ _____
3 I / speak English ✓ _____
4 We / ride a horse ✗ _____
5 You / run fast ✓ _____
6 He / swim ✗ _____

3 Use the ideas in Exercise 2 and write sentences that are true for you.

1 cook — <u>I can / I can't cook.</u>
2 dive _____
3 speak English _____
4 ride a horse _____
5 run fast _____
6 swim _____

4 Memory test! In pairs, take turns to give a number for your partner to say what the person in the picture in Exercise 1 can/can't do.

Number two.

They can't sing.

5 Speak and complete the table for you and your partner. Tick (✓) or cross (✗).

	fly	sing	fix things	act	draw	climb
You						
Partner						

I can't fly! And you?

© Pearson Education Limited 2017 PHOTOCOPIABLE

5.3 Grammar

1 Draw a line to match 1–6 to a–f.

1. Can you swim?
2. Can they dance?
3. What can they do?
4. Can he play the piano?
5. Can we speak English?
6. Can she ride a horse?

a. Yes, we can.
b. No, he can't.
c. Yes, I can.
d. Yes, she can.
e. No, they can't.
f. They can jump.

2 Read the questions. Are they correct? Tick (✓) or cross (✗). Then correct the mistakes.

1. ✗ He can play the piano?   *Can he play the piano?*
2. ☐ Can you cook well?   _____
3. ☐ Can it fly?   _____
4. ☐ What we can do?   _____
5. ☐ Can they skateboard?   _____
6. ☐ She can speak English?   _____

3 Write questions and short answers with *can* or *can't*.

1. he / swim? ✗   A: *Can he swim?*   B: *No, he can't.*
2. we / dive? ✓   A: _____   B: _____
3. they / speak Chinese? ✓   A: _____   B: _____
4. I / act? ✗   A: _____   B: _____
5. your cat / jump? ✓   A: _____   B: _____
6. you / draw a cartoon? ✗   A: _____   B: _____

4 Write questions about the people in the pictures using *can*. Then in pairs, take turns to ask and answer. Tick (✓) or cross (✗).

1. ✗ *Can she ride a horse?*
2. ☐ _____
3. ☐ _____
4. ☐ _____
5. ☐ _____
6. ☐ _____

Can she ride a horse?

No, she can't!

6.2 Grammar

1 Complete the text with the words in the box.

My Day

I ¹ **get up** early. I ² _____ breakfast at home and then I ³ _____ to school. After school I ⁴ _____ my homework and I ⁵ _____ my room. I ⁶ _____ TV after dinner.

Box: go, have, watch, do, ~~get up~~, tidy

2 Write the third person form of the verbs in Exercise 1.

1 *gets up*
2 _____
3 _____
4 _____
5 _____
6 _____

3 Complete the sentences with the correct form of the Present Simple.

1 My sister *makes* (**make**) dinner on Saturdays and I _____ (**make**) dinner on Sundays!
2 We _____ (**have**) breakfast at home. Next, we _____ (**go**) to school.
3 I _____ (**have**) lunch at school. My best friend _____ (**have**) lunch at home.
4 I _____ (**listen**) to music before dinner and my sister _____ (**do**) her homework.
5 I _____ (**tidy**) my room and my sister _____ (**play**) computer games.
6 I _____ (**hang out**) with my friends and my sister _____ (**watch**) TV.

4 Complete the sentences. Then test your memory in pairs! Take turns to give a sentence for your partner to say *Katy* or *Jackie*.

	Jackie	Katy
get up	late	early
go to school	with her brother	with her mum
have lunch	at school	at a friend's house
do homework	on the bus	in her bedroom
play computer games	before dinner	after dinner
watch TV	before bed	before bed
go to bed	late	early

1 Jackie *gets up* late but Katy _____ early.
2 Jackie _____ to school with her brother but Katy _____ to school with _____ .
3 _____ does her homework in her bedroom but _____ does her homework on the bus.
4 They _____ before bed.

> She goes to school with her brother.

> Jackie!

© Pearson Education Limited 2017 PHOTOCOPIABLE

6.3 Grammar

1 The adverbs of frequency are in the wrong place! Rewrite the sentences so they are correct.

1. My brother gets up <u>always</u> late. — *My brother always gets up late.*
2. I hang out with my friends at the weekend <u>often</u>. _____
3. My <u>never</u> parents play computer games. _____
4. My sister <u>usually</u> is late. _____
5. We go <u>sometimes</u> to the cinema. _____
6. You do <u>always</u> your homework. _____

2 Complete the sentences with the adverb of frequency and the correct form of the verb.

1. He <u>never goes</u> (**go** / **never**) to bed early.
2. Dad _____ (**make** / **usually**) dinner.
3. We _____ (**hang out** / **sometimes**) with friends after school.
4. I _____ (**do** / **always**) my homework at school.
5. They _____ (**play** / **often**) computer games in the evening.
6. Sara _____ (**watch** / **never**) TV before dinner.

3 Use the ideas in Exercise 2 to write sentences that are true for you.

1. *I often go to bed early.*
2. _____
3. _____
4. _____
5. _____
6. _____

4 Look and complete the sentences. Then in pairs, take turns to make sentences for your partner to say *true* or *false*.

	Richard	Danny
always / Saturdays	football	hot dog
often / after school	music	friends
usually / Sundays	book	eating
sometimes / Wednesdays	cooking	guitar
never / at the weekend	skateboard	cakes

> Richard sometimes plays the guitar on Wednesdays.

> False! It's Danny.

1. Richard always <u>plays football</u> on Saturdays.
2. Danny often _____ after school.
3. Richard _____ does his homework on _____.
4. Danny _____ .

© Pearson Education Limited 2017 **PHOTOCOPIABLE**

7.2 Grammar

1 Draw a line to match 1–6 to a–f.

1. I don't usually get up
2. My parents don't like
3. He wants a pet but his mum
4. My uncle and aunt don't often
5. Jasmin doesn't usually go
6. Our pet tortoise

a watch TV.
b doesn't eat a lot.
c early at the weekend.
d doesn't like animals.
e our neighbours' dog.
f to the cinema.

2 Circle the correct answer.

1. Jason *doesn't want* / *don't want* a parrot.
2. The girls *doesn't walk* / *don't walk* to school.
3. My granny *doesn't play* / *don't play* computer games.
4. My pet cats *doesn't eat* / *don't eat* a lot.
5. We *doesn't do* / *don't do* our homework on Saturdays.
6. My phone *doesn't work* / *don't work*.

3 Complete the sentences with the correct form of the words given.

1. Mum and dad **don't want** (**want** / ✗) a pet snake.
2. Matt _____ (**tidy** / ✗) his room at the weekend.
3. Rachel and Jack _____ (**like** / ✓) classical music.
4. We _____ (**listen** / ✗) to music in class.
5. Our English teacher _____ (**speak** / ✗) very fast.
6. My little sister _____ (**eat** / ✓) a lot.

4 Guess and write sentences about your partner, his/her friends and family. Then in pairs, read the sentences for your partner to say *true* or *false*. Tick (✓) or cross (✗).

1. Your brother/sister / make cupcakes ☐ _____
2. You / like ice-skating ☐ _____
3. Your best friend / like snakes ☐ _____
4. Your grandparents / go to bed early ☐ _____
5. You / sometimes cook dinner ☐ _____
6. Your parents / go to concerts ☐ _____
7. Your neighbours / speak English ☐ _____
8. You / like classical music ☐ _____

> Your brother doesn't make cupcakes.

> False. My brother makes good cupcakes.

7.3 Grammar

1 Put the words in the correct order to make questions.

1. parents your Do help you ? — *Do you help your parents?*
2. English speak Does your granny ? _____
3. have music lessons we Do ? _____
4. I well Do speak English ? _____
5. his room your brother tidy Does ? _____
6. our parents Do go to the gym ? _____

2 Match the answers to the questions in Exercise 1.

a [5] Yes, he does.   c [ ] No, they don't.   e [ ] Yes, we do.
b [ ] Yes, you do.   d [ ] Yes, I do.   f [ ] No, she doesn't.

3 Complete the dialogue with the words in the box.

| Yes, I do.   Does she like   Yes, they do.   ~~Do you take~~   Does your sister want |

A: ¹ *Do you take* your dog for a walk every day?
B: ² _____
A: Do your parents help you?
B: ³ _____
A: ⁴ _____ a pet?
B: No, she doesn't.
A: ⁵ _____ animals?
B: Yes, she does.

4 Imagine you are a reporter for a magazine and write questions.

1. What / you do / relax? — *What do you do to relax?*
2. you / hang out with friends / every day? _____
3. you / listen to music / before breakfast? _____
4. your parents / do sport? _____
5. your best friend / speak English? _____
6. What / you do / on Sundays? _____

5 Read the questions in Exercise 4 again. Note your answers. Then interview a partner and note his/her answers.

Question	Me	My partner
1		
2		
3		
4		
5		
6		

What do you do to relax?

I play with my hamster and …

© Pearson Education Limited 2017   **PHOTOCOPIABLE**

8.2 Grammar

1 Circle the correct answer.

1. I love cycle / **cycling**.
2. My mum hates cook / cooking.
3. My classmates don't like skateboard / skateboarding.
4. David doesn't like do / doing taekwondo.
5. You love eat / eating my cupcakes!
6. We hate get / getting up early.

2 Put the words in the correct order to make questions.

1. your cat Does your sister like ? — *Does your cat like your sister?*
2. spiders your mum Does like ? — _____
3. your parents Justin Bieber like Do ? — _____
4. our class our teacher Does like ? — _____
5. like skateboarding Do you ? — _____
6. I ice-creams Do like ? — _____

3 Read the answers to the questions in Exercise 2. Complete them with *does, doesn't, do* or *don't*. Then write what the underlined words refer to.

1. Yes, it *does*. It loves <u>her</u>! — sister
2. No, she _____ . She hates <u>them</u>! — _____
3. No, they _____ . They don't like <u>him</u>. — _____
4. Yes, he _____ . He likes <u>us</u>. — _____
5. Yes, I _____ . I love <u>it</u>! — _____
6. Yes, you _____ . You love <u>them</u>! — _____

4 Read the questions and complete the *Me* column. Use ☺☺ (love), ☺ (like), ☹ (don't like) or ☹☹ (hate). Then ask and answer in pairs and complete the rest of the table.

Do you/they like … Does he/she like …	Me	My partner	My partner's brother/ sister/parents
getting up early?			
swimming?			
reading?			
speaking English?			
cooking?			
eating fruit?			
skateboarding?			

Do you like cooking?

No, I don't. I hate it!

8.3 Grammar

1 Circle the correct answer. Then draw a line to match 1–6 to A–F.

1 ____ do you live?
  a Who   (b) Where   c What
2 ____ is your birthday?
  a When   b What   c How
3 ____ is your favourite singer?
  a Whose   b Who   c How
4 ____ is your mum?
  a Where   b When   c Whose
5 ____ is that pen?
  a Who   b Whose   c How many

A It's my pen.
B Beyoncé.
C I live in Liverpool.
D On March 1st.
E In the garden.

2 Correct the underlined words.

1 A: <u>Who</u> many photos have you got? B: Ten. <u>How</u>
2 A: <u>When</u> do you do to relax? B: I do sport. ____
3 A: <u>Who</u> do you have guitar lessons? B: On Mondays. ____
4 A: <u>How many</u> is my phone? B: On the sofa. ____
5 A: <u>Whose</u> is your English teacher? B: Mr Smith. ____

3 Read the answers and complete the questions.

A: ¹ <u>How many brothers and sisters</u> have you got?
B: I've got two brothers and one sister.
A: ² _____ their names?
B: Their names are Brian, Jamie and Alice.
A: ³ _____ are they?
B: Brian is 15, Jamie is 13 and Alice is 9.
A: ⁴ _____ best friend?
B: My best friend is Sarah.
A: ⁵ _____ hang out?
B: We hang out after school and at the weekend.

4 Work in groups of four. Ask and answer the questions in Exercise 3 and note your partners' answers.

Question	Partner 1	Partner 2	Partner 3
1			
2			
3			
4			
5			
6			

How many brothers and sisters have you got?

I haven't got any brothers or sisters but I've got two cousins.

1.4 Communication

1 Read the dialogues. Where's the best place for the extra sentence? Draw an arrow (→).

Dialogue 1

Dave: Dad, this is Jonas. Jonas, this is my dad.
Dad: Hello, Jonas. Nice to meet you.
Jonas: Nice to meet you too, Mr Smith.

Extra sentence:
He's my classmate.

Dialogue 2

Robbie: Mark, this is Anne. She's my cousin.
Mark: I'm Robbie's classmate.
Anne: Nice to meet you too, Mark.

Extra sentence:
Nice to meet you.

2 Work in groups of three. Roleplay these scenarios, changing roles. Use Dialogues 1 and 2 to help.

Roleplay 1

Student A: Introduce your neighbour to your mum/dad.
Student B: You are Student A's mum/dad.
Student C: You are Student A's neighbour.

Roleplay 2

Student A: Introduce your new classmate to your brother/sister.
Student B: You are Student A's brother/sister.
Student C: You are Student A's new classmate.

Roleplay 3

Student A: Introduce your cousin to your best friend.
Student B: You are Student A's best friend.
Student C: You are Student A's cousin.

2.4 Communication

Put the words in the correct order to make questions. Answer for you. Then interview three partners and note their answers. Who is most like you? Tell the class!

Questionnaire!

	You	Partner 1	Partner 2	Partner 3
1 name your What's ?				
2 you How old are ?				
3 you from are Where ?				
4 favourite music your What's ?				
5 your Who's favourite singer ?				
6 favourite sport your What's ?				
7 Who's sports person your favourite ?				
8 film favourite What's your ?				
9 actor Who's your favourite ?				

© Pearson Education Limited 2017 PHOTOCOPIABLE

3.4 Communication

Student A
- Cut out your half of each dialogue.
- Order the dialogues with a partner. Then act them out, changing roles.
- Act out the dialogues again but change the highlighted words. Make them funny!

Student B
- Cut your half of each dialogue.
- Order the dialogues with a partner. Then act them out, changing roles.
- Act out the dialogues again but change the highlighted words. Make them funny!

Dialogue 1 You are at home.

A: Would you like a biscuit?

A: Hello. Please, come in.

A: Would you like a sandwich?

Dialogue 1 You are at a friend's house.

B: Yes, please! I love chocolate biscuits!

B: No, thanks.

B: Thank you.

Dialogue 2 You are at a friend's house.

A: Thanks! Where's the bathroom, please?

A: Oh, no! Where's my phone?

Dialogue 2 You are at home.

B: It's on the sofa.

B: It's upstairs. Let me show you.

4.4 Communication

Put the sentences in the correct order to make dialogues and act them out in pairs. Then replace the underlined words with your own ideas or use the pictures. Act out the dialogues again.

Dialogue 1

- [ ] **A:** Are you sure?
- [ ] **B:** No problem.
- [ ] **B:** Yes, I'm fine.
- [ ] **A:** Oh, no! My <u>orange juice</u> is on your <u>sofa</u> … I'm so sorry …

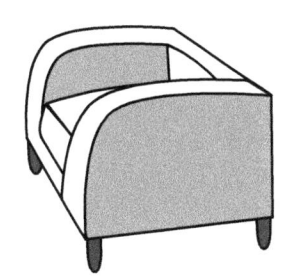

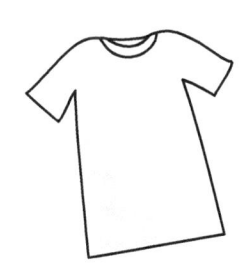

Dialogue 2

- [ ] **B:** Sorry, my mistake. Here you are.
- [ ] **A:** This isn't my <u>phone</u>.
- [ ] **A:** OK. Thanks.

Dialogue 3

- [ ] **A:** That's all right.
- [ ] **B:** I've got it!
- [ ] **A:** Where's my <u>bag</u>?

5.4 Communication

1 Use the words in the box to complete the dialogue.

| agree | can | go | ~~do~~ | beach |

Sarah: Let's ¹ *do* something fun!
Rob: I ² _____ . 🙂
Sarah: We ³ _____ go to the park.
Rob: I'm not sure. 😐
Sarah: OK. Let's ⁴ _____ ice-skating.
Rob: It's not a good idea. 😟 I can't skate.
Sarah: Let's go to the ⁵ _____ .
Rob: Let's do that! 🙂 We can dive too.
Sarah: Great idea! 🙂

2 Cut out one set of cards. Then in pairs, take turns to make a suggestion for your partner to react to. Use Exercise 1 to help.

go ice-skating 🙂	skateboard 😐	go to the park 😟	go to the cinema 🙂
go to the beach 😐	play football 😟	ride our bikes 🙂	make cupcakes 😐
go to the swimming pool 😟	go to the zoo 🙂	draw 😐	climb 😟
dive 🙂	listen to music 😐	play the guitar 😟	sing 🙂

6.4 Communication

Read the dialogue. Then ask and answer in pairs and complete the times.

Alice: What time is the game?
Ben: It's at five to four.
Alice: What time is it now?
Ben: It's ten to four.
Alice: Let's run! / Let's go then!

Student A

The English lesson:	The party:	The film on TV:	The football game:
Now: 10:45	Now: 19:15	Now: 20:20	Now: 9:35
Lunch? _____ Now? _____	Dinner? _____ Now? _____	Art club? _____ Now? _____	Dance club? _____ Now? _____

Student B

The English lesson?	The party?	The film on TV?	The football game?
_____ Now? _____	_____ Now? _____	_____ Now? _____	_____ Now? _____
Lunch: Now: 2:30	Dinner: Now: 19:40	Art club: Now: 17:10	Dance club: Now: 16:05

7.4 Communication

Read the dialogue. Two words are in the wrong place. Find and circle them. Then roleplay the scenarios in pairs.

Man: Hello. Can I help you?
Bill: Can I have two tickets to the concert, thanks?
Man: That's twenty-one pounds fifty.
Bill: Here you are.
Man: These are your tickets.
Bill: Please.

Student A

Roleplay 1   At the theatre

- Buy three theatre tickets.
- Student B starts.

Roleplay 2   At the football match

- You work at a football club.
- One ticket is £11.50.
- You start. Say: 'Hello. Can I help you?'

Roleplay 3   At the cinema

- Buy one cinema ticket.
- Student B starts.

Roleplay 4   At the swimming pool

- You work at a swimming pool.
- One ticket is £3.60.
- You start. Say: 'Hello. Can I help you?'

Student B

Roleplay 1   At the theatre

- You work at a theatre.
- One ticket is £5.50.
- You start. Say: 'Hello. Can I help you?'

Roleplay 2   At the football match

- Buy two tickets for the football match.
- Student A starts.

Roleplay 3   At the cinema

- You work at a cinema.
- One ticket is £3.20.
- You start. Say: 'Hello. Can I help you?'

Roleplay 4   At the swimming pool

- Buy one ticket for the swimming pool.
- Student A starts.

8.4 Communication

Read the dialogue. Then ask and answer in pairs and complete.

> **Sam:** What's the weather like in Spain in winter?
> **Jamie:** It's often sunny but it's sometimes cold and rainy.

Student A

Spain / summer ?	The UK / spring?	Poland / winter?	Italy / autumn?	Australia / winter?
The USA / winter — sometimes	Scotland / summer — usually	France / spring — sometimes	China / spring — often	Spain / winter — sometimes

Student B

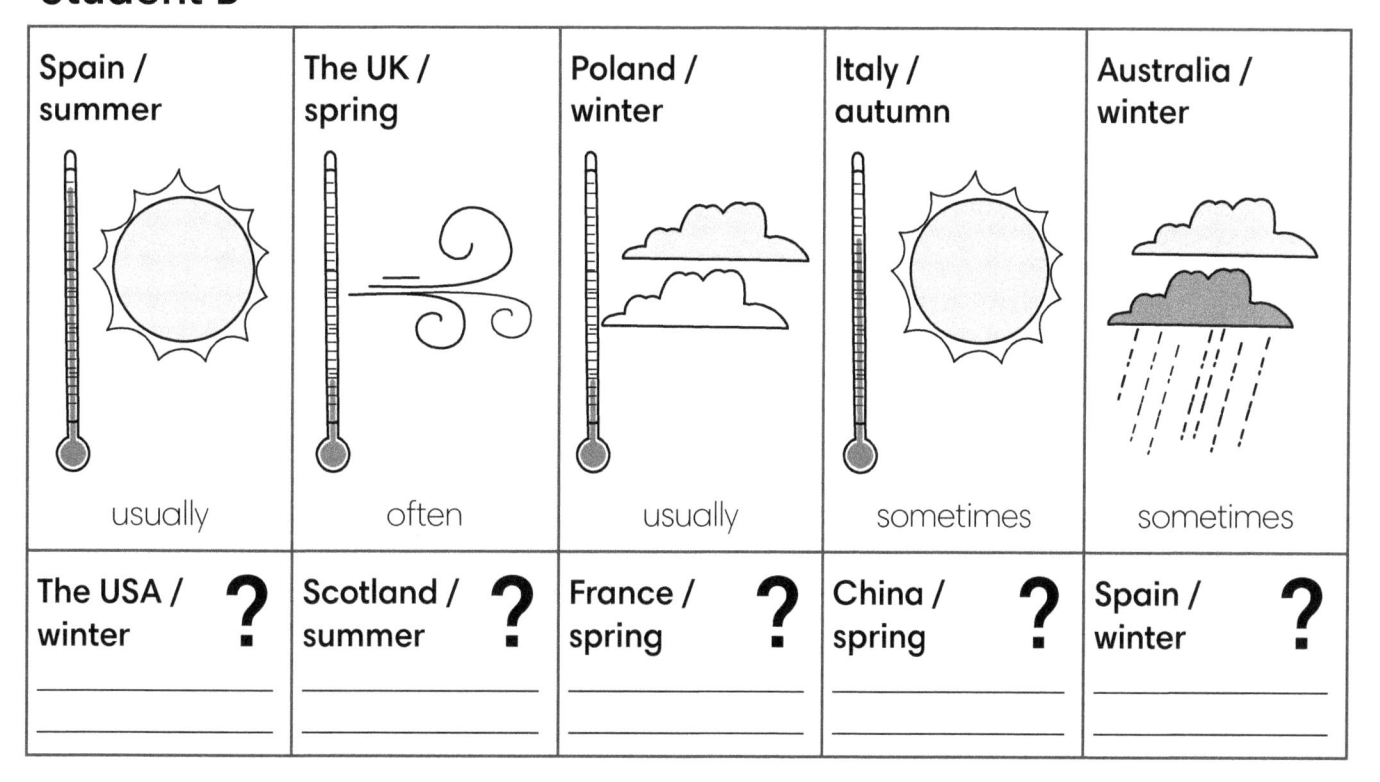

Spain / summer — usually	The UK / spring — often	Poland / winter — usually	Italy / autumn — sometimes	Australia / winter — sometimes
The USA / winter ?	Scotland / summer ?	France / spring ?	China / spring ?	Spain / winter ?

© Pearson Education Limited 2017 PHOTOCOPIABLE

Play

Where's the chocolate?

The characters

The Jones family

Sam: 12; sporty clothes

Mandy: Sam's sister; 10; clever; cool clothes, glasses

Mum: can sing well, a long dress

Dad: very strong; trousers and a shirt

Granny and Grandad: helpful, sometimes very funny; Granny usually has good ideas; their clothes aren't cool

Other characters

Jo: Sam's best friend; 12; loves computer games; a T-shirt, jeans, glasses

Mr Grim: the Jones' new neighbour; long nose, his hair is different colours, green face; black clothes

Aliens: six or more; long noses, their hair is different colours, green faces; white alien suits

Narrators: two girls and two boys with very nice party clothes

Zongie (zongaroo): a friendly alien pet. You can invent it!

Scene 1

[The Jones family and Jo are in the garden. Mum, Dad and Granny are on the chairs. Mandy has got a book. Grandad is speaking on his mobile phone. Sam and Jo have got a laptop.]

Narrator 1: Hello, everyone. Welcome to our play!

Narrator 2: Meet the Jones family. This is Sam!

Sam: Hi, everyone! *[Sam waves to the audience.]*

Narrator 2: Sam is twelve. He's sporty. *[Sam mimes running.]* Jo is his best friend.

Jo: Hello! *[Jo waves to the audience.]*

Narrator 2: He's twelve too. He *loves* playing computer games! *[Jo points to his computer.]*

Narrator 3: And this is Mandy.

Mandy: Hello! *[Mandy waves to the audience.]*

Narrator 3: She's Sam's sister. She's ten. She's *very* clever. *[Mandy points to her head to show she's clever.]*

Narrator 4: Meet Mum and Dad!

Mum and Dad: Hi! *[Mum and Dad wave to the audience.]*

Narrator 4: They are Sam and Mandy's parents. Mum loves music and can sing very well. *[Mum sings 'La! La! Laaaaa!']* Dad's very strong! *[Dad shows his muscles.]*

Narrator 2: Meet Granny and Grandad too. They are often very funny! *[Grandad laughs.]* Granny usually has good ideas. *[Granny puts her finger up to show 'I've got an idea!']*

Granny and Grandad: Hello! *[They wave to the audience.]*

Narrator 1: It's Saturday afternoon and the Jones family are in the garden.

Narrator 2: Their neighbour, Mr Grim, comes into his garden with his funny pet. *[Mr Grim walks into his garden with a very big box and puts it on a table. His pet, a zongaroo, is with him. They stand next to the garden fence so they can see the Jones.]*

Mandy: What time's dinner, Mum?

Mum: It's at seven o'clock. Would you like a chocolate? There's a big box of chocolates in the fridge.

Mandy: Yes, please!

Sam: Me too!

Jo: And me, please! *[Mandy, Sam and Jo run into the house.]*

Mum: *[shouting to the children]* IT'S UNDER THE CHOCOLATE CUPCAKES!!!

[The children are in the garden again.]

Sam: Mum, there isn't a box of chocolates in the fridge.

Jo: And there aren't any cupcakes!

Dad: Let's eat Granny's chocolate cake then.

Grandad: It's very good!

Sam: *[Sam runs into the house again.]* DAD, … IT ISN'T HERE!

Granny: What? My fantastic chocolate cake? *[Granny is sad.]*

Mandy: There isn't any chocolate in the kitchen.

Grandad: *[to the adults]* Let's look again. *[Mum, Dad, Grandad and Granny go into the house.]*

Sam: *[to Mandy and Jo]* Come on you two. We can play football.

Mandy and Jo: Cool!

Narrator 3: Who's got Mum's box of chocolates? Where are the chocolate cupcakes?

Narrator 4: And what about Granny's fantastic chocolate cake?

[The box of chocolates, the chocolate cupcakes and Granny's chocolate cake are in Mr Grim's big box! He takes them out of the box, puts them on his table and has a chocolate. He gives a chocolate to his pet too. He thinks it's very funny…]

Scene 2

[Sam, Jo and Mandy have got a football. Mandy – back to the fence, Sam – back to the Jones' house, Jo – opposite Mandy.]

Narrator 1: Sam, Mandy and Jo all love playing football so they're happy.

Sam: *[ball to Jo]* Jo, ... here you are!

Jo: OK! Mandy, this one's for you!

Sam: Jo, be careful!

Jo: *[Ball to Mandy ... but the ball goes into Mr Grim's garden.]* Oh, no! I'm sorry. Where's the ball?

Mandy: It's in Mr Grim's garden.

Sam: Not again!

Jo: Who's Mr Grim?

Sam: *[to Jo]* He's our new neighbour.

Narrator 2: Sam goes into Mr Grim's garden.

[Mr Grim sees Sam. He quickly puts the chocolate in the box. He puts the football under the table so Sam can't see it.]

Mr Grim: *[smiling]* Ah. It's you again, Sam. How are you?

Sam: I'm fine, thanks. Mr Grim, I'm very sorry but our ball is in your garden.

Mr Grim: Where is it?

Sam: Oh ... it isn't here. That's strange! I'm sorry about that. Bye!

Mr Grim: Bye, Sam.

[Sam is back with Mandy and Jo. Mr Grim sits in his garden and has another chocolate!]

Mandy: Have you got the ball, Sam?

Sam: No, I haven't. It isn't there.

Jo and Mandy: *[surprised]* What?

[The aliens arrive in their spaceship. They run round the Jones' garden. Mr Grim sees them and hides inside his house. He watches them!]

Narrator 4: Look at the aliens! They are from the planet Zong. Aliens from Zong are usually very friendly. They speak a funny language. Listen!

Alien 1: *[to the aliens]* Oooooiiiiiiiiii!

Alien 2: Zongozongozongozongooo!

Alien 3: Eeeeeeeeeeeeeeeeeeeee!

Alien 4: Bing bong! Bing bong!

Alien 5: Wizzzzzz, woooooo, zing!

[Sam, Jo and Mandy are scared. They run behind the tree but the aliens see them.]

Alien 6: *[to the aliens]* Hang on. Look! Three children!

Alien 1: *[to the children]* Oh, good afternoon.

Mandy: *[to the aliens]* Who are you? Why are you in our garden?

Alien 1: *[to the children]* It's OK! It's OK! Please relax! We're friends. My name's Wong. These are my friends Bong, Dong, Nong, Gong and Song.

Aliens 2–6: *[smiling and waving]* Hi!

Mandy, Jo and Sam: Nice to meet you. *[They aren't behind the tree now.]*

Sam: I'm Sam. This is my sister, Mandy. Jo's my best friend.

Jo: *[to the aliens]* Where are you from?

> **Alien chant 1**
> We're from Zong.
> We're from Zong.
> Look at our noses.
> They're very long!

Alien 2: Zong is the name of our planet!

Mandy: Excuse me, but why are you in our garden?

Alien 4: We're here because we want to find Grimoaldo.

Alien 5: Grimoaldo is from Zong too. He isn't very friendly.

Alien 6: And he isn't very nice. He's got Zongie.

Jo: Who's Zongie?

Alien 1: She's our pet. *[The aliens are very sad again.]*

> **Alien chant 2**
> Zongie's cute, Zongie's cool.
> Zongie's our pet zongaroo!

Sam: *[to Alien 1]* Pardon? A kangaroo?

Alien 3: No, no. A *zongaroo*! We love zongaroos on the planet Zong. *[The aliens look sad.]*

Mandy: What other pets do people from Zong like?

> **Alien chant 3**
> People from Zong hate cats and dogs.
> Our favourite pets are znakes and zrogs!

Sam: *[to all aliens]* We can help you find Zongie!

Mandy: I've got an idea. Let's meet in the garden tomorrow morning at eleven o'clock. We can make a plan!

All aliens: Thank you!

Mum: *[She's in the house.]* SAM! MANDY! JO! DINNER'S READY!

Sam, Mandy, Jo: Bye! *[The children walk to the house, waving.]*

Aliens: Bye! *[The aliens walk away.]*

Narrator 1: The children have dinner and the aliens go to their spaceship.

Scene 3

[The children are in the garden. Mr Grim is in his garden again with his funny pet.]

Narrator 2: The children are in the garden and Mum, Dad, Granny and Grandad are in the house. It's eleven o'clock.

[Mr Grim sees the aliens and runs into his house.]

All aliens: Hello, hello, hello! We're here!

Sam, Mandy and Jo: Hi!

Sam: MUM, DAD! GRANNY AND GRANDAD! [The adults run into the garden.]

Dad: What's wrong? Oh! … [The adults see the aliens, stop and look.]

Sam: [to his family] It's OK. These are our new friends.

All aliens: Nice to meet you!

Mum: [to all aliens] Would you like an apple?

Alien 3: [to Mum and Granny] No, thanks. We don't eat apples on Zong.

Jo: [to all aliens] What do you eat?

Alien chant 4

Chocolate, chocolate,
We love chocolate!
Chocolate cake, brown and green,
Chocolate pizza and chocolate ice-cream!

Sam: Mum, our friends have got a big problem.

Alien 4: [to Mum, Dad, Granny and Grandad] Grimoaldo has got our pet zongaroo. Grimoaldo is from Zong too but he isn't very nice.

Grandad: [to all aliens] What does Grimoaldo like doing?

Alien 6: [to Mum, Dad, Granny and Grandad, thinking] He likes playing football …

Alien 1: … and, he's from Zong so he *loves* eating chocolate.

Granny: I know! I've got a plan! Sssshhh!

[All the characters stand next to Granny. She tells them her plan. Mr Grim wants to listen but he can't hear. He isn't happy.]

Narrator 3: What's Granny's idea? Look!

Scene 4

[The Jones family, Jo and the aliens are in the Jones' garden. Granny goes into the house and brings out a fantastic chocolate cake. She puts it on the table. Then they all go inside the Jones' house saying 'Sssssshhhhhhh'.]

Narrator 4: The Jones, Jo and the aliens wait inside. They are next to the window and they can see the garden.

[Mr Grim comes into his garden with Sam's football and the zongaroo. He looks over the fence and sees the chocolate cake. He jumps over the fence with the zongaroo and has some cake. He's very happy!]

Narrator 1: The Jones, Jo and the aliens run into the Jones' garden! Grimoaldo sees the aliens. He is scared …

Sam: It's Mr Grim, our neighbour!

Alien 1: No, it isn't. It's Grimoaldo!

Mandy: GRIMoaldo …

[Mr Grim / Grimoaldo runs. Everyone helps stop him. Now Zongie is next to Alien 2. She's very happy.]

Dad: [to Mr Grim / Grimoaldo] I've got you! [Mr Grim / Grimoaldo takes off his black clothes. He has a white alien suit under them.]

Granny: [not happy] Where are our cakes and chocolate?

Grimoaldo: [sad] I'm sorry, I'm sorry, I'm sorry …

Alien 2: How are you, Zongie?

Zongie: I'm fine, thanks.

Jo: [to all] Wow! Zongaroos can speak!

Zongie: Here's your football, Sam.

Sam: Thank you, Zongie!

Alien 1: Thank you, friends! Please come to Zong for a holiday in the summer.

Grandad: Thank you. But now let's have a chocolate party!

Mr Grim / Grimoaldo: Ooooh! Can I come?

Zongie: Grimoaldo hasn't got any friends on the planet Earth. That's why he wants a pet. He isn't very bad.

Granny: Would you like a chocolate, Mr Grim … I mean, Grimoaldo?

Grimoaldo: Yes, please!

Alien chant 5 (with Grimoaldo)

We're from Zong.
We're from Zong.
Look at our noses.
They're very long!
We love Sam and Mandy and Jo.
We like planet Earth. We don't want to go!

Project worksheets

Get Culture!
English around the world

Step 1
Work in groups of four. Choose one of these countries. Where is it? Circle it and find it on the map in the Student's Book, page 20.

The Republic of Ireland / New Zealand / The Republic of South Africa / Canada

Step 2
Find information about your country and photos on the Internet. Search for the name of the country and the words below.

number of people	capital city		
big cities	languages	map	flag

Step 3
Write about your country and add photos of the map, flag, cities / interesting places. Make slides for the presentation. Use the ideas below to help.

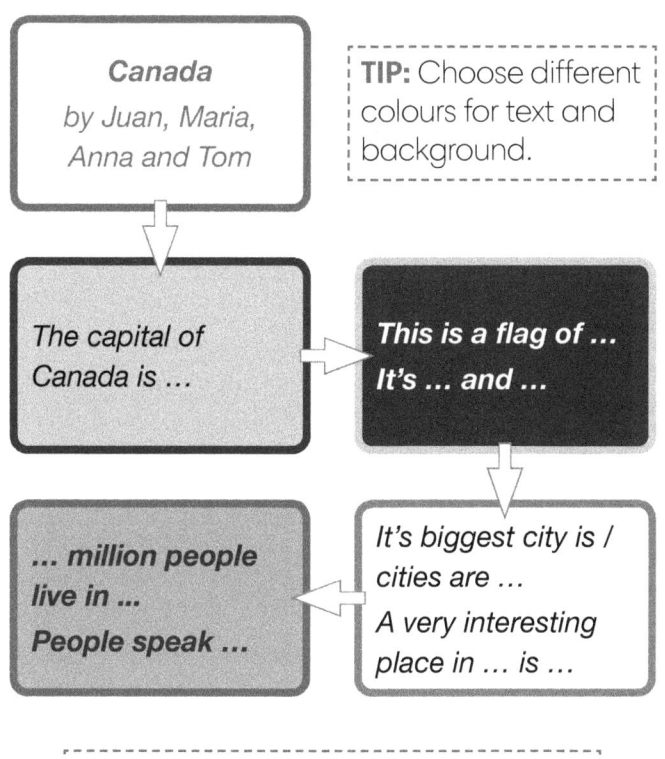

- **Canada** by Juan, Maria, Anna and Tom
- **TIP:** Choose different colours for text and background.
- The capital of Canada is …
- This is a flag of … It's … and …
- … million people live in … People speak …
- It's biggest city is / cities are … A very interesting place in … is …

TIP: Check spelling. Ask your teacher about spelling-check programmes.

Step 4
Share the presentation with the class. Take turns so that all students in the group talk about one slide. You can start like this:

This is a project about …

Get Culture!
Houses in my area

Step 1
Work in groups of three/four. Choose the house for your group. Where is the unusual house? What type of house is it? Circle.

detached house / semi-detached house / terraced house / block of flats / cottage / houseboat / palace

Step 2
Take photos of the house or find them on the Internet. Choose the best photos.

Step 3
Write a description and add different photos of the house. Make slides for the presentation. Use the ideas below to help.

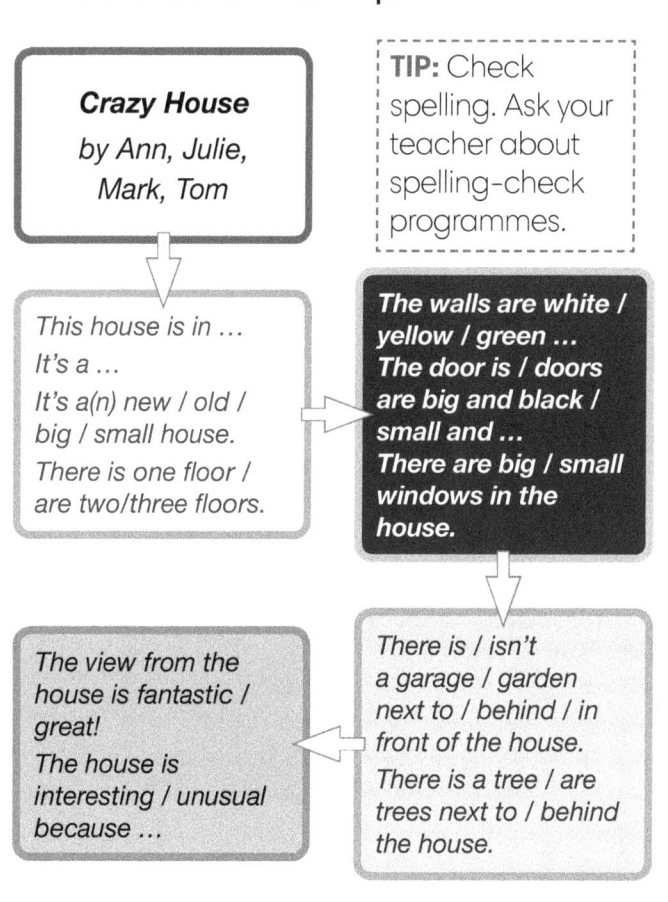

- **Crazy House** by Ann, Julie, Mark, Tom
- **TIP:** Check spelling. Ask your teacher about spelling-check programmes.
- This house is in … It's a … It's a(n) new / old / big / small house. There is one floor / are two/three floors.
- The walls are white / yellow / green … The door is / doors are big and black / small and … There are big / small windows in the house.
- The view from the house is fantastic / great! The house is interesting / unusual because …
- There is / isn't a garage / garden next to / behind / in front of the house. There is a tree / are trees next to / behind the house.

TIP: Choose different colours for text and background.

Step 4
Share the presentation with the class. Take turns so that all students in the group talk about one slide. You can start like this:

This is a project about … This house is in …

Get Culture!
Fun things to do in ...

Step 1
Work in pairs. What are the fun places in your area? Circle them or add your own. Then choose 3-4 places.

park / garden / sports centre / school / cinema

Step 2
Look for photos of these places on the Internet or take photos yourself. Remember to ask for permission.

Step 3
Write about the places and add photos. Use the ideas below to help.

TIP: Use ready templates in your word processor.

TIP: Choose different colours for text and background.

Fun things to do in ...*

- This is ...
- It is in/near/next to/at ...
- You can play football / skateboard / see a film there.

*Add the name of the place where you live.

TIP: Check spelling. Ask your teacher about spelling-check programmes.

TIP: The leaflet can have 1-4 pages.

Step 4
Print a few copies of the leaflet or share your digital leaflet with the class. Vote for the top three fun places.

Get Culture!
My pet

Step 1
Look at the questions and think about a pet for your photo album page.
1. Have you got a pet? What is it?
2. Would you like to have a pet? What is you ideal pet?

Step 2
Take photos of your pet or find photos of your ideal pet on the Internet.

Step 3
Write a short text about your pet / your ideal pet. Use the ideas below to help.

TIP: Use nice colours for text and background.

TIP: You can make 2 pages to show more interesting photos of your pet.

> This is my pet rabbit / ideal pet.
> It's a rabbit / dog / parrot.
> His/Her name's ...
> He's/She's cute / clever ...
> He/She eats ...
> He/She can ...
> Here's a fun fact about rabbits ...

TIP: Check spelling. Ask your teacher about spelling-check programmes.

Step 4
Make a class pet photo album. Use the ideas below to help.
1. Choose three volunteers to create the album. Email the pages to them or print them.
2. Put the pages together to create the album. Put the pages in alphabetical order or put animals in groups.
3. You can download a special computer programme to help you make and present the album. Ask the teacher or parents for help.
4. Share the album with the class.

Grammar video roleplays

Unit 1 It's Granny's birthday!

The characters: Narrator, Sophie, Jen, Alex, Dad, Mum, Megan

Part 1
Scene 1
[Jen, Alex, Sophie, Mum and Dad are in Granny Sophie's living room. Everybody is wearing smart clothes. Sophie is standing in the middle of the room and Mum, Dad and Jen are around her. Alex is taking off his coat.]

Narrator: Today is Sophie's birthday. She is seventy years old. Sophie is Jen and Alex's grandmother. They are at her house.
Sophie: *[hugging Jen]* I'm so happy you're here.

Scene 2
[The doorbell rings and Alex goes to open the door. It's his aunt Megan. She's got a box with a birthday cake, a present in a bag and a card.]

Alex: It's aunt Megan!
Megan: *[to Alex, passing him the box with the cake]* Hello, Alex! Hold this, please! Be careful! It's Granny's birthday cake.
Alex: It's OK. I've got it!

Scene 3
[Megan, without her coat now, is in the living room and is giving the present and the card to Sophie. Alex is giving the box to his mum.]

Megan: Happy birthday, Mum! Here's your present.
Sophie: Thank you, my darling. Where's your son?
Megan: Jason is in Spain with his class. They're on a school trip. *[giving the card to Sophie]* Here's a card from him.
Sophie: Oh, it's a lovely card!

Scene 4
[Sophie and Megan are hugging. Dad is waiting for the cake.]

Dad: Hello, sister! We're ready for the cake!
Mum: *[Mum is oppening the box and is looking at it with surprise.]* Oh, no!

Part 2
Dad: What?
Mum: *[surprised]* Look at the cake.
Megan: Oh, no! It's the wrong cake.
[They all laugh as they speak.]
Jen: It's a baby's cake! Look!
Sophie: 'Happy birthday baby Luke!'
Alex: Luke is one today!
Dad: *[eating the cake]* And the cake is yummy!
Jen and Alex: Dad!

Unit 2 That's my T-shirt!

The characters: Narrator, Jen, Alex, Mum, Dad

Part 1
Scene 1
[Mum and Jen are in the living room. Mum is ironing and Jen is holding a laundry basket for Mum. She's also talking on the phone.]

Mum: Jen, put these clothes away, please.
Jen: *[to Mum]* OK, Mum. *[talking on the phone]* Oh, hi! What's up? What? No!

Scene 2
[Jen is sitting on the bed in her bedroom. The basket with clothes is on the floor.]

Narrator: Ten minutes later …
Jen: *[finishing the phone conversation]* Bye, Holly! … *[to herself, checking the clothes from the basket]* Hang on, what are these? These aren't my jeans. They're too long! These are Mum's jeans! [Jen is taking a big top from the basket.] Yep, this top is Mum's too!

Scene 3
[Jen's mum is standing at the door of Jen's room. She's got a pair of jeans in her hand.]

Mum: *[pointing at the jeans]* Jen, these are your jeans. They're too small for me!
Jen: Oops! Sorry, Mum!
Mum: *[Mum is pointing to the big top on Jen's bed.]* And that's my top over there.
Jen: Yes, it is. Here you are! *[Jen is giving the top to her mum.]*

Scene 4
[Jen is in Alex's bedroom. There are some T-shirts on his bed.]

Alex: Jen? … Jen, where's my new T-shirt?
Jen: *[Jen is pointing to the T-shirts on the bed.]* It's over there with your old T-shirts!
Alex: No, those are Dad's T-shirts!
Jen: Oh, then your T-shirt is …

Part 2
[Dad is standing in front of a mirror.]
Alex: *[angry]* Dad! That's my T-shirt!
Dad: Yes, it's cool, isn't it? My T-shirts are boring!
Alex: But dad …
Dad: Bye now!
Jen: … it's too small for you …

Unit 3 There's a phone on the sofa!

The characters: Jen, Alex, Lian

Part 1
Scene 1
[Jen, Alex and Lian are in the kitchen. Jen is taking some glasses out of the cupboard. Alex is standing in front of the open fridge. He's holding the fridge door open with one hand. He's got his phone in his other hand.]

Alex: Jen, where's the orange juice?
Jen: It's in the fridge.
Alex: Where?
Jen: It's in front of you. *[Jen is pointing at the orange juice in the fridge.]*
Alex: No, it isn't.
Jen: Right there! There's a carton next to the milk.
Alex: Oh, there it is!

Scene 2
[Alex, Jen and Lian are sitting on the sofa in the living room. Lian has her phone in her hands and is showing something to Alex. There's a mobile phone on the sofa.]

Alex: Where's my phone? *[Jen is standing to look under the coffee table.]*
Lian: *[pointing at the sofa]* There's a phone on the sofa.
Jen: No, that's my phone. *[Jen is picking her phone from the sofa.]*
Lian: Maybe it's under the table.
Jen: No, it isn't.

Scene 3
[Alex is looking for his phone behind the sofa.]

Lian: Is it behind the sofa?
Alex: No, it isn't but there are two DVDs.
Jen: Hey! Those are my DVDs!

Scene 4
Alex: Wait! There are some sweets under the sofa!
Jen: Yuck! They're old!
Alex: But where's my phone?
Lian: Hang on! *[Lian is trying to call Alex.]*

Part 2
[Sound of a mobile phone ringing in the distance. Children walk to the kitchen.]

Lian: Shhh!
Jen: It's in the kitchen.
Alex: Yes, but where?
Lian: It's in the fridge!
Jen: Yes, it is!
Alex: What …
Lian: Oh, Alex!

Unit 4 I haven't got big feet!

The characters: Narrator, Jen, Alex, Mum

Part 1
Scene 1
[Alex and Jen are at a bookshop with their mum. Jen is standing close to Alex. Mum is at the back of the shop, looking for a book.]

Narrator: At the bookshop.
Alex: *[Jen is trying to get a book from a shelf and is stepping on Alex's foot.]* Ouch, my foot! Be careful!
Jen: It isn't my fault! You've got long legs! And you've got big feet!
Alex: I haven't got big feet! I'm tall!

Scene 2
Jen: You've got long arms too! Like this! *[Jen mimics having long arms that are close to the floor.]*
Alex: Yeah, but I haven't got a big head, like you!

Scene 3
[They go to Mum.]

Jen: My head is fine! Mum? Is my head big?
Mum: Stop it, you two! Jen, your brother hasn't got big feet. Alex, your sister hasn't got a big head! Now, hurry up with the books! We haven't got a lot of time.

Scene 4
Jen: Oh, they've got *Yummy Cupcakes*. Great! *[Jen is trying to get a book but it's too high for her.]* Oh, no! It's too high! Alex? Help me, please!

Part 2
Jen: That book over there? Please?
Alex: So my long arms are OK, now?
Jen: Come on! Be a good brother!
Alex: Oh, all right! *[Alex takes the book from the shelf.]*
Jen: Thank you!
Alex: *[pointing at the pictures of cupcakes in the book]* But I want these cupcakes! Ooh, and these! And these too!
Jen: Fine!

Unit 5 I can fix it!

The characters: Jen, Alex, Lian, Lucas

Part 1
Scene 1
[Jen, Alex, Lian and Lucas are hanging out in Lian's room. Lian is making a film for her granny in Shanghai.]

Lian: *[holding a video camera and filming Lucas, who's playing the guitar.]* Guys, this video is for my granny, in Shanghai. Granny Lin, this is my friend, Lucas.
Lucas: *[Lucas stops playing and is waving at the camera.]* Hello!
Lian: Lucas is very talented! He can play the guitar and he can sing!
Lucas: Well, I can't sing very well but …

Scene 2
Lian: Oh no, not again!
Alex: What's wrong?
Lian: It's the camera. I can't see a thing! *[Lian is showing her video camera to Alex.]*
Alex: Let me see … Hmm, I can fix it.
Lian: *[Lian's filming Alex.]* Thanks! Alex is a genius! He can fix things! He can do very clever things with computers too!

Scene 3
Jen: Yes, very clever – he can play computer games all day! *[offering Lian a cupcake]* Cupcake?
Lian: *[with a mouth full of a cupcake]* Jen is a fantastic cook! These cupcakes are yummy!

Scene 4
Alex: But what about Lian?
Lucas: Yes, what can she do?

Part 2
Lian: I can skateboard and I can draw.
Lucas: *[surprised]* But where are the cupcakes?
Lian: *[laughing]* And I can eat cupcakes very fast! Sorry, Lucas!

Unit 6 I listen to classical music.

The characters: Narrator, Jen, Alex, Lucas

Part 1
Scene 1
[Alex, Jen and Lucas are at school. Lucas is asking Jen and Alex about their daily routine for a school survey.]

Narrator: Lucas asks Jen and Alex about their daily routine for a school survey.

Scene 2
Jen: I get up early. I get ready for school and I have breakfast.
Alex: Me too. Breakfast is very important. Jen makes pancakes!
Jen: Then we walk to school.
Alex: We're never late for school.

Scene 3
Jen: After school we do our homework. In the evening, …
Alex: I listen to classical music and Jen plays the piano. *[Jen starts laughing.]*

Scene 4
Lucas: Come on, guys! Alex listens to classical music! Jen plays the piano! Seriously?
Jen: *[laughing]* Oh, Alex. Lucas, let me tell you what Alex really does!

Part 2
Jen: Alex gets up late! He hasn't got time for breakfast. We run to school because he's late. In the evening he watches TV and he plays computer games! He never listens to classical music.
Alex: But I'm still your favourite brother!
Jen: That's because I've got only one brother!

Unit 7 I don't like cats!

The characters: Jen, Alex, Mum, Dad

Part 1
Scene 1
[Jen, Alex, Mum and Dad are in the living room. Mum's watching TV. Dad's reading a newspaper. Jen is doing something on her smartphone. Alex is entering the room and is showing something to Mum on his tablet.]

Alex: Mum? I want a dog like this! Please?
Mum: Aww … I like dogs but they are hard work, Alex.
Alex: I don't mind!

Scene 2
Mum: Can you get up early and take it for a walk? Every day?
Jen: Poor dog! Alex doesn't get up before twelve o'clock at the weekend.
Dad: Big dogs eat a lot.
Alex: But it's small! It doesn't eat a lot.
Dad: Because it's a puppy! These dogs are usually very big!
Alex: Oh, all right.

Scene 3
[Jen and Dad are looking at Alex's tablet too.]

Jen: How about a cat? People don't take cats for a walk.
Alex: I don't like cats! And I'm allergic!
Dad: [smiling and pointing at the tablet] Look, these are perfect for you! They don't eat a lot and you are not allergic to them.

Part 2
Alex: A … goldfish? Dad! I can't play with a goldfish!
Jen: Well, it is cute …
Alex: This is not funny …

Unit 8 Let's go to summer camp!

The characters: Jen, Alex, Lian

Part 1
[Jen, Alex and Lian are sitting in the kitchen. They're discussing summer camps.]

Lian: Hey guys, do you want to go to summer camp with me?
Alex: Maybe. What do you do there?
Lian: Horse-riding, rock climbing … I like rock climbing.
Jen: I don't like it!
Lian: [pointing at a leaflet] How about water sports? There's sailing, windsurfing …
Alex: No, thanks. I don't like getting wet.
Jen: That's true. Lian, you like sports. We like them, but we want to do other things too. Cooking, for example?
Lian: There's a cooking camp in …
Alex: No, thanks. I love eating but I hate cooking!
Lian: Let's find a camp we all like.

Part 2
Alex: How about tech camp? It sounds good!
Jen: No …
Lian: [pointing at a leaflet] Look here!
Jen: Not another sports camp!
Lian: No, not the sports camp. The fun camp. There are lots of different activities.
Jen: That's good!
Alex: Hang on! What time do you get up at summer camp?
Lian: Early?
Alex: No, thanks! But you can go. Have fun!
Jen: Oh, Alex!